Images of Kingship in Early Modern France

Louis XI, known as "The Spider King" because he wove many intricate plots, lives on in popular imagination primarily as a villain and a cruel, cunning, rather unscrupulous character. By contrast, during the early modern period, Louis XI was alternately praised and excoriated. Absolutists fled to his banner whilst constitutionalists reviled him as a murderous tyrant. In *Images of Kingship in Early Modern France*, Adrianna Bakos uses the changing nature of Louis XI's historical reputation to explore the intellectual and political climate of early modern France.

Images of Kingship In Early Modern France examines the aims of those who wrote about Louis XI's reign and how these aims informed their writings. The manner in which political writers and polemicists evoked and manipulated multiple images of Louis XI testifies to the complex ideological landscape of early modern France. Adrianna Bakos challenges the traditional interpretation of constitutionalism and absolutism as discrete and opposed, positing instead a discursive "web" wherein these two theories are intertwined. *Images of Kingship in Early Modern France* is an important contribution to European historiography and to debates on historical versus political interpretations of kingship.

Adrianna Bakos is Assistant Professor at the University of Rochester, Rochester, New York.

Images of Kingship in Early Modern France

Louis XI in Political Thought, 1560–1789

Adrianna E. Bakos

London and New York

First published 1997
by Routledge
11 New Fetter Lane, London EC4P 4EE

Simultaneously published in the USA and Canada
by Routledge
29 West 35th Street, New York, NY 10001

Typeset in Garamond by Routledge
Printed and bound in Great Britain by Redwood Books,
Trowbridge, Wiltshire

British Library Cataloguing in Publication Data
A catalogue record for this book is available from the British Library

Library of Congress Cataloguing in Publication Data
Bakos, Adrianna E.
Images of Kingship in Early Modern France: Louis XI in Political
Thought, 1560–1789/Adrianna E.Bakos.
Includes bibliographical references and index.
1. Louis XI, King of France, 1423–1483–Influence. 2. France–
History–Louis XI, 1461–1483–Historiography. 3. Monarchy–
France–History–16th century–Historiography. 4. France–
Intellectual life–Historiography. I. Title.
DC106.3.B33 1997   96–42013
944'.027'092–dc20   CIP

ISBN 0–415–15478–2

For my parents

Contents

Preface

> I at least have so much to do in unravelling certain human lots, and seeing how they were woven and interwoven, that all the light I can command must be concentrated on this particular web, and not dispersed over that tempting range of relevancies called the universe.
>
> (George Eliot, *Middlemarch*)

I first came across a reference to the "tyrant" Louis XI when reading François Hotman's *Francogallia* in a graduate course on early modern political thought in the fall of 1985. I was intrigued by Hotman's portrait of Louis XI, and became even more so when it seemed that the "Spider King" made an appearance in almost everything I read thereafter. I was persuaded that the image of Louis XI, so obviously evocative for political writers, offered an opportunity to approach early modern political thought from a fresh perspective. Moreover, perhaps because I began to see everything in arachnoid terms, I became convinced that the idea of a web would be useful in reconsidering the evolution of political thought in France over the course of more than two centuries. To that end, I have chosen not to proceed chronologically, but rather to attempt to isolate and examine different sections of what I see as a discursive web. The book thus ranges back and forth across time in order to pursue separately the constitutionalist and absolutist visions of Louis XI, before attempting to understand the ways in which these strands are tangled together.

Wherever possible I have chosen to use the modern critical editions of the primary sources considered here. In many cases, no modern edition exists, in which case, whenever possible, I have tried to work from either first editions or editions considered particularly important by contemporaries. Unless otherwise noted, all the translations from French to English are my own. In cases where my translation might be open to challenge, or when I felt the phrasing of the original text to be particularly significant, I have included the original in the notes.

Some material in Chapter 1 was previously published in a different form as "The Historical Reputation of Louis XI in Political Theory and Polemic during the French Religious Wars," in *The Sixteenth Century Journal* 21 (1990): 3–32. I would also like to thank the *Journal of the History of Ideas* for kind permission to reprint here as Chapter 5 my article entitled, " 'Qui nescit dissimulare, nescit regnare': Louis XI and *Raison d'Etat* during the Reign of Louis XIII," which appeared in volume 52 (1991): 399–416.

I am grateful to the Giles B. Whiting Foundation and the Social Sciences and Humanities Research Council of Canada for grants which enabled me to travel to France and complete my research in the early stages of this project. My thanks also to the University of Rochester for allowing me to take a timely academic leave in order to complete the writing of this book. I would especially like to thank the knowledgeable staffs at the Firestone Library, Princeton University; the Rush Rhees Library at the University of Rochester; the Houghton Library, Harvard University; and the Folger Shakespeare Library. Although I return again and again to the Folger ostensibly on account of their tremendous and ever-expanding collection in early modern politics and ideology, the truth is that few places offer as hospitable an environment in which to work.

Among the many individuals who contributed to this book in so many ways, I should like to make special mention of the following. First and foremost I owe a debt of gratitude to John Salmon, whose guidance first as a dissertation advisor and then as a cherished friend have meant so much to me. At a critical juncture I benefited enormously from conversations with John Guy, who helped me to clarify not only what I wanted to say but how I ought to say it. Orest Ranum and Mark Greengrass read the whole manuscript and offered immensely useful suggestions which refined both style and substance. David Bell generously agreed to read several chapters at a particularly busy time in his own life; his comments led me to rethink important aspects and are greatly appreciated. I would also like to thank my colleagues at the University of Rochester, especially my fellow French historians Alice Conklin, Jean Pedersen and Jeff Ravel. Linda Levy Peck patiently listened as I poured out a litany of complaints and frustrations; her ability to cut to the heart of the matter often pointed to a solution that had eluded me. Despite the tremendous input of all these gifted historians, I freely confess to all sins of omission and commission which remain.

It has been a pleasure to work with the staff at Routledge. I would especially like to thank Claire L'Enfant and Heather McCallum, who have created a truly fine history list, of which I am honoured to be a part. I am grateful to my friend Laura Abrahamsen, who provided a personal 24-hour "Latin hotline" to help with particularly troublesome translations. Finally, loving thanks to my husband, Glen Donaldson. His boundless support (not to say prodding) made the completion of this book possible.

Introduction

"Le roi araignée"

Louis XI (r. 1461–1483) lives on in the historical imagination primarily as a villain, a cruel and cunning, rather unscrupulous character worthy of the name by which French schoolchildren still refer to him: *le roi araignée*, the Spider King. This wily and enigmatic figure continues to captivate Frenchmen, as is evidenced by the recent publication of a book of cartoons about Louis XI, entitled *Je ne suis pas celui que vous croyez*.[1] Unlike his near contemporary Richard III, however, Louis XI has no devoted group of modern defenders intent on rescuing him from general opprobrium. Modern historians have, it is true, attempted to provide a more balanced account of a complicated man ruling in difficult times, but Louis XI's negative popular reputation persists despite these efforts.[2] After all, villains do make better copy.

In the past two decades, historians have begun to study the historiography of kingship and of individual kings. In 1976, W. F. Church published *Louis XIV in Historical Thought*, which examined how Louis XIV fared at the hands of historians from Voltaire to the *annalistes*.[3] Two years earlier, an article by Michel Tyvaert appearing in *Revue d'histoire moderne et contemporaine* analysed representations of different French kings in histories written during the seventeenth century. Tyvaert went so far as to tabulate rankings of "good" and "bad" kings by seventeenth-century historians,[4] Charlemagne, Philippe Auguste and Louis XII ranked among the "good" kings, whose qualities most closely approximated those of the contemporary kingly ideal of piety, justice, and liberality. By contrast, Louis XI is numbered among the "bad" kings, a list which also included among others Chilperic and Charles IX. Nevertheless, Tyvaert acknowledges that the portrait of Louis XI drawn by seventeenth-century historians is an ambivalent one, and it is precisely this ambivalence which makes an investigation into the reputation of the Spider King both fascinating and worthwhile.

The historiography about Louis XI is particularly interesting because of the light it sheds on the complicated intellectual climate of early modern France. Indeed, the significance of this study lies in the effective use of the image of Louis XI as a prism through which to examine political discourse of the time. This book intends to explore the landscape of early modern

French political discourse, using as its guide the historical reputation of Louis XI. It is not my intention to right some historical wrong done to the reputation of Louis XI. Any re-evaluation of his reign is relevant only in so far as it pertains to the question of why Louis XI is such an enduring symbol of tyranny and immorality. To what degree have his historiographical fortunes been influenced by the political aims and assumptions of those who wrote about his reign? I believe that Louis XI's historical reputation was created not so much by biographers and historians as by political writers and polemicists who, in the centuries since his death, constructed the negative image of Louis XI. A general survey of political literature from the early modern period reveals the frequency with which he is mentioned by sixteenth-, seventeenth- and eighteenth-century writers. With few exceptions, Louis XI is among the most commonly cited of past French monarchs. His ubiquitous presence testifies to the evocative power of his image. We are forced to ask what it is about the Spider King that repeatedly brought him to the attention of early modern writers.

Having discovered the extent to which Louis XI functioned as a touch-stone for political writers, it seemed useful to invert the methodology and begin to use him as a means to gain a new *entrée* into the literature. It quickly became evident that there was indeed some correlation between views expressed about Louis XI and stances taken by politically attuned Frenchmen on a whole range of issues. Studying the ways in which references to Louis XI were used to justify and legitimize opposing political theories provides a fresh approach to authors and ideas that have been the subject of much scholarly debate.

In some respects the landscape of early modern political thought is remarkably uniform. Prior to the outbreak of the French Religious Wars in 1562, there existed a traditional view, to which the majority of Frenchmen adhered, that, while the power of the king was not absolute, limitations on the exercise of his authority were purely self-imposed. The tensions in this system of "absolute self-limitation" were exacerbated by the conflict which intensified throughout the second half of the sixteenth century. Under the stress of factional and religious strife, ideas of authority and limitation began to detach themselves from one another and move into mutual opposition. The new "constitutionalists", whose view was radicalized by the atrocities of St Bartholomew's Day in 1572, argued, among other things, that institutional limitations placed upon the crown prevented the misuse of authority that had been delegated to the ruler by the people. Using historical examples, they sought to prove that the representation of the "nation" in government was a long-established practice in France, laid out in the "ancient constitution." On the other hand, the *politique* absolutists, who were desperate to maintain order and preserve the state from disintegration, argued that the king must remain unfettered by institutional restraints in order to be able to govern in the best interests of the commonwealth.

This uncoupling of authority and limitation intensified through the course of the seventeenth century; constitutional and absolutist ideologies evolved as the two views of kingship drew further apart.[5] The seventeenth-century absolutists, for example, were more adamant in their enunciation of the principle of unfettered monarchical rule than had been the *politique* writers of a century earlier. Constitutionalists (that is, those who advocated the institutional limitation of royal power) now emphasized the authority of law over the king's actions, rather than concentrating on the role of the estates general in protecting the people against the excesses of absolute rule. These differences are linked to the changed composition of French government: by the early seventeenth century, the estates general was recognized as ineffectual, and the sovereign courts increasingly assumed the role of checking the royal abuse of authority.

During the eighteenth century, the constitutionalist struggles against absolute rule assumed a decidedly noble cast. *Nobiliaire* ideology echoed some of the principles of the sixteenth-century resistance theorists, but the nobles were substituted for the people as the "nation" and given an historic role to prevent royal actions injurious to the state. At the same time, a new debate arose between supporters of the now-defunct estates general and those of the Parlement of Paris as to which institution could best represent the interests of the people and protect individual liberties from encroachment by the crown.

Admittedly, in defining the tension which characterized political discourse between 1572 and 1789 as essentially an intensifying struggle between "constitutionalism" and "absolutism," there is a risk of oversimplification. Because of this, some working definitions are necessary, especially for the term "absolutism." I recognize that using the word absolutism is fraught with potential hazards but I do so deliberately because I believe that, despite the current academic discomfiture with the term, absolutism continues to be a viable concept when discussing *ancien régime* political thought. For the most part, I agree with historians who question the applicability of the term when characterizing the political reality of, say, France under Louis XIV, but the realm of theory, while undoubtedly connected to the socio-political context, merits separate consideration in this regard. We know, for example, that political writers and polemicists from the sixteenth to the eighteenth centuries referred to *puissance absolue* with notable frequency. The nature of authority in France was always open to debate and those advocating untrammelled monarchical power were no less vociferous than were opponents of the crown. That contemporaries argued over the limits of authority (or lack thereof) should be sufficient evidence that absolutism, at one end of this spectrum of debate, merits continued attention from historians of political thought. In no way do I mean to assert that "absolutism" was a static construct across three centuries. Obviously, what contemporaries meant by *puissance absolue* changed over time; the meaning and extent of absolute authority differed substantially as articulated by Claude de Seyssel, Jean Bodin and Cardin Le Bret. The balance between consent and limitation shifted in the course of the sixteenth and seventeenth centuries.

For the purposes of this study, "absolutism" refers to that stable strand of French political thought that, throughout the early modern period, emphasized the essential indivisibility of monarchical authority and recognized no *institutional* checks on the exercise of that authority. Defenders of royal authority never advocated the completely unlimited exercise of royal power, which they saw as arbitrary, not to say despotic, and which they clearly distinguished from *puissance absolue*. Absolute monarchs were always bound by natural and divine law, as well as the fundamental laws of the kingdom. The king was also prohibited from obstructing the citizen's access to, and enjoyment of, his own private property.[6] The key to understanding absolutist ideology, and the core of the working definition of absolutism employed in this book, is the recognition that for defenders of absolute monarchy the limitations placed on the exercise of royal authority were self-imposed. Perhaps naively, these writers believed that monarchs felt morally obliged to contain their actions within the parameters of divine and natural law and that they willingly adhered to the fundamental laws of the realm and prohibitions against incursions into the private property of their subjects. The emphasis here is on the notion of monarchical self-limitation. The scope of the limitations that the king was morally bound to observe, however, alternatively diminished and expanded throughout the early modern period in conjunction with the course of political events and the application of theories of reason of state. These contractions and expansions of the sphere of moral constraint within which the king operated are paralleled by increases and decreases in the volume of constitutionalist discourse.

Constitutionalism is a term which has caused even more trouble to historians of political thought. Some historians define constitutionalism as that theory which views the latent authority of the people as a necessary component of ideal government.[7] Others apply the term to denote the conception of the state as an organic entity, within which the king's powers are limited by the existence of a unified system of law moderating the actions of all the elements within the commonwealth.[8] Where these two senses of the term constitutionalism intersect is the starting point of our working definition: the recognition that the limitations placed on royal power are not merely self-imposed but consist of institutional restraints as well. The emphasis placed by some historians on a requisite sovereign community, and the focus of others on the restraining power of a corpus of law, highlight the central problem in obtaining a clear picture of constitutional ideology. The designation of the appropriate institution empowered to restrain the king changed over time. During the sixteenth century, constitutionalist writers invested the estates general with the responsibility and authority to limit monarchical abuse of power. In the course of the seventeenth century, however, *parlementaire* writers accentuated the function of the sovereign courts as guardians of the laws in an effort to enhance their role within government. Moreover, corporate rivalries complicate our understanding of constitutional ideology and may well have helped to undermine the force of constitutionalist arguments at the time.[9] Although the definitions employed in this study may seem broad, I believe that absolutism and constitutionalism are terms which continue to be useful in the examination of political thought in the early modern period. Indeed the analytical strength of the discussion lies in the breadth and flexibility of these constructs. This conceptual fluidity does not, of course, prohibit the evolution of these concepts into distinctly different ideologies about the nature of government. The interaction and reciprocal responsiveness of constitutionalist and absolutist ideas have not been adequately explored; the study of the way in which constitutionalist and absolutist writers evoked the memory of Louis XI forms the first step in such an analysis.

This study is informed by the notions of linguistic context championed by Quentin Skinner, John Dunn and J. G. A. Pocock.[10] My own understanding of how we ought to ascertain the meaning of a given text falls somewhere between Skinner's quest for authorial intent[11] and Pocock's call to learn the language(s) of political discourse.[12] I believe that the retrieval of the author's intent is essential to an understanding of a given text, although the meaning the author ascribes to his own work may be, as Pocock points out, only one of a number of meanings perceived by generations of readers. While the author cannot control all the meanings attributed to the text by its readers, he certainly controls the meaning he himself invests in his own work and, for that reason, what the author intends to do in writing is of significance. The manner in which the author participates in the political discourse is certainly as important as the cognitive and linguistic limitations that the available discourse places upon him. The character of the author's engagement with political language, ranging from wholesale acceptance to deliberate subversion, provides us with information about the status of political discourse at that particular moment.

It seems clear that, during the early modern period, out of a unified traditional "language" of politics there evolved two increasingly distinct dialects that assigned different meanings to the same words. The study of the historical reputation of Louis XI amply demonstrates the separation, opposition, and entangling of absolutist and constitutionalist discourse. The establishment of "linguistic context," which is the methodological cornerstone of the history of political discourse, requires a shift away from the concentration on so-called great works. This book employs such a technique in addressing Louis XI's historical reputation. Along with well-known works of political theory, I examine minor tracts by lesser-known authors, anonymous pamphlets and a few histories, in order to discern the pervasiveness of Louis XI as an evocative symbol. I have attempted to avoid the pitfalls associated with distinguishing between "elite" and "popular" culture; to the extent that pamphlets directed at a wider, albeit still literate audience, parallel interpretations of Louis XI found in more theoretical works, it seems that the language of political discourse permeates the popular/elite barrier. Nevertheless, while the reputation of Louis XI among the urban working poor and rural inhabitants, as expressed in poems and ballads, is a rich and worthwhile topic, such a cultural study lies beyond the scope of this book. My interests focus more on how interpretations and reinterpretations of Louis XI are employed as rhetorical strategies within early modern political thought.

Before proceeding to the examination of the historical reputation of Louis XI in the sixteenth, seventeenth and eighteenth centuries, it may be helpful to recount the major events of his reign. Louis XI was born at Bourges in 1423.[13] During much of his early life he was separated from his father since the uncertain circumstances of the Hundred Years War in the 1420s and 1430s required that the Dauphin be moved from place to place relatively often. Many of those early years were spent at the grim fortress of Loches. If one were given to psychological explanations, one might cite this early lack of permanence as the reason behind Louis XI's later insecurity, bordering on paranoia.[14] It is certainly true that Louis did not form any close family relationships, and he demonstrated singularly unfilial sentiments when he led the revolt against his father in 1440–1, known as the *Praguerie*.[15] After the failure of the revolt, in an effort to keep his restless son occupied, Charles VII gave Louis administrative control over Dauphiné; after further intrigues had widened the gap between father and son to irreconcilable proportions, Charles exiled Louis XI to that province. Louis governed Dauphiné as if he were completely independent and he pursued a foreign policy which was often at odds with that of his father. Finally, in 1456, when the threat of armed intervention by Charles VII in Dauphiné seemed imminent, Louis fled to Burgundy to seek the protection of his uncle, Philippe le Bon. He remained at the court of Burgundy until his accession to the throne of France in 1461.

Upon his succession, Louis engaged in a major administrative reorganization which alienated many of the great lords of the realm. A number of his father's loyal servants were deprived of their offices and "new" men, sometimes of lesser social standing, were appointed to these posts. Louis also set to work regaining territories which had been lost to France; in the pursuit of this goal, he was simultaneously undermining the autonomy of the princes in various provinces.[16] It has been persuasively argued that Louis deliberately attempted to transform the relationship of the nobles to the king from one based on vassalage to the more purely political one of non-contractual subjection.[17] Louis XI encountered particular resistance to his centralizing efforts in Brittany; François II, duc de Bretagne, refused to render the homage to Louis XI which the king felt was his due, and furthermore manifested an aggravating tendency to take on the trappings of autonomy. The two men clashed over who possessed the right to appoint bishops in Brittany. The duke pointed to Louis XI's threatening manner and actions as evidence of his intention to deprive the nobles of their privileges and powers. Thus motivated, the discontented nobles formed a coalition against Louis, called the League of the Public Weal, and placed at their head the king's brother, Charles of France, also known as the duc de Berry.[18] Other great seigneurs arrayed against the king included the comte de Charolais (the son of the duc de Bourgogne), and Jean de Bourbon. The major battle of the war which ensued, known as the War of the Public Weal, was fought at Montlhèry in July of 1465; it ended inconclusively. Louis decided to treat with the Leaguers and, after listening to the advice of an assembly of notables held in September, he acceded to all the demands of the rebellious nobles. Although the calling of an estates general and the formation of a committee of thirty-six deputies designed to reform the administration of the realm were part of these demands, the Treaties of St Maur and of Conflans, signed in October of 1465, consisted more of concessions to the particularist desires of each of the rebel magnates. The most important of these concessions was the granting of Normandy to Louis XI's brother, Charles, as an appanage.[19]

The issue of Normandy set the stage for the second phase of the conflict. Louis was uncomfortable about having Charles in such close geographic proximity to the duc de Bretagne. At the first opportunity he seized the pretext of protecting the territorial integrity of Normandy to occupy areas of the province.[20] Louis offered to give Roussillon to Charles in exchange for Normandy, but Charles refused. The dukes of Brittany and Burgundy supported the heir presumptive in his resistance to the king and the three concluded an alliance with the duc d'Alençon. The volatile situation did not erupt into open violence as it had in 1464–5, since Louis was able to defuse their potential force through the conclusion of separate treaties with each of the parties. Louis finally called an assembly of the estates to meet at Tours on 1 April 1468. The assembly only lasted six days, and, far from introducing reforms in administration, its sole purpose appears to have been the convenient exposition of the fundamental law that Louis could not alienate Normandy. The assembly decided that Charles could only be granted an appanage worth 12,000 *livres tournois* per year in rent (in addition to which Louis would give Charles another 60,000 *livres tournois* as a pension). In September 1468 a peace was signed between Louis XI and François II of Brittany; it was followed by the Treaty of Péronne signed in October by Louis and Charolais, who had succeeded his father as duc de Bourgogne in 1467.

The dénouement of the War of the Public Weal occurred at Tours in November of 1470, when Louis held an assembly of notables. The members of this assembly concurred with the monarch that he was not obliged to uphold any of the treaties signed between 1465 and 1468 because they had been obtained by force. From this point on, although Louis repeatedly came into conflict with the dukes of Brittany and Burgundy, there was never again the unified opposition to the crown which had characterized the activities of the great nobles during the 1460s. A number of factors contributed to the relative ineffectiveness of the grandees during the later years of Louis XI's reign. As of 1470, Charles of France was no longer heir to the throne, since Louis's second queen, Charlotte of Savoy, gave birth to a son on 30 June. Within two years, the brother of the king, the focus of all the rebels' aspirations, was dead. At that time Louis was accused of having ordered his brother's murder and the nobles rebelled once more in the summer of 1472. The rebellion was a short-lived affair; after ravaging the countryside without accomplishing any concrete goals, the Burgundians concluded a peace with Louis in November of 1472. Similarly, the duc de Bretagne was constrained to accept peace in October of the same year, after Louis had invaded his duchy once more. From that point on, the duc de Bourgogne, the real leader of the opposition to the king, was primarily occupied with military campaigns in Lorraine until his death on the battlefield of Nancy in 1477. With Charles of France dead, the duc de Bretagne quiescent and the duc de Bourgogne occupied elsewhere, the nobles were deprived of effective leadership.

This brief account of the War of the Public Weal cannot convey the complicated web of intrigues practised both by the Universal Spider and by his enemies. Other important aspects of Louis XI's reign, such as his relationship with the church[21] and his commercial policy,[22] were also influential in the subsequent construction of his historical image. The alternating periods of conflict and cooperation between Louis XI and the papacy, especially over the issue of the Pragmatic Sanction, were of particular interest to Gallican writers active at the turn of the seventeenth century. Sixteenth-century constitutionalists often cited the onerous levels of taxation under Louis XI as evidence of the king's tyranny. Moreover, during the latter half of the seventeenth century, comparisons were made between Louis XI's economic policies and the mercantilism practised by Colbert. Nevertheless, writers arguing about the nature of kingship and the state, with whom this book is primarily concerned, relied predominantly on Louis XI's dealings with the great nobles and the sovereign courts. Of particular interest was the episode when the Parlement of Paris successfully defied the king. Under the leadership of *premier président* La Vacquerie, the parlement refused to register one of Louis XI's edicts which it considered to be unjust. The spirited resistance of the parlementaire members in the face of Louis XI's evident displeasure, and the latter's subsequent acquiescence, were repeatedly cited by political theorists as constitutionally portentous.

Louis XI's personality should not be overlooked as a factor in the interpretations of later writers. Much was made of his superstitious and suspicious nature, attributes which allegedly intensified toward the end of his life. His political sagacity and willingness to disregard moral considerations in pursuit of a goal became very important in the debate between proponents of *raison d'état* and advocates of traditional morality in the early seventeenth century. Most importantly, Louis XI's wilful nature and his refusal to countenance any perceived encroachments on his authority were described extensively by writers on both sides of the theoretical divide.

Despite the strong disagreement over the nature of his reign and the character of Louis XI himself, no one could deny that he left France with much needed peace when he died. Of course, this may be due as much to the fact that he managed to outlive all of his worst enemies as to any action taken on his part! As Michelet was to write in the nineteenth century, Louis XI's most loyal associate was Death; Edward IV of England, Louis's brother Charles, and Louis's nemesis, Charles le Téméraire, all pre-deceased him. The fortunate demise of René of Anjou (the so-called "King of Naples") and his heirs meant that Anjou, Maine and Provence escheated to the royal domain. Louis XI himself finally expired on 30 August 1483 after several years of illness, punctuated by attacks of apoplexy.

This synoptic treatment of these critical events serves merely to provide the necessary background to a discussion of Louis XI's historical reputation in the sixteenth, seventeenth and eighteenth centuries, which seems, as already suggested, to have been primarily based upon various interpretations of the War of the Public Weal.

In order to analyse the views held by later authors about Louis XI, one must be aware of the sources available to them. An attempt has been made here to examine a few relatively well-known works that are representative of the large corpus of contemporary and near-contemporary works about the king. Jacques Le Long's bibliography makes clear that a vast array of material was available to writers interested in Louis XI, although, for the most part, the manuscripts and books listed by Le Long were secondary accounts not based primarily on documentary sources.[23] We do know, however, that documentary evidence such as letters and manifestos were available to historians and political writers; certainly, by the end of the seventeenth century, Joachim Legrand's massive biography of Louis XI is replete with references to such primary sources. Therefore, I begin this – admittedly selective – survey of contemporary accounts with a brief look at a few of the documents pertaining to the War of the Public Weal, as these provide us with first-hand information about seigneurial attitudes toward Louis XI, as well as clearly indicating avowed and actual motives for the rebellion.[24]

The idea of Louis XI as the oppressor of "le pauvre peuple" appears repeatedly in the declarations made by the rebelling lords. Very early on in the conflict, Jean, duc de Bourbon, who, along with the duc de Bourgogne's son, the comte de Charolais, led the noble forces arrayed against the king, outlined his ostensible motives for rebellion:

> Dear and good friends . . . before and since the beginning of the reign of *monsieur* the king who currently rules, the deeds of this kingdom have been conducted and governed more by will than reason, and all exactions, oppressions, wrongs, griefs and other infinite ills have been done and

given and are still being done and given each day, as much against the churches [and] nobles as against the poor and middling people . . . [25]

Similarly, in a later manifesto made by the comte de Charolais, the plight of "le pauvre peuple" is the constant theme. Charolais, in speaking to the citizens of Amiens, reviews the abuses related to him in a letter from the duc de Berry. Charolais uses terminology in referring to Berry which gives a hint as to his real intentions. Charolais refers to the duc de Berry as being willing to receive "aid and counsel from the princes and lords of his blood and other notable men of *his kingdom.*"[26]

The warring nobles' constant references to the issue of taxation as one of their motivations for rebellion did not go unnoticed by Louis XI. He responded by neatly turning the tables, asserting that such burdensome levels of taxation were the fault of the nobles since the bulk of the king's revenues were spent on their pensions.[27] The documents demonstrate equally well the other major issue which coloured histories written about Louis XI in the fifteenth century: the struggle of the old feudal lords against the newly marshalled forces of centralization. Even if the nobles sincerely believed they were fighting on behalf of "le peuple menu," the element of self-preservation was at least as strong a motivation. This is most clearly demonstrated in letters written by Charles, duc de Berry, immediately after the Treaty of Conflans was concluded, in which he was given Normandy as an appanage. It became apparent to the duke that Louis XI did not intend to fulfil the articles of the treaty concerning Normandy. Charles realized full well that Roussillon for Normandy was not a fair exchange, since he would have to spend large amounts of money on the maintenance of troops in order to keep the ever-rebellious Catalans in line. Louis had only recently asserted control over the region, which he held as a trust against payment of 200,000 crowns from John II of Aragon, who had needed French troops to help quell the uprising of Catalan rebels in the province.[28] In lamenting his situation to Charolais, Charles outlined the implications of the way the royal offer had been tendered:

> The form in which this matter proceeded against me touches all the peers of France, who possess the dignity and privilege that the king cannot and must not proceed against them without the assembly and consent of the other [peers]; consider also that at present it is a question of the ancient and natural peerages of France.[29]

In expressing these concerns, the duc de Berry was touching upon constitutional questions which will re-emerge in more formulated and encompassing form in the following centuries. Both these concerns, the injustice of taxation without consent and the inherent rights of the nobility, are specific aspects of the broader and more important question of the nature of royal government.

The struggle to come to grips with this problem forms the underlying theme of another major documentary source, Jean Masselin's *Journal des Etats*

Généraux de France tenus à Tours en 1484. The *Journal* clearly raises the constitutional questions which occupy such a central role in French political thought. Furthermore, there is the everpresent, though almost always subliminal, connection between the discussion of these questions by members of the assembly and antipathy toward the memory of the late king. The juxtaposition of a dialogue about the constitution and the wholesale rejection of Louis XI's policies regarding taxation sets the stage for assertions that Louis XI in fact deliberately undermined the ancient constitution of France.

Jean Masselin's account of the proceedings is lucid, interesting, and informed. This is not surprising since he seems to have occupied a position of some importance within the assembly and was generally regarded by other members as being an honest man and an eloquent orator. Almost nothing is known about his early years. He appears to have received a doctorate in both civil and canon law, becoming a canon at the Cathedral of Rouen. It is as an official in the service of the archbishop of Rouen that Masselin became one of the four deputies from that *bailliage* at Tours.[30]

It seems to have been generally understood by the deputies that one of the main reasons for the calling of the estates was the necessity of establishing a regency council in light of Charles VIII's minority. The first paragraph of the journal is devoted to explaining why the estates were called to Tours. Since the crown has come down to a minor, "the guarding of the prince and the disposition of the kingdom have devolved to the men of the three estates."[31] The assembly was very conscious of the larger issues involved in deciding what role the estates would play in the choosing of the new king's councillors. Masselin summarizes the problem that faced the deputies:

> This question: what is the power of the estates? sustained a thousand debates during all our meetings and in all the public discussions. Some believed that because the supreme authority of the kingdom is in the estates, they must never resort to supplications . . . but that it is necessary rather to decree and command, at least until the estates have instituted a council that will receive from them sovereign power. Others maintained by contrast that it is not the estates but the princes of the blood to whom, as legitimate guardians, the law gives the government of the kingdom; that in the rigour of law it is not necessary to ask the consent of the estates, except to levy taxes, and if one nevertheless does [ask consent] it is purely the favour of the princes and indulgence on their part.[32]

In the debate described by Masselin, the first position was eloquently expounded by Philippe Pot, Seigneur de La Roche. In one sentence Pot summarizes the essential conflict underlying the question of the regency council: "How can flatterers attribute sovereignty to the prince who takes his existence from the people?"[33]

Despite the repeated expressions of such constitutional principles, the role of the assembly in choosing the king's councillors came under steady and successful attack, both from aristocratic elements within the assembly itself and from agents of the young king who were loath to give up their present positions of influence. Factional struggle ensued between the sister and brother-in-law of the new king, Anne and Pierre de Beaujeu, on the one side, and the heir to the throne, Louis D'Orléans, on the other. The involvement of the assembly was whittled away through successive royal interventions until its right of nomination was completely undermined and it was left with the sole function of confirming the choices of Charles VIII, or rather of the Beaujeu faction, which succeeded in asserting control over the king.[34] The question of the regency council was only successful in bringing the constitutional questions into sharper focus. In terms of actually affecting the role of the assembly in government, it could be argued that the struggle resulted in the complete victory of the crown and the abasement of the assembly's prerogative.

A similar dichotomy exists between the theoretical and actual exercise of authority over the issue of taxation. The king's councillors asked for a total annual *taille* of 1,500,000 livres; initially, the estates were only willing to grant 250,000. The great seigneurs, noting with some exasperation the independent-mindedness of the assembly, commented: "We think that you have pretensions to write the code for an imaginary monarchy and to suppress the ancient laws."[35] Eventually, the assembly grudgingly agreed to grant the sum demanded by the king, but then the unity of the assembly was shattered by quarrels over the way in which the burden of the *taille* was to be distributed among *bailliages*. Though consent was nominally required of the estates, it seems apparent that they were incapable of translating the theory of their ultimate authority, so eloquently expounded in the record, into actual, sustained opposition to the demands of the king and council.

It is not surprising that Louis XI is first referred to in the context of the discussion about finances. Direct references to Louis in the text, however, are few and far between. It seems almost as if the assembly as a whole was studiously avoiding any mention of the king himself. Nevertheless, attacks on Louis XI are implicit throughout the proceedings, since the plight of a people burdened with taxes is a constant theme. There is one lengthy diatribe made against Louis by a Parisian judge named de Forez which is so scathing and vehement an attack that, even on its own, it could account for Louis's poor reputation in the following years:

> You know that formerly, in the time of Louis, the entire state and the church were dishonoured, elections were fixed, indignities performed against episcopates and benefices, the goods of the church stolen, the most holy persons abandoned without dignity, how shall I say it, abandoned to a vile and ignominious condition. The nobility, for its part, did not suffer less damage: it saw itself denied its rewards, tormented by the calling of the *bans* and military expeditions, deprived of its privileges and its honours. It is not necessary to call to your memory the informers and calumniators against innocence admitted throughout the court, given

honourable titles and public offices, nor to those avid men, inventors of new profits, placed in charge of levying taxes and in the highest administration, for the most wicked of men were the most loved . . . [36]

The historical portrait of Louis XI takes on an even more sinister hue if we turn to chronicles. Georges Chastellain's work, *Chronique des derniers ducs de Bourgogne*, is an excellent example of the character assassination in which fifteenth-century chroniclers seem to have indulged. Although the *Chronique* was not published until the nineteenth century, it did circulate in manuscript throughout the early modern period and was well known as a source for Burgundian history as well as offering insight into fifteenth-century French politics.[37] Chastellain's negative attitude can be understood in part as the product of his provincial consciousness. Chastellain's whole career was connected with the court of Burgundy; he became official historiographer in 1455. It is no wonder that he did not view Louis favourably since, as a loyal Burgundian, he reacted with open hostility to Louis's centralizing policies.

Chastellain's chronicle is a monument both to the court of Burgundy and to Georges Chastellain himself. Its pages are filled with pageantry and chivalrous sentiments; its intent seems to have been less to portray historical events than to evoke a general glorious ambience. Louis XI, with his often less than noble demeanour and his political machinations that constituted the antithesis of the chivalric code, does not fare well at the hands of the Burgundian chronicler. Right at the beginning of his chronicle, Chastellain provides us with his opinions of Louis. Although he presents Louis as being grateful for his uncle Philippe le Bon's protection in his years of exile from the French court, Chastellain quickly undermines this initially favourable impression by pointing out the gross disparity between Louis's pretty words and his subsequent mistreatment of Philippe.[38]

As the chronicle progresses, condemnations of Louis are interspersed with depictions of the grandeur of the Burgundian house. The most interesting chapter in the chronicle is Chapter 54 of the third part, in which Chastellain feels compelled to recount a dream or vision he experienced concerning Louis XI. In this vision a woman appears in Louis XI's chamber (significantly, after having been barred from entering by some of the king's minions). Through the vehicle of this celestial image, Chastellain is able to criticize the king unreservedly, with an undisguised hatred lacking in his other condemnations of Louis:

> Louis, king of France, the time has come that the royal French dignity has descended to a bestial man and the most worthy and holy crown on earth is poised on the head of a non-man! Oh, cursed time for you and cursed the reign of such a king who will abuse [the crown] thus![39]

The harangue against Louis constitutes one of the most vitriolic attacks made on the monarch during the fifteenth century.

Through the vehicle of the dream, Chastellain can make what are obviously his own personal opinions synonymous with divine revelation and eternal truth, especially since the woman may well represent the Virgin Mary.[40] The woman ends her oration with a plea for Louis XI to reform his ways: "Cease, Louis, cease, I beg you. Return to yourself and your royal nature . . . and moderate the extreme viciousness that brings you blame, wounds and damage finally to your salvation."[41]

Chastellain's ideas about Louis XI filtered down to later writers by a number of means. We know that Chastellain's *Chroniques* circulated in manuscript form. In addition, it is possible that the writings of Jean Meschinot, the Breton poet, contributed to the spread of Chastellain's negative attitudes toward Louis XI. It is certain that there were letters exchanged between the two writers, and their careers at the courts of Burgundy and Brittany follow a similar pattern. The primary reason for associating the two men with reference to the reputation of Louis XI is the existence of what may well have been a collaborative effort entitled the *Vingt-Cinq Ballades*. Although there has been some debate among modern scholars about the actual subject of the *Ballades*, internal evidence would seem to support the contention that they are political verses directed specifically against Louis XI.[42]

The contention that the *Vingt-Cinq Ballades* are indeed directed against Louis XI is supported by a character description which, although leaving the subject unnamed, includes all the unfortunate traits commonly assigned to him. Furthermore, the plight of the people is a constant theme in the work.[43] All of Louis XI's vices listed by Chastellain appear in Meschinot's work. The connection between Chastellain's chronicle and Meschinot's poetry is demonstrated even more clearly in another ballad by Meschinot, written in the form of a dialogue between Louis XI and France. If we conclude that the apparition in Chapter 54, Part 3 of Chastellain's chronicle was meant to be France, it could be asserted that it is this character who also makes an appearance in Meschinot's ballad. Although concrete evidence is lacking, this assertion merits consideration since Meschinot's ballad does recall Chastellain's vision in terms of its vehemence and the specific crimes with which it charges Louis XI.

> Sire . . . – Que veux? – Entendez . . . – Croy? – Mon cas.
> Or dy. – Je suys . . . – Qui? – La destruicte France!
> Par qui? – Par vous. – Comment? – En tous estats.
> Tu mens. – Non fais. – Qui le dit? – Ma souffrance.
> Que souffres-tu? – Meschief. – Quel? – A oultrance.
> Je n'en croy rien. – Bien y pert. – N'en dy plus!
> Las! si feray. – Tu perds temps. – Quelz abus!
> Qu'ay-je mal fait? – Contre paix. – Et comment?
> Guerroyant . . . – Qui? – Voz amys et congus.
> Parle plus beau. – Je ne puis, bonnement.[44]

A few lines later in the dialogue, Louis XI says that his subjects owe him obedience, but when asked what he owes them, he responds, "Rien."

Meschinot's *Vingt-Cinq Ballades* appeared as a supplement to his more famous work, *Les Lunettes des Princes*, in the edition published in Paris in 1495, and was included thereafter in all the subsequent editions. *Les Lunettes des Princes* was a tremendously popular work in the first half of the sixteenth century, with no less than thirteen editions published in Paris, Rouen and Lyons before 1540.[45] Although Meschinot's works were probably of somewhat less interest to political writers, since *Les Lunettes* was merely one in a long and increasingly tedious succession of handbooks for princes, it seems clear that his work was popular at some level, contributing in no small measure to the growing legend of the tyrannical king Louis XI.[46]

The two most important contemporary histories about Louis XI are Thomas Basin's *Histoire de Louis XI* and Philippe de Commynes's *Mémoires*. Whereas the chronicles rarely penetrate beneath the surface of events, these two histories are remarkable in the extent to which they attempt to understand and communicate issues of causation which lie behind the battles and treaties. They are also distinct from the chronicles in that they possess a didactic quality, although this didacticism is primarily moral in the case of Basin, and pragmatic with regard to Commynes.[47] This tendency, both to analyse events and to employ them as examples illustrating truths which transcend the historical context, makes these two works much more important to later writers engaged in precisely the same sort of enterprise of utilizing history to support moral or political axioms.

In this respect, Basin's work is by far the most damaging testimony about Louis XI's reign. Not only does he condemn Louis on the grounds of morality, he also depicts the opposition to the monarch as completely justified and in accordance with both Scriptural law and laws regarding the governance of a commonwealth. Basin makes no claim to be impartial; his duty as a historian is to portray the truth *as he sees it*. Basin notes that, because he depicts Louis XI as such an extreme and malevolent character, his readers will doubt both the veracity of the portrait and Basin's objectivity.

> At the time I began to write, I felt doubtful and uncertain. . . . I was afraid, in fact, that by revealing his subtle, malicious, perfidious, sottish, pernicious, cruel deeds, some of our readers, little inclined to take us at our word, might take me for a slanderer rather than a historian . . .[48]

It is indeed tempting to characterize Basin as a "slanderer," given the scurrilous nature of this potted description, but Basin's hostility is understandable in light of his experiences. He was born in 1412 into a rich Norman merchant family. He received a civil law degree at Pavia and a canon law degree at Louvain. At twenty-three years of age he entered the Church and rose through the clerical ranks to become Bishop of Lisieux in 1447. Basin had helped to thwart the Dauphin Louis's attempt to take Normandy from Charles VII and later he was actively involved in the War of the Public Weal. It is no wonder, then, that Louis XI harboured a lasting animosity toward the Norman bishop and forced him into exile in 1471.[49]

Basin never seems able to restrain himself from vilifying Louis XI. In several chapters at the end of Book 7,[50] Basin describes Louis's character in unrelievedly hostile terms. The chapters have headings describing positive attributes, which Basin proceeds to demonstrate are completely lacking in the king. In fact, Louis XI possessed the contrasting vice in abundance. When Basin entitles a chapter "Sa générosité", he really means to discuss how Louis drained the life blood from France. In Chapter 12, entitled "Sagesse et prudence du roi Louis," Basin uses extremely pejorative language: "By a great number of his words and actions he showed himself to be so ridiculous and foolish that there is very little difference between him and a crazy person."[51] Among Basin's most searing indictments of Louis XI is Chapter 15, which deals with the king's methods of distributing justice.[52] Moreover, according to Basin, Louis XI was an alcoholic who committed his worst actions while in a drunken haze.[53] The list of vices which Basin attributes to Louis is seemingly endless. More important than Basin's moral condemnation, however, is the conclusion the author draws from the recognition of the king's moral bankruptcy.

Basin anticipates the Huguenot resistance theorists in his complete justification of the League of the Public Weal. The coalition of the nobles was motivated by their desire to reform the realm.[54] In a significant passage, Basin refutes the argument that the princes may under no circumstances try to correct the king's behaviour through the use of force. Basin employs the ship analogy, ubiquitous in political theory: people on an imperilled ship, whether they be slaves, mercenaries, or free men, are permitted to resist an incompetent or insane captain. It is important to note that Basin includes among the marks of a "captain" unfit to lead, an unwillingness to take the counsel of wise men.[55] Basin then recounts the specific crimes of Louis XI and asks: "Therefore why, I ask, cannot *les grands* and the nobles, seeing the state reduced to such devastation, assemble together for the common good and to bring a remedy for evils of which there are so many as can hardly be recounted."[56]

This support for the actions of the nobles during the War of the Public Weal was couched in broad enough terms to be viewed as a general theory of resistance to a ruler who no longer gives the welfare of the state his first priority.[57] Coupled with the moral condemnation of Louis XI, Basin's views on the legitimacy of noble resistance may well have contributed to the later constitutionalist vision that equated Louis XI with tyranny.

The prosecution has all but laid the case to rest. It is time for the defence to speak and, in Philippe de Commynes, Louis XI has an advocate of no mean ability. Commynes's *Mémoires* are the only important example of a fifteenth-century source that portrays Louis XI not only as a capable king, but even as an exemplar of the political sagacity necessary to reign over a kingdom as vast as France. It is no wonder that Commynes is an admirer of Louis XI; he was one of the king's councillors for more than ten years and appears to have been one of Louis XI's closest confidants. In terms of recounting the major events of the period, Commynes had the added advantage of having spent a number of years at the Burgundian court before changing loyalties in August of 1472.

Commynes was born about 1447. He entered the service of the Duke of Burgundy in 1464 and held the offices of councillor and chamberlain. Commynes may well have thought the advancement in the Burgundian court too slow and lacking satisfactory emoluments. So, on the night of 7 August 1472, he betrayed his lord and fled to the camp of Louis XI. Apparently Commynes was already receiving a pension from Louis in 1471. There is no doubt that transferring his loyalties to the king of France had its financial advantages. Immediately upon entering the king's service, Commynes received the principality of Talmont, and in 1473 he married Hélène de Chambes and secured the title of Seigneur d'Argenton.[58]

In reading the *Mémoires*, one is immediately struck by the most obvious difference between this work and all the chronicles and histories discussed thus far. Louis XI is presented here as a flawed but generally competent monarch. In keeping with the other personalities found in the pages of the *Mémoires*, Louis XI possesses a complexity which successfully undermines the reader's ability to make a quick judgement about his character. The attribute which Commynes admires most about Louis is his political sagacity. Louis XI understood perfectly the way in which the game of politics was played and he was himself a consummate player. Most of Louis XI's other admirable qualities appear to be harnessed to this shrewd political sense. Louis XI was characterized by a general modesty of demeanour and was willing to admit when he was in error, a trait which Commynes values highly. Moreover, Commynes truly believes that, despite the conflicts that plagued Louis XI's reign, which seem to have been the result of some major miscalculations in the early years, Louis always kept the good of the state uppermost in his mind.

Commynes often points out defects in Louis's character which are considered especially undesirable because they undermine the king's ability to make wise deliberations. Commynes finds a way to lessen the negative impact of these faults, however, by saying that if one must possess defects, and all humans do, then these, especially suspicion, are not the worst to have since they may occasionally be turned to one's advantage. Commynes would rather see the state ruled by a wise and suspicious king than by a foolish and trusting one.[59]

Commynes's positive view of Louis XI sets the *Mémoires* apart from the other contemporary sources available to later theorists. This in itself, however, cannot account for the tremendous popularity of the work; the *Mémoires* was first published in Paris in 1524 and new editions of the book appeared thereafter with astonishing regularity. Already by 1560 there were at least sixteen French editions.[60] By the end of the sixteenth century, the *Mémoires* had been translated into Latin, Italian, Dutch, German and English, with a Swedish edition being published a little later in 1624.[61]

The popularity of the *Mémoires* and the frequency with which writers of all intellectual hues referred to it could be due to the presence of two provocative theoretical elements in the work. The first is Commynes's ambiguous view on constitutional issues. By quoting out of context, both absolutists and resistance theorists could find an ally in Commynes. The second element is a certain political pragmatism, inadequately labelled "proto-Machiavellian," which was employed by some writers wishing to assert the extensive powers of the crown without being stigmatized as followers of the Florentine. A brief discussion of Commynes's political theory (unformulated as it was) demonstrates both his ambiguous view of the commonwealth and the pragmatism which made the *Mémoires* of continual use to later polemicists.

At a time when over-mighty nobles were threatening to devastate France, one needed the type of strong monarchy which could contain these rebellious subjects. Commynes does not appear to have regarded with any great alarm the lack of assemblies of the estates during the reign of Louis XI; the consultative machinery necessary for good government was available to the king in the form of counsellors, and Commynes devoted a substantial amount of space to the necessity of obtaining good counsel. This was the prerogative of the king and the calibre of the counsellors depended upon the king being able to make intelligent choices.

The edifice of absolutism implied by Commynes's concentration of decision-making power in the king lacks a cornerstone, however. With regard to taxation, Commynes is adamant about the necessity of obtaining the consent of the estates before levying any new taxes. In Chapter 18, Book 5 of the *Mémoires*, to which the sixteenth-century constitutionalists most often refer, Commynes describes a commonwealth in which the powers of the king are distinctly limited: "Was there ever a king or lord on earth who had the power, outside his [personal] domain, of levying one *denier* on his subjects without the permission and consent of those who must pay it, except through tyranny or violence?"[62] He refers more specifically to France when he says: "Our king [who] is the lord of the world has the least cause to say, 'I have the privilege of levying on my subjects whatever I please to do.' "[63]

On the other hand, it would be a mistake to employ these examples as an illustration of Commynes's commitment to limited monarchy. Commynes based all his ideas about the relationship of the king to the commonwealth on a surprisingly naive assumption that friction would not occur between the king and the estates. The king may well require the consent of the estates for taxation, but the latter would never refuse a request for funds because the deputies were all loyal subjects of the monarch.[64] Commynes thought that the meeting of the estates enhanced rather than undermined the king's authority. It is difficult to arrive at a conclusion about Commynes's views on the relationship between king and commonwealth, largely because he himself felt no need to analyse the institutions of France. His political ideas are largely centred on the psychological combat which characterized relations between princes. The emphasis he places on the ability of the individual to influence his surroundings, for good or ill, precludes anything but the most cursory of discussions about institutions.

We have seen that Commynes's work is characterized by a certain political pragmatism; he often justifies unscrupulous actions as necessary for the attainment or preservation of the best interests of the state. Pragmatic considerations exist in tension with those of morality, however, and Commynes is never able to resolve which of these should be upheld when making political decisions. On the one hand, Commynes espouses many of the tenets held as valid in the discourse of "normal" Renaissance politics.[65] He does believe that a prince will suffer divine retribution if he acts iniquitously. Some scholars have even maintained that Commynes possessed a concept of the ideal prince.[66] Whether we agree with this assertion or not, it cannot be denied that Commynes quite willingly countenanced radical departures from this ideal moral framework in the pursuit of desirable political goals.

The fact that Commynes was nowhere near as "godless" as Machiavelli in the eyes of sixteenth- and seventeenth-century writers accounts, at least in part, for his acceptance into the mainstream of political thought.[67] His continued and indeed increasing popularity at the end of the sixteenth century was linked, as well, to renewed study of the works of Tacitus. Tacitean political philosophy was employed in most analyses of Machiavellian ideas, both to support and to refute them. Commynes and Guicciardini were viewed as the modern thinkers whose ideas most closely resembled Tacitean politics, and thus, because they shared a number of ideas with Machiavelli, they were employed, along with Tacitus, in discussions of Machiavellian ideology.[68] It seems apparent, then, that any assessment of Louis XI's historical reputation in the sixteenth century must be related to the various and contrasting interpretations of Commynes's *Mémoires* which are made possible by the work's own internal inconsistencies. The juxtaposition of vaguely formulated constitutionalist doctrine and "proto-Machiavellian" precepts makes the *Mémoires* the perfect "all-purpose" source for the conflicting political ideas of the sixteenth, seventeenth and eighteenth centuries.

We turn finally to the views of Claude de Seyssel, who, although not quite contemporary with the other sources cited, is far enough removed from the later sixteenth-century writers to constitute a historical source, at least in their eyes. As with Commynes, Seyssel's ideas can be found in treatises on both sides of the constitutional issue, since his most famous work, *La Monarchie de France*, is characterized by a balanced view of government whose expression is sometimes ambiguous and therefore easily distorted for the purposes of more polemical writers. Seyssel's idea of *freins* can be interpreted to mean a system of institutional limitations imposed on the king's authority, or, alternatively, it can be understood in more absolutist terms if one places the emphasis on the voluntary element evident in the work. Some of the ideas expressed in *La Monarchie* find illustration in his panegyric to Louis XII, the *Histoire de Louis XII*, and at times his views of Louis XI appear to be a product of these political conceptions.

Claude de Seyssel was born into a noble Savoyard family sometime around 1450. The Seyssel family was aligned with the French camp in Savoy, and Claude de Seyssel's career followed a dual path in pursuit of both French and Savoyard interests. His education was primarily legal; he studied civil law at the University of Turin, where, after receiving a doctorate, he taught for several years. In 1492 he left Savoy to enter the service of Charles VIII. Throughout the 1490s, Seyssel's dual loyalties were manifest: in 1496 he became a counsellor to Savoy, and in 1498, following the accession of Louis d'Orléans as Louis XII, he became a member of the Great Council. Simultaneously with establishing his courtly political credentials, Seyssel also advanced in his ecclesiastical career. Although he had not yet taken priestly orders, he accepted a benefice in Mondavi. Eventually, in 1503, after obtaining a dispensation, Seyssel finally entered the priesthood. In 1511, Louis XII awarded the bishopric of Marseilles to Seyssel, although Seyssel did not take up the post until after the king's death in 1515. He later petitioned for, and was granted, a transfer to the archbishopric of Turin, where he spent the years until his death in 1520. Seyssel was sent on missions to the Emperor Maximilian, as well as to a number of Italian cities, thereby gaining useful diplomatic experience and putting his legal education to good use in the service of the French king.[69]

The *Histoire de Louis XII* was written in response to criticism of an oration Seyssel had given at the court of Henry VII in England. Seyssel had been sent to England to explain why the marriage of Claude of France and Charles of Austria was not going to be carried out. His speech, recounting the glories of France, was published in Paris in 1506.[70] It was followed by an attack which forced Seyssel to justify his stance in the earlier oration. Seyssel's response was the even more mawkishly patriotic *Les Louenges du roy Louis XIIe* (retitled the *Histoire de Louis XII* in the two subsequent editions of 1558 and 1587). The obsequiousness of his prose regarding Louis XII led Jacques Poujol to award him a place "de choix parmi les thuriféraires des Rois de France."

The *Histoire* is basically a comparison of Louis XII with all the previous monarchs of France. It is not surprising that Louis XI is portrayed in a less than favourable light in the *Histoire*, since no other French king can quite measure up to the quality of Louis XII. Even Charlemagne suffers at the hands of Seyssel.[71] Seyssel devotes a separate section of the work to Louis XI and he apparently feels a particular need to demonstrate Louis XII's superiority over Louis XI because, he writes, there are men who speak incessantly "of [Louis XI's] deeds, of his sayings, praising him almost to the sky, saying that he was the most wise, and the most powerful, the most liberal, the most valiant and the happiest [king] that ever was in France."[72]

Seyssel seems determined to set the record straight singlehandedly. In contrast to Louis XII, "le père du peuple," Seyssel maintains that Louis XI was, in fact, unpopular because of the burdensome taxes he levied. Moreover, he was hated by much of the nobility whom he had deprived of positions after succeeding to the throne. Interestingly enough, however, Seyssel speaks of the War of the Public Weal in terms very similar to those of Commynes. He sees the rebellion as the product of the discontented nobles who only pretended to fight for the good of the commonwealth.[73]

After recounting the misfortunes of Louis XI's reign, Seyssel engages in a direct comparison between the two kings. Seyssel makes much of the fact that Louis XI was unwilling to venture outside France to engage in military endeavours designed to redound to the glory of France, as Louis XII did in Italy. This point is surprising considering Seyssel's viewpoint about the hazards involved in conquering countries, as expressed in *La Monarchie*. This is also a direct refutation of Commynes who admires Louis XI for never having risked troops and funds on unnecessary enterprises outside the borders of France. Seyssel asserts that Louis XI could not have done so even if he had wanted to since he was constantly occupied in keeping his own discontented subjects obedient. As well, Seyssel compares the two kings in terms of their piety. His argument with regard to piety is inconsistent since he criticizes Louis XI for making grand but insincere demonstrations of piety. He applauds Louis XII, however, for the frequent occasions when he would "cure" scrofula, which is arguably among the most visible manifestations of piety imaginable. Finally, Seyssel compares the kings with regard to their habits of dress. Again, what could be construed as a positive attribute, Louis XI's modest attire, is criticized by Seyssel who says that it is too extreme, "so that he often seems to be more a merchant or a man of low condition than a king, which is not seemly for a great prince."[74] This relates to Seyssel's notion of a flexible but well-defined social order; by dressing in a fashion inappropriate to his station, Louis XI is inviting the contempt of the lower classes, which detracts from the continued harmonious operation of the established hierarchy.

Rather disingenuously, Seyssel completes the comparison of the two kings by disclaiming the desire to malign anyone. He merely feels it his duty to point out when the acts of a king are reprehensible. Of course, it is difficult to take Seyssel at his word in this regard, since his hero, Louis XII, does not seem to have perpetrated any act at all which is deserving of even the slightest criticism in Seyssel's eyes, whereas all the previous kings of France, Louis XI not least among them, have utterly failed to attain such heights of perfection.

This completes our brief survey of selected contemporary and near-contemporary works about Louis XI that were available to later writers in one form or another. Considering the unmitigated hostility manifested in most of the works discussed, it is puzzling that Louis XI received any favourable press at all in the following centuries. It could be argued that the influence of one work, that of Commynes, far outweighed the others. It was the best known of the works discussed; certainly it was the most frequently cited. We are confronted with a paradox: if the works condemning Louis XI were perhaps less familiar to sixteenth-, seventeenth- and eighteenth-century writers, while the one work extolling his positive attributes was constantly employed by them, why did Louis XI's historical reputation suffer so grievously at the hands of a number of political writers? It seems apparent that the contemporary works negatively disposed to Louis XI successfully created a climate hostile to the king, even though they may not have been influential as individual works. This view was certainly inherited by sixteenth-century writers, some of whom then employed the negative aspect to weight their arguments about resistance. Others, in attempting to refute these assertions, had of necessity to revise the historical reputation of Louis XI in order to deprive the resistance theorists of one of their main symbols. Commynes's *Mémoires* proved a valuable source, since it possessed contradictory elements which could be isolated and employed by polemicists of both persuasions.

The remainder of this book is divided into three sections. I have deliberately chosen not to proceed chronologically in this survey of Louis XI's historical reputation because it seems to me that the contrasting interpretations of the Spider King each deserve their own detailed and sustained analysis. Part I explores the enduring image of Louis XI as a tyrant whose wilful acts and blatant disregard for established representative institutions set a disturbing precedent. This section takes as its starting point the St Bartholomew's Day Massacre, which polarized political opinion and contributed to the initial bifurcation of political thought into constitutionalist and absolutist discourses. The constitutionalist aspect in seventeenth-century political thought is followed in Chapter 2. Through a discussion of the *thèse nobiliaire/thèse royale* controversy in Chapter 3, I indicate how opposed, and yet how entangled, constitutionalist and absolutist strands had become by the eighteenth century. Through the nuances in Louis XI's reputation I hope to highlight both the continuity and the changes wrought in constitutionalism between 1560 and 1789.

Part II explores the image of Louis XI as sage. In the sixteenth century, coupled with efforts to support assertions about the value of strong, purely self-limiting monarchy, *politique* absolutists portrayed Louis XI positively as a shrewd monarch whose devotion to the advancement of French interests ought to be emulated. Changes in absolutist theory throughout the late sixteenth and seventeenth centuries correspond with alterations in the reputation of Louis XI. Chapter 4 thus explores absolutist theory from the outbreak of the Religious Wars to the sunset years of Louis XIV, using the reputation of Louis XI as a map to guide us through the shifting landscape. Chapter 5 examines the contribution of emerging *raison d'état* to the reputation of Louis XI and to absolutist thought in general. Known for his cunning and his disregard for the moral niceties, Louis XI was an excellent role model for Gabriel Naudé and others, who argued that the morality governing state affairs did not necessarily correspond exactly to that governing the behaviour of private individuals.

In the context of a discussion about the idea of counsel, Part III recounts how opposing portraits of Louis XI created in the sixteenth and seventeenth centuries elided in some cases and collided in others. As the ambivalence of the Parlement of Paris about whether it was a monarchical or representative institution deepened, so did the presentation of Louis XI by parlementaire writers begin to slip between praise and condemnation and back again. Renewed calls for the convocation of an estates general were accompanied, not surprisingly, by extremely hostile references to the tyrant, Louis XI. On the other hand, as the advocates of the Parlement of Paris fought to provide a precise political role for the court in the government of France, Louis XI was once more cautiously lauded as an example of a great king who paid heed to the wise counsel of his magistrates.

A book such as this encounters some rather large methodological obstacles that can be only partially overcome. The selection of which sources to include is problematic; clearly there are numerous works other than those examined here in which Louis XI is mentioned. This is certainly true, for example, in the multitude of Mazarinade pamphlets produced during the Fronde. In many cases, however, these citations prove to be much of a muchness. The inclusion of additional such references would not alter the discursive web I am attempting to explicate but would, I believe, lengthen that explication unnecessarily. Although I have limited my search for references to Louis XI primarily to both major and minor political literature from the period 1560 to 1789, within those parameters an effort has been made to choose as randomly as possible in the belief that random selection provides as accurate a picture as the examination of every mention of Louis XI would.

The second methodological problem is how to evaluate the "density" of references to Louis XI. In some cases, the discussion of Louis XI is central to the argument of the author; in others, references are more tangential. I have attempted to incorporate both "thick" and "thin" citations in the belief that, even in those instances where Louis XI appears as a supporting rather than a central character, his very presence in the text provides an important signal about the author's intentions. Moreover, even somewhat more off-hand references can indicate the pervasiveness of Louis XI as an ideological symbol at a particular historical moment.

The third methodological issue concerns the unacknowledged borrowings of one author from another and the sometimes unrecognized status of a work as a response to an earlier unknown piece. With regard to phrases by and anecdotes about Louis XI, I have tried to trace back to the original source wherever possible. This becomes less problematic later in the period under investigation as marginal citations and footnoting apparatus become more common and expected elements in non-fictional prose. To some extent, although the origin of key elements in Louis XI's historical image is undoubtedly important, for our purposes the commonness of such phrases is perhaps more revealing of the Spider King's place within the early modern ideological landscape at any given moment.

Related to this question of unacknowledged sources is the problem of how to address changes in historical method throughout the sixteenth, seventeenth and eighteenth centuries. One might think that assessments of Louis XI would be determined at least in part by the availability of different types of sources and how they were interpreted by authors within different contexts. While it is clear that documentary evidence such as letters and official records was more likely to be used by the end of the 1600s than had been the case a century earlier, what is remarkable is the extent to which the use of additional material from the reign of Louis XI did not substantially change the interpretation of the king. Political writers of all persuasions were more likely to continue to employ the image of Louis XI to suit their rhetorical purposes than to attempt a re-evaluation of the Spider King based on new or hitherto unknown sources. Of course, Louis XI's reputation did undergo changes, but my basic premise is that this had much more to do with the shifting ideological landscape than with the discovery of new evidence about the king or the application of a different historical method.

According to John Pocock, texts outlive their authors and are reinvested with meanings as the language of political discourse evolves.[75] As historians, we acknowledge but seldom explore the notion that actions outlive their agents, to be reinterpreted within new political and linguistic contexts. The study of the historical reputation of Louis XI demonstrates not only the importance of "texts as events" but also of *events as texts*.

Part I

"Le roi hors de page"

Solon used to say that speech was the image of actions . . . that laws were like cobwebs, – for that if any trifling or powerless thing fell into them, they held it fast; while if it were something weightier, it broke through them and was off.

(Diogenes Laertius, *Solon*, Book X)

1   The architect of tyranny

It is a truism that people feel compelled, both in their personal lives and collectively as a society, to fashion and refashion the past to meet the requirements of the present. In France, such a need was most keenly felt during the tumultuous era of the French Religious Wars, when the only solution to the deepening chaos seemed to lie in a return to a glorious French past. Intensified interest in the origin and evolution of the French monarchy, coupled with the scholarly efforts of legal humanists to discover the roots of French law, contributed to the emergence of the historical and evidential sensibility considered central to "modern" historiography.[1]

The sixteenth-century interest in the original form of the French monarchy, its "ancient constitution," has received considerable attention from historians, although the French side has never elicited the same sustained study that English historians have devoted to the ancient constitution in early Stuart England.[2] Two things seem apparent from a comparative examination of the French and English contexts. First, John Pocock, and more recently and emphatically Glen Burgess, have stressed the early Stuart vision of the English constitution as a living thing. The ancient constitution, although immemorial, evolved in tandem with the changing circumstances of the commonwealth, always perfectly suited to the English people. New or modified customs could be accommodated without altering the fundamental nature of the constitution. In contrast, French writers such as François Hotman and Theodore Beza possessed a much more static interpretation of the French constitution. These authors acknowledged that changes had taken place over the centuries since the days of Clovis, most notably the institutional alterations that had accompanied the transfer of authority from the Merovingians to the Carolingians and later to the Capetians. They nevertheless insisted not only on an awareness of origins but also on an outright return to the institutions that were the concrete manifestation of the original constitution. For them, change to a great degree equalled perversion and degeneration.

Second, and more important, if the view taken by most English historians is correct, contemporary ideas about the ancient constitution were distinct from a vision of popular sovereignty based upon natural rights theories.[3] In

France, on the other hand, the two visions were much more closely connected, even mutually reinforcing. Although André Lemaire has asserted that François Hotman's *Francogallia* formed a turning point at which time the emphasis on an ancient constitution gave way to the discussion of more abstract notions of natural rights, I would argue that, for Hotman, Beza and other resistance theorists, arguments based on universalist pleas for the existence of natural rights were always balanced with an attention to and exposition of the particularities of French constitutional origins.[4] It does seem that throughout the course of the seventeenth century we do see a drift away from an interest in the ancient constitution in favour of positions predicated upon reason and natural rights. Critics of Louis XIV, such as the anonymous author of *Les soupirs de la France esclave*, preferred to characterize absolute monarchy as an illegitimate form of government *per se* rather than as a deviation from established customary relationships. By the eighteenth century, however, in the form of the well-known *thèse royale/thèse nobiliaire* controversy, writers once again wedded arguments concerning sovereignty based upon natural rights with renewed attention to, one might say obsession with, the excavation of the French past.

Louis XI is central to all of these discussions. Even during the seventeenth century, when polemicists such as the author of *Les soupirs*, and more temperate voices like that of Fénelon, tried to construct reasoned arguments transcending a limited French context, frequent references to Louis XI can be found. The ubiquitous appearance in these works of Louis XI, as well as other figures from the French past, testifies to the consistent and profound importance of historical example not just as diverting anecdote but as critically bracing support for their arguments. Throughout these shifts of emphasis, the use of Louis XI remains a constant weapon in the battle against absolutist ideology. Louis XI functions not merely as an illustrative example of the inherent flaws of monarchical government; he is *the* usurper, the diabolical perverter of the French constitution. He is, paradoxically, both cause and effect; simultaneously an agent of cataclysmic change and the monstrous creation of a people that has shirked both its rights and its responsibilities as a sovereign community. In the next three chapters we will explore how images of Louis XI amplify arguments based on the ancient constitution, on natural rights and on some melding of the two.

The St Bartholomew's Day Massacre, which began on 24 August 1572, stands out as one of the most important events of early modern French history.[5] The massacre is generally believed to occupy a pivotal position in the history of French political thought,[6] and indeed Louis XI receives his harshest criticism from polemicists moved by the horrors of the weeks following the assassination of Admiral Coligny, the leader of the Huguenots, on 24 August. I have chosen to begin my examination of the historical reputation of Louis XI with the cataclysm of St Bartholomew's Day because I firmly believe that the massacre, and the French religious wars in general, caused a bifurcation of traditional political theory into two clearly defined and opposing camps of constitutionalism and absolutism. Obviously political treatises were produced between 1516, when Seyssel published *La Monarchie de France*, and the outbreak of the religious wars in 1562, and several of these do mention Louis XI, but the portraits they draw lack the passionate rage or admiration found in works produced during the tumultuous decades after 1560. This moderate appraisal of Louis XI in the first half of the sixteenth century corresponds, I would argue, with a corpus of political thought which, for all its internal gradations, possesses a unity and cohesiveness that was effectively and irrevocably shattered by civil war. Although *regalians* like Charles de Grassaille and Jean Ferrault emphasized the expansiveness of royal authority, while Etienne Pasquier and Bernard du Haillan stressed the importance of consultative governmental institutions such as the Parlement of Paris and the estates general, all of these individuals believed that monarchical limitation and monarchical authority formed two halves of an organic whole.[7] After the outbreak of the religious wars, and more particularly after the St Bartholomew's Day Massacre, this whole was torn asunder so violently that limitation and authority could never again fit comfortably together.

The murder of Coligny and other Huguenot leaders was made pathetically easy by their presence in the capital for the wedding of Henri de Navarre and Marguerite de Valois, the sister of Charles IX. This fact was not lost on the Huguenot writers. It led many of them to believe, as did the author of *Le Reveille Matin*, that the massacre was in fact a premeditated plan fully endorsed by the king.[8] It was speculated that the plan for the elimination of the Huguenots had been formulated as early as 1565 when Catherine de Médicis met with the Duke of Alva at Bayonne.[9] Whether or not the massacre was premeditated, the results were the same: about 3,000 Huguenots were murdered in Paris and 10,000 in the provinces.[10] This already lamentably high figure was inflated by Huguenot writers to more than 100,000, thus endowing the massacre with apocalyptic proportions.[11] The magnitude of the event impelled Huguenot writers to renew their polemic against the government, specifically against the Guisard manipulation of royal policy.

The St Bartholomew's Day Massacre ushered in a new phase in French political theory, since the Huguenot works produced after the massacre exhibited a radical new posture.[12] The tone of Huguenot polemic sharpened; the commitment to institutional checks on the crown was now unswerving. The recognition that the estates general could well function in this capacity was not, however, new. Well before 1572, the estates general had become the focus of Huguenot hopes for governmental reform. This is certainly not surprising given that, at the estates general of 1560 and 1561, both the second and third estates did seem inclined to endorse toleration.[13] Among works of the 1560s calling for the assembly of the estates, two stand out both in terms of the vehemence with which they expounded the need to assemble the estates, and the connection made between the support for the estates and the denigration of Louis XI. The emphasis on the estates general, not coincidentally coupled with vigorous attacks on Louis XI, I would argue, marks a dramatic shift away from the sort of political literature produced before the outbreak of war.

The first of these two anonymous works, the *De la Necessité d'assembler les Estats* is actually a short pamphlet composed of extracts from other sources extolling the virtues of the estates general. The first extract is from Book 5, Chapter 18 of Philippe de Commynes's *Mémoires*. This chapter is the one most often cited by sixteenth-century writers searching for statements on the desirability and indeed necessity of holding frequent meetings of the estates. By isolating Commynes's opinions about the value of the estates from the corpus of the *Mémoires*, this short extract grossly distorts his general views about the limitations on kingship. The characterization of Commynes in this pamphlet is consistent with that of most other sixteenth-century authors: he is perceived as a forerunner of the Huguenot brand of constitutionalism.[14] The extract includes the famous rhetorical question posed by Commynes: "Was there ever a king or lord on the earth who had the power, outside his domain, of levying one *denier* on his subjects without permission and consent of those who had to pay it, except by tyranny and violence?"[15] The work also includes an extensive quotation taken from later in the chapter where Commynes argues against those who say that it is *lèse majesté* to speak of assembling the estates.[16] The Huguenot writers derive from this passage an endorsement of institutional checks on the crown. Although originally deployed by the Huguenots, Commynes's view on the estates makes its way into the absolutist arsenal by way of Gentillet and Bodin. These authors agree that calling for the convocation of the estates general is not an act of *lèse majesté*, although their reasons are wholly different from those of their opponents. Absolutists argued that calling for the estates general did not undermine the authority of the crown since that body only served to enhance the king's power and prestige through the process of supplications.[17] The tactic of reinvesting examples and primary material used by one's opponents with a directly contrasting meaning was common among early modern writers of all political stripes. Charting such semantic inversions, especially those surrounding Louis XI, whose complex personality and chaotic reign supplied just the sort of material needed for these manipulations of meaning, provides us with invaluable information about the ebb and flow of early modern political discourse.

The other two extracts which make up the rest of the pamphlet are from the speech of Charles de Marillac, Archbishop of Vienne, to the court at Fontainebleau in August of 1560, and Michel de L'Hôpital's address to the estates general assembled at Orléans in 1561. In Marillac's speech, utility appears to be the main consideration. If the people are not succoured they will become desperate and will then more willingly listen to the words of seditious men.[18] On the other hand, L'Hôpital's address emphasizes the more positive aspect of how the calling of the estates facilitates the administering of the realm.[19] Together, the three extracts provide the spectrum of arguments about why the estates general should be called. The importance of the work lies in the implicit association of the estates with Louis XI through the inclusion of the extract from Commynes. The Huguenots writing after 1572 create out of this connection an inverse relationship between the estates and Louis XI, wherein the more the former is elevated, the more completely the latter is condemned.

The anonymous *Mémoires des occasions de la guerre, appellee le Bien-Public* (1567) contributes in no small measure to the development of this inverse relationship between the estates general and Louis XI. Like *De la Necessité d'assembler les Estats*, it calls for the holding of an assembly as imperative for the welfare of the realm, but the argument in the *Mémoires des occasions* is constructed in a manner far more detrimental to Louis XI's historical reputation. Drawing on a number of different contemporary and near-contemporary accounts, the writer describes the events surrounding the so-called War of the Public Weal. According to the author France had been in a similar situation, a century earlier, to the one in which she found herself in the 1560s; reform of the administration was needed in order to preserve the health of the commonwealth. In 1465, the princes and great lords of the realm met secretly to discuss the "plaintes et doléances" which had been communicated to them. They decided to take up arms to force Louis XI to call an assembly of the estates:

> as that [thing] which at all times before had been the only and sovereign remedy for public disorder in the kingdom and which alone had the right and authority to cure such disorder, the monarchy of France having been from the beginning tempered by the authority of the nobility, and the communities of the provinces and great towns of this kingdom.[20]

The work contains as strong a statement about the sovereignty of the estates as any found in the works of the writers after 1572: "In effect, the issue is nothing else but that the king, no matter how great, aged, shrewd and well-advised he is, must submit himself to this assembly."[21] In order to bring the rebellion of the nobles to an end, Louis XI agreed to the appointment of thirty-six commissioners who were called "les Reformateurs du Bien Public." It seems apparent that the author chose the events surrounding the War of the Public Weal to support his assertions about the necessity of holding estates precisely because of Louis XI's reputation as a strong-willed, politically shrewd monarch. If a king with Louis's noted disregard for counsel could be induced to call the estates and agree to the formation of a council of thirty-six deputies, then the assembly could be said to have had an entrenched place in the constitution which could not be denied even by the most wilful of monarchs.[22]

At first it seems paradoxical that the author would present Louis XI in an almost laudatory light, writing of the king's greatness and sagacity. Yet the very fact that Louis XI was loath to call the estates but felt compelled to do so by the force of circumstance only serves to strengthen the author's arguments regarding the importance of the institution. The reputed unwillingness of Louis XI to share his authority is thus powerfully juxtaposed with his ultimate reliance on the estates general. In other words, by elevating Louis XI, the author is also enhancing the prestige of the estates, since such a great prince was willing to acknowledge the necessity of holding an assembly in order to reform the realm.

If this argument had been sustained throughout the work, perhaps Louis XI would have been judged less harshly by later writers. The author changes tactics, however, when he discusses how Louis XI called another assembly of the estates (actually an assembly of notables which met in 1470) in order to take his revenge on the nobles and to renege on the promises he made in 1467. At this point Louis XI is roundly criticized for manipulating this second assembly into helping him to execute his selfish aim of vengeance rather than pursuing the common interests of all the members of the commonwealth. The author laments that the "estates" of 1470 accomplished nothing and in fact plunged the commonwealth into yet another war. "How did [Louis XI] profit from this, except to ignite a new war, so hard and bitter that it lasted thirteen or fourteen years?"[23] The author then launches into a comparison between the reign of Louis XI and that of Charles IX. The author implies that, no matter how unfortunate conditions were under Louis, they are much worse under the present king, and consequently the need to call the estates general in order to reform the realm is even more urgent. The author ends by asserting that the present condition of France is so deplorable that, instead of order, the commonwealth is characterized by misery and anarchy.

In two respects, the *Mémoires des occasions* provided the material which later Huguenot writers would utilize in their condemnations of Louis XI. First, the rejection of a positive interpretation of Louis XI's relationship with the estates during and immediately following the War of the Public Weal, found in the second half of the pamphlet, sets the stage for the transformation of a noble reaction into a grand constitutional struggle. Second, the similarity noted by the author between the 1460s and the 1560s did much to ensure that, from then on, the reign of Louis XI would be subject to partisan scrutiny in the effort to find fifteenth-century precedents for dealing with the injustices of a sixteenth-century monarch.

Although both *De la Nécessité* and *Mémoires des occasions* strongly urge the assembly of the estates general, they differ from post-Massacre literature by espousing similar views in several significant ways. While the pamphlets from the 1560s were critical of Charles IX, they still appear to be predicated upon a belief in the king's genuine desire to do good. If only he could be convinced that the situation had become critical, Charles IX would put aside his personal will in favour of the common good. The implication was that the estates general could counsel the king about the best course of action. If he listened to the estates, rather than the self-interested denizens of the court, peace and prosperity would be restored. After the St Bartholomew's Day Massacre, writers abandoned almost wholesale the "evil counsellor" trope in favour of direct attacks on the king and on the concept of kingship. When the king becomes the main target of criticism, the function of the estates general changes as a result.

This leads one to consider the second crucial distinction between pre- and post-Massacre constitutionalist literature. Prior to 1572, most writers presented the estates general as a consultative body, called to provide information to the king that might have been hidden from him or misrepresented by his closest advisors. After the Massacre, the estates were increasingly viewed, not merely as a consultative body, but more impor-tantly as the repository of popular sovereignty.[24] It is the case that both pamphlets from the 1560s are bits of ephemera and, consequently, we should not be surprised to find little in the way of weighty theoretical exposition. While the works published after 1572 are more substantial, they are similarly rooted in contemporary circumstance, written to convince the king to pursue a certain course of action. The differences in content have more to do with the changing political scene than with changing polemical goals. Throughout the 1570s the religious war intensified and became embittered. Huguenots were increasingly characterized by their opponents as not being truly French. Consequently, constitutional arguments made on their behalf, drawn solely from an examination of the French past (both distant and more recent), no longer sufficed, since Huguenots were arguably not "real" Frenchmen. In the work of François Hotman, Theodore Beza, Mornay, and the Scotsman George Buchanan, we find extended discussion of the idea of popular sovereignty alongside historical investigation in an effort to broaden and place on a firmer footing the constitutionalist standpoint.

Among those who emphasized the primacy of the estates general, François Hotman stands out. In his most famous work, the *Francogallia*, Hotman makes explicit the connection between the ancient constitution and the concept of popular sovereignty. One of the foremost legal theorists of the sixteenth century, Hotman pursued his legal studies at Orléans in the late 1530s and then moved to Paris to practise his chosen profession.[25] From there he went to Geneva, where he met Theodore Beza in 1548, and the two collaborated in the teaching of classics at Lausanne. This would not be the last time the two theorists exchanged ideas. From Geneva Hotman travelled in 1556 to Strasbourg, where he came into contact with a number of English Protestants who had fled to the continent in the years of restored Catholi-cism in England under Mary. The influence of these early experiences and contacts can easily be discerned in the *Francogallia*. The work possesses a fully-articulated theory of resistance, showing similarities to the works of the Marian exiles, including John Ponet, Christopher Goodman and others.[26] *Francogallia* is framed, however, as a historical analysis based on the examination of custom, which owes a great deal to Charles Du Moulin, who did so much to codify and systematize French customary laws.[27] The fact that the *Francogallia* is such an amalgam of different influences has led to some controversy about the exact intention of the work.[28]

An examination of Hotman's political ideas in the *Francogallia* is complicated by the fact that Hotman made substantial revisions to the work between editions. Whereas in the 1573 and 1576 editions Hotman lays heavy emphasis on the election of French monarchs in order to add weight to his argument about the sovereignty of the people, by the 1586 edition political changes led to a markedly more royalist view on succession, thus undermining his assertions about the people as the continuing fount of authority. We can also perceive a change in Hotman's attitude toward the Parlement of Paris between the editions of the 1570s and that of 1586. In the earlier versions, Hotman has reserved his harshest words for the sovereign court, calling its members "sycophants and flatterers of royalty." But in the 1586 edition, in an effort to muster all the support he can for the cause of Henri de Navarre, Hotman refers to the *parlementaires* as the protectors of the fundamental laws, one of the most important of which is the law of succession. Bearing the differences between the editions in mind, we will concentrate on the drift of Hotman's thought through the 1570s. It is his emphasis on the sovereignty of the people which is most important here, since it is in this context that Hotman reviles Louis XI.

Because Hotman views customary usage and procedure as one of the determining factors in the legitimacy of contemporary governmental behaviour, he looks to the origins of institutions and then discusses how and why they changed. Any efforts at objective historical enquiry are compromised, however, because of Hotman's desire to find evidence to support the claim that the sovereignty belonged to the people and was exercised on their behalf by the estates general. By recounting the "history" of Francogallia, Hotman seeks to prove that the estates did indeed once exercise the extensive powers which legitimately still belong to them but which have been usurped by tyrannical kings, notably Louis XI.

First and foremost among these powers were those of election and deposition. They were regularly exercised by the estates in order to ensure that the commonwealth remained well administered. Hotman provides a number of examples from the early history of the Francogallic state to prove that "the kings of Francogallia were constituted by the authoritative decision and desire of the people, that is, of the orders, or, as we are now accustomed to say, of the estates, rather than by any hereditary right."[29]

The powers of election and deposition are not the only ones possessed by the estates. Hotman refers to the estates as the "highest administrative authority in the kingdom of Francogallia."[30] This position entails the following responsibilities: the making of war and the negotiating of peace; the legislation of public laws; the appointment of all officials of the commonwealth; the assigning of the deceased king's patrimony; and the making of all decisions which involve the levying, collection and administration of revenues from taxation. This list of powers and responsibilities is concluded with the blanket statement that the estates have authority over "all those issues which in popular speech are now commonly called affairs of state."[31]

Hotman has attributed all the powers which are usually associated with the monarch to the estates, and the ruler's function is reduced to one of administration. The king possesses no power of initiative; the first fundamental law of the ancient constitution is that the king may not do or decide anything affecting the commonwealth without the authority of the public council. Hotman asserts that the vestiges of this ancient law are to be found in the Parlement of Paris which "has appropriated to itself the authority of the ancient parliament [i.e. the public council]."[32] While, as was mentioned earlier, Hotman's attitude toward the parlement undergoes a considerable change by the later editions of *Francogallia*, it would be fair to assert that Hotman's view is never one of full endorsement; at best he is ambivalent about the parlement because he always assumes that real authority is vested in and ought to be exercised by the estates. It should be noted that the negative statements about the parlement found in the last chapter of the *Francogallia* in both the 1573 and 1576 editions remain in the 1586 edition, even though in other parts of the work he refers to the institution positively as the protector of the constitution. One could speculate that his earlier, more clearly negative opinion about the parlement added to his already condemnatory opinion of Louis XI, since he appeared to have cooperated with the courts (at least when forced to do so) in contrast with his even less successful relationship with the estates. For those who viewed the parlement as representing the people in some way, the harsh judgement of Louis XI would be mitigated. For Hotman, however, who at least initially views the parlement as a collection of pettifoggers and royal sycophants, the cooperation of Louis XI with the courts is only another indictment both of his tyranny and of the royalist collusion of the parlement.

Hotman underscores the subjection of the king to the assembly by asserting that the royal majesty is distinct from the monarch; the monarch only assumes majesty when he is enthroned in the assembly. In other words, the majesty exists in the assembly itself and is only "donned" by the monarch when he enters.[33] Hotman makes use of the Aragonese coronation oath, to which a number of constitutionalist writers refer, to demonstrate that, from the moment of his installation, the king is cognizant of his inferior status in relation to the assembly.[34]

Although this happy state of affairs existed in ancient Francogallia, France is no longer governed according to such constitutional principles. Hotman chooses to fix the blame for the corruption of Francogallia's pristine constitution on Louis XI, and he devotes an entire chapter to the discussion of his tyranny. The chapter is entitled "The memorable authority of the council against Louis XI", and it recounts the events surrounding the formation of the League of the Public Weal. Hotman transforms the rebellion by *les grands* into a great constitutional struggle, saying that the magnates,

> who were aroused by the continued queries and complaints of the com-
> mon people, assembled their local forces and began to prepare an army to
> secure the public welfare and, in the words of Philippe de Commines, "to
> be able to show the king by force the corruption of his administration of
> the commonwealth . . . Hence the war that was undertaken was said to be
> for the public welfare, and it was commonly called the War of the Com-
> mon Weal."[35]

An examination of the corresponding passage in Commynes undermines
Hotman's credibility in the accurate citation of sources. Commynes describes
the incident thus: "And this war was since called [the war of] the Public
Good because it was undertaken *under the guise of being for the public good of the
kingdom.*"[36]

Hotman goes on to state that, although Louis XI agreed to accept the
commission of the thirty-six men, consisting of twelve deputies chosen from
each of the three estates, the king later reneged on his promises.[37] Consequently, states Hotman in language highly reminiscent of the pamphlet
Mémoires des occasions, "a most lamentable war was kindled in Francogallia,
which lasted for nearly thirteen years. In this way the king's perjury was
expiated both by his own disgrace and the ruin of the people."[38] Clearly,
Hotman places all the blame for contemporary misery on the tyrannical
behaviour of Louis XI a century earlier. The king refused to honour the will
of the people, expressed in the assembly of the three estates, and, in that
refusal, he subverted the fundamental laws of the realm. For Hotman, who
holds the estates general to be the only institution capable of righting the
wrongs being perpetrated in the commonwealth, Louis XI must bear
ultimate responsibility for beginning the process of degeneration which
robbed the assembly of all its legitimate authority, thus bringing France to
its present chaotic state.

Hotman's conflicting desires to emphasize Louis XI's perfidy and demonstrate the vitality of the estates create within the chapter a tension similar to
that found in *Mémoires des occasions*. On the one hand, Hotman wants to
portray Louis XI as a tyrant who suppressed the authority of the estates
general, thus bringing ruin to the French commonwealth. On the other
hand, he is concerned to show the basic strength of the institution by
asserting that it still functioned under the most tyrannical of kings. Indeed,
marked similarities in the arguments of the *Francogallia* and the *Mémoires des
occasions* prompt one to speculate. It is entirely possible that Hotman drew
some, if not all, of his ideas regarding Louis XI and the League of the Public
Weal from the *Mémoires des occasions*. This assertion is supported by the fact
that, although it was first published in 1573, large parts of the *Francogallia*
were composed in 1567 and 1568. Hotman is unlikely to have derived his
ideas from another source; the *Mémoires des occasions* appears to be the first

instance where one finds the War of the Public Weal interpreted as a constitutional struggle. Indeed, the parallels are so striking on this point that one could make a case for Hotman's authorship of the pamphlet. If Hotman had already written the chapter on Louis XI in 1567, might he not have published the excerpt anonymously? The relationship between the *Mémoires des occasions* and the *Francogallia* cannot be established with certainty, but that there was some connection is apparent from similarities both in the language employed and the interpretations placed upon the action of Louis XI and his disobedient nobles.

If we turn our attention to the work of Theodore Beza, we find that the balance of Beza's argument has shifted farther away from an emphasis on the ancient constitution and toward more universalist appeals to natural rights. His characterization of Louis XI is, however, consistent with that of François Hotman. From the beginning, Beza was even more actively involved in the Huguenot movement than was Hotman. Beza was Calvin's second-in-command until the latter's death, whereupon Beza took over the leadership of the movement.[39] It seems apparent that Beza was already formulating theories of resistance in the 1550s, the theory of the right of magistrates being found in conjunction with the "evil counsellor" theory used to explain unjust actions committed by the government. He was closely associated with the military leaders of the Huguenots, acting as chaplain to the Prince de Condé in 1562–3 and counsellor to Condé's son in the 1570s. At the time when the *Du Droit des magistrats* was written, 1572–3, Beza was in contact with Hotman as the latter had again taken refuge in Geneva. It is evident that there was considerable exchange of ideas between the two men at this time; the *Du Droit* is often regarded as a theoretical explication of ideas more empirically grounded in the *Francogallia*.

Although the *Du Droit des magistrats* follows the *Francogallia* closely in its line of argumentation, Theodore Beza places less emphasis on the estates general than does Hotman. Nevertheless, Beza reaffirms Hotman's assertion that the sovereign authority reposes in the estates. Beza provides examples of both ancient and modern states to support his view that the assembly possesses the right to elect and depose rulers. Ironically, Beza holds up England under Elizabeth as "the happiest [country] that exists in the world today, God keep it in its tranquility . . . "[40] Yet Elizabeth manipulated her parliament in a way which Beza would not have found very admirable. Like Hotman, Beza utilizes the Aragonese coronation oath to support his idea of monarchical subjection to the assembly. He concludes his list of ancient and modern examples of the estates exercising authority over kings with a discussion of France. He makes the statement that, if the kingdom was not elective, neither Pepin nor Hugues Capet would have had a legitimate title to the crown when they became kings, since they were not of the house within which the crown had previously been passed. Beza does not provide as detailed a list of the functions and responsibilities of the estates as does Hotman, but it is clear that Beza believed that the estates did at one time possess wide-ranging powers "to establish and depose the principal officers of the crown, or at least to keep an eye on what the king does in that regard, and over the imposition of *tailles* and other principal affairs of government in peace and in war."[41]

Beza's views on the estates general correspond with his negative appraisal of Louis XI. While Hotman focuses on the actual War of the Public Weal, Beza seems most interested in the appointment of the thirty-six commissioners. This emphasis would correlate with Beza's more extensive discussion of the magistrates who, under the direction of the estates, are empowered to resist the tyrannical behaviour of a ruler. He says of Louis XI and the commission of the thirty-six:

> In the year 1467, King Louis XI who, as much as he could, transformed the monarchy of France into a tyranny (which royal flatterers refer to as placing kings *hors de page*), being charged with good reason of administering the kingdom very badly, received from the estates assembled at Tours thirty-six persons as curators, by whom he would be guided and governed.[42]

Louis XI's main sin against the commonwealth was that he broke his oath to accept the guidance of these thirty-six men. He paid for his deceit, Beza remarks, by personal suffering in the remainder of his own life and by the execration of posterity.

An accurate rendering of the phrase *hors de page* is crucial to our understanding of the historical evolution of Louis XI's reputation, yet its meaning is initially elusive. In the *Grand Larousse*, *hors de page*, while literally translated as "outside the page," actually means something like, "to become master of oneself," or "to master one's chosen *métier*." In Emile Littré's *Dictionnaire de la langue française*, *hors de page* is defined figuratively as "être tout à fait son maître. Il n'a pas de tuteur, il est hors de page."[43] From what we know about Beza's view of Louis XI, and the context of the passage quoted above, we should probably assign a more pointedly pejorative meaning to Beza's use of the term. *Mettre les rois hors de page* is probably most accurately translated as "to place kings beyond constraint." It is so crucial to grasp the meaning of this phrase because, over the course of several centuries, Louis XI is repeatedly characterized in this way, either as having placed kings *hors de page* or as being himself a king *hors de page*. I have not found the phrase used in conjunction with any other French monarch, nor am I familiar with its use in any other context. Beza's *Du Droit des magistrats* appears to be the first instance of such an association, but it is far from the last time Louis XI is characterized in this way. Uniquely associated with Louis XI, *mettre les rois hors de page* eventually becomes a shorthand way of evoking a host of images and assumptions about the nature of his reign.

Although the *Vindiciae contra tyrannos* is often included with the works of Hotman and Beza as an example of Huguenot constitutional theory, it is different from the first two since it places much less emphasis on the estates general and more on the functions of the inferior magistrates.[44] This difference can be accounted for, at least in part, by the fact that the *Vindiciae* was published in 1579, and a great deal had happened in the political realm since the St Bartholomew's Day Massacre. Charles IX was dead and Henri III was reigning. The extreme Catholics had organized into a League, dedicated to the extirpation of the Huguenots. It seemed, moreover, that Henri III was throwing in his lot with the Leaguers, who were consequently infiltrating government at all levels. With the Leaguers increasing in influence and likely to be able to take control of the estates general, it is hardly unexpected that the author of the *Vindiciae* was wary of placing too much emphasis on the authority of that body.

Nevertheless, the author does maintain that at one time the estates general did possess sovereign authority in the realm. He sketchily outlines their responsibilities: "The authority of this assembly was always such that, whatsoever it decided, whether it had to do with treating for peace or making war, or creating a regent for the kingdom, or imposing a new tax, was held to be firm and inviolable."[45] The author of the *Vindiciae* views the estates as an extraordinary assembly which, although possessing sovereign authority, exercises that authority in a direct manner only infrequently. The estates general, "which are nothing other than the epitome or collection of the kingdom,"[46] appoints officers, or magistrates, who administer the commonwealth on a day-to-day basis. The king is only the first among these magistrates; the lesser magistrates:

> are like assessors of the king in the administration of justice, participating in royal power and authority, having in their hands the management of affairs of state, neither greater nor lesser than that of the king, who is, moreover, like a president, only holding first place amongst them.[47]

According to the author, the magistrates are appointed by the estates general to act as intermediaries between the people and the king. While the author devoted most of the work to a description of the rights and duties of these magistrates to resist a tyrannical king, it is clear that these rights derive from their appointment by the people, i.e. by the estates. (Here the author appears to be talking about the provincial estates, which has led to some speculation that the *Vindiciae* envisioned some sort of federal republic.) Even though direct discussion of the estates is limited in the *Vindiciae*, the premise of the work is a belief in the supreme authority of the people, as vested in the estates. The idea of an ancient constitution is implied but gives way before a thoroughgoing theory of the people's sovereign rights. In the case of France, the people have endangered their rights by abandoning ancient practices that confirmed their sovereign status. The abandonment of ancient forms does not, however, in any way "prejudice the right of the people." When an argument based on ancient constitution is found lacking, the author easily shifts his emphasis to more theoretical ground.

Despite some differences, the argument of the *Vindiciae* is sufficiently like that of Hotman and Beza to suggest a similarly negative opinion of Louis XI. The author spends some time refuting the legitimacy of rights accumulated by rulers over the years, including the right of life and death over subjects, the right of pardon, and the right to confiscate and dispense with the property of subjects. Moreover, the king may not alienate any part of the royal domain. This is demonstrated by the many instances when newly crowned kings have issued ordinances revoking the unlawful alienations made by their predecessors. In this regard, Louis XI had overstepped the bounds of his authority by alienating portions of the domain without reference to the estates, an abuse which was rectified by his successor, Charles VIII. Although the language is by no means as condemnatory as that employed by either Beza or Hotman, the author does view Louis XI as a usurper of rights belonging to the assembly. Like the *Francogallia*, however, the *Vindiciae* possesses an inner tension which is the result of trying to demonstrate the tyranny of Louis XI and the strength of the estates at one and the same time. The author of the *Vindiciae* asserts, "It was not long ago that the estates constrained Louis XI, a very strong-willed prince, to receive thirty-six curators, under the guidance of whom he would be forced to govern the affairs of state."[48]

This view of Louis XI travelled beyond France, making its way, along with other key components of Huguenot resistance theory, into the works of the Scottish monarchomach George Buchanan. I have chosen to mention Buchanan briefly here because his theories on resistance were highly influential both among the Huguenots and, later, among the Catholic Leaguers.[49] While Louis XI does not appear in *De Jure Regni Apud Scotos* (1579), which is after all a pointed polemic justifying Mary Queen of Scots' forced abdication, evidence of Buchanan's opinion about the Spider King can be found in the *Rerum Scoticarum Historia*, often published together with *De Jure Regni*. In Book 12 of *Rerum Scoticarum*, when discussing Louis XI, Buchanan parenthetically refers to him as the king who converted legitimate kingship in France into tyranny (*qui Regnum legitum Francorum in tyrannidem converterat*).[50] Although Buchanan's advocacy of tyrannicide in certain situations goes a good deal beyond the Huguenot vision of a monarchy in which the sovereignty of the people limits the ability of the king to do ill, the broad outline of his ideas accords with that of writers like Hotman and Beza. He shares with them, moreover, a highly condemnatory view of Louis XI. In evoking the tyrannical image of Louis XI, Buchanan deliberately plucks the strings of collective memory that resonate to the fear of misgovernment and oppression. For Buchanan, fearful memories work wonders in the effort to persuade people of the rightness and necessity of constitutionally-limited monarchy.

Although by no means an exhaustive investigation, the examination of Louis XI's historical reputation in these selected monarchomach treatises supports the original assertion that this king's image played an important role in the articulation of resistance theory. At the hands of resistance theorists, Louis XI functioned paradoxically both as a focus of blame for the deterioration of the French polity and as an illustration of the essential strength of the estates general, even when confronting the most wilful of monarchs. He also made appearances in otherwise non-historical discussions of popular sovereignty, as an illustrative example of the horrors of unrestricted royal power. In such analyses, he is always blamed for perverting the constitutional structure, implying the continued acceptance of the idea of an ancient constitution, even when arguments are more focused on ahistorical notions of natural rights.

Louis XI's historical reputation finds little respite in the changing political circumstances of the 1580s, for, just as the Huguenots begin to retreat from their extreme stance of legitimate resistance to a monarch, the Leaguers take up their pens and Louis XI is paraded once again as the personification of tyranny.

The political situation was drastically altered by the death of the duc d'Alençon et d'Anjou, the heir and last remaining Valois claimant to the throne. The succession now became a hotly debated issue because the next in line was the Protestant Henri de Navarre. Although the Catholic League was founded in the 1570s, it received added impetus from the events of the 1580s. Henri III was moving away from his earlier support for the Leaguers and in fact ensured their opposition when he had the duc de Guise assassinated during the estates general at Blois in 1588.[51] The Leaguers replaced the Huguenots as the party of opposition to the crown and they took up many of the Huguenot ideas of resistance, in many cases reformulating them in even more radical manner. This is evidenced by Jean Boucher's justification of Jacques Clément's assassination of Henri III in 1589. Although the main purpose of Boucher's work, *De Justa Abdicatione Henrici Tertii*, was to justify the deposition of Henri III, in passages added after the regicide, Boucher praised Clément as a martyr for the faith.

Not only does Boucher propound the sort of constitutional theories previously held by the Huguenots, he even uses the same historical examples to support his assertions. In speaking of the bridles placed on royal authority, Boucher mentions the peers, who have tutorial responsibilities, and, of course, the estates. It is the estates "who always prescribe what is to be done publicly, and also kings have often been deposed [by them] when [the kings] displayed private offences and lusts against the kingdom."[52] Boucher notes that the ancient stature of the estates can be perceived through the remnants of their authority in his day. They are still empowered to appoint guardians during the reign of a minor. But the power of the estates is clearly not what it used to be and, like the Huguenots, Boucher blames Louis XI for the decimation of their authority. In fact, Boucher indicts Louis XI even more forcefully than do the Huguenots:

If it had not been for the fact that this rule was diminished by Louis XI, who was quite evidently the first architect of tyranny in France (for the flatterers of kings say that kings should be defended from servitude and that royal liberty should be unfettered) and if it had not been for his [assumed] devotion for the Virgin, just as Henry [III] used deception by the pretence and mask of his ascetic and flagellant order, then we should perhaps have preserved this role in its entirety and not be tortured by the wound of an oppressed public liberty.[53]

Although the passage is embellished somewhat, its core seems to have been lifted almost entirely from Beza's *Du Droit des magistrats*; the parenthetical condemnation of flatterers, following the indictment of Louis XI's tyranny, is almost the same construction as found in Beza. And the phrase "mettre les Rois hors de page" which is in the corresponding passage of Beza is part of the marginalia in Boucher. Clearly, Boucher derived his opinion about Louis XI from the Huguenots.

Although Boucher's work, *De Justa Abdicatione Henrici Tertii*, is probably the most famous of the Leaguer works, there was a prodigious production of tracts espousing Leaguer views in the late 1580s and early 1590s. The Leaguer camp was not, however, monolithic in its views on the relationship between crown and nation, as the anonymous *Dialogue du Royaume* (1589) makes clear. The tract is ostensibly the recounting of a discussion taking place at the house of one of the participants. The first speaker inveighs against the institution of monarchy, and his diatribe against the kings of France goes on uninterrupted for almost forty pages.

Even within this wholly negative context, the assessment of Louis XI stands out. The speaker says of him:

He was fickle, wily, hypocritical, mocking, deceiving and false, as timid as he was desirous of being feared; more than any other king, he crushed his people with tributes and taxes. It would be redundant for me to elaborate further on his behaviour.[54]

A second speaker enters the discussion, roundly criticizing the first's unwillingness to recognize the good qualities of such kings as Saint Louis and Charlemagne. He then proceeds to redraw the sketches of successive monarchs along much more favourable lines. He even has a more positive, though hardly convincing, view of Louis XI. While acknowledging his "esprit subtil," the speaker maintains that Louis XI deserves approbation for recapturing the Somme towns lost to the Burgundians, as well as for attempting to establish one code of law throughout the kingdom.[55]

There are many pamphlets which far exceed the *Dialogue du Royaume*, both in the hostility of their attacks on Henri III and in their open endorsement of armed resistance. Particularly notable in both these respects is a short tract entitled *L'Atheisme de Henri de Valoys: où est monstré le vray but de ses dissimulations et cruautez* (1589). *L'Atheisme* takes up the theme of the *Dialogue* regarding the reasoning behind the original creation of monarchy. Prior to the institution of kingship, God ordained that the Hebrews should elect from among themselves the wisest and most experienced men to govern. These were known as "Princes du peuple." As with the Huguenot resistance theorists, Old Testament examples of people electing their leaders provide the necessary evidence for the Leaguer assertion: "In truth, the people could do without princes and kings, but [rulers] could not do without [the people] by whom they are created and upon whom their estate depends, and without whom they cannot subsist."[56] According to the author, the avarice of the children of Samuel led to the divine determination that the Israelites should be governed by a king chosen from among themselves: "Finally, notwithstanding all the reproofs, they wanted to have a king, and to great regret, they were accorded one; this was not done, then, with the advice and consent of divine counsel."[57]

The author's negative opinion of monarchy leads him to condemn French kings in a manner similar to that of the first speaker in the *Dialogue*. The author of *L'Atheisme* asserts that he searched through the chronicles of France to discover which of Henri III's ancestors the present king most closely resembled in character: "several have been perfidious and as for the majority: some have been greedy, others cruel and bloodthirsty." Henri III surpasses even his most villainous ancestors, however, because "he has been discovered to be the worst enemy of our Christian religion."

Louis XI is the object of particularly strong invective since he is considered by the author to be the French king that Henri III most emulated in his actions. "Louis XI deceived and dissimulated as much as possible; there was no security in his word . . . " Even the perfidious Louis XI, however, would not break his word once he had sworn an oath, unlike Henri III. Similarly, when the author compares crimes which the two monarchs perpetrated against the great nobility, those of Henri are considered more heinous since Louis XI's actions were at least clothed in a semblance of legality. The comparison between the two villainous kings extends still further and concludes as follows:

> Thus, in a word, [Henry III] compares best with Louis XI in insupportable extortions with which he tortured the people, and the mistrust he conceived against the princes, and the scorn he levelled at them, elevating thieves, and principally in his dissimulation.[58]

The deceitful natures of the two monarchs are then compared. While Louis XI's deceitful nature made it impossible to trust him, Henri III's dissimulating tactics verged on the diabolical: "[Henri] plays the monk, the penitent, the hermit; he wears his faith on his belt, he beats his breast, while inside there is nothing but a cesspool of all filth and wickedness."[59] Given the obvious intent of the work to place Henri III in the worst possible light, the extended comparison of the monarchs would seem to be based on the view that Louis XI was among the most tyrannical and oppressive kings the French nation had ever known, at least prior to the surpassingly wicked Henri III.

Although Louis XI was rarely a popular figure in French political thought even before 1572, it is clear that both the Huguenot response to the massacre and the Leaguer response to the perfidies of Henri III converted Louis XI's image into the paradigm of the tyrant. From 1572 onwards, opposition to the crown no longer felt inclined to couch attacks on the government in the "evil counsellor" theory, which had been proven inadequate and indeed fictitious by the events of August 1572. But although the target of attack was now the king himself, it was still appropriate to delve into history to provide a model of tyranny which was the necessary concomitant of the demand to reform the rampant abuses in the realm.

The Huguenot writers effectively combined historical analysis of the ancient constitution with theoretical discussion about the natural rights of man. For them, the usefulness of an ancient French constitution lay in its dual nature: it was both rooted in a historical moment of the revered French past and transcendent in its manifestation of the principle of popular sovereignty. Significantly, Louis XI functions as a linchpin holding these two discursive modes together. He is at once singular and archetypal, functioning both as scapegoat and spectral warning: the ghost of what was and what may be again. In employing Louis XI to illustrate and amplify their arguments, Huguenot and Leaguer resistance theorists evoked an image of tyranny which their opponents would be hard pressed to dispel. Indeed, the success of the absolutists lay not in negating that image but in manipulating it to serve their own ideological ends. This image of Louis XI as architect of tyranny is remarkably resilient, despite the best efforts of royalist writers. As we shall see, for advocates of popular sovereignty in the next century, Louis XI remained the archetype of the tyrant who was unfortunately emulated by French monarchs intent on keeping authority indivisibly vested in themselves.

2 A spider at Versailles

The reign of the Sun King, Louis XIV, threw a new, dark shadow across the reputation of Louis XI. In the early years of the seventeenth century Louis XI had been partly rehabilitated, due in large measure to the efforts of *raison d'état* writers like Gabriel Naudé and Louis Machon. As pragmatism edged out morality in the arena of politics, so the Spider King's webs of intrigue were re-spun as manoeuvres of shrewdness and sagacity. Both his domestic and international dealings were re-evaluated and placed in a more favourable, even sometimes highly laudatory light. This rehabilitation was greatly facilitated by royalist writers more or less closely affiliated with Richelieu's literary stable. In the first half of the seventeenth century, writers more frequently presented Louis XI as laying the groundwork for France's future greatness by vanquishing the narrowly self-interested nobles, thus preparing the way for the great accomplishments of the Bourbons.[1]

This glow of approbation faded somewhat as the seventeenth century wore on until, by the last years of Louis XIV, the reputation of Louis XI reached a new nadir. Seemingly in lockstep with the growing opposition to Louis XIV's foreign wars and domestic policies, images of Louis XI took on an ever more sinister hue. A return to a traditional moral framework for politics, most clearly espoused in Bishop Bossuet's *Politique tirée de la Sainte Ecriture*, did much to ensure that, even among those devoted to the idea of absolute monarchy, Louis XI was not necessarily showered with praise. Temperate critics like Abbé Fénelon used Louis XI as a didactic device to illustrate emphatically the "don'ts" of kingship. Pierre Bayle, a supporter of strong monarchy, showed a marked ambivalence toward Louis XI, praising his political sagacity but wary of too openly endorsing the type of rule Louis XI had by now come to represent.

Most significantly, in the years after the Revocation of the Edict of Nantes, Huguenot exiles began to link Louis XI and Louis XIV. In the flood of pamphlet literature pouring into France from beyond its borders, one can find numerous examples of double-barrelled condemnations of Louis XI and Louis XIV as twin pillars of tyranny. Within the body of exile-produced polemic, portraits of Louis XI are remarkably consistent with those produced and perpetuated a century earlier. Once again, writers evoked the image of Louis XI as a tyrant who had destroyed the ancient constitution. Through guilt by association, Louis XIV is condemned not only for his own actions but also for cloaking himself in the same mantle as that worn by the tyrannical Louis XI. In emulating, even surpassing the crimes of his progenitor, Louis XIV put the capstone on the edifice of despotism that Louis XI had begun to build some two hundred years before. Moreover, the association of the two kings by political writers and polemicists cut both ways; as Apollo's lustre dimmed, so too the reputation of Louis XI darkened perceptibly. From the more tempered criticisms of Fénelon to the vitupera-tive volleys contained in the anonymous pamphlet *Les Soupirs de la France esclave*, Louis XI finds few supporters and fewer genuine admirers. The pervasiveness of this hostility is in marked contrast to that of the sixteenth century, when condemnations of Louis XI were, by and large, limited to writers of a decidedly constitutionalist bent. This chapter considers why, in the last quarter of the seventeenth century, negative opinions of Louis XI spanned the spectrum of political orientation. Casting our eyes over the references to Louis XI in this period we hope also to give added contour to the general ideological landscape of France as the sun was setting over Versailles.

François de Salignac de la Mothe-Fénelon was a pivotal figure in the last years of Louis XIV's reign. His famous dispute with Bishop Bossuet was rooted in the religious and intellectual tensions of the last quarter of the seventeenth century. Not only were Fénelon's Quietist and ultramontane inclinations destined to bring him into conflict with Bossuet and the government but also his participation in the *Cénacle*, a group led by the ducs de Beauvilliers and Chevreuse, would result in further ostracism from the corridors of power. Although appointed tutor to the king's grandsons in 1689, he lost the post ten years later, ostensibly on account of his uncom-promising defence of the Quietist, Madame Guyon. Yet it seems likely that his political views, coupled with religious unorthodoxy, made him unpopular with the king. Although by no means openly opposed to the policies of Louis XIV, the gentle and indirect criticisms of the king in his masterpiece, *Télémaque*, demonstrate an unhappiness with the regime which could hardly be countenanced.[2]

Télémaque recounts the adventures of Ulysses' son. Fénelon uses the epic format to point out to his young pupil the necessity for preparation and education in order to govern justly and effectively. The seemingly endless journey of Telemachus to find his father parallels the voyage which must be undertaken to attain wisdom. Similarly, the trials and tribulations endured by Telemachus are analogous to the pitfalls of kingship. Throughout the work, Fénelon reiterates his belief that ruling is not a pleasure but rather an onerous task with but few rewards, the most valuable of which is the peace which accompanies the knowledge that one has governed solely with the good of the people at heart.[3]

Fénelon does not advocate an institutionally-limited monarchy. He believes that by educating the heir to the throne in all the proper moral virtues, the monarchy would, in the natural course of events, come to embody all those virtues of self-restraint which guarantee the well-being of the state. Yet the very fact that Fénelon perceived a need to re-emphasize these virtues implies a criticism of the contemporary state of affairs. That these moral criticisms could form the kernel of a much more seditious form of opposition was a possibility which could not be overlooked. Given its mythological setting, it is not surprising that Louis XI does not appear in *Télémaque*. Fénelon's opinion about Louis XI may, nevertheless, have influenced the work. Jacques Le Brun, the editor of the modern edition of Fénelon's complete works, speculates that Louis XI's character had such an impact on Fénelon that he later gave many of the monarch's traits to the character of the evil Pygmalion in Book 3 of *Télémaque*.[4]

The moral criticisms contained in *Télémaque* also form the core of a collection of *dialogues des morts*, written by Fénelon sometime between 1692 and 1695. These dialogues remained in manuscript form prior to 1700, although numerous copies were made and contemporaries were probably aware of their existence. From 1700 to 1712 some of the dialogues were published piecemeal, but it was not until after Fénelon's death in 1715 that the dialogues were published *in toto* with Fénelon's name on the title page.[5]

Louis XI figures very prominently in these dialogues, appearing in six of them, more than any other historical character. Each of the six dialogues addresses a character flaw for which Louis XI was well known, but they also have a larger significance in that some appear to lend themselves easily to a discussion of contemporary events. Dialogue fifty-seven, the first of those in which Louis XI appears, is between him and Cardinal Bessarion who, at the behest of Sixtus IV, had attempted in 1470 to reconcile the rulers of France, England and Burgundy in the hope that they could be persuaded to participate in a new crusade against the Turk. The dialogue centres around the importance of classical education. Bessarion addresses Louis XI with a tone of disrespect and accusation: "I see in you all the barbarie of the Latins, among whom a desolated Greece, after the taking of Constantinople, tried in vain to open up the mind and letters."[6] Apparently Fénelon subscribed to the traditional view of Louis XI as an ignoramus, a view that Gabriel Naudé had tried so hard to dispel in his *Addition à l'histoire de Louis XI*.[7] Louis XI responds by complaining of the "savants" to whom he had mistakenly listened while at the court of Burgundy before he came to the throne:

they were pedants and imbeciles like you; they understood little of affairs; they knew little of the diverse characters of men; they knew not how to dissimulate, nor to keep quiet, nor how to insinuate themselves, nor how to enter in the passions of others; nor to find resources in difficulties, nor to divine the designs of others; they were vain, indiscreet, contrary, always concerned with useless words and deeds, full of subtlety that convinced no one, incapable of learning to live and restrain oneself. I could not suffer such beasts.[8]

Fénelon seeks to have Louis XI indict himself through an unabashed declaration of those qualities, condemned by society, which the Spider King prizes most highly. Fénelon voices his own opinion on the views of Louis XI through the mouth of Bessarion: "I greatly prefer to be a pedant than a traitor, a tyrant and an enemy of the human race."[9]

From a dialogue demonstrating Louis XI's lamentable denigration of education, Fénelon moves to a discussion of Louis XI's bad choice in ministers. Louis XI's combatant in this debate is Cardinal Balue. Fénelon's choice of Balue is especially significant, since Balue had betrayed his master, Louis XI, by providing intelligence to the king's arch enemy, Charles le Téméraire. That Balue should be the voice of Fénelon's criticism only serves to heighten the negative portrait of Louis XI. Balue criticizes Louis XI for employing only those of base condition in the key positions of state. He contends that, for Louis XI, merit was a quality at once odious and suspect. Balue emphasizes the difference of degree between them when he says: "I admit that I was a dishonest man but it was because of this that you preferred me to others."[10] Balue appears to be implying that, since his malevolence was circumscribed by his lesser position, his infamy will be of a similarly lesser degree. Louis XI, on the other hand, possessing a higher responsibility, bears also greater guilt because his evil-mindedness had much broader consequences.

The next dialogue pits Louis XI against his own biographer, Philippe de Commynes. The two men engage in a discussion about the necessity of writing royal histories. Louis XI expresses his opinion that the dead are better left in peace, but Commynes defends his *Mémoires*, pointing out that Louis XI's reputation "was strangely blackened" and that his own work helped to ameliorate the negative impression of the monarch passed down to posterity. Louis XI remains dissatisfied with Commynes despite the latter's defence because he recorded the king's worst idiosyncrasies. Commynes then counters with vehemence: "Do you believe that a king can be hidden after his death as you hid certain intrigues during your life? I would save nothing for you by my silence and I would dishonour myself."[11] Here again, as in *Télémaque*, we see the importance of posterity for Fénelon. A king ought to be aware that he cannot control events after his death as he did in life. Therefore, he ought to act with an eye to his posthumous reputation since iniquities will inevitably surface and rebound to his eternal infamy.

Dialogue sixty-one, between Louis XI and Louis XII, is particularly compelling because it brings together two monarchs whose respective reputations were so very different. In comparison with Louis XI, posterity has been overwhelmingly kind to Louis XII. The contrast between the two kings could not be more stark: Louis XI was stooped and unattractive, suspicious and vindictive, ignorant and parsimonious, and, above all, unconcerned with the plight of the people of France. Louis XII, on the other hand, was reputed to have been kind and generous, and manifested his love for his subjects at every opportunity. He was especially beloved for keeping the tax levels low (although, by the end of his reign, the war in Italy forced a rise in the *taille*). Consequently, Louis XII gained the approbatory nickname: *le père du peuple*, the father of the people.[12]

The dialogue is also interesting in light of the series of pamphlets styled in this manner published during the Fronde.[13] At the beginning of the dialogue, Louis XI does not recognize Louis XII and asks who he is. When *le père du peuple* answers, Louis XI asks with a deliberately possessive tone, "How did you govern my kingdom?" What follows is a predictable debate on the best means of governing France. Louis XI is disparaging of Louis XII's claim that he gave succour to the people of France, always preferring their repose to any glory which might be obtained through the vanquishing of enemies. Louis XI says:

> You understood the art of reigning very poorly. It is I who placed my successors in a position of authority without limits. It is I who dissipated the leagues of princes and lords. It is I who levied enormous sums. I discovered the secrets of others. I knew how to hide my own. Shrewdness, arrogance and severity were the maxims of government. I greatly fear that you spoiled everything and that your softness destroyed all my work.[14]

Once again, Louis XI indicts himself by advocating precisely those qualities which Fénelon has taken pains to denounce. It is also significant that Louis XI brags about having placed kings beyond restraint; although Fénelon does not use the by now familiar phrase, *hors de page*, he clearly acknowledges Louis XI's reputation as the architect of tyranny.

The final dialogue between Maximilian I and Louis XI focuses on Louis's suspicious nature, a character flaw which resulted in the loss of most of the Burgundian lands to the Habsburg Empire. Louis XI admits that he did not foster the marriage between his son, Charles, and Marie of Burgundy because he feared that, in becoming powerful, his son might well have ambitions to displace him as king. Knowing his own lack of filial loyalty, Louis XI was afraid his son would act on similar impulses if given a sufficient power base from which to work.[15] Maximilian sounds a moral note at the end of the exchange: "When one has abandoned the path of probity, one no longer walks with one's family among the chasms; one is miserable and deserves it."[16]

Fénelon was clearly very interested in Louis XI and was intent on utilizing him as a figure for condemnation. His criticism of Louis XIV's policies could thus be implied through an attack on Louis XI by his own contemporaries or by highly respected figures like Louis XII. Fénelon's choice of Louis XI as a major participant in these dialogues served to confirm the connection between the Spider King and the Sun King forged in the common imagination.

The use of Louis XI in Fénelon's *dialogues des morts* is only one of several examples of the importance attached to Louis XI by writers of this enduring sub-genre of political literature. The re-publication of the *Dialogue d'Estat* (1652) in 1691 testifies to a renewed interest both in this particular pamphlet format and in the character of Louis XI. This would seem to be supported by the publication of another *dialogue des morts* in 1690, *Entretien de Louis Onze and Charle Hardi Duc de Bourgogne*. Published in Amsterdam and consequently beyond the reach of French governmental censorship, the anonymous pamphlet addressed contemporary circumstances much more directly that did the veiled references of Fénelon. Drawing upon the evocative force of Louis XI's historical reputation, the author seeks to heighten the effect of his arguments by comparing and contrasting contemporary France with the events of Louis XI's reign, and the character of Louis XIV with that of his progenitor.

Louis XI opens the dialogue by noting how, in the Elysian fields, erstwhile enemies were reconciled.[17] Charles the Bold answers that this is because they have drunk from the river of forgetfulness, i.e. the Styx. Louis XI also yearns to drink from that source because the memory of his wicked life tortures him. In contrast to previous dialogues, Louis XI is presented as remorseful and ashamed. By portraying Louis XI as humble and penitent, the author creates a striking contrast with the arrogance of the Sun King.

Louis XI and his old nemesis, Charles the Bold, begin to discuss the events of their own lifetimes in an effort to reconcile, but as the conversation progresses, it becomes increasingly apparent that they are equally concerned with the intensification of hostilities in the late 1680s. When Louis comments on Charles's initial refusal of advantageous peace terms after the successful siege of Nuits with the result that the duke later had to accept less advantageous terms, Charles points out that Louis XIV is about to make the same mistake. After the pope's confirmation of the emperor's candidate to the archbishopric of Cologne in 1688, Louis XIV, disgruntled by the pope's willingness to support Habsburg interests against those of the French crown, seized Avignon, invaded the Palatinate and took Philippsburg. The Truce of Ratisbon, fragile at the best of times, was shattered.

French troops initiated a scorched-earth policy upon their eventual retreat from the Palatinate in the summer of 1689. Louis XIV's unwillingness to accept the desirable *status quo* established at Ratisbon resulted in the cementing of the alliance against France and, with the addition of the United Provinces to the League of Augsburg and the support of William of Orange, now king of England, the tide was definitely turning against France. Louis XIV now relied upon the good offices of the pope to retain something of the advantages gained before Ratisbon. As Charles the Bold comments in the *dialogue*, it is not at all clear that the Allies will respect the mediation of the pope. Louis XI agrees with his opponent's assessment of the situation and predicts that Louis XIV should surrender all in the hopes that he will not lose all and "the mediation of the pope will serve as a small cloak to cover his shame."[18]

The two rulers return to a discussion of their own time with Charles asking Louis XI to recount the events of his reign. Louis XI refers to his early rebellion against his father (known as *La Praguerie*) and his mismanagement of the government of Dauphiné. After his succession to the throne, Louis says,

> I was as bad a king as I was a son. Scarlet was the colour of the mourning clothes I put on at [my father's] death, and from the time I mounted the throne of the *fleur de lis*, I rendered myself so odious to all of France that all the princes formed a league which they called [the league] of the public good.[19]

Louis XI maintains that if he had had the power that Louis XIV possessed, he would not have been obstructed in his unworthy goals. Charles points out that whereas Louis XI had not possessed Louis XIV's power, the latter does not have either Louis XI's skill or the good fortune to exploit it to its fullest potential:

> [Louis XIV] moves heaven and earth in order to break the universal league, but far from dissolving it, he only affirms it and strengthens it: his power and his successes make all the world fear him and each one unites with [the league] in order not to be overcome in isolation.[20]

Louis XI and Charles leave the discussion of current conditions to focus once more on their own histories, with Louis referring to his humiliation at Péronne when Charles captured him and forced him to accompany him to Liège. They then discuss Philippe de Commynes, who had defected from Burgundy's camp to enter the service of Louis XI.[21]

Finally, in the last pages of the pamphlet, the two discussants redirect their attention to Louis XIV and contemporary affairs. Commenting on the revocation of the Edict of Nantes, Louis XI remarks that Louis XIV has cause to regret his actions in driving the Huguenots into exile since, in doing so, he has simply provided his enemies with a supply of motivated soldiers. Charles compares the Catholicity of the two French kings, arguing that Louis XIV betrayed his faith by allying with the Infidel. Louis XI now says that he is sorry he did not drink from the river of forgetfulness, but Charles the Bold invites him instead to raise a cup of ambrosia to the health of king William of England, in the fervent hope that he would not soon count himself among the inhabitants of the Elysian fields.[22]

The approach of using a comparison between Louis XI and Louis XIV to highlight the latter's defects is carried much further in a series of three pamphlets published in Cologne in 1694. The *Miroir historique de la ligue de l'an 1464, ou peut se reconoitre la ligue de l'an 1694* and the two subsequent pamphlets written on the same topic are cited by Bayle in his article on Louis XI in the *Dictionnaire historique et critique*.[23] The pamphlets are directed against the militaristic policies of Louis XIV, and they appeal to the international coalition raised against him not to negotiate peace terms which would redound only to the advantage of the Sun King himself.

In the early 1690s the French troops were enjoying some limited successes in the field, especially in the Spanish Netherlands and Northern Italy. Continuous French pressure on Turin compelled the Duke of Savoy, Victor Amadeus II, to desert the League and join France. The duke's defection was an ominous sign of the League's continued fragility. The possibility of its disintegration owing to military losses, combined with the seductive prospect of financial rewards for any newly-acquired friends of the French, greatly alarmed the author of the *Miroir historique*. The author seeks to draw a parallel between the League of Augsburg and the League of the Public Weal in order that he might demonstrate what could be accomplished by the current league if it holds firm and, by contrast, what is to be feared "if it is so weak as to dissolve itself before having forced a peace on France that does not permit it to set Europe at odds any longer."[24]

According to the author, the League of the Public Weal was formed at the outset by the duc de Bretagne, who had been engaged in a struggle with Louis XI over the autonomy of the region. The duke maintained that if Louis XI tried to usurp his authority over Brittany, the king would surely try to undermine the independent power of the other great nobles as well. In order to add legitimacy to their struggle, the magnates placed at their head Charles, duc de Berry, the brother of the king. It is significant that the author does not dwell on the intentions of the rebelling princes. Whether their appeal to the public good was sincere or fraudulent seems not to be at issue. What is important is how Louis XI dealt with their association. He acceded to all their demands with a great show of conciliation, although, of course, his accommodating demeanour was all a ruse:

> Louis XI, who was resolved to purchase the rupture of the League at whatever price, consented that thirty-six experienced and prudent men be drawn from the three estates in order to regulate all that they judged to be necessary for the reformation of the kingdom, that there would be no revision or appeal of what they decreed and that they would remove all new taxes.[25]

Of course, Louis XI had no intention of abiding by promises made for the sole purpose of securing the dissolution of the League of the Public Weal.

Later, at Péronne, when he was negotiating with the comte de Charolais, Louis XI easily acceded to the comte's conditions because he felt his life to be seriously threatened. But his willingness to defer to Charolais's wishes evaporated quickly when he was no longer in danger. The author's point in reciting the history of Louis XI's successful dissipation of the League of the Public Weal is clearly stated at the end of the pamphlet. The author begs the question: "If Louis XI was able to do this with a limited power, what could not France do, with its incomparable forces?" The author does not intend to argue that Louis XIV will follow the same course of vengeance as had Louis XI, but simply to show that what happened in the past might serve as a clue for the future. That clue, according to the author's interpretation, was that the allies must construct a peace "so advantageous that France is not able to recover from it, nor to exact revenge for frivolous quarrels, against those who have been in the League at this time."[26]

The second pamphlet, *Avis d'un amy à l'autheur du miroir historique de la ligue de l'an 1464*, is addressed to the author of the first pamphlet, praising him for the illustrative comparison of the two leagues. The parallel drawn by the first author ostensibly motivates the second (though in fact the two writers were probably one and the same) to produce a similar comparison of Louis XI and Louis XIV. The author clearly perceives Louis XI as the prototype of Louis XIV; the latter's actions function almost as an echo of the earlier king's perfidy:

> One sees the living Louis XIV clearly in the shadow of Louis XI: the copy is superior to the original, and many sad events have provided and continue daily to provide us the bloody proof that the disciple has surpassed the master.[27]

A comparison then follows wherein the *guerre du bien public* is likened to the *Fronde*; Louis XI's impatient sojourn in Dauphiné is compared with Louis XIV's desire to invade his father-in-law's Spain. History records Louis XI's intrigues against the English, the Burgundians, and the Liègeois. Louis XIV's sole ambition has been to intrigue against Holland. The attack on Louis XIV by way of a comparison with Louis XI becomes absurd when the author focuses on the physical appearance of both kings. According to the author, although Louis XI was born ugly and Louis XIV handsome, nevertheless the parallel is valid since the deceits and machinations employed by Louis XIV have left their mark on his previously attractive face.

The author conjures up a long historiographic tradition when he writes that Louis XI had "mis les Roys de France hors de page," although he departs from the tradition in attributing this accomplishment to Louis XI's success in corrupting ministers from foreign powers rather than his suppression of institutions like Parlement of Paris and the estates general. Louis XI may have begun the process of royal liberation from restraint, but his emulator took royal authority to new heights:

> If Louis XI placed the kings of France beyond restraint . . . even the most passionate Frenchman is unable to disagree that Louis XIV goes much farther, having forced the ecclesiastical estate to submit to his will, the princes of the blood to his laws, and without response, crushed the nobility beneath his feet and generally reduced all his subjects to slavery. As much as he has done, he will deal even more severely, alas, with the people of his conquests.[28]

The author asks his audience: "Would you not say that this comparison would serve to make one imagine the transmigration of souls from one body to another?" He then digresses to discuss the connection of names to character traits and argues that the rise and fall of nations is often framed by reigns with kings possessing the same name. The comparison being completed, the author returns to his original intention of commenting on the *Miroir historique*. It being evident that Louis XIV wants to rupture the League in order to tackle each member individually, it is important for each state to recognize its particular interests.

The third pamphlet in this series, *Pensées sur l'avis d'un amy à l'autheur du miroir historique de l'an 1464*, has little to say about Louis XI directly. The author does seem intent, however, on discussing some of the historic treaties signed by French kings. An example is the Treaty of Arras, signed between Charles VII and Philippe de Bourgogne, in 1435, in which the French king was forced to accept humiliating terms. The other major point this pamphlet makes is the inability of Louis XIV to keep his word. In this regard, the author elaborates on the previous pamphlet's discussion of Louis XI's dissimulation by adding a relatively unknown anecdote. He recounts the incident when Louis XI signed a treaty with the leaders of a peasant revolt. Perceiving a danger in their great numbers, Louis XI reneged on the agreement and sent in the military to arrest the labourers. Moreover, Louis XI violated the treaty struck between France and Burgundy, when he ravaged the lands of the orphaned princess of Burgundy almost immediately upon the death of her father, duke Charles.[29]

These pamphlets indicate several important new factors influencing the reputation of Louis XI by the end of the seventeenth century. First, concerns about developments on the international scene in the 1680s and 1690s were reflected in new attention to similar aspects of Louis XI's reign. The portrait of Louis XI drawn in these pamphlets becomes coloured by considerations of his diplomatic and military tactics in addition to an on-going interest in his relationship with institutions such as the Parlement of Paris and the estates general. The second, and more important, development was the link forged between Louis XI and Louis XIV. Opponents of Louis XIV could amplify the impact of their criticisms by yoking him with Louis XI, whose malevolence and tyranny were, by this time, firmly entrenched in the collective memory of France. The association of the two kings, so powerful and enduring, would continue to affect both of their reputations well into the eighteenth century.

One of the great polemical exchanges of the seventeenth century took place in the wake of the Glorious Revolution of 1688. The assumption of the English throne by William of Orange was of enormous interest to the Huguenots living in Holland. Within the community of Huguenot exiles, a pamphlet war ensued in which more narrow considerations about the legitimacy of the English case gave way to much broader, more theoretical discussions about the nature, scope, and limit of royal authority. The most vehement pamphlets were those exchanged between Pierre Bayle and Pierre Jurieu, whose increasingly embittered personal relationship was played out in print alongside their obvious political disagreements.[30] Frequent mention of Louis XI can be found in both their works; interpretations of the monarch appear to be congruent with their respective views on kingship. A closer examination of references to Louis XI by Bayle and Jurieu will simultaneously shade our understanding of the differences between them and, on the broader canvas, add more texture to our picture of late seventeenth-century political ideology.

Although an advocate of absolute monarchy, Pierre Bayle was not an admirer of Louis XIV, and for obvious reasons. Bayle's Protestant beliefs did not, however, result in antagonism toward the French monarchy. Although raised as a Huguenot, Bayle briefly converted to Catholicism only to return once more to Protestantism. The vagaries of his religious life convinced him of the need to discount denominational differences in order to focus on the core of Christian faith. He believed that a strong government was necessary for the preservation of the individual's right to express that faith as he chose.

Born in 1647, the son of a Protestant pastor, Pierre Bayle spent his early years being educated at home by his father. After his older brother Jacob finished his studies, Pierre was allowed to travel to Puylaurens to begin his own formal education. Frustrated by the low standards at Puylaurens, Bayle travelled to Toulouse where he enrolled in a Jesuit college. His conversion to Catholicism, which occurred during his stint with the Jesuits, did not outlast his college days. Shortly after attaining his master's degree, he returned to Protestantism and travelled to Geneva to study at the Academy there. After a series of tutorial appointments, Bayle secured the chair of philosophy at the Academy of Sedan. Eventually, along with other prominent Protestants, Bayle settled in Rotterdam, where he developed his ideas concerning civil toleration. His dedication to the idea of absolute monarchy and his fervent endorsement of continued Huguenot loyalty to the French crown brought Bayle into constant conflict with Jurieu, the vigorous supporter of popular sovereignty In 1693 Jurieu succeeded in having Bayle's chair at the Ecole Illustre suppressed.[31]

Bayle's support for absolute monarchy, tinged as it was by his experience as an exile, results in an ambivalent attitude to Louis XI. In his *Nouvelles de la république des lettres*, Bayle reviewed Antoine Varillas's history of France, dealing with each section of the work in turn. Regarding the piece on Louis XI, Bayle says: "It is only a morsel, but it is a morsel of great price." Bayle praises Varillas for his success in presenting an unvarnished portrait of the fifteenth-century monarch, without flattery or disguises.[32] Bayle's own opinion of Louis XI can be ascertained in his "Consideration particulière des sentiments de Louis XI," which forms Chapter 152 of his *Pensées diverses à l'occasion d'une comete*. Bayle tries to get at the truth about real piety. He maintains that the invocation of saints or of the Holy Spirit when one is lying on a deathbed proves little about true piety, since the desire to be cured is the true motivation of such prayers. As an example, Bayle cites the voyage of the Minim father, Saint François de Paul, to the court of Louis XI. It is hard to believe, according to Bayle, that a schemer such as Louis XI, a prince who would gain his own ends through fraud and other nefarious means, could truly be a pious man. Bayle says that a true conqueror, of the type of Alexander, is at least open and honest about his ambitions.[33] Yet despite these indications to the contrary, Bayle argues that Louis XI did have true piety, as demonstrated by his private prayers for the forgiveness of his part in the poisoning of his brother. Bayle's assertion that Louis XI did possess a sincere faith must be seen in the context of his arguments on behalf of toleration. The point Bayle is attempting to make is that piety is not necessarily accompanied by other moral virtues: "Thus we have in his person the example of a perfect agreement between a very wicked soul and a belief in the existence of God which gives rise to the most excessive religious bigotry."[34]

If we examine the entry for "Louis XI" in the *Dictionnaire Historique et Critique*, we find Bayle's view of the king to be condemnatory, but not unequivocally so. Bayle writes that Louis XI was "a prince well versed in the art of reigning." Though he was skilled at political intrigue, he was sometimes caught in a muddle because of his propensity for extreme behaviour of one sort or another.[35] Bayle goes so far as to praise Louis XI in a limited fashion for his negotiations with Edward IV, which resulted in peace between England and France. Although it was not a glorious event in French history, Bayle asserts that Louis XI acted with prudence in this instance, since he had many powerful enemies at that juncture and "a man ought not to pretend to a Roman courage out of season."[36] Bayle also points out Louis XI's laudable rigour in forcing soldiers to pay for their quarters promptly. Thus, Louis XI helped France to grow rich by ensuring that money circulated regularly through the economy. This is the first instance of Louis XI's economic policies being praised and it perhaps points in the direction of another new element contributing to his reinterpretation. The importance of economic reforms would grow in succeeding years and might well result in some alterations in Louis XI's portrait. Bayle's conclusion, drawn from this praise, is "how the ill qualities of a monarch are sometimes compensated with others [and], all things considered, make the people as happy as under a good and well-natured king."[37]

Though Bayle clearly acknowledges the oppressive regime endured under Louis XI, he still maintains that:

[Louis XI] had eminent qualities, and such as were absolutely necessary to him; for without these he never could have maintained the monarchy against domestic and foreign enemies ... He not only preserved his dominions in the midst of so many attempts, but also enlarged them; for he reunited Anjou, Maine and the duchy of Burgundy to the crown, and acquired Provence.[38]

Bayle also notes that Louis XI's alleged illiteracy was sufficiently disproved by Gabriel Naudé. All in all, Bayle seems to have formed a relatively detached opinion of Louis XI, remarking on both his good and bad points. Nevertheless, one could argue that his treatment of Louis XI might be more coloured by contemporary concerns than it might at first appear. Bayle's approval of Louis XI's peace negotiations with England, which sacrificed glory for practicality, may well be a criticism of Louis XIV's militaristic policies. The attack is all the more pointed since, as we have seen, Louis XI was often likened to, and was here being employed as an example against, Louis XIV. Second, Bayle's concerns are illustrated as much by what he omits as what he includes. Gone are the references to Louis XI's manipulation of the estates general, seen so frequently in sixteenth-century condemnations of the king. That institution had ceased to function as a viable counterweight to the king's unfettered will, as indeed had the Parlement of Paris, in Bayle's view; or rather, the Parlement was an assembly of sycophants who no longer wielded their considerable power on behalf of anyone except themselves and the king. This was perhaps even more dangerous, because it maintained the fiction of restraint on royal power. Bayle is openly hostile to parlement, as is demonstrated in his article on *premier président* La Vacquerie. Rather than applauding parlement's refusal to register an offending edict, Bayle argues that this precipitated evil. He maintains that Etienne Pasquier would not have supported the claims of parlement so assiduously if he had known that the inflexibility of the courts was not infrequently detrimental to the state.[39]

The fact that Bayle places some importance on economic issues and the territorial aggrandizement of France clearly indicates that more new elements are entering appraisals of Louis XI. Despite his absolutist leanings, Bayle is generally condemnatory of Louis XI and he does devote a large footnote in the entry about the king to a discussion of how he oppressed the people of France.[40] Nevertheless, Bayle's view of Louis XI is temperate; his support for Louis XIV, mitigated by criticisms of some of the king's harshest policies, is reflected in a judicious treatment of Louis XI in which the personal defects of the king are weighed against his successful efforts on behalf of France.

With the publication of *Les Soupirs de la France esclave, qui aspire après la liberté* (1694), on the other hand, Louis XI's historiographical fortunes plunged to a new low. Although the work is anonymous, I have chosen to follow Guy Dodge's attribution to Pierre Jurieu.[41] The work is a truly vitriolic attack on the French monarchy, using many of the same arguments which first emerged among resistance theorists during the French Wars of Religion.[42] In addition to arguments resurrected from the previous century, the author also incorporates new elements from the works of seventeenth-century writers to buttress his assertions about the oppressive regime which Louis XIV inherited and continued to maintain.

The pamphlet takes the form of fourteen *mémoires*, apparently written on a monthly basis. The first *mémoire*, dated 10 August 1689, launches the first volleys against the edifice of absolutism by recounting the oppression of the Church, the courts, the nobles and the towns. The rest of the entries describe the nature of despotic government and by what means the court of France maintains its control. Louis XI figures prominently in many of the entries. He makes his first appearance in the third *mémoire*, which purports to discuss "the unhappy effects of the arbitrary and despotic power of the court of France." Louis XI and Louis XIV are compared with regard to their respective levels of despotism and cruelty, in which, of course, neither king emerges any better by way of the comparison:

> In order to blacken the name of Louis XI it was noted that he had caused to die four thousand of his subjects, and because of this, one justifiably considers him a cruel Prince. Today the clemency of Louis XIV is praised, and nevertheless one can prove that he has caused thirty to forty thousand people to be hung, burnt, beaten, massacred, and to perish in prisons and in exile. This is ten times more than Louis XI.[43]

Most importantly, the work argues that such arbitrary power on the part of the monarchy is a perversion of the true constitution of France, a usurpation of authority originally vested in both the estates general and the parlement. With regard to the estates general, the author echoes the arguments of resistance theorists found in works such as Hotman's *Francogallia* and the *Vindiciae contra tyrannos*, even using the same historical examples. The author cites the assembly at Tours as an example of the continued power of the estates general.[44]

The author goes on to discuss the authority of parlement, noting the La Vacquerie episode wherein Louis XI demonstrated "all the characteristics of a tyrant and, in effect, did more to ruin the liberty of the people and the parlement than had all his predecessors combined."[45] Before the usurpation of their sovereignty by French kings, the people lived happy, free lives, unburdened with oppressive taxation or continuous billeting and victualling of troops. Although Charles VII was the first to establish troops in times of peace,

> Louis XI, son of Charles VII, knew well how to profit from this new institution, and those who have read history know how he empowered himself by this means, and began to lay the foundations of tyranny under which we groan today.[46]

The author concludes by appealing to Frenchmen to return to their ancient constitution. He maintains that it has not been even four hundred years since France was the most free country in Europe. Moreover, "its slavery only truly began under Louis XI and reached its height under Louis XIV. Thus, one must count the total duration of the tyranny as only two hundred years."[47]

Les Soupirs is a pivotal work in the historiography of Louis XI. It owes a debt to the past, combining disparate elements such as resistance theory from the sixteenth century and parlementaire ideas from the "Fronde" era, but it is also a harbinger of things to come, pointing in the direction that French political thought will take during much of the following century. As the ideas developed by resistance theorists during the French civil wars, ignored for much of the seventeenth century, resurface in *Les Soupirs*, so too is the portrait of Louis XI as a tyrant reinvigorated. The author also discusses the constitutional importance of the Parlement of Paris, so earnestly promoted during the "Fronde." To these elements from the past, the author of *Les Soupirs* added the consideration of issues arising from a specific set of contemporary circumstances. Concerns about the international situation resulted in a new attention to Louis XI's relations with other European countries, particularly England. Although economic questions did not figure prominently in *Les Soupirs*, Pierre Bayle's emphasis on Louis XI's fiscal policy ensured that such considerations would henceforth form part of any discussion of the king.

The international struggles that had become, by the 1680s and 1690s, an endemic feature both on the domestic French scene and Europe-wide, provided renewed impetus for the examination of kingship. Once again the very basis of kingly authority in France came under scrutiny. Because of his vexed personal history with institutions like the estates general and the Parlement of Paris, Louis XI was bound to fare badly at the hands of those challenging the legitimacy of Louis XIV's military campaigns and the domestic policies in place to support those campaigns. But even for those who, like Fénelon and Bayle, professed support for absolute monarchy (though for different reasons, to be sure), Louis XI was a problematic figure. In their desire to support the *idea* of absolute monarchy, these writers were compelled to point out the sorts of extreme royal wilfulness that could seriously undermine perceptions of legitimacy. If Louis XIV could not be criticized directly, his conscience might be prodded by references to his flawed ancestor. If the pricks of conscience did not work, detached consideration of Louis XI's troubled reign might spur royal reflection and behaviour modification. Louis XI finds genuine admirers only among the few writers who, like Joachim Legrand, were truly devoted to the sort of state-king deity that Louis XIV had "fabricated" at Versailles.[48]

Interestingly enough, although the combination of all these factors resulted in a thoroughly unflattering portrait of Louis XI drawn by late seventeenth-century writers, the re-examination of these issues in the eighteenth century resulted in a reputation that was far from uniformly bad. As the relationships between constituent elements of the French state were recast and redefined, Louis XI was caught again in the crucible of political debate. In the eighteenth century, the collective memory of Louis XI was once more manipulated to suit the requirements of adversaries on both sides of another powerful debate: the *thèse nobiliaire/thèse royale* controversy.

3 Louis XI and the French nation

[Mazarin's] whole care and attention was now turned to the annihilation of dignities and rank by any means he could find, and to depriving persons of quality of every sort of authority, and, for that purpose, removing them from all posts in State affairs, and putting in men of base extraction like himself, whose offices he magnified in power, distinctions, influence, and wealth, persuading the king to consider all nobles and *seigneurs* the natural enemies of his authority, and to prefer, for the handling of State affairs, men of no account, whom he could on the slightest discontent reduce to nothingness by taking away their posts as easily as he had given them . . . [1]

At times Saint-Simon's *Mémoires* seems little more than the collected complaints of a peevish courtier too long overlooked. But, from a broader perspective, the *Mémoires* are also a product of the profound discontent felt by many sword nobles at the beginning of the eighteenth century. Along with those of Henri de Boulainvilliers, Fénelon and a host of lesser-known writers, Saint-Simon's words are reflective of what has come to be known as the "aristocratic reaction", which began in the last years of Louis XIV's reign. The arguments for more noble involvement in government have been characterized as an attempt to restore the conditions which existed prior to Louis XIV's and especially Mazarin's efforts to undermine the independent status of the nobility. As William Doyle points out, however, the whole idea of an "aristocratic reaction" in the eighteenth century may be ill-conceived, even unfounded.[2] G. Chaussinand-Nogaret also argues against the prevalent conceptualization of the eighteenth-century nobility as being uniformly reactionary, maintaining that a substantial section of the nobility subscribed to the ideas of the Enlightenment and actively promoted political reform.[3] Certainly, the appeal to some ideal past in which the nobles were responsible for restricting the arbitrary will of the king could be called reactionary by virtue of its very emphasis on the past, but the idea of power-sharing, so coherently expounded by Montesquieu,[4] is clearly much more than a simple knee-jerk response to new royal policies. There is little doubt that the ideas of Boulainvilliers and other reform-minded individuals contributed to the creation of an intellectual environment which challenged the old regime.

Indeed, the *nobiliaire/royale* debate has often been placed within the much larger framework of the interplay between constitutionalism and absolutism, with writers like Boulainvilliers considered as the intellectual heirs of François Hotman and Theodore Beza.[5] Clearly there are substantial differences between the *nobiliaire* ideology expressed by Boulainvilliers and others during the eighteenth century and the resistance theories propounded by Hotman, Beza and Buchanan. The sixteenth-century writers sought to justify an already-existing state of affairs; their constitutional arguments grew out of the need to legitimize radical resistance to the crown. By contrast, the *nobiliaire* writers advocated reform of the system to allow for more aristocratic involvement in government. Nevertheless, this chapter is premised on the assumption that, despite some differences between theories expounded in the sixteenth and eighteenth centuries, the theoretical conflicts of the later period were motivated by the same general goals. The constitutionalist ideas propounded by Hotman and Junius Brutus in the sixteenth century were recast in the aristocratic mould of *nobiliaire* ideology, but the principle of monarchical limitation remained constant. The same holds true for the absolutists of the sixteenth century and their *royaliste* heirs.

The connections between the sixteenth-century resistance theorists and their eighteenth-century *nobiliaire* counterparts should not, however, obscure the fact that the distance between them is more profound than one of mere chronology. For writers like Boulainvilliers, the concept of "la nation" has become central to their arguments about the historical and contemporary importance of the nobility. While use of the term *nation* was already widespread by the sixteenth century, it was used almost exclusively to designate a group sharing either ethnicity or geography, as for example in the reference to German or English "nations" at the University of Paris. For eighteenth-century *nobiliaire* writers, by contrast, *nation* possessed a specific political meaning: the nation was synonymous with the French nobility. In this noble definition, nation encompassed a racial, caste quality, but also, importantly, a political dimension lacking in earlier formulations. Their participation in the earliest Frankish assemblies on the *champs de mars* established the nobles as an integral component in the functioning of the French constitution. Later usurping kings, most notably Louis XI, had ousted the nobles from the political process. *Nobiliaire* writers were trying to re-establish the right ordering of the ancient constitution, including the reactivation of the (noble) French nation.

Clearly this "noble" nation is something quite different from the nation as articulated in the years immediately preceding and during the French Revolution. What is rather surprising is that, up until recently, there has been little discussion about the relationship between these two distinct meanings of *nation*. In his article on "Nation" in *A Critical Dictionary of the French Revolution*, Pierre Nora asserts that "the quasi-official advent of the 'nation' was . . . precisely contemporaneous with the very beginning of the Revolution, that is with the meeting of the Estates General."[6] Others who have written about the nation and the "rise" of nationalism see a similar disjuncture between the *ancien régime* and revolutionary meanings of *nation*.[7]

While historians have begun to turn their attention to a discussion of "national identity" and "national consciousness" in early modern France,[8] it seems remarkable that historians have thus far paid very little attention to the idea of *nation* in the context of the *nobiliaire/royale* controversy, wherein it clearly possessed a political meaning in addition to its rather archaic ethno-geographical sense. Liah Greenfeld has recently addressed this important *lacuna* in *Nationalism: Five Roads to Modernity*. In the hundred pages devoted to France, Greenfeld posits that eighteenth-century nobles, dismayed by a perceived diminution of their power, sought to forge a new identity, that of a "nation," in order to reclaim their lost political role. While I share some of David Bell's reservations regarding the evidence Greenfeld marshals in support of her thesis,[9] I endorse her general assertion that the nobility's efforts to redefine itself were influential in the evolution of the concept of the nation.

The *thèse royale/thèse nobiliaire* controversy has been discussed in its general outlines elsewhere.[10] For our purposes, a comparison of Henri de Boulain-villiers, the defender of the aristocracy, with the Marquis d'Argenson and other less well-known royalists such as Damiens de Gomicourt and P. L. C. Gin, highlights the contrasting interpretations of Louis XI found in *nobiliaire* and *royale* thought. Louis XI is the monarch most often blamed for debasing the ancient French nobility. Among eighteenth-century noble writers, the revolt of the great magnates during his reign represented a watershed in French history. The failure of the revolt resulted in the abrogation of the rights of the nation. Louis XI had dealt a blow to the nobility from which it had yet to recover. Although other kings who came after him, most especially Louis XIV, would also play their part in maintaining and extending the pitiable dependence of the once-proud nobility, Louis XI initiated the process of noble disempowerment. Because of his special role in this regard, eighteenth-century interpretations of Louis XI by *nobiliaire* and *royale* writers would seem to offer an interesting vantage point from which to examine the political meaning of a noble *nation*, and perhaps to suggest explanations of how, in the course of the eighteenth century, *nation* took on its more familiar revolutionary connotations.

The *thèse nobiliaire* was most ably and vehemently expounded by Henri de Boulainvilliers. The contradictions in Boulainvilliers' work have given rise to characterizations which run the gamut of the socio-political spectrum: he has been called both a racist[11] and an "incipient socialist."[12] Harold Ellis has referred to Boulainvilliers as an "aristocratic reactionary," despite the overuse of the term, because *le comte* advocated a return to a past in which nobles took an active governmental role.[13] If such a restoration could be accomplished, noble power and glory would enjoy a resurgence that would certainly benefit the French state and assure the well-being of its people.

Born in 1658 into a noble family of ancient extraction, Boulainvilliers was educated at the Oratorian Academy at Juilly and, for a time, pursued a military career. Like Fénelon, he became part of the duke of Burgundy's circle, although there was some distance between Boulainvilliers and the rest of the circle because of his emphatic endorsement of feudalism, which the other members rightly believed could not be wholeheartedly supported in view of the duke's imminent possession of absolute authority.[14] Boulainvilliers himself was not immune to the blandishments of the Bourbon monarchy, finding himself part of the court he criticized. After the death of the duc de Bourgogne, Boulainvilliers became part of the Regent's entourage, and he wrote several important treatises under the aegis of Philippe d'Orléans. According to Ellis, much of Boulainvilliers' work, especially during his period of tenure with the Regent, was produced as a direct result of events like the *affaire du bonnet* and the *affaire des princes*, which encapsulated the constitutional struggles that bedevilled the early years of the Regency.[15]

Boulainvilliers' ideas concerning the importance of noble participation in French government are put forward in his *Histoire de l'ancien gouvernement de la France* and the *Essais sur la noblesse de France* which, like almost all his works, appeared posthumously (in 1727 and 1732, respectively). The *Essais sur la noblesse de France* is perhaps the more theoretical of the two works. Consequently it contains more obvious inconsistencies which cannot be buried in a welter of historical examples. The *Essais* are more wide-ranging in subject matter, as Boulainvilliers attempts to prove that classical Rome and, less convincingly, Greece possessed aristocratic forms of government during their heyday.[16] The persuasive thrust of the work is hampered, however, by Boulainvilliers' acknowledgement at the outset that all men are naturally equals ["naturellement égaux"]. Boulainvilliers argues:

> It is certain that in the common law all men are equal. Violence introduced the distinctions of liberty and slavery, of nobility and common rank; but although the origin is vicious, it has been established through usage for such a long time that it is a natural law.[17]

By admitting that at one time in the primeval past men lived as equals, Boulainvilliers unwittingly undermines his own arguments about nobility, since, if prescription could legitimize the substitution of a system based on freedom for some and slavery for others over one in which all men were free, could time and usage not also conceivably legitimize the replacement of a more recent system with one in which all men were equally slaves (with the exception of the king)? This somewhat backhanded acknowledgement of universal equality may be one reason why the ideas of Boulainvilliers and other *nobiliaire* writers are utilized by more radical theorists on the eve of the Revolution.

Boulainvilliers sidesteps potential problems associated with an acceptance of theoretical equality by affirming that the possession of "la vertu" distinguishes some men from the ranks, and that this strength of character can be passed on to the next generation (although, as Ellis effectively argues, Boulainvilliers places more emphasis on education and environment than on heredity).[18] Moreover, such "vertu" is, in fact, a much-needed commodity and the chaos of government requires the participation of men possessing the wisdom to steer the ship of state clear of the shoals.[19]

From these general introductory remarks, Boulainvilliers directs his attention to the development of the monarchy in France which, from before its inception, was inextricably bound up with the nobility. Even before the Franks conquered the Gauls, nobility characterized government in the geographic region which eventually became the kingdom of France. Before the Romans conquered them, the Gauls were governed by nobles under the authority of several kings, "and it was presumed that the dignity of the nobility was, among the people, as ancient as their government."[20]

When the Romans invaded Gaul, they discredited the "autorité d'usage" in order to firmly establish their control over the region. Boulainvilliers asserts that the emperor Caligula was determined to wage all-out war on the Gallic nobles. A new "nobility" emerged, consisting of magistrates who oversaw the implementation of Roman law throughout the province. With the arrival of the Franks, this Roman nobility was dissipated and a number of these magistrates went into ecclesiastical administration.[21]

The most important thing to the invading Franks was the preservation of their unbridled liberty (though these freedoms did not, of course, extend to the newly-liberated Gauls). In describing the political liberties of the Franks, Boulainvilliers offers a radical reinterpretation of French history, diminishing the role of the Frankish kings even more than did the resistance theorists of the sixteenth century, with whom he has been compared.[22]

> They regarded the right to choose their captains and their kings as the surest means of avoiding oppression and they obeyed them only at war. During times of peace, kings or captains retained credit only in proportion with their exploits; they took part in public or private deliberations only if they merited the confidence of the people by their actions, or if they had more eloquence than others in order to influence them in their sentiments.[23]

Boulainvilliers proclaims the significance of the Frankish conquest of Gaul in the *Histoire de l'ancien gouvernement de la France*: "it is the foundation of the French state in which we live ... " He is distressed by the fact that, although a number of historians praise the event, they do not consider what it meant for the French nation. Rather, these unnamed historians have quite erroneously interpreted the Frankish conquest to be the foundation of absolute monarchy because, by virtue of the Frankish victory over the Gauls, France became the patrimony of Clovis and his successors.[24] Boulainvilliers believes that the conquest had the greatest ramifications for the nation, and although we must understand that by "nation" Boulainvilliers means only the conquering Franks, the nobles, his consistent evocation of the concept may have endeared him to later writers who, in turn, broadened the concept of the nation and imbued it with its well-known revolutionary implications.

As a consequence of the Frankish conquest, the French as a nation (remembering Boulainvilliers' narrow definition of the term) have certain liberties which have been eroded through the course of time. Boulainvilliers emphatically refutes the common contention that Clovis exercised complete royal authority over his Frankish as well as his new Gallic subjects; he maintains by contrast that the Franks were not actually subjects, in the most rigorous sense of that term.[25]

Boulainvilliers admits, however, that this idyllic state of French liberty did not last. As the power of the Franks extended, the credit of their ruler grew and so, as a consequence, did his authority. The accretion of power culminated in the reigns of Charles Martel and Pepin. When Pepin assumed control of the throne, the hitherto free and independent French, who had so often conquered their enemies through the force of their valour and perseverance, were themselves conquered, "not as a foreign nation but as a private family."[26] Although, as part of his oppressive rule, Charles Martel abolished the assemblies which had been held at the Champs de Mars, his descendant, Charlemagne, restored them and gave them their most perfect form. It is clear that, despite the inroads made into French liberty under the later Merovingians and under Pepin, Charlemagne managed to restore France to its full glory, most amply demonstrated in the re-establishment of the ancient assemblies. Boulainvilliers waxes eloquent about this, Charlemagne's greatest accomplishment:

> All the dignity of the Nation and of its kings themselves resided in this august assembly that was moreover the good [product] of the union and concord of all the people subject to the French monarch with their sovereign.[27]

The second of Boulainvilliers' *Lettres historiques sur les parlemens ou états-généraux*, which are appended to the *Histoire de l'ancien gouvernement de la France*,[28] deals with the assemblies held under Charlemagne at greater length. Here again Charlemagne is praised for his understanding of the French nation and his recognition of the people's loyalty to him, which convinced him to give back to these assemblies all of the power that he had himself accrued. Unfortunately for the French nation, "none of the kings since him have ever understood that the French were originally a free people," and consequently, the assemblies which were so highly valued by Charlemagne were denigrated by his successors and, especially under the Capetians, manipulated and corrupted to such an extent that they were no longer the guarantors of ancient French liberties.[29]

In this regard, Louis XI is among the most reviled of the Capetian kings. Along with Philippe le Bel, who is equally despised by Boulainvilliers, Louis XI functions as a scapegoat for many of the ills which have befallen France since the glorious days of Charlemagne. The last two *Lettres historiques* are devoted to a discussion of Louis XI's reign and, more particularly, to the farcical estates general held at Tours in 1467. Boulainvilliers rather grudgingly admits that Louis XI possessed some facility for government. He manifested "a clarity and marvellous keenness of judgement, a singular quickness of imagination, much art and facility of expression, courage in war and liberality worthy of the first heroes."[30] These qualities were, tragically for France, overshadowed by his "amour-propre;" Louis XI thought of his own interests before those of the state. Moreover, since the time of Louis XI, "amour-propre" has always been supreme in the hearts of the French kings (with the possible exception of Louis XII).

Although Boulainvilliers does not characterize the War of the Public Weal as a constitutional struggle, he does point out that it was the actions of the nobles that forced Louis XI to admit the errors he had made and to agree to repair the disorders of the realm caused by his behaviour. Boulainvilliers does not, however, believe that Louis XI's change of heart was genuine. His self-interest was again clearly manifested in his conduct toward the estates general held at Tours in 1467, discussed in the final letter.

Louis XI manipulated the estates general to accomplish his own goals and, when these were attained, he immediately dissolved the assembly. Once he managed to gain the assembly's support for his decision to renege on his grant of Normandy as an appanage to the duc de Berry, he dismissed the deputies. Interestingly, Boulainvilliers links Louis XI with his Bourbon successors, Louis XIII and Louis XIV, and remarks rather wryly on Louis XI's contribution to the building of the absolutist system, which perhaps Louis XIII and Louis XIV took for granted:

> Louis XIII covered his ears with both hands when one dared to cite him some established rights or privileges, and he bellowed that this was only a privilege against his will. Louis XIV, more of a formalist, but not less concerned with the effective end to which all kings tend, did not let any [such privileges] subsist. But, as Louis XI could only make a start on the great work of despotism, he could only go step by step. It's this that makes one regard the success of this assembly of the estates of the kingdom as one of the most remarkable strokes of his politics.[31]

One aspect of the estates held at Tours was particularly irksome to Boulainvilliers. The seating plan of the assembly indicated Louis XI's intention to erase all visible signs of noble privilege. The nobles who were not attached to the court in some official capacity were seated among the members of the third estate. This intermingling of ranks was a pernicious precedent set by Louis XI, only one of numerous actions taken by the king to destroy the existence of the nobility as a separate order. This social levelling was seen by Boulainvilliers as an effort to reduce all members of society to the same abysmal state of subjection.[32]

In the *Essais sur la noblesse*, the theme of tragic noble debasement is further explored and, again, Louis XI's actions figure prominently in Boulainvilliers' account of the downfall of feudal government and the decline into despotism. By obscuring the distinctions between nobles and *roturiers*, by making the nobles reliant on the king's favour for advancement, and by developing the infantry which successfully abolished the military need for nobles, Louis XI effected nothing less than a revolution in government. Louis XI contributed to the debasement of the nobility by elevating men of little account to positions of power and influence.[33] At the same time that he was elevating "des petits gens" to positions of influence, Louis XI was undermining the independent power of the nobles in another way: he was tying the nobility more firmly to himself. He established the new chivalric order of Saint Michel in order to break the bonds of the old nobility and to create a reliance on the monarchy for noble marks of honour.[34] Finally, by making the newly-established infantry the backbone of his armed forces, Louis XI deprived the nobility of its one true service to the state, reducing the nobles in one fell swoop to useless parasites, contributing nothing to the well-being of the state.[35]

Boulainvilliers believed that Louis XI facilitated the French descent into despotism more than did any other French king. His simultaneous debasement of the nobility and elevation of the third estate, his efforts to create noble reliance on the central monarchy, and his obstruction of the only true avenue of service for the nobility, created a system of despotic government which flourished and indeed became the illegitimate *status quo* under Louis XIII and Louis XIV. Despite the fact that, like other writers contributing to the *thèse nobiliaire/thèse royale* debate, Boulainvilliers concentrated on the origins of the French state, Louis XI is pivotal in his discussion of the development of despotism.

While it is true that Boulainvilliers' work provides the most clear-cut example of the noble thesis, no study of this debate would be complete without at least a brief look at the views of Montesquieu. Although the multi-faceted nature of Montesquieu's work makes it extremely difficult to place him solidly within any one particular intellectual camp, for our purposes the *nobiliaire* aspects of his work will be emphasized, although, of course, there are substantial differences separating him from *nobiliaire* writers like Boulainvilliers.

Born in 1689, Montesquieu's background was strongly *robiniste*, although, like Boulainvilliers, he was educated at the Oratorian Academy at Juilly. After Juilly, Montesquieu studied law at the University of Bordeaux, then went to Paris for a few years. Upon his father's death in 1713, he returned to Bordeaux to take the place in the Bordeaux parlement previously held by his father. In 1716 he succeeded to his uncle's post of *président à mortier* which he held until his resignation in 1726.[36] In the meantime, Montesquieu was busy pursuing literary and scientific interests as well, and he became a member of the *Académie de Bordeaux* in 1716. He gained instant fame when, in 1721, his *Lettres persanes* were published. In 1727, Montesquieu was elected to the *Académie Française*, though not by unanimous vote. At that time, the Abbé Dubos was the secretary of the Académie Française. Montesquieu's fame was ensured, though at that point it rested almost completely on the success of the *Lettres persanes*. Throughout the remainder of his life, Montesquieu travelled, first to Italy and then to England, and devoted himself to the study of the interactions of societies with their forms of government. He died in 1755.[37]

Montesquieu's place among the *nobiliaire* writers is uncertain. One radical author calls Montesquieu a "red reactionary" and argues that his views were "toutes favorables à l'aristocratie," galvanizing feudal theorists who had been strangely quiescent in the years between 1732 (the year the *Judicium Francorum* was republished) and 1748.[38] On the other hand, Montesquieu has been interpreted by other modern scholars as a strong advocate of monarchy, albeit limited monarchy, whose ideas were a synthesis of those expressed by both Boulainvilliers and the *royaliste* Dubos.[39] Despite these conflicting interpretations, based on different aspects of the admittedly complex *Esprit des lois* ("Spirit of the Laws"), some assumptions can be considered common to most interpretations of his work. Montesquieu did believe that governmental authority, regardless of the form of the state, must be diffused among two or more agencies, in order to protect the people against the arbitrary use of power by any one agent. In terms of the debate between constitutionalists and absolutists, reconfigured as *nobiliaires* and *royalistes*, this fact alone effectively separates him from those who sought to justify indivisible monarchical sovereignty by appeals to the origins of the French state. His belief that, at least at some point in French history, the feudal nobility fulfilled the function of counterbalancing royal authority links Montesquieu more firmly with the *nobiliaire* camp. Moreover, Montesquieu's view of Louis XI conforms to those expressed by writers intent on demonstrating that absolute authority was achieved through the usurpation perpetrated by the French kings against the constitution established at the inception of the French state.

Montesquieu agrees with Boulainvilliers that the Franks invaded Gaul and liberated its inhabitants from Roman rule. He denies abbé Dubos's assertion that the Franks were invited by the Gauls, arguing that Clovis did, in fact, plunder villages. Moreover, Dubos's "proof" of the transfer of Roman *imperium* to the Franks in Justinian's renunciation of the rights of empire over Gaul in favour of Clovis's descendants contains flawed logic: "What did this foreign assignment of rights do to an establishment already formed?"[40] On the other hand, Montesquieu does not subscribe to Boulainvilliers' assertion that the Gauls were reduced to servitude under the Franks. His biographer, Robert Shackleton, sums up Montesquieu's opinion of these two ideological combatants admirably: "Montesquieu describes the system of Boulainvilliers as a conspiracy against the *tiers état*, and that of Dubos as a conspiracy against the nobility."[41] Nevertheless, Montesquieu is ideologically much closer to Boulainvilliers, and he reserves his harshest criticism for Dubos. Like Boulainvilliers, he believes that the nobility shared sovereign authority with the king, although the two authors hold different views of French history.

While Boulainvilliers (and Dubos for that matter) conceptualizes French history as essentially static, Montesquieu possesses a dynamic and developmental view of history and he does not hark back to France's ancient origins to justify modern reformism.[42] Instead, he searches throughout French history for a situation in which the principle of checks and balances was best manifested. There is, in fact, no one moment in French history which provides Montesquieu with an example that one could follow to reform the government of eighteenth-century France. For Montesquieu the process of change is much more significant than any single event. He points to the process by which fiefs were established and later became hereditary as demonstrating, in varying degrees, that system of balance which best ensures the liberty of the people and the preservation of the state. Montesquieu does not call for a return to full-blown feudalism; he is as aware of its flaws as he is of its advantages. He does want to indicate, however, how the feudal system worked to prevent the arbitrary exercise of power. In Book XXXI, Montesquieu argues that the power of the nobles counterbalanced the tyranny of the corrupt regencies of Fredegonda and Brunehaut.[43] The Carolingian coup somewhat later is explained by the fact that the nobles placed their faith and loyalty in the mayor of the palace, rather than the king. The mayors eventually became so strong that they combined royalty with mayoralty. The ability of the nobles to counterbalance the power of the king was confirmed by the integral role they played in the replacement of the Merovingian by the Carolingian dynasty.

> In the mixture of these two authorities [mayoral and royal], a kind of reconciliation occurred. The mayor had been elective, and the king hereditary: the crown, at the beginning of the reign of the Carolingians, was elected because the people did the choosing; it was hereditary because they always chose from the same family.[44]

Feudalism achieved its most complete form after the death of Charlemagne because, in the partition of the empire, it was declared that every freeman whose lord died could choose to become the vassal of whomever he wanted.

> Thus, those who were formerly directly under the power of the king, in so far as they were freemen under the count, became imperceptibly vassals of one another, for each freeman could choose the lord he wanted, whether the king or another lord.[45]

At the same time, Charles the Bald passed the important regulation making fiefs hereditary. The independence of the nobles was complete. Feudalism, thus articulated, contained the seeds of its own destruction and the destruction of the balance between the king and the intermediary powers of the nobility. For now the great vassals refused to obey anyone and the kingship was merely nominal, occupied by the holder of the greatest fief. From this situation of unquestioned domination of his own lands, the king could expand his borders through the use of force or the negotiation of alliances without having to endure the fetters which restricted the actions of previous kings. The kingdom was characterized by anarchy and violence. Thus the Capetians began the process of territorial accumulation and expansion of authority against which Boulainvilliers fulminates but which Montesquieu merely regrets as the almost unavoidable result of the loss of balance. Differing in the degree to which they lament the progressive Capetian assumption of complete control, Montesquieu and Boulainvilliers share the belief that contemporary France needs to be reformed and that the clues to the nature of this reform can be discovered in the study of pre-Capetian France. Do they share a similarly hostile view of Louis XI?

There are no references to Louis XI in the *Spirit of the Laws*, which is not surprising since the historical sections of the work stop well before his reign. A number of references to Louis XI in other works, however, testify to Montesquieu's interest in the king. In fact, Montesquieu composed a history of Louis XI, the manuscript of which was apparently burned by accident.[46] Louis XI also occupies a prominent place in the outline Montesquieu prepared for a proposed history. The thumbnail sketch was entitled "Morceaux de ce que je voulais écrire sur l'histoire de France." In it, Montesquieu summarizes his view of French government under the Capetians:

> The constitution . . . under this race, was reflective of the fate that formed it. It was a monstrous body which, in a great fief where no one obeyed, contained an innumerable number of small states, in which obedience was sometimes limitless and sometimes almost nonexistent. The public good consisted only in the exercise of certain private rights that some claimed to have over others and which were not founded on any general view.[47]

Clearly, this anarchic situation could easily degenerate into tyranny, and just such a lamentable result occurred under Charles VII and, especially, under Louis XI. In keeping with the ideas expounded in the *Spirit of the Laws* regarding the correlation of the spirit of the people with the type of government under which they live, Montesquieu maintains that the spirit of the people under Charles VII and Louis XI was different from what it had been earlier. "Arbitrary power was raised and formed in an instant. At the end of [Louis XI's] reign, there was not a *seigneur* who could be assured of not being assassinated."[48] The subsection dealing specifically with Louis XI begins unequivocally:

> The death of Charles VII was the last day of French liberty. In an instant one saw another king, another people, another policy, another patience; and the passage from liberty to servitude was so great, so prompt, so rapid and the means so strange and odious to a free nation, that one could only characterize it as a spell of dizziness falling all at once over this kingdom.[49]

There is some inconsistency in Montesquieu's portrait of Charles VII's reign. By contrast with his earlier criticism of Charles VII, for the purposes of his discussion of Louis XI, Montesquieu writes about the preceding reign in glowing terms. The English had been driven out, the finances were in good condition. Louis XI did not have to do much to become "that prince of Europe most loved by his subjects and most respected by foreigners."[50] Louis XI did not, however, capitalize on the happy state of affairs that existed upon his succession to the throne. Instead, he abolished the Pragmatic Sanction and alienated the nobility. His was a tragic reign for France and he himself was fortunate to have had in Commynes a biographer who tried to mitigate the justifiably harsh judgement levelled at him by posterity.

Louis XI also appears in another of Montesquieu's incomplete works, *Réflexions sur le caractère de quelques princes et sur quelques événemens de leur vie*, which was to form part of a larger work entitled *Le Prince*. Here Louis XI is compared to Tiberius at some length. According to Montesquieu, the two rulers shared courage in battle and timidity in private life. They were similar as well in their ability to deceive and their establishment of arbitrary rule.[51] But even Tiberius fares better at the hands of Montesquieu than does Louis XI, and gets the better of the French king in further comparison:

> But if one examines these two princes, one will sense right away how much the one is superior to the other. Tiberius sought to govern men, Louis considered only how to trick them . . .
>
> Finally, Louis had finesse; Tiberius profundity. One could, with little effort, defend oneself against the artifices of Louis; the Roman put shadows in front of minds and hid himself as soon as one began to see him.
>
> Louis, who had for his art only false caresses and minor flattery, won over men through their own weakness; the Roman, through the superiority of his own genius and an invincible strength that carried them along.[52]

Louis XI was not only malevolent but petty as well, and Montesquieu held him in contempt, while retaining some respect for Tiberius's abilities, although he considered him a tyrant.

It is clear that Louis XI was precisely the kind of monarch that Montesquieu feared would take advantage of a situation in which monarchical authority was unfettered. In the sort of monarchy France had become, where the king was merely the greatest of the fief-holders whose power was unchecked by intermediary bodies in his own domain, tyranny was a real and ever-present possibility. Louis XI's reign was the tragic consequence of the process by which the necessary balance that was the essence of the French monarchy was lost. Although the emphasis on dynamic social change separates him from other *nobiliaire* writers like Boulainvilliers, Montesquieu shares with them a belief that a group of free (noble) Frenchmen is necessary for the proper functioning of the polity. Like Boulainvilliers and Saint

Simon, Montesquieu manifests a deep distrust of unbridled monarchical authority and a corresponding dislike for Louis XI.

If we now turn our attention to writers on the other side of this debate, we find that, once again, portraits of Louis XI are coloured by a very specific understanding of the French "nation" and its place in the political process. The central figure among the *thèse royale* writers is the Abbé Dubos[53] and, although his *Histoire critique de l'établissement de l'ancien gouvernement de France* (1734) deals exclusively with the early years of the French monarchy, Dubos's "Romanist" thesis provides the foundation upon which later royalists predicated their views of government. Dubos maintained that the Frankish conquest was a myth. Clovis did not lead a band of freedom-loving warriors on an expedition to invade Gaul and liberate its inhabitants from the yoke of Roman oppression. Quite the opposite, in fact, occurred. According to Dubos, the Romans hired the Franks as soldiers; Clovis came at the behest of the Roman government in Gaul. If, as Dubos argued, the Franks entered Gaul by invitation rather than conquest, the consequences for the French monarchy are tremendous. The Franks were co-opted into the Roman system, a system which had at its core the idea of an absolute ruler whose authority was in no way dependent on the consent of the people. The Franks adopted this form of government; from its beginning, then, France was a legitimate absolute monarchy. Contemporary significance attributed to Dubos's *Histoire critique* is indicated by the fact that at least five editions of the work were published between 1734 and 1742.[54]

Auguste-Pierre Damiens de Gomicourt, writing somewhat later in the eighteenth century, sought to defend Dubos's thesis and to examine later periods of French history in light of this "Romanist" view. Gomicourt was born into a successful commercial family of Amiens in 1723. Declining to enter the family business, Gomicourt pursued his interests in languages and history. He was a founding member of the *Académie d'Amiens*, eventually becoming its director. Along with his works of history, of which the *Mélanges historiques et critiques* (1768) is the most well known, Gomicourt translated William Blackstone's *Commentaries* and wrote some minor works on linguistics and poetry. All of his works were either pseudonymous or anonymous.[55]

The *Mélanges historiques* consists of a collection of essays on the development of the French monarchy. Before embarking on his historical enquiry, Gomicourt attempts to define the opposing concepts of liberty and despotism, and it appears he was influenced by Montesquieu in some of his initial assumptions if not in his subsequent conclusions. This is especially the case when Gomicourt defines liberty:

> True liberty is entire when a man can do all that is permitted by law; man is free when he can work for his well-being without being troubled therein by others; man is free when he can enjoy his goods and his estate under the protection of the law, under the same conditions as other members of the State; finally, it does not deprive man of liberty to oblige

him to observe the law and to request of him for the general good of the State a part of his goods or a service that is in proportion with those of other citizens.[56]

Gomicourt is also, like Montesquieu, willing to acknowledge the legitimacy of different forms of government and even to recognize that there may be different types of monarchy. Gomicourt reveals his absolutist bias, however, when he asserts that despotism should be defined by the motivations of the ruler rather than the extent of his power.[57] It follows that the much-proclaimed protection of liberty under the law is essentially meaningless in an absolute monarchy if the ruler's ability to create law is unfettered.

While Gomicourt readily admits that monarchy may be either limited or absolute, his main intent is to prove that France conforms to the latter type. There are only two fundamental laws in France: the law of succession and the right to trial by jury.[58] Other than by fundamental laws, authority can also be limited through the division of power between the king and people. Such a division of power has never taken place in France, however, and, given Gomicourt's minimalist interpretation of fundamental law, it is clear that the authority of the French king is, and has always been, unlimited.[59] Gomicourt goes on to outline the powers of the absolute monarch: to perform justice, to assemble and arm subjects for the defence of the state, to make declarations of war and treaties of peace, to levy subsidies in the amount he judges to be necessary, and to create magistrates. Even if a king breaks a law, the people cannot require of him an account of his actions because, by doing so, they would become magistrates in a republic.

His discourse is primarily an attack on Boulainvilliers, and Gomicourt devotes considerable attention to a point-by-point refutation of Boulainvilliers' evidence. Gomicourt maintains that it is foolish to believe that the Franks who settled in Gaul possessed the same character as when they inhabited the forests of Germany.[60] After addressing a number of issues which he felt Boulainvilliers misrepresented, Gomicourt rather disdainfully declares the *comte's* "system" both unhistorical and untenable.[61] Departing from Dubos's theory somewhat, Gomicourt argues that the Franks did indeed conquer Gaul, but he goes on to support Dubos in asserting that, from the very first, they employed hereditary succession; a son followed his father on the throne without the need for the consent of the people.[62] On the issue of a national assembly, Gomicourt asserts that its members were chosen by the king "under the name of *placite* but they did not represent the nation."[63] Regarding taxes and subsidies, Gomicourt argues that the right to these was "essentially attached to the sovereign power because it watches over the conservation of the state, as much within as without."[64] Gomicourt also states that parlements, which do not, in his view, correspond to the early Frankish assemblies, were established by the French kings, and, in what is probably a response to the heightened significance placed on the registration process by *parlementaire* writers, Gomicourt emphatically declares: "This registration is a form of promulgation established by the king, consecrated by usage and which will cease at the moment the sovereign commands it."[65]

Gomicourt had a personal axe to grind with the Parlement of Paris: he came into conflict with several of the sovereign courts, stemming from the inclusion in the *Mélanges historiques* of a memorandum from Colbert to Louis XIV in which the minister referred to the *Chambre des Comptes* as an unnecessary institution because he believed that the functions of the chamber could be carried out by two or three members of the parlement. The *Chambre des Comptes* passed an *arrêt* condemning the work as injurious to the magistrature, but parlement construed this act as a violation of its own rights and declared the act of the *Chambre* to be null. However, parlement obviously agreed with the assessment made by the *Chambre*, because the court still moved to suppress the *Mélanges historiques*.[66]

Gomicourt's denigration of the parlement's right of registration high-lights the significance of the on-going struggle between the Parlement of Paris and the crown in the writings of both *nobiliaire* and *royaliste* writers. Successive conflicts between the Parlement of Paris and the crown, including the forced registration in 1730 of the royal edict endorsing Unigenitus (the papal bull declaring Jansenism heretical); the flare-up of the controversy surrounding the refusal of sacraments in the mid-1750s; and the resignation in 1765 of the Parlement of Brittany, whose struggle with the provincial governor the duc d'Aiguillon was the catalyst for Chancellor Maupeou's coup in 1771, formed a backdrop to the *nobiliaire/royale* debate.

Having seen how Gomicourt's ideas clearly conflict with those expressed by Boulainvilliers, one is curious to see if that opposition is echoed in Gomicourt's treatment of Louis XI. Louis XI does figure quite prominently in two of Gomicourt's "dissertations," especially the one dealing with the suppression of the position of the Constable of France. This short essay begins with the statement: "Louis XI formed the project of abasing the great nobles of his kingdom." He sought every means possible to deprive them of the great power they had enjoyed since the reign of Hugues Capet, who, according to Gomicourt, sacrificed his legitimate authority to become king:

> The civil wars that desolated France, under the successors of this prince, weakened their power still further and augmented that of the great nobles; the more the kings had need of their help the more the nobles contributed to the defence of the state and the more they became forward, bold, often even audacious . . . believing themselves to be the equals of their masters, they dared oftentimes to claim it and attempted very often to make the people over whom they tyrannized believe it.[67]

Gomicourt's interpretation of developments under the Capetians reverses that of Boulainvilliers. Noble replaces royal usurpation and consequently Louis XI's role is re-evaluated. The worst offender among the nobles trying to usurp power was the comte de Saint Pol, and Louis XI dealt with him properly, in accordance with his laudable design "to reduce the great nobles

of his kingdom to the point where they are only the first of his subjects."
Unfortunately, the tumultuous times which followed the reign of Louis XI
all the way through the sixteenth century prevented his successors from
furthering his project to reclaim rightful authority. In fact, the nobles
continued to increase in strength. Happily for France, a period of relative
calm coincided with the appearance of "un grand politique": Richelieu. In
fact, Gomicourt seems to admire Richelieu even more than he does Louis XI,
although it is clear that the cardinal was only following the path already laid
out by Louis.[68] Gomicourt believes that Richelieu was successful in restoring
the absolute monarchy, but his success was due in large measure to the
initial efforts made by Louis XI. The connection between the two figures
recalls the absolutist literature of the early seventeenth century, in which the
pragmatic policies of Richelieu were often compared to the efforts of Louis
XI.[69] For Gomicourt, then, Louis XI was not a despot who corrupted the
ancient constitution by depriving the nobles of their power and levelling the
distinctions among the members of French society in order to better ensure
his tyrannical control. On the contrary, he was the first of the French kings
to begin the process of reclamation; his efforts to reduce the nobility to its
proper position within society (as only the first among the king's subjects)
were the first steps on the road back to absolute monarchy which was the
ancient, and thus legitimate, form of government in France.

It seems very clear that Gomicourt's idea of the nation differs substantially from the noble vision articulated by Boulainvilliers. In his discussion
of the *assemblée de la nation*, for example, Gomicourt is adamant that,
although a group of royally-chosen bishops and great nobles may sometimes
assemble around the king, by no means do they represent the nation.[70]
Significantly, Gomicourt cites the Aragonese coronation oath as an example
of how the people can consent to be governed absolutely by their monarch.[71]
The Aragonese coronation oath was, of course, cited to support very different
claims about the nature of royal authority made by resistance writers in the
sixteenth century. Within the ideological context of Huguenot resistance to
the crown, the oath was used to argue historical precedents for popular
sovereignty; for Gomicourt and other royalist writers two centuries later, the
oath proves that *le peuple* voiced its approbation for absolute monarchy as the
legitimate form of government in France.

It is important not to envision too rigid a schema regarding the *thèse
nobiliaire/thèse royale* debate, as there is considerable diversity in the views of
writers in both camps. René-Louis de Voyer de Paulmy, marquis d'Argenson
(1694–1757), is an example of a writer whose ideas do not conform to the
narrow definition of the *thèse royale*, yet he does possess the same hostility to
the feudal nobility that characterizes the other royalist writers. As a
consequence of this, d'Argenson also demonstrates the same admiration for
Louis XI as does Gomicourt.

D'Argenson's is a classic case of unsatisfied ambition. His memoirs are
filled with his desires, most often unrealized, to attain a position of influence

within the government. As Nannerl Keohane phrased it, "The marquis confided to his journals a cherished fantasy that he would one day be given full power to reorder France, so that he could play Sully to Louis XV's Henry IV."[72] Though his political role was more modest than perhaps he had envisioned, d'Argenson was appointed minister for foreign affairs in 1744. He engaged in complicated and largely unsuccessful diplomatic manoeuvrings which were made no easier by the apparently aimless military campaigns of the latter stages of the War of the Austrian Succession. He was dismissed by Louis XV in January of 1747. Like many others, he was too often caught up in the factionalism of Louis XV's court to be able to secure a position from which he could oversee the implementation of the reforms that he believed were necessary for the preservation of the state and the well-being of the people.[73]

In his work, *Considerations sur le gouvernement ancien et present de la France* (1764), d'Argenson outlines the changes he advocates to achieve the ideal, a democratic monarchy. D'Argenson places his emphasis on local administrative autonomy. Each community was to have its own "magistrats populaires" who would oversee local issues of police and finances, though d'Argenson did refer judicial matters to royally-appointed judges. D'Argenson is adamant that this decentralized system by no means threatens the monarchy because the competing interests of various communities would keep them from ever uniting against the crown.[74] The country itself would be divided into departments smaller than the existing *généralites*, and at the head of each would be a royally-appointed intendant. The apparent democratic thrust of d'Argenson's work is considerably blunted when it is noted that these intendants were to be responsible for appointing the magistrates in each community (although they were required to gather evidence on the worthiness of potential appointees from the members of the community). D'Argenson's anti-noble bias is evident here in his desire to replace the provincial control based on traditional noble power structures with a bureaucracy on the one hand monarchical and on the other, "democratic."

This hostility to the feudal nobility is at the core of the *Considerations*. In the "Avertissement," d'Argenson describes the intent of the work "to establish what are the imperfections of feudal government." D'Argenson deals only briefly with the early years of the French state because he believes the polity was not fully developed at that time. The Gauls and the early Franks were too concerned with making war, engaging in the chase and securing the basic necessities of life to be involved in developing and refining their form of government. Under the Merovingians, civil wars caused divisions in the country and the nobles gained in strength. Under the Carolingians, "the nobles elevated themselves under weak kings and formed feudal government . . . almost so that he who was not a noble became a slave."[75] Finally, under the Capetians, the great struggle against the feudal nobility began when the third estate was constituted, found a deliberative voice, and allied itself decidedly with the monarchy.

What is the place of Louis XI in this struggle between the feudal nobility and the monarchy? Not surprisingly, d'Argenson praises Louis XI for his efforts to suppress the overweening power of the nobles. D'Argenson is more guarded in his admiration of Louis XI than is Gomicourt, however, and he attributes much of the son's success to the father's efforts, especially in chasing the Burgundians and the English out of France. D'Argenson recognizes the valuable contribution made by Louis XI, nonetheless, and although he expresses some mild reservations about Louis XI's manner, d'Argenson has no doubts about Louis XI's actions being for the good of the state:

> Louis XI went quickly to the source of the resistance he felt . . . On all
> sides, the appanages of the princes of the blood seemed closer to sover-
> eignties than to simple domain honorific possession as they are today.
> Thus to have given them in order to subsist Normandy or Guyenne
> would be to resurrect in the middle of the monarchy as many sovereign-
> ties more dangerous that those that had existed three hundred years
> before. Whether by luck or good counsel, Louis XI overcame all his rivals
> with an address perhaps a little too nimble for a French king: he demon-
> strated well his design to reign arbitrarily but finally he won out.[76]

D'Argenson interprets the War of the Public Weal as a sham perpetrated by the nobles at the expense of the people: "Under Louis XI there was made a league and a war of the public good; it was concerned with nothing else but to render some great *seigneurs* most powerful and insolent."[77] Finally, despite his qualms about the nature of French government in his own time, d'Argenson possesses an essential faith in the French monarchy and believes in the unbreakable bond between the monarchy and the people and between order and liberty. His devotion to the monarchy is further demonstrated in the brief essay appended to the *Considerations* in which he argues that France should play a pivotal role in European politics. Again, Louis XI is men-tioned favourably, this time for his contribution to the preservation of French power and influence on the international scene.

> When France wanted to provide for Europe the happiness it enjoyed, it
> applied all its forces to repress the ambitious; and no one applied himself
> more than did Louis XI, Richelieu and Louis XIV to extend our fron-
> tiers.[78]

D'Argenson's view of Louis XI is less overtly laudatory than that of Gomicourt, which is entirely in keeping with the former's reformist plans for the French monarchy.

Although not strictly pertaining to the debate between the *nobiliaires* and the *royalistes*, two other works dealing with Louis XI bear brief examination within the general framework of this discussion: the *Histoire de Louis XI* by Charles Pinot Duclos, and Voltaire's *Essai sur les moeurs*. In different ways, the interpretations of Louis XI expounded by these two writers deviate from the general picture of Louis XI provided by the *royalistes*, with whom they can be loosely grouped. Duclos makes much more of Louis XI's relationship with the third estate than do others like Gomicourt, while Voltaire levels a much harsher judgement on the king than do other royalist writers, despite his advocacy of absolute monarchy, albeit in the form of "enlightened" despotism.

Charles Pinot Duclos was born in Dinan on 12 February 1704. He was briefly a *sous-lieutenant* in a regiment of Limousin, but he quickly gave up the post and went to Paris, where he became a clerk of an *avocat* to the Conseil d'Etat. He became part of the literary group of which Maurepas was also a member, and the latter succeeded in having Duclos admitted to the *Académie des Inscriptions et Belles-Lettres*, despite the fact that Duclos had not yet written anything! In 1744, Duclos returned to Dinan and became mayor of the town. During his time in the "provinces," Duclos received a commission to write a history of Louis XI, using all the materials collected by Joachim Legrand. He became a member of the *Académie Française* in 1747, and in 1750 he filled the post of royal historiographer vacated by Voltaire. He was ennobled in 1755 and became the permanent secretary of the *Académie Française*.[79]

Although Duclos trumpets his own efforts at objectivity in the *Histoire de Louis XI* (1745) and roundly criticizes both Thomas Basin and Claude de Seyssel for their prejudice against Louis XI, he obviously brings certain strong ideological biases to his study which make him favourably predisposed to the monarch. While he is not slavish in his praise, it is clear that Duclos views Louis XI as a positive figure who handled many problems of his reign admirably, and who left France strong and at peace when he died. Contrary to the standard interpretation of Louis XI, even by his supporters, that portrays the king as initially misguided and in some sense responsible for the troubles which bedevilled him during the early years, Duclos does not portray Louis XI as even slightly at fault. Rather, Duclos places the blame for the War of the Public Weal squarely on the shoulders of François II, duc de Bretagne. The conflict between Louis XI and the great nobles was due entirely to the boundless ambition of the duke. While Louis XI was willing to iron out the differences between him and the duc de Bretagne, the latter remained obdurate: "this prince was resolved to deliver Brittany to the English rather than submit himself to the king." Not only was the duke determined to withhold his allegiance from the king of France but he also actively campaigned to turn the other great nobles against Louis XI.[80]

Duclos is quite emphatic that *le bien-public* was only a pretext for the noble rebellion. Speaking of Charles, duc de Berry's manifesto, which outlined the ostensible reasons for the rebellion, Duclos writes,

> The retreat of this prince was the signal that made the storm that had been forming for some time break; the malcontents openly declared themselves under the name of the League for the Public Good, which was always their pretext, and rarely their motive.[81]

When the conflict was nearing its conclusion, and Louis XI was successfully undermining the unity of the noble camp by proffering land and positions of power and influence within the government, the true nature of the noble motivations was revealed, despite their half-hearted efforts to appease the people:

> When everyone was unhappy, they spoke vaguely about the public good [but] nothing was decided; and the people, often the pretext and always the victim of the ambition of the great nobles, were still oppressed to satisfy the greed of those who proclaimed themselves their protectors. Dammartin had reason to write some time afterward to the comte de Charolais, later the duc de Bourgogne, that this league had been the league of the public ill.[82]

In fact, according to Duclos, Louis XI was infinitely more concerned about the well-being of his subjects than were the nobles who made so much of their desire to help the people. It was, in the end, the people who suffered most as a result of the war which the ambition of the nobles ignited; it was necessary to levy new taxes to pay for the pensions which Louis XI had promised the nobles in return for an end to the war.[83] Although "buying off" the nobles was perhaps not the best solution, Duclos believes Louis XI was always motivated by the laudable desire to spare the people from further carnage whenever possible:

> It is true that, excepting his devotions and his offerings, which were very onerous, all his expenses had as their goal the public good and especially the conservation of his subjects; this caused Molinet, a historian of Duke Maximilian, to say that Louis would rather lose ten thousand *écus* than to risk the life of one archer.[84]

Nor did Louis XI spend all the kingdom's revenues on bribes, pensions and spies, as some authors have written. According to Duclos, Louis XI strengthened the army, fortified or rebuilt towns, established industries, constructed buildings and made rivers navigable. Duclos then questions the motives of those who have so maligned Louis XI, given that "one sees nothing in this tableau of the life of Louis XI that merits the satires [*répandus*] against him."[85]

The reason for the hostility of a number of writers, in Duclos's opinion, is that Louis XI effected a revolution in government. He overturned the order of French society by suppressing the nobility:

> One sees, so to speak, a revolution in government. This prince seemed to plough a road to arbitrary power. It is this that causes one to say, as an expression which for being popular is not less just, that Louis XI placed the kings *hors de page*; but at least the people ceased to be the slaves of the great nobles, and it was the latter who spread the libels against this prince.[86]

With Duclos all but justifying arbitrary rule, it is hardly surprising that a proponent of the estates general like Jacques Baptiste Britard should attack his work with such venom almost forty-five years later.[87] And yet what is most interesting about Duclos's statement is his belief in the strong relationship between Louis XI and the people.

Voltaire passes a much more rigorous judgement on Louis XI in his *Essai sur les moeurs*. He is harshly critical of Louis XI's personal failings, the discussion of which takes up most of the few short pages devoted to the king. In fact, Voltaire appears to place altogether too much stock in the various stories about Louis XI's cruelty. Voltaire believes, for example, that Charles VII did indeed die from starvation because he feared that his son was intent on poisoning him. Voltaire also argues that, although there is no solid proof, Louis XI's role in the death of his brother is highly suspect. Worst of all, Voltaire endorses a story about the children of the duc de Nemours being placed under the scaffold, on Louis XI's orders, so that when their father was decapitated his blood would splatter down on them.[88] Voltaire maintains that, by the very force of his wicked personality, Louis XI changed the mores of France. By contrast with the preceding reign, France under Louis XI had lost its moral grandeur:

> Never was there less honour than under this reign. Judges did not blush to partake of the goods of those they had condemned . . . Preceding times had inspired proud and barbarous morals in which one saw heroism sometimes burst forth. The reign of Charles VII had the Dunois, the La Trimouille, the Clisson, the Richemont, the Saintraille, the La Hire {families} and magistrates of great merit, but under Louis XI not one great man. He debased the nation. There was no virtue; obedience took the place of everything and the people were finally as quiet as convicts in a galley.[89]

Voltaire's hostility toward Louis XI is reflected in his condemnation of Commynes. He refers to the writer as the "celebrated traitor who, having for a long time sold the secrets of the house of Burgundy to the king, finally passed into the service of France . . . " Voltaire's criticism extends to the *Mémoires* as well: "one values the *Mémoires*, despite their having been written by a courtier who feared to tell the truth, even after the death of Louis XI."[90] Voltaire's opinion about the worth of the *Mémoires* is unexpected; generally speaking, Commynes's work was praised by writers both before and after Voltaire as a balanced view of the monarch. Commynes himself was considered to be one of the best historians and authors France had ever known. Voltaire's repeated references to Commynes as a traitor are unique among the many commentaries on the man and his work throughout the early modern period.

Yet, for all his criticisms of both the monarch and his biographer, Voltaire is still willing to admit that Louis XI possessed some qualities and performed some actions which were valuable to the state. Voltaire acknowledges that Louis XI had courage. Louis XI also understood human motivations and affairs of state. He established the postal service in France, albeit initially for his own personal use as an information network. He repopulated Paris after the city had been devastated by contagion; though its new inhabitants were originally brigands, Louis XI's brutal police force eventually transformed them into law-abiding citizens. He wanted to establish one set of weights and measures throughout the kingdom as it had been in the time of Charlemagne. Voltaire concludes, "Finally, he proved that a wicked man can work for the public good when his private interest is not contrary to it."[91] This view of Louis XI as the unpleasant medicine needed to cure France's ills, namely the disunity which characterized feudal government, was quite common. Louis XI's character flaws have to be weighed against the long-term benefits which France enjoyed as a result of his reign. Voltaire's ambivalence regarding the achievement of Louis XI is summed up as follows:

> We have seen by how many happy attempts Louis XI was the first king of absolute Europe, since the establishment of the great feudal government . . . but he did this by colouring the scaffolds with the blood of Armagnac and Luxembourg, in sacrificing all to his suspicions, in paying dearly the executioners of his vengeance.[92]

Voltaire's view of Louis XI is much more negative than those of the royalist writers who used the king for polemical purposes. Like Duclos and other royalist writers, however, Voltaire comments on the relationship of Louis XI with "le peuple," and he offers praise for Louis XI's accomplishments, albeit with some reserve.

Finally, let us turn to Pierre-Louis-Claude Gin, another example of a royalist writer who laid all the troubles of contemporary France at the feet of the feudal nobility. His dedication to the absolute monarchy of Louis XV and Louis XVI is demonstrated in his political career as much as in his writings. Born in Paris in 1726, Gin was the son of a barrister. There was enough family money to secure the purchase of the office of *secrétaire du roi* for Gin when he was twenty-seven years old. Although initially supportive of the *parlementaires*, Gin became a thoroughgoing supporter of the crown; he became a councillor in the Maupeou parlement and then in the Grand Conseil. He and his family were imprisoned at Port Royal for almost a year in 1793, where he composed (or edited) the *Court plaidoyer pour Louis XVI*. Upon release, Gin went to Clermont where he was named as mayor, but he refused to take the oath against the monarchy. He died in November 1807.[93]

Gin's *Les Vrais principes du gouvernement françois* (1777) is emphatically absolutist in tone. He begins with a politely-worded rebuttal of Montesquieu's ideas. Although he obviously respects the Baron de la Brède, he is distressed by the dangerous interpretations placed on the *Esprit des lois* by later writers.[94] Gin is especially concerned to show that mixed government is not possible because the struggle among the bodies or individuals between whom the authority is divided will inevitably result in the violent victory of one over the others, ending ultimately in despotic rule. Like most royalists, Gin does believe that there are fetters on the king's power, although these come in the form of fundamental laws. One such fundamental law is the necessity for a king's council. Gin is very adamant and specific when he states that this council would have "a right of representation, not of resistance because this would suppose a double sovereignty which is incompatible with monarchy."[95]

Gin's advocacy of the absolutist ideal is best indicated in two situations discussed in the work. First, Gin praises the empire of China, long considered by many theorists as the prime example of an oriental despotism. Gin is effusive in his admiration: "The famous legislator Confucius knew no other principle of government than that of paternal power. He so impressed this principle in the hearts of the Chinese that they regard themselves as members of an immense family of which the emperor is the father."[96] Rather unconvincingly, Gin asserts that the liberty of the Chinese people is "proven" by their prodigious population and the care they take with agriculture, commerce and industry.

Gin's concluding remarks do much to belie his apparent desire to guard against the despotic exercise of the royal will. Gin ends by quoting a statement made to the Parlement of Paris by Henri IV in which the king "paints so vividly the true character of monarchical government: [an] image of paternal power." Speaking of the Edict of Nantes, Henri exclaimed, "I have made the edict, I wish it to be observed; my will must serve as reason, one never resists a prince in an obedient state. I am king now, I speak to you as a king, I want to be obeyed."[97]

Having dealt with more theoretical questions in the first part of the book, Gin turns to the history of France where he intends to demonstrate the perfection of French monarchical government. According to Gin, the troubles plaguing France were all caused by the division of the sovereignty. The weakness of the last Merovingian kings allowed the mayors of the palace to appropriate part of the royal power, and eventually the sovereignty was reunited in the new Carolingian kings. Under the Carolingians, the officers of the crown gained power at the expense of the king and, under the last Carolingians, the lords were able to make their lands patrimonial, severing their last ties of dependence to the king. "Hugues Capet brought the great domains that he possessed to the crown but he lost the plenitude of power that the kings his predecessors enjoyed in the territory of the great vassals."[98] Feudal government was substituted for true monarchy with the result that the king needed the consent of all his vassals before he could implement policies for the good of all his subjects. Fortunately, several French kings since Hugues Capet, Louis XI not least among them, successfully countered the feudal nobility's continuing efforts to remain independent. Gin argues that the troubles of Louis XI's reign were based not on the king's actions but on attempts at noble usurpation:

If you look for the cause, it is not the power of the monarch to which one ought to attribute it but rather to the resistance to [the crown's] legitimate power that feudal government introduced at the end of the second race of our kings; to this pretended league of the public good that formed in the first years of this reign; in a word to the struggle against authority, the sole pretext that can distract a sovereign in a pure monarchy from the happiness of his people to which his personal interest is inseparably attached.[99]

The discussion of Louis XI is immediately followed by a reference to Richelieu, who was also forced to act severely because of the opposition to authority manifested during the reign of Louis XIII. By contrast, Louis XIV's reign was one of public tranquillity, according to Gin, and all aspects of French culture flourished as a result. Louis XI's rather harsh actions are also explained away in the *Origine des malheurs de la France*, published much later in 1797, where again Louis XI's name is coupled with that of Richelieu. Gin argues that, while subtler methods of noble control are effective in most circumstances, "the intrigues of powerful men, the furies of fanaticism necessitated several rigorous actions under the reign of Louis XI and under the ministry of Cardinal Richelieu."[100]

As a magistrate, albeit as a handpicked member of the Maupeou parlement, it is not unexpected that Gin manifests a certain ambivalence resulting from seemingly opposed *parlementaire* and monarchical loyalties. In fact, in *Lawyers and Citizens: The Making of a Political Elite in Old Regime France*, David Bell asserts that Gin's attacks are levelled much more against his erstwhile colleagues among the magistracy than against *nobiliaire* writers such as Boulainvilliers (and, to a lesser degree, Montesquieu), and Bell is no doubt correct in emphasizing the anti-*parlementaire* thrust of Gin's thought.[101] Nevertheless, it is also clear that Gin was responding to the attempts by Boulainvilliers and others to resurrect the political claims of the old nobility, and it is this trajectory of Gin's thought that is traced here. Clearly, the anti-*parlementaire* and the anti-*nobiliaire* strands of Gin's thought are considerably entangled. As it did for Montesquieu and Gomicourt, each in their different ways, for Gin the conflict between the king and the magistrates shadowed the discussion about the relationship between the king and the nobility.

This is nowhere as evident as in Gin's discussion of Louis XI's special role in protecting *parlementaire* liberties. Unlike Boulainvilliers and *parlementaire* writers like the author of the *Judicium Francorum*, who argue that parlements had their roots in the ancient *placita*, Gin postulates that the courts were created by Saint Louis solely for the handling of judicial affairs. Nor does the parlement appear to be a *cour des pairs* in the sense of consisting of ancient nobles providing advice to the king. Gin maintains that the families of the ancient peerage were totally extinct by the middle of the fifteenth century. Though the magistrates were royally-appointed, laws were passed limiting the king's right to remove officers at will. Even Louis XI, known for his arbitrary exercise of authority, willingly renewed the ordinance of Charles le Chauve prohibiting the conferring of an office unless vacated through death, voluntary demission or forfeiture. According to Gin, Louis XI so clearly recognized the wisdom of this law that he made his son, the future Charles VIII, swear to continue to uphold it.[102] Gin's accolades for Louis XI regarding the king's treatment of his officers are similar to those repeatedly expressed by many *parlementaire* writers of the eighteenth century, whose views will be examined more closely in Chapter 7 of this book. At the same time, Gin wanted to preserve the plenitude of monarchical power, and his willingness to abandon *robiniste* pretensions in favour of royal authority is demonstrated as much in his participation in the Maupeou parlement as it is in his writing.

Gin is essentially an absolutist thinker; his laudatory appraisal of Louis XI's willingness to "limit" his own power is a classic absolutist formulation. His discussion of parlement, however, hints at the problem experienced by many eighteenth-century *parlementaire* writers. The admiration of *parlementaire* writers for Louis XI seems surprising, unless one recognizes the essential ambivalence of many members of the *noblesse de robe*. Their unwillingness to turn their backs on a system of which they are an integral part means that they can never entirely "fuse" with their more vehemently anti-absolutist sword counterparts, despite the modern arguments for just such a fusion.[103]

Although Gin shares with his colleagues an understanding of the dilemma facing the magistracy, not surprisingly his solution to this quandary is rather more absolutist than most. And yet perhaps Gin has merely shifted the landscape of the problem without in fact resolving it. Gin's absolutism is predicated upon two relationships: the irremediably adversarial relationship between the great sword nobility and the king; and the affiliation between the king and *le peuple*, based on their recognition of a shared antagonism against the great nobles. In fact, Gin's argument in favour of absolute monarchy is primarily based upon the monarchy's ability to protect the liberty of individuals. He goes so far as to state that absolute authority is enshrined in fundamental law precisely because protection of liberty *requires* such a plenitude of power.[104] The great nobility had to be defanged and domesticated in order to ensure the safety and "liberty" of the people; only a monarch with absolute power could accomplish the domestication of the Sword.[105] Such a specious argument, however, constructed from a combination of worn-out paternalism and limp pronouncements about liberty, could not withstand the tempest of swirling *parlementaire*, *nobiliaire* and absolutist ideologies that characterized the twenty years prior to the Revolution. Taken together, the arguments of Boulainvilliers and Montesquieu on the one hand, and those of Gomicourt, d'Argenson and Gin on the other, present all the elements necessary for a new, potentially revolutionary interpretation of the nation. By conflating the nobility's claims about its status as a nation and the monarchy's emphasis on its role as protector of *le peuple* against the nobility, an innovative thinker could forge a powerful new concept of the nation, powerful precisely because it could simultaneously resonate with the past and yet point to a revolutionary future. The abbé Sieyès was well-placed to take up such a task.

If, as Pierre Nora has suggested, *la nation* was born in 1789, then the thorny abbé Sieyès was its improbable midwife. Sieyès has been called the "key to the French Revolution,"[106] and indeed his appearances in the political arena punctuate the phases through which the Revolution passed. He was most active from 1789 to 1791, during which time he was a member of the National Assembly and served on the committee charged with drafting the constitution. He was also elected to the republican National Convention in 1792, but his level of involvement declined with the passage of time. His irascibility and arrogance ensured that he had few associates and even fewer friends; he retreated further into the shadows during the years of the Terror. He reappeared in 1795 when he was elected to the legislature under the Directory, and from then on gained in prominence, becoming president of the Council of Five Hundred (1797), ambassador to Prussia (1798), and a member of the Directory (1799). While he participated in Napoleon's *coup d'état*, Sieyès was not a prominent member of Bonaparte's government, though, in a deeply ironic twist, Sieyès was named a count of the Empire in 1808.[107]

Sieyès's greatest accomplishments were, of course, as a theorist and polemicist, not as a politician.[108] The pamphlets he wrote in 1788 and early 1789 mark the moment at which the Third Estate found its revolutionary voice; some historians have asserted that these pamphlets collectively constitute a "script" for the early phases of the Revolution. Until recently, scholars have viewed these early pamphlets, especially Sieyès's most famous work, *What is the Third Estate?*, as consistently radical, ignoring both internal ambiguities and any possible similarities to pre- and even anti-Revolutionary political thought. Yet *What is the Third Estate?* in fact contains an intriguing discursive web of reform and revolution that manages both to energize the Third Estate through an appeal to its quasi-corporate vanity and self-interest, and to transform its particular ambitions into universal aspirations.[109] The radical nature of the political solutions proposed in *What is the Third Estate?* is explicit. Louis XVI's agreement to convoke the estates general in May of 1789 focused public attention on the potential of this assembly but also on its inherent problems. Writing in this environment of mixed anticipation and doubt, Sieyès laid out the minimum reforms that would have to be made to the estates general if it could have a chance of functioning as a body representing Frenchmen. Sieyès was certainly not alone in calling for the doubling of the number of deputies representing the Third Estate, coupled with a fundamental change in the deliberative process: voting by head rather than by order. But Sieyès went much further than his fellow pamphleteers by creating an alternative scenario, should the clergy and the nobility not wish to implement these changes. The denial of even these modest requests for reform would demonstrate the callous disregard for the needs of 99 per cent of the French population. Even if such a division into orders was laid out in a constitution, an eventuality which Sieyès highly doubts, the inequity of the situation and the manifest unhappiness of the Third Estate would cast serious doubt on that constitution, if not abrogate it completely.[110] The absence of a constitution would require the formation of an extraordinary constituent assembly. Sieyès is adamant that the Third Estate alone can function in this extraordinary capacity. It can do so because the Third Estate *is* the French nation; its deputies to the estates general are the representatives of the nation and need no other source of legitimization as a constitutive body.[111] We will return to Sieyès's discussion of the nation in a moment.

While there is no doubt that the revolutionary scenario Sieyès constructed rested on philosophical rather than historical foundations, it is possible to overemphasize Sieyès's ahistoricity.[112] Sieyès had, in fact, a clearly developed sense of the past and of the current critical situation's relationship to that past. Within his work, an acknowledgement of the French past provides an unobtrusive background for the bolder patterns of radical change and reconfiguration. Whether this nod to the past is genuine or strategic is difficult to establish, and probably beside the point. Sieyès's references to the French past underscore the fact that political legitimization through history continues to be viable even on the eve of revolution.

Although Sieyès's evocation of the French past is rarely explicit, at critical points in the narrative of *What is the Third Estate?*, history is employed to emphasize his political philosophy. This is nowhere more evident than in his discussion of *la nation* in the second chapter. Sieyès is clearly responding to the *nobiliaire* theorists when he writes:

> If the aristocrats try to repress the People at the expense of that very freedom of which they prove themselves unworthy, the Third Estate will dare challenge their right. If they reply "by the right of conquest," one must concede that this is to go back rather far. Yet the Third Estate need not fear examining the past. It will betake itself to the year preceding the "conquest;" and as it is nowadays too strong to be conquered it will certainly resist effectively.[113]

French history is nothing but a seemingly endless account of noble usurpation; the estates general "simply a *clerico-nobili-judicial* assembly."

It is not perhaps surprising that Louis XI once again makes an appearance, though admittedly as a supporting character. Sieyès asserts that France was never actually a monarchy:

> If you consult history to verify whether the facts agree or disagree with my description, you will discover, as I did, that it is a great mistake to believe that France is a monarchy. With the exception of a few years under Louis XI and under Richelieu and a few moments under Louis XIV when

it was plain despotism, you will believe you are reading the history of a Palace Aristocracy. . . . [The People] has always considered the King as so certainly misled and so defenceless in the midst of the active and all-powerful Court, that it has never thought of blaming him for all the wrongs done in his name.[114]

It is not coincidental that Louis XI is once more cited in association with his "disciples," Richelieu and Louis XIV. One could argue that even though Sieyès refers to Louis XI's reign as "pure despotism," these years also offered the greatest protection of the people against the predations of the nobility. For Sieyès, the nobility, enjoying all its privileges at the expense of the Third Estate, had a greater negative impact on the vast majority of Frenchmen than one bad king ever could. After all, the weight of royal despotism was much more likely to fall on courtiers and nobles in close proximity to the king than on merchants and artisans in Rouen, Lyons or Nîmes. I am by no means asserting that Sieyès was a closet monarchist. I do find the juxtaposition of Louis XI and fellow French despots alongside discussion of the nation provocative, and I would argue that they point to a rather remarkable respinning of the discursive web. Sieyès twines together a *nobiliaire* thread, that has for decades emphasized the rights of the (noble) nation to participate in government, and an absolutist thread, that increasingly predicated legitimacy upon the monarchy's ability to protect the people. The conflation of *la nation* and *le peuple* is thus both indebted to a long tradition of competing ideologies and a radical reworking of that tradition.

La nation is, of course, a central focus in *What is the Third Estate?*, and most of the modern commentary on Sieyès's thought has hinged upon an understanding of his definition of this term.[115] In the effort to underscore Sieyès's originality, however, little attention has been paid to how he fuses two older definitions of *la nation* and *le peuple* to create a new, hybrid entity. Although Sieyès was not entirely alone in equating nation and people, as is evidenced by the debate over what to call the Third Estate after it had separated itself from the other two orders,[116] the forceful manner in which he combined *la nation* and *le peuple* provided the ideological shift which was a necessary precursor of the Revolution. The very manner in which the Third Estate and the nobility are placed in opposition throughout much of *What is the Third Estate?* testifies both to Sieyès's debt to the earlier *nobiliaire* formulation of *la nation* and to his vehement rejection of its premise.

Sieyès maintains that "a nation is made one by virtue of common laws and common representation."[117] These characteristics hold true for a noble nation, if it is considered without regard to other elements in society. Sieyès maintains that all nobles are governed by one law and possess representation; it is only in relation to the much larger mass of common folk that this law becomes invidious privilege, this representation mere caste interest. What Sieyès wanted was not to take away the political rights of the nobility but to extend these rights of representation and legal equity to all French citizens. The claim of the nobility to rights based on its status as the nation was to

Sieyès both repulsive and perhaps provocative. If nationhood conferred political rights, then the French people must be a nation.

Sieyès explicitly identifies *le peuple* with *la nation*. And whereas his vision of *la nation* owes something to *nobiliaire* ideology, his evocation of *le peuple* echoes absolutist thought, albeit faintly. It is noteworthy that, in a series of articles published in *Le Moniteur* in 1791, Sieyès asserted, writing against Tom Paine, that the people's rights might be better protected in a monarchy rather than in a republic.[118] Granted that the intervening two years between the publication of *What is the Third Estate?* and the articles in *Le Moniteur* were not easy ones for Sieyès. He became increasingly disillusioned with the progress of the Revolution, but I think it would be incorrect to interpret Sieyès's backhanded support for monarchy as a complete aberration in the evolution of his thought. Certainly, at least on the surface, Sieyès's ode to absolutism does not accord with his strident calls for popular political action. And yet it may be this apparent incongruity that accounts for the powerful way in which his words resonated with the public. Sieyès wove a strand of *ancien régime* paternalism in amongst the threads of bourgeois self-determination to create a pattern at once revolutionary and mildly nostalgic; a mixture of wines from two old casks poured into one new bottle.

The extent to which, from the St Bartholomew's Day Massacre until the French Revolution, constitutionalist literature relied upon the trope of Louis XI as tyrant is quite remarkable. The ubiquitous presence of Louis XI, and the unremittingly negative light in which he is presented in so many political works, ranging from pamphlets to full-blown treatises, illustrate some important points about constitutionalist thought. First, despite different emphases at different times, those opposed to absolute monarchy – from *monarchomachs* in the sixteenth century, through Huguenot exiles in the seventeenth century, to discontented nobles in the eighteenth century – shared a complex set of assumptions about kingship, law and sovereignty. The phrases they repeatedly used, the images they invoked, not only highlight the extent to which they differ from their opponents, but also how much commonality and consistency of belief characterize constitutionalist ideology across more than two centuries. Second, although some scholars have argued that political thought shifted away from an emphasis on the past and empirical arguments to arguments based on abstract philosophies, such as natural rights, it seems clear that evidence derived from history continues to function as a major pillar supporting contentious assertions about power, property and the extent of political participation. Third, one finds embedded in the textual surface of constitutionalist writing (and political literature in general) rhetorical nodes, consisting of images, phrases, and anecdotes taken from French society's collective memory. These nodes may be placed within the text deliberately or even unconsciously by the author, but, once encountered by the reader, they trigger associations on a visceral level that complement the conscious reception of the author's message. I maintain that these images, like that of Louis XI, not only persuade the reader about the correctness of an author's response to a particular political context but also of the deep-down truth of – in this case – the constitutionalist vision of France. Finally, as the work of Sieyès makes clear, even for the most avid proponent of popular sovereignty, the absolutist perspective of Louis XI was influential, if only in a minor way. Perhaps other aspects of absolutist ideology filtered into constitutionalist literature as well. Let us now move gingerly to another part of this discursive web to examine in greater depth the absolutist vision of the Spider King in the sixteenth and seventeenth centuries.

Part II

"Le plus sage de nos roys"

"Will you walk into my parlour?" said a spider to a fly;
"'Tis the prettiest little parlour that ever you did spy."
(Mary Howitt, *The Spider and the Fly*)

4 Unfettered king, unlimited greatness

Much of the most recent scholarship devoted to the *ancien régime* has been directed to challenging previously accepted characterizations of the nature of French government. Scholars have quite appropriately called into question the all-too-pat early modern French schema which outlines the relentless emergence of absolutism. According to this schema, in the course of the sixteenth and seventeenth centuries, the French government was transformed from one which possessed a consensual, if elitist, foundation to one in which all remnants of participation were eradicated. The culmination of this process by which medieval constitutional practices were eroded and replaced by an absolutist apparatus was to be found in Louis XIV's government, summed up in the apocryphal statement, "l'état, c'est moi." The years leading up to the French Revolution amply demonstrated the bankruptcy of the absolutist system, a fact confirmed by the cataclysm of the Revolution itself.

There is no doubt that so simplistic an interpretation is suspect.[1] At the same time, the best revisionist intentions may run amok. The increasing discomfort with the term absolutism is a case in point. Historians of early modern France have attempted to deal with the problem of "absolutism" in two ways. A considerable amount of attention has been devoted to the question of whether early modern French government was ever, in practice, an absolute monarchy. Drawing on local and regional histories, scholars have provided persuasive evidence of the crown's inability to extend authority into the corners of the kingdom.[2] Other works have stressed how factionalization inhibited the exercise of absolute authority even at the political centre.[3] Most of these revisionist efforts have been focused on the reign of Louis XIV, on the assumption that in the second half of the seventeenth century France came closest to being ruled by an absolute monarch.[4]

Historians have also directed their energies to the rather more problematic issue of definition. It is one thing to analyse the contemporary definitions of absolutist writers[5] and another to provide a modern definition to fit the demand of a retrospective institutional schema.[6] On the whole, however, attempts to define the theory of absolutism are less common among historians of France than studies of absolutism in practice. Historians of Tudor and Stuart England, by contrast, have been engaged for the past decade, at least, in defining terms like absolutism and divine-right kingship. Obviously, there is a very real difference between absolutism in theory and in practice. For, even if we acknowledge that "absolutism" *never* existed in France, absolutism should still be discussed as a concept over which political thinkers and polemicists continuously disputed. After all, "absolutism" is a concept which grew out of early modern society; it is contemporaneous with the government to which it was often applied by individuals who lived under its rule. Moreover, modern historians define absolutism too starkly. For authors of the early modern period, *puissance absolue* meant something quite different from what most scholars mean when they refer to early modern French government as absolute, and, indeed, "absolutiste" is not a term used during the early modern period. Nevertheless, *puissance absolue* did appear in contemporary parlance in reference to a type of government which retained elements of both consent and limitation. Absolutism did not equal arbitrary rule because both natural and fundamental laws were always and everywhere held to bind the ruler's actions. At this point, one might be tempted to argue that "absolutists" and "constitutionalists" were not really so different after all. Such an argument, however, requires turning a blind eye to the differences contemporary political thinkers perceived among themselves. If Jean Bodin and George Buchanan in the sixteenth century, and Pierre Bayle and Pierre Jurieu in the seventeenth century, viewed each other as protagonists, we ought to give their avowed differences serious consideration.

If we are going to consider *ancien régime* absolutism, however, it is imperative to keep in mind that the notion of *puissance absolue* as a description applied to their own government by contemporaries still changed over time. While the characteristic emphasis on monarchical self-limitation remained constant throughout the sixteenth and seventeenth centuries, the balance between the scope of the monarch's rule by will on the one hand and the binding quality of natural and fundamental law on the other shifts over time. In the sixteenth century, *politiques*[7] such as Jean Bodin and Innocent Gentillet endorsed much greater monarchical authority and less "popular" political participation than writers such as Hotman and Beza. *Politiques* nevertheless attempted to prevent the most potentially egregious royal behaviour by outlining a substantial corpus of fundamental law, including laws governing the succession, distribution of royal lands and the faith of the monarch. *Politiques* also invoked natural law to prohibit, among other things, royal expropriation of citizens' private property. It should be remembered that, while these laws were neatly laid out by sixteenth-century absolutists, they still reluctantly maintained that the people had no recourse if a monarch chose to contravene these laws. During the course of the seventeenth century, the balance between royal authority and limitation by law shifted progressively toward the former. This was accomplished by narrowing the scope of natural, and especially fundamental, law. Not surprisingly, portraits of Louis XI drawn by absolutists, while always complimentary, grew ever more flattering as the seventeenth century wore on, especially after the succession of the Sun King, with whom he was so often associated, both in glory and in shame.

Since, as we saw in Chapter 1, Louis XI's reputation in the sixteenth century seems firmly linked to views held of institutions such as the parlement and the estates general, it would be reasonable to assume that a political theory advocating a much smaller governmental role for such institutions would be accompanied by a marked elevation of Louis XI's historical stature. This would indeed seem to be the case when one examines the views of writers who opposed theories of popular sovereignty espoused by the Huguenot "monarchomachs," and upheld the supreme civil authority of the king. These theorists have been labelled absolutists, although they never advocated the completely unrestricted exercise of monarchical power. Nevertheless, they did maintain that sovereignty was lodged indivisibly in the king, and they rejected the idea of a contract between the king and the people which asserted that legitimacy was based on adherence to the conditions contained within the contract. Consequently, the absolutists viewed the institutions of the Parlement of Paris and the estates general as purely consultative in nature.

Ironically, for *politique* writers, as for Huguenot resistance theorists, the St Bartholomew's Day Massacre confirmed their beliefs about where ultimate power in the state ought to be located. *Politiques* viewed the massacre as agonizing proof of the need for a plenitude of monarchical authority. Only a very strong monarch could prevent the warring factions from dismembering and devouring France between them. From 1572 until the death of d'Alençon in 1584, the *politique* viewpoint, with all its absolutist implications, was tremendously influential. Even after the duke's death, *politiques* continued their vigorous calls for peace; the ultimate success of Henri IV was due, in large measure, to the efforts of absolutist writers like Jean Bodin, Innocent Gentillet and Pierre Belloy, among others.

Through the years, Innocent Gentillet's *Discours Contre Machiavel* has received almost uniformly bad press. In 1689, A. Baillet wrote that the *Anti-Machiavel*, as the treatise had come to be known, was the work "of a zealous Calvinist but a mediocre scholar and a very minor *politique*."[8] Baillet was at least partially mistaken on all three counts. If anything, Gentillet was a "zealous" *politique*, as evidenced both in the *Anti-Machiavel* and in another work entitled *Remonstrance au Tres Chrestien Henry III de ce nom Roy de France et de Pologne.*[9] As for being a mediocre scholar, while that may have been true with regard to his reading of Machiavelli, Gentillet's work is suffused with apposite classical references and his knowledge of Philippe de Commynes's *Mémoires*, which he uses repeatedly to refute Machiavelli, is extensive.

Gentillet was born around 1535 in Vienne. Sometime after 1547 he was a page at the court of Henri II and his name remained on the court rolls for twenty-nine years, although he was not always present at court during that time. He went to Geneva for a time after the St Bartholomew's Day Massacre, where he wrote and published the *Anti-Machiavel*.[10] His association with the *politique* faction is confirmed by his involvement in the publication of the duc d'Alençon's *Protestation* after the meeting of some moderate Catholics and Huguenots at Millau in the summer of 1574. Gentillet was appointed to the *chambre mi-partie* of the Parlement of Grenoble through the good offices of the duc d'Alençon, and he was nominated to the presidency of that court in 1581.[11]

The *Remonstrance au Tres Chrestien Henri III de ce nom Roy de France et de Pologne* was written in 1576. It is a standard *politique* treatise appealing to the king to maintain peace in the realm. The work is divided into three sections, the first asserting that nothing beneficial can come from a king making war on his subjects, the second pointing out the miseries already endured by the people of France in the present civil war, and the third refuting the pessimistic position that it would be impossible to establish a good and lasting peace in France.

In the first section, Gentillet supports his assertion by relating the historical example of Louis XI. Here, Gentillet is not as admiring of that king as he is in his more famous work, the *Anti-Machiavel*, saying that Louis XI was "as shrewd and cunning a prince as there had ever been in France" and one who governed badly upon his succession. Nevertheless, Louis XI is worthy of commendation because he willingly acknowledged his error and "sought by all means possible for him to end this war, following the advice of Francisco Sforza, the duke of Milan, his good friend, who counselled him that in order to have peace he should never refuse anything that is asked of him."[12] According to Gentillet, the king was unwilling to jeopardize the kingdom on something as uncertain as a battle. While Louis XI is not presented as the ideal prince in the *Remonstrance*, he is held up as an example of a king who both recognized his error and was willing to do his utmost to prevent that error from causing irreparable damage. The *Remonstrance* is clearly not a theoretical treatise extolling the benefits of absolute monarchy; Gentillet wants only to demonstrate the advantages of peace.[13] Thus it is not surprising that Louis XI is not fully endorsed as a model monarch. Nevertheless, the reference to Louis XI in this tract indicates Gentillet's willingness to employ Louis XI as an instructional example, a tendency which was much more apparent in another work of the same year, the *Discours contre Machiavel*.

Although the *Anti-Machiavel* has often been dismissed as little more than an extended effort to lay the blame for the troubles France was experiencing at the door of the Italians, the work can be understood as a much more theoretical piece. It constitutes a major weapon in the growing arsenal of absolutist theory.[14] More than once, Gentillet asserts the absolute power of the monarch and he states unequivocally that, should the monarch choose to circumvent civil laws of his own creation, " . . . it is nevertheless necessary to obey him, because God commands [obedience]."[15] Although an argument for Gentillet's support of limited monarchy has often been made, based on his distinction between *puissance absolue* and *puissance civile*, the very strong emphasis placed on the discretionary quality of this second type of authority, i.e. that the king chooses when and how and even if he will be limited by civil laws, is an indication of Gentillet's desire to support unquestioned royal authority. While this idea of discretionary self-limitation is one of the main tenets of traditional formulations of royal authority, the vehemence with which Gentillet asserts this power, coupled with a positively "Bodinian" view of the king's relationship to the estates, establish him more clearly as an absolutist than a traditional *regalian*. On one point, Gentillet separates himself definitively from the earlier writers: he does not view the right of consent to taxation as a natural law. (This is a much more radically absolutist assertion than any Bodin would make.) Gentillet asserts that kings possess complete control over the goods and persons of their subjects. Furthermore, the king may indeed tax his subjects without their consent, although it would be unwise for him to do so.[16]

While the *Anti-Machiavel* can be understood as a treatise of political theory, it must not be forgotten that its avowed purpose was the refutation of those "pernicious doctrines" of Machiavelli imported by the Italian contingent at court.[17] Interestingly, one of the primary sources on which Gentillet relies to counter the maxims of Machiavelli is the *Mémoires* of Philippe de Commynes. Ironically, for a number of later French writers, Commynes was to become "notre Machiavel."[18] Gentillet asserted that Commynes "understood better how one must govern the affairs of a great kingdom than Machiavelli did a simple manor."[19]

Such a heavy reliance on Commynes as a source results in a consistently positive view of Louis XI. Gentillet's praise for the king is even fulsome at times. Louis XI was:

> very humble in his habits, speech and in all things; he knew enough to recognize his errors and to amend them, and these virtues were the means by which he extricated himself from great affairs that he had to grapple with as soon as he came to the throne.[20]

In refuting the Machiavellian notion that one should never conclude a dishonourable peace, Gentillet employs Louis XI much as he did in the *Remonstrance*. He notes the concessions made by Louis XI to the rebelling nobles, in order to secure peace in the realm:

> Commynes, his chamberlain, says that [Louis XI's] humility and recognition of his faults saved his kingdom . . . What dishonour can there be to a Prince in using small and lowly means, provided that he renders his country peaceful, his estate secure and his subjects happy and obedient?[21]

Gentillet's views on the right of the king to tax his subjects without their consent results in a reversal of the standard interpretation of one of the most criticized aspects of Louis XI's reign: the burdensome taxation. Again,

Gentillet relies completely on Commynes's account for the justification of the heavy *tailles* levied on the people. Gentillet writes that, although Louis XI levied many *deniers* on his subjects, he spent all such revenues wisely and for the good of the kingdom.[22] How ironic for Gentillet to take such a stand on the proper use of levies: using taxes to corrupt foreigners and buy their services is nothing if not a decidedly Machiavellian activity! Gentillet departs from Commynes, however, in that Commynes considered taxation without consent as violating natural law, despite his justification of Louis XI for doing so. On the other hand, Gentillet does not see taxation without consent (as required by urgent circumstances) as a violation of natural law. The distinction Gentillet draws between *puissance absolue* and *puissance civile* stems directly from a discussion of this passage on taxation in Commynes, which Gentillet believes to be much misinterpreted by earlier writers. Gentillet asserts that those reading Commynes perceive a far greater degree of limitation on the king than the memorialist actually endorsed. After outlining the differences between the two types of power, Gentillet concludes his explication of Commynes with the statement that Commynes was only speaking of civil power:

> one must understand that Commynes was referring to this second power in the passage in question, and not to the absolute power of the Prince. Because, with regard to the latter, it is certain that the Prince has the power to undertake wars and levy taxes on his subjects without their consent . . . for [Commynes] wrote that [the king] has entire power over the goods and persons of his subjects.[23]

With respect to taxation, then, Gentillet's support for Louis XI's actions is given more freely even than that of Commynes. He notes that the people will bear patiently the burden of taxation as long as the taxes are levied by just one man.[24] Although this view is based on the idealistic assumption that the Prince will indeed always apply the revenues received from taxes for the welfare of the realm, the principle remains even if such revenues are misused.

There are other ways in which Louis XI is depicted in a positive light. Gentillet notes honour and integrity among his virtues. In one instance, when offered the services of an assassin for the proposed elimination of the duc de Bourgogne, a man whom he had every reason to hate and fear, Louis XI warned the duke of the attempted betrayal. Suspecting the king's motives, the duke did not believe Louis and so helped to bring about the destruction of the Burgundian house.[25] This was only fitting, according to Gentillet, as just retribution for the duke's perfidy in his treatment of the comte de Saint-Pol.[26]

Finally, Gentillet's favourable view of Louis XI finds its counterpart in Gentillet's subordination of the independent role of the estates general. Much like Bodin, Gentillet sees the assembly of the estates as enhancing the authority lodged in the king, rather than limiting it. The advantage of taking counsel is that it adds weight to the king's authority since it demonstrates his moderation. This does not imply, however, that if a king chooses not to consult the estates, his authority is in any way diminished.[27] Specifically regarding the estates general, Gentillet sees the utility of such an institution to the king because of the contact the deputies have with the most isolated and remote areas of the realm. The deputies are capable, therefore, of imparting valuable information about the condition of the commonwealth. One particular passage on the estates, written by Gentillet, corresponds very closely with its counterpart in Bodin's *Six Livres de la République*:

> Kings assembled their estates because numerous persons assembled from all parts of the kingdom can better inform [the king] about all the abuses and corruption committed there than could some small number, and can also more effectively remedy these problems in much the same manner as there is no better physician than one who knows well the malady and the causes thereof.[28]

In the work of Jean Bodin we find the decisive absolutism which, finally and definitively, rejected the irresolution of political thought in the first half of the century. Accordingly, we find in Bodin's treatises on government a portrait of Louis XI which provides a strong contrast to that drawn by Hotman and the resistance theorists.

Bodin's theoretical framework is not without its inconsistencies, however. A number of modern scholars have argued persuasively that a transformation in Bodin's political ideas took place between the time he wrote the *Method for the Easy Comprehension of History* and the composition of the *Six Livres de la République*.[29] A case could be made, on the other hand, that there is less of a radical change in his ideas than appears to be the case, and that his later works merely provide more precise definitions of concepts already present in less articulated form in his earlier works. In any case, the complexity and depth of his political thought can perhaps be accounted for by the rather tortuous path his life took.

Born in Angers round 1530 into a lower-middle-class family, Jean Bodin was admitted to the Carmelite order at an early age and was educated at the University of Angers, then at Toulouse. He was an *avocat* at the Parlement of Paris in the 1560s. Bodin was probably imprisoned for a period of almost eighteen months during 1569 and 1570 in the Conciergerie, and some scholars have concluded from this evidence, coupled with a possible stay at Geneva, that Bodin possessed definite Protestant sympathies at this stage in his life.[30] Like Gentillet, he was an adherent of the duc d'Alençon's party and went to England in 1581 as a part of the duke's entourage in his effort to woo Queen Elizabeth. After the duke's death in 1584, he retired to Laon, where he took over the position of *procureur du roi*, which had been left vacant by his brother-in-law's death. Between the years 1589 and 1593 he appears to have supported the League, and this apparent reversal in his religious and political allegiances has been variously interpreted.[31] From his own experiences Bodin was able to gain insight into all aspects of the religious and political conflict and his treatises must always be considered in the light of these experiences.

The *Method for the Easy Comprehension of History* was first published in 1566 and it is customary to view this treatise as the product of the more constitutionalist phase in Bodin's thought. Indeed, the emphasis on the limitations imposed on the king is much stronger here than it is in the *Six Livres*. Furthermore, his concept of sovereignty, which is precisely defined in the *Six Livres*, seems much less formulated in the earlier work, which has led to considerable difficulty in deciding whether the *Method* is absolutist or constitutionalist in character. In the *Method*, he states that sovereignty in the commonwealth is exercised by the individual or institution which carries out the following five functions: (1) creating the most important magistrates; (2) proclaiming and annulling laws; (3) declaring war and peace; (4) receiving final appeal from all magistrates; and (5) adjudicating the verdict of life or death.[32] Although all these marks of sovereignty are repeated in the *Six Livres*, the second point, the power of legislation, is elevated to become the primary mark of sovereignty into which all the other marks are subsumed. In this rearrangement, scholars have perceived a centralization of unlimited authority which was distinctly lacking in the *Method*.

Nevertheless, it can be argued that absolutist tendencies are evident in the earlier work that support the idea of a theory which was vaguely absolutist and became more clearly so in the *Six Livres*. The idea of the indivisibility of sovereignty, which has been regarded as one of the major tenets of Bodin's absolutist theory, is already formulated in the *Method*. In the earlier work Bodin also asserts that "those who decree law ought to be above it, that they may repeal it, take from it, invalidate it, or add to it, or even, if circumstances demand, allow it to become obsolete. These things cannot be done if the man who makes legislation is held by it."[33] Granted, the king is still, of course, restrained by natural law and should, according to Bodin, voluntarily submit himself to the laws of his own creation. But this self-limitation is very like Gentillet's *puissance civile*; if the king chooses not to limit himself, he still rules by right and cannot be disobeyed.

It is in the context of the limitations imposed by natural laws of justice that Bodin refers to Louis XI. He recounts the story of the king's conflict with the Parlement of Paris over the latter's refusal to register an unjust edict. What is interesting about this passage is the parenthetical comment made by Bodin that Louis is said to have been the first to have liberated the kings from servitude.[34] Obviously, although Louis was submitting himself to the judgement of parlement, he was free to choose whether to do so or not; the edict would still be binding without registration by the parlement. Bodin was using this episode to demonstrate how a king ought to limit himself, but the implication remains that the king is free and submits himself neither to an individual nor to an institution unless he chooses to do so.

Even if we assert that the *Method* is characterized by veiled absolutism, it cannot be denied that some modifications and additions were made to Bodin's political thought in the decade between 1566 and 1576. The absolutist strain in Bodin's thinking is, indeed, much more pronounced in the *Six Livres*, and Louis XI's status as a role model is correspondingly enhanced. Throughout the work, Louis XI is portrayed as an absolute but not tyrannical king. He behaved impulsively, and sometimes foolishly, but he never went beyond the bounds of his legitimate authority. If, as with the incident involving parlement noted above, Louis XI was made to see the injustice of his behaviour, he willingly changed his ways and tried to act in accordance with the dictates of natural law.

Another aspect of Bodin's thought which is considerably amplified in the later work is his view on the estates, which, as already indicated, is quite similar to that expressed by Gentillet. Bodin believes the estates general are an important body, but of a purely consultative nature. He asserts that, although it is entirely within the authority of the sovereign prince to make laws without the consent of the assembly, it is not "courteous" for him to do so.[35] Furthermore, the assembly is useful because it provides the arena in which the king may hear the complaints of his subjects:

> For where can things for the curing of the diseases of the sicke common-weale, or for the amendment of the people, or for the establishing of lawes, or for the reforming of the Estate, be better debated or handled, than before the prince in his Senat before the people.[36]

In fact, nowhere is the king's majesty and sovereignty so clearly displayed as when he is present in the assembly of the three estates. For nothing more explicitly declares the ruler's authority than when the people assemble and request him to assist them in some way. An assembly is not the demonstration of the people's authority but rather an affirmation of their submission to the sovereign authority of the king.[37]

Finally, Louis XI is mentioned in another work by Bodin, his *Journal* of the estates held at Blois in 1576–7.[38] Here, the connection between Bodin's view of Louis XI and his belief in the limited advisory role performed by the estates is made explicit. In response to a proposal to send deputies to advise the king, Bodin argued that it was not within the power of the assembly to send a committee to the king uninvited. At other points in the *Journal*, Bodin reiterates the view that the assembly can do nothing except by command of the king.[39] He goes on to assert, however, in purely pragmatic terms, that it would be unwise to send deputies to the king because they would be intimidated and unable to stand up to him. The king would then be in a position to enforce his will while maintaining the fiction of consent. This, according to Bodin, was the case with Louis XI, who, "with the eighteen people he convoked in the form of estates, arranged everything that he wanted and made it seem like it was done by the estates, and in this way placed kings *hors de page*."[40] The influence of the Huguenot resistance theorists is evident in Bodin's use of the phrase "hors de page," though, of course, Bodin was not implying that Louis XI was usurping power in order to liberate the French kings from the restraining hands of the estates, as is the case with the Huguenots. Bodin maintains that the estates should not delegate members to meet with the king not only because such initiative was disallowed by the purely consultative nature of the institution, but also because by further reducing the number of deputies who interact directly with the king they were undermining the nature of the assembly as a body representing all of France. The fact that Louis XI's manipulation of the deputies is used by Bodin as a warning to his colleagues not to send delegates to the king might suggest a less positive view of the monarch than that expressed by Bodin in earlier works. Nevertheless, the reference remains devoid of any implication that Louis XI acted in a manner contrary to the authority of the crown.

The apparent ambivalence that Bodin expressed in his journal can be accounted for by the duality of Bodin's position at the assembly. As a member of the estates, Bodin must have felt that he was representing the people of France and was obliged to promote the common interest. This would help to explain his repeated assertions about the restricted nature of the charge given to the deputies by their constituencies. On the other hand, he was always aware of the limited power of the estates general in their relationship with the king. The journal is a record of actual events, and the contradictions contained within it reflect both Bodin's awareness of his responsibility to those he represented and his conception of the assembly as an institution of royal administration which was employed by the king for more effective governing of the realm.

Ironically, Bodin records Louis XI as establishing the perpetuity of offices; resistance theorists who looked to parlement were doubtless scandalized by Bodin's depiction of Louis as the builder of at least part of the constitutional edifice which they thought he had done his utmost to destroy! Bodin notes Louis XI's actions in dismissing all his father's councillors when he became king, but it seems that, although Bodin may have considered this action ill-advised, he had no doubts about its legitimacy as a manifestation of sovereignty. It is notable that Bodin makes no reference to the War of the Public Weal when discussing Louis XI's dismissal of the councillors. Furthermore, Louis did establish the perpetuity of offices later in the reign, which would seem to suggest that, while he may have been impulsive, he did not act tyrannically.

As the religious wars entered their final phase, after the assassination of Henri III in 1589, the ultra-Catholic ranks became split between those who agreed, albeit with great reluctance, that the crown should pass to Henri de Navarre, and those for whom the Catholicity of the monarch was paramount and who consequently viewed the hitherto Protestant Navarre as anathema.

The duc de Mayenne, in his capacity as lieutenant-general of the kingdom, called for an assembly of the estates general to meet in Paris. Both contemporaries and modern historians have questioned the legitimacy of the estates held at Paris in 1593 because of the unorthodox manner of its convocation and the fact that the deputies were overwhelmingly drawn from strongly Leaguer regions of France, primarily from the immediate environs of Paris. A number of the most vehemently Leaguer delegates pushed for an invitation to be issued to the Infanta of Spain to assume the French throne. All such efforts were halted by the timely conversion of Henri of Navarre and by the Parlement of Paris's vehement objections both to the idea of placing a woman on the throne (which would contravene Salic law) and to the very notion that the estates had a right to elect a king at all.[41]

The famous pamphlet *Satyre Ménippée*, first published in 1593, ridiculed the bogus estates and the patently insincere Catholic piety of many of its delegates. As a ringing indictment of chaos and bloodshed caused by decades of war, the *Satyre Ménippée* contributed to the rising chorus of calls for an end to war and, above all, stability – stability that could only be achieved and maintained by a strong monarchy.

The premise of the *Satyre Ménippée* is that, before speaking to the assembly of the estates, representatives of the different orders as well as the leaders of the convention each drank a truth serum of sorts that forced them to reveal their true intentions and motivations. Monsieur d'Aubray, the member designated to speak on behalf of the third estate, rises to condemn the war and the naked self-interest of the Leaguers, disguised as religious zeal. In a digression that discusses the pitiful state to which Paris has been reduced because of the wars, d'Aubray cites the War of the Public Weal. He maintains that although the duc de Berry, the comte de Charolais and the princes of France claimed that they took up arms on behalf of the people and the kingdom, when it came to negotiating a peace settlement, each one looked to his own well-being and advancement, "without making mention of the public any more than they did of the Turk." If you looked in the annals of France, d'Aubray continued, you would find that the intention of the chiefs of the Burgundy and Orléans factions was to "encroach on the authority of the kingdom, and to benefit one great house over the other . . . "[42] By the end of the religious wars, then, the War of the Public Weal was characterized by absolutists not as a grand constitutional struggle but instead as the petty squabbling of tinpot princes, a fifteenth-century mirror reflecting the pernicious factionalism plaguing France a century later.

If we turn to advocates of divine-right theory, we find that Louis XI once again fares well. Divine-right theory avoids the whole question of whether a king is good or bad, moderate or tyrannical. A king is appointed directly by God and is responsible to God alone. He is legitimate if he is the next in line of succession because of the existence of a perpetual kingship. The heir becomes king at the very instant the old king dies and coronation ceremonies are superfluous.[43]

Despite his belief in the divine right of kings, Pierre de Belloy's work, the *Apologie Catholique*, is also a strongly *politique* work which places religious considerations beneath the welfare of the state in the hierarchy of priorities. Although a Catholic, Belloy supported the succession of Henri de Navarre because he was the next in line to the throne. In addition to the fact that Navarre was the legitimate successor, Belloy was firmly convinced that the bloodshed somehow had to cease. Much of the work is an eloquent plea for peace as the only Christian solution. He notes that it is not only morally wrong but also ineffective to use physical force to try to convert the Protestants: "If someone is in the shadows, one brings him into the light; one doesn't cut his throat."[44]

The *Apologie Catholique* is also a lengthy exposition on the Salic law and rightful succession. Belloy also makes clear his view that there can be no earthly judge of a legitimate king since he is endowed with an almost mystical quality which effectively separates him from the lesser members of the commonwealth. By way of support for the assertion of divine ordination, Belloy assumes a Gallican posture. He argues that the pope cannot possibly have any temporal authority within the kingdom of France since God himself ordained the French kings, and they have no superior save God himself. It is in this context that Belloy makes a reference to Louis XI. Louis XI's involvement in ecclesiastical affairs is often overlooked by sixteenth-century writers, so it is interesting to note Belloy's opinion in this regard. He praises Louis XI for having taken action to ensure that the church was contained within the state. In 1467 Louis XI had confirmed the laws in France denying papal authority, "without which remedy, priests would have formed another monarchy and more powerful than the royal [one] . . . "[45]

Belloy's belief in the sovereign authority of the king is also vigorously expressed in an earlier work entitled *De l'Autorité du Roy*. He states that, of the various forms of government, monarchy receives the most approbation from God and the most praise and esteem from peoples. Belloy could not be more explicit about his views of monarchy when he writes "the estate and royal majesty contains the right, power and authority to command alone, as monarch and sovereign in his republic."[46] His unequivocal views on the nature of monarchical authority lead Belloy to condemn the activities of the Catholic League which he sees as attempting to cover its efforts to undermine the power of the king with the cloak of a holy war against the Huguenots. Although himself a strong Catholic not averse to fighting the Huguenots, Belloy would only endorse such a course of action if decreed by the king himself.[47] Belloy compares the activities of the Catholic League with those of the rebellious nobles of the previous century, especially during the reign of Louis XI. Belloy notes the practice of the members of the League of the Public Weal to meet in the Church of the Magdalene in order to give their assemblage the guise of a religious brotherhood. Realizing the real intent of those present at the gatherings, Louis XI forbade any more meetings without his own presence.[48] Belloy asserts that the religious intentions of the Holy League in his own time are as false as those of the League of the Public Weal. The other alleged purpose for the formation of a league, the desire to work for "le bien public," is a similarly bogus pretext for conspiracy. He says disparagingly of such ostensibly high-minded individuals, "O quels restaurateurs!"[49] For Belloy, the League of the Public Weal serves as an excellent example of personal ambition being disguised as altruism; the rebellion of the nobles under Louis XI, like the activities of the League in the late 1580s, was really a conspiracy designed to bring the king to his knees for the purposes of private gain. Although the nobles had been fractious under Charles VI and Charles VII, they did not frame their ambitions as grand struggles on behalf of the people. Under Louis XI, by contrast,

> the relics of the [noble rebellion] bore a new configuration, under the title of the public good and reformation of the estate of the king, of which the dukes of Berry, Burgundy and Brittany were the chiefs, more for their advancement and commodity than for the care of the poor people, as their deportment clearly showed.[50]

Belloy's co-religionists had no more right and no better cause to attempt to usurp the rightful authority of the king than had the Huguenots. It is through this prism of complete devotion to the concept of monarchical sovereignty that Belloy interprets the tumultuous and, by this time, much examined events of the previous century.

The representations of Louis XI in the writings of such diverse writers as Bodin, Gentillet and Belloy indicate that, despite differences in emphasis, sixteenth-century absolutists from all shades of opinion saw in Louis XI a strong monarch who unified and expanded his kingdom, confirmed the superiority of state over church and left the kingdom at peace when he died. That his methods may have been harsh was not at issue; he may have snubbed the nobility and refused counsel at times, but he was perfectly within his rights to do so. Louis XI had enough political sagacity to realize when he had pushed too hard and he did his utmost to repair any damage that might have been incurred by his wilfulness. It could be argued as well that, in consistently employing Louis XI as a historical example of both the effectiveness and the legitimacy of absolutist government, the proponents of absolutism were largely reacting against the resistance theorists; there is no better way to refute an argument than to demonstrate the misrepresentation of facts upon which the argument is based. By presenting Louis XI in a positive light, the absolutists attempted to deprive the monarchomachs of the target against whom they launched much of their invective. In this way they demonstrated that resistance theories were based on a fallacious interpretation of history, and thus undermined their appeal in a period when history was believed to be the major source for answers to contemporary problems.

During the last ten years of the Civil Wars, France seemed poised on the brink of anarchy; increasingly, absolute monarchy seemed the best, perhaps the only, way to re-establish social and political order out of apparent chaos. As the end of the century approached, absolutist ideas, which writers such as Gentillet and Bodin had already endorsed during the 1560s and 1570s, were voiced with greater frequency and vehemence. Moreover, with the triumph of Henri IV, absolutists received added impetus to re-articulate ideas developed during the course of the conflict. By the third quarter of the seventeenth century, this more uncompromising form of absolutism came to be represented by the famous, if apocryphal, declaration, "l'état, c'est moi." Though the maxim attributed to Louis XIV was in many ways a simplification of absolutism as it developed in the seventeenth century, it does suggest the direction absolutist ideas were taking under the Bourbon monarchy. Absolutist theory in the years after the triumph of Henri IV diminished the limitation on the king's power posed by the fundamental laws of the realm. The sanctity of the king, as developed by divine-right theorists like Belloy, was expounded more emphatically as part of the justification for royal incursions into hitherto protected areas of subjects' private property rights. Absolutists also encouraged the development of the concept of the state as an identifiable entity separate from society, the control of which carried with it absolute authority. The difference in degree between the sixteenth- and seventeenth-century formulations of absolutist theory is perhaps most evident in the change of importance attributed to the past. Unlike sixteenth-century writers who made appeals to the "ancient constitution" in order to support the idea of absolute government as legitimate, seventeenth-century absolutists, while prepared to mine the past for useful examples, were equally willing to discard the distant past in favour of arguments based on usage. In their view, absolute rule existed in France; in some sense, its legitimacy rested on that very existence as much as anything else. Their denial of the ancient constitution as relevant to contemporary discussion did not, however, prevent these writers from referring to historical figures and events as a means of amplifying their arguments. The reputation of Louis XI is largely rehabilitated through the efforts of these seventeenth-century writers, and the laudatory appraisals he receives at their hands illustrate, as much as anything else, the differences between sixteenth- and seventeenth-century formulations of absolutism.

Charles Loyseau was one early seventeenth-century writer whose ideas clearly demonstrate the new direction taken in absolutist ideology. Born in Paris in 1564, Loyseau was an *avocat* at the Parlement of Paris. His family had only recently entered the ranks of the magistracy; his grandfather had been a *laboureur* (a well-to-do cultivator) in Nogent-le-Roi.[51] Loyseau is perhaps best known as a proponent of the privileges and responsibilities of the robe. His three major works, *Traité des Seigneuries* (1608), *Cinq livres du droit des offices* (1609) and *Des Ordres et simples dignités* (1610)[52] offer such a breadth of topics and complexity of treatment that a number of contrasting interpretations of Loyseau's thought have been put forward by modern scholars.[53] There is a consensus, however, that with regard to the issue of sovereignty, upon which so much of the debate between constitutionalists and absolutists is premised, Loyseau ought to be placed with the latter group.[54] A comparison of Loyseau's ideas on sovereignty with those expressed by the *"politique* absolutists" such as Jean Bodin and Innocent Gentillet should help to demonstrate some of the modifications made to absolutist theory in the early years of the seventeenth century.[55]

Loyseau describes sovereignty in the context of his discussion of *seigneurie*, which he defines as the ownership of land. In the *Traité des Seigneuries*, Loyseau examines different types of *seigneuries* and the rights and responsibilities associated with the ownership of such domains. Loyseau makes an important distinction between two types of ownership which derive from the same domain. By *seigneurie in abstracto*, Loyseau means the possession of all rights and authority associated with the possession of the land. *Seigneurie in concreto* refers to the land itself.[56] These related aspects of possession which refer respectively to *puissance et propriété* are especially significant with regard to the control of the state. Sovereignty is a function of *seigneurie in concreto*. The king derives his authority from his "possession" of the land which comprises France. By virtue of his possession of the *seigneurie* of France, the king also possesses sovereignty over it.[57]

Loyseau is not, however, arguing that the monarch's sovereign power allows him to act tyrannically. Loyseau is careful to distinguish between public and private *seigneurie*. Public *seigneurie* "consists in the superiority and authority that one has over persons or over things," i.e. power over the public activity of citizens and over revenues collected from them applied to the good of the domain. Private *seigneurie* approximates direct ownership.[58] The king of France enjoys public *seigneurie* since it is clear that private *seigneurie* over Frenchmen would be a sort of slavery which has never existed in France.

Loyseau further subdivides public *seigneurie* into *suzeraineté* and *souveraineté*. Loyseau describes how *seigneuries* were originally established at the time the Franks conquered Gaul. The chieftain divided the land among his best warriors, allotting to each a parcel of a size commensurate with individual merit and the number of soldiers each commanded. These were known as fiefs because of the new owner's obligation to assist the chieftain in times of war. In time, these fief-owners usurped aspects of administrative control from the overlord, the process having been legitimated through prescription. Loyseau calls this level of authority *suzeraineté*.[59]

Chapter Two of the *Traité des Seigneuries* deals specifically with *seigneuries souveraines*. It is at this point that Loyseau departs dramatically from the *politique* absolutists. Loyseau has already laid the groundwork of his assertion about the nature of sovereignty by emphasizing the territorial quality of *seigneuries*. He successfully alters the direction of absolutist theory by declaring the unequivocal identification of sovereignty with the territorial state. He cites the example of the separation of Flanders from France:

> when the French king gave up the sovereignty of Flanders, as a consequence Flanders was separated and removed from the state of France and became a state apart. Because, in short, sovereignty is the form that gives existence to the state, the "state" and sovereignty taken "in concreto" are synonyms and the state is thus called because sovereignty is the height and end of power to which the state must direct and establish itself.[60]

Loyseau goes on to address the rights of sovereign *seigneuries* and maintains that what Jean Bodin asserted in the *Six Livres de la République* to be the only mark of true sovereignty, the authority to make law, is actually one of many characteristics of sovereignty. Supreme legislative authority is one aspect of the sovereign's rights as they pertain to power. Not surprisingly, other elements of sovereign power as laid out by Loyseau are precisely those which Bodin subsumes into the right to make law in the *Six Livres* and distinguishes separately in the *Method*: the right to create officers, arbitrate in peace and war, coin money, and the right to judicial last resort.[61] Two things which distinguish Loyseau's position from that of Bodin are Loyseau's denigration of customary law and his belief about the sovereign's right to levy impositions.

Customary laws are those customs and traditions that developed differently in different regions of France, which, though unwritten, attained the force of law through time and usage. The status of customary laws was a thorny issue to political thinkers because they were both an obstacle to policies of centralization and the manifestation of certain individual rights which many considered to be inviolate. Bodin, for example, argued that one must be above the law, in order to be able to add to, subtract from or modify it. Nevertheless, he was hesitant to allow the king limitless power to alter or abrogate the customary laws of France. Loyseau, on the other hand, views customary law as the same as civil law: customs only become law when they are sanctioned by the king and registered in his parlement, following the procedure established for all new civil laws.[62]

Loyseau is circumspect in acknowledging that, at one time, the consent of the people was required for the levying of new impositions. As with his treatment of the origins of the French monarchy, however, Loyseau once again argues for legitimacy through prescription. Citing Philippe de Commynes, Loyseau asserts that when the *tailles* were neither regular nor perpetual, they were only levied with the consent of the people. He goes on to argue, however, that in his time, the opposite is true:

> one must no longer doubt that in France (which is today possibly the most pure and perfect monarchy in the world) our king, having almost no other foundations of finance, can levy monies without the consent of the estates, which, as I have proven in the preceding chapter, has absolutely no part in sovereignty.[63]

The adamant quality of Loyseau's position effectively separates him from Bodin and Gentillet, both of whom allow for the levying of taxes without consent in cases of extraordinary urgency. Nevertheless, even Gentillet, who supports extraordinary levies with less reluctance than Bodin, hedges his statement with the warning that the king may not attack the personal belongings of his subjects, thus suggesting a certain ambivalence. Loyseau, by way of contrast, argues that the sovereign does have control over both persons and goods within his kingdom. Loyseau's elaboration of this assertion proceeds as follows: sovereigns have control over persons and goods; control over persons does not necessarily equal slavery; in the same way, control over goods does not necessarily equal *seigneurie privée* or perfect, direct ownership.[64]

In the context of his discussion regarding the rights of sovereignty, Loyseau makes two brief references to Louis XI. One of the attributes associated with sovereign power is the right to coin money. A dispute over the duc de Bretagne's coining of specie was one of the reasons why Louis XI undertook the war against the duke. In a similar manner, friction between the king and the duke was created through the latter's usurpation of sovereign honour by using the phrase "duc par la grâce de Dieu."[65] Louis XI made war on Brittany because he felt his sovereign status to be challenged. Loyseau's interpretation of this aspect of the War of the Public Weal puts Louis XI's actions, and those of the nobles, in a whole new light. No longer is Louis XI's conduct to be viewed as oppressive or tyrannical. The nobles are not trying to re-establish their rightful places in the French constitution, but rather they are usurping powers belonging solely to the French king. This view of the War of the Public Weal reflects Loyseau's view of noble *suzeraineté* as usurped powers which eventually became legitimate through time and usage.

Loyseau recognizes the grave error Louis XI made upon his accession to the crown in dismissing all his father's advisors. In the *Cinq livres du droit des offices*, Loyseau notes the danger to the state created by the wilful behaviour of Louis XI. When he came to the throne, Louis XI:

> changed most of the principal officers of the kingdom, which was one of the primary causes of this memorable civil war, called the "Public Good": this being well known, he ordained in 1467 that henceforth the officers of France could not be deprived of office without duly judged forfeiture. Knowing by experience the great usefulness of this ordinance, and fearing that after his death it would be no more observed than that of Philippe le Bel, fifteen years later on his deathbed, he made Charles VIII his son and successor to swear to uphold it, reminding him (as the story goes) that the observation of the ordinance would be one of the great assurances of his state; and not being content to have him swear, he sent right away to the Parlement the act of this oath to have it published and registered.[66]

In much the same manner as Bodin before him, Loyseau points out Louis XI's mistake but emphasizes more Louis XI's recognition of this error and his efforts to effect reparation. Although Louis XI does not figure largely in Loyseau's major works, the brief mentions of him bear no real hint of condemnation. Rather, it seems Louis XI acted within the proper confines of monarchical sovereignty which, as Loyseau defined them, were the broadest yet to be envisioned.

The idea of the kingdom as property, articulated by Loyseau, underlay the arguments of another absolutist, M. I. Baricave. In his *Defense de la monarchie française et d'autres monarchies*,[67] Baricave argues that the alienation of domain is indeed permissible. Prior to this time, alienation was deemed unlawful, even by the *politique* absolutists, by virtue of fundamental law. By permitting alienation, Baricave implicitly questions the validity of the entire corpus of fundamental law, hitherto considered one of the foremost constitutional restraints upon the monarch, therein demonstrating the theoretical gap separating sixteenth- and seventeenth-century conceptions of absolutism.[68] Baricave maintains that kings are called "Seigneurs proprie-taires du Domaine" and, according to the laws of property, a proprietor cannot be deprived of the land by any means and may do with it as he wills. On a practical note, Baricave argues that the grant of land may be the only form of reward which a king is able to give loyal servants. As proof, Baricave cites a number of historical examples of royal alienation, including a reference to Louis XI's gift of lands to his chancellor, Guillaume de Rochefort.[69]

Baricave's book is a lengthy refutation of the *Vindiciae contra tyrannos*; it is hardly surprising that he takes a hostile view of the War of the Public Weal and a correspondingly laudatory view of Louis XI. Citing Robert Gaguin's chronicle,[70] Baricave clearly believes the publicly-stated intentions of the rebelling nobles to have been nothing more than a ruse to cover their own selfish goals:

> And the pretext of this league was to deliver the people from the oppres-sion that they suffered from the *tailles* and subsidies imposed by the king. But the peace and the deal that they made thereafter with the king show that their entire design was nothing other than ambition and avarice.[71]

Baricave goes on to refute the *Vindiciae's* account of the estates general held at Tours in 1467. The constitutionalist interpretation of this event had always been that it provided proof of the innate strength of the assembly, as demonstrated in its convocation even by the most wilful of monarchs. Baricave uses the assembly at Tours to support precisely the opposite assertion:

> This example clearly shows that the estates never had any authority or power in France, seeing that the convocation of it and the decisions made therein did nothing to appease the troubles and factions, for which purpose they had been convoked . . . Above all the good of the state

depends on the wisdom of the king and on his worth (as everything bad is based on his imprudence or stupidity) without which neither the estates, nor anything else has the power to bring any remedy.[72]

In Baricave we find the same belief as in Loyseau, articulated in a slightly different manner: the state lives or dies with the sovereign; no other person or institution possesses any power to change the state, either for good or ill. In this sense, the lifeblood of the state flows through the monarch, and his strengths and weaknesses are reflected in the character of the realm.

As the resistance theorists did, so, too, the absolutists often used catch phrases to encapsulate their views on Louis XI and kingship. The use of the phrase "mettre les rois hors de page" was commonly and consistently connected with Louis XI by the first quarter of the seventeenth century.[73] The absolutist interpretation of the phrase "mettre les rois hors de page," appears in Pierre Matthieu's *Histoire de Louis XI*. In a eulogy of the king which precedes the work, the assessment of Louis XI's achievement is as follows: "He carried nothing from the place which he left, but the proud title to have freed the kings of France from subjection or wardship, capable to command, not a Realm only, but the whole world."[74]

Best known as a poet and an historian, Pierre Matthieu was born in 1563. He obtained a law degree at Valence and began his practice in Lyon. During the Religious Wars, he allied himself firmly with the Catholic League but when, in 1593, Lyon submitted to royal authority, Matthieu became one of the deputies sent to Paris to render homage to Henri IV. From that point on, Matthieu became one of the most zealous supporters of Henri IV, organizing all the festivals when the king travelled to Lyon in 1595. Seizing the moment, Matthieu went to Paris where Henri IV commissioned him to write his *Histoire de Louis XI*. He died in Toulouse in 1621.

In the *Histoire de Louis XI*, Matthieu's intention is not solely to present a history of Louis XI's reign, but also to erect a monument to his hero, the king who commissioned the book, Henri IV. The *avertissement* contains a comparison of the two kings in which Henri IV is depicted as superior to Louis XI in every way. Although the latter had all the raw qualities of a good king, these were tempered by vice rather than virtue: "His wisedome had a touch of cunning, his justice of severitie, his valour of rashness, his clemencie of fear, his liberalitie of profusion, and his pietie of dissimulation."[75] Henri IV, on the other hand, "takes delight to be what he appeares, and to appeare what he is." Louis XI is not to be denigrated, however, simply because he falls short of some of Henri IV's great personal qualities and achievements. The comparison of Louis XI and Henri IV adds to the lustre of the latter's reputation because he surpasses in virtue and capability the one king greater than all the rest in the art of government. Matthieu writes:

This Historie doth truely show the diversitie of the two portraits, and gives the King an incredible content, to see that the raigne of a great,

mighty, redouted and wise King, may not enter into comparison with his
by the difference which hee hath set in order of his treasure . . . and in the
restablishment of the publike safety and felicitie.

Henri IV was aware of, and encouraged, the parallels between himself and
Louis XI. According to Rodolphe Le Maistre, who was commissioned by
Henri IV to produce a translation of the first six books of Tacitus, Henri
commanded Matthieu to write a history of Louis XI because he felt the life
and reign of the Spider King was among the most illustrative of all of
Henri's predecessors.[76] Repeated comparisons between the two kings were
made during the course of the seventeenth and eighteenth centuries. Both
strong monarchs known for their ability to unify a divided France, Henri
and Louis were portrayed as two sides of the same coin, with Henri's shining
face brightly visible and Louis's visage hidden in shadow on the reverse. In
discussing the format of his work, Matthieu writes that the first ten of the
eleven books will concern the events of Louis XI's reign and the last will
compare "that which was done in those times, and . . . that which is done
now, to show that Lewis hath been as much inferiour to Henry, as he was
held superiour to other Kings."[77]

Matthieu is by no means complimentary when he discusses the events
preceding the War of the Public Weal. He criticizes Louis XI's harshness in
depriving his father's officers of their dignities and oppressing *le peuple menu*
with extraordinary impositions. The war is nevertheless characterized as
noble pretensions couched in public concern. Louis XI is praised for his
unwillingness to put the lives of his subjects at risk, though his actions
sprang from the recognition that the chaos created by a lengthy war would
endanger the throne more than an ignominious peace, rather than from any
pure-hearted concern for his subjects.[78]

Matthieu follows the absolutist interpretation of the estates general held
at Tours as a manipulated assembly convoked to "rubber-stamp" Louis XI's
intention to renege on the promises made at Conflans.[79] Louis XI's character
is further called into question when Matthieu notes his apparent pleasure at
hearing of his brother's death.[80] Despite a predominantly negative appraisal
of Louis XI's character, however, Matthieu yet believes him to have been an
effective monarch. Circumstances beyond his control forced Louis XI to
behave in such a manner as to ensure the safety of the state but also to
guarantee a harsh moral judgement from posterity.

The role of necessity in determining and justifying Louis XI's actions is
an important new development in interpretation of his reign and it is a
trend which emerges in Matthieu's history. While not abandoning the
existing moral framework within which the king was supposed to operate
(as evidenced by his praise for Henri IV as both effective and moral),
Matthieu maintains that actions must be judged according to both the
circumstances which brought them about and the ends to which they are
directed. Viewed through the light of necessity, Louis XI's conduct takes on
a much more praiseworthy aspect. In speaking of the peace achieved with

the Burgundians, the importance of necessity as a mitigating factor is clearly articulated:

> It is true that if necessitie, which hath no law, did not excuse the proceedings of this Prince, and if the honour of the action did not remaine to him that hath the profit, there might be exceptions taken to that which the King did to have this Peace. A wise Prince and less fearefull would have adventured a Battell, rather than be subject to his enemies pride, but these high and generous formes of treating are buried in the ruines of proud and triumphant Rome, and there is nothing remaining but admiration which History represents.[81]

One could argue that the anarchic condition of the previous fifty years had created in writers such as Matthieu a certain pessimism about the true motivations of men and their ability to live peaceably with one another. Given the fractious nature of men, it may well be appropriate to use what could be construed in other circumstances as vicious methods to keep the peace. Matthieu justifies most of Louis XI's actions on the grounds of necessity. Regarding excessive taxation, Louis XI "was forced to mow the Medow as often as he had need," because of the great affairs in which he was engaged.[82] If he acted harshly upon his accession to the crown, it was because "he found such savadge humours, and so accustomed to liberty, that as the intemperance of the patient justifies the severity of the Physician, he was forced to use fury to make mad men wise."[83]

Despite his emphasis on the mitigating nature of necessity in considering Louis XI's conduct, Matthieu believes that Louis possessed good qualities. Citing the episode when Louis XI tried to warn the duc de Bourgogne of the count of Campobasso's intended treachery, Matthieu praises Louis XI's display of honour.[84] Moreover, at the beginning of the eleventh chapter, Matthieu cites Commynes's famous statement that, though all kings possess both virtues and vices, Louis XI was notable in that he had fewer bad qualities than the rest. Matthieu continues in this vein: "This great authority which hee preserved unto his last gaspe, and carried into death, was supported by three mighty pillars, which his own wisdome had raised, Severity, Constancy, and Reputation."[85]

Matthieu's work thus seems poised between the old morally-grounded ideology and the newly-emerging pragmatic view of politics. On the whole, he condemns Louis XI's character but applauds his politics. A new conception of Louis XI appears to be forming. No longer is his reign to be judged on moral or constitutional grounds, but rather on whether his actions, as driven by necessity, benefited the state. This pragmatic view seems predicated on the unity of authority in the sovereign. In this manner, we see that *raison d'état* arguments logically emerge in an environment which accepts as doctrine the absolute and indivisible sovereignty of the monarch.

Although Matthieu's work points to interesting new developments in the historical reputation of Louis XI at the hands of later *raison d'état* theorists, the king was also portrayed positively by absolutist theorists unwilling to give way to the new pragmatic current. During the first half of the seventeenth century Louis XI's historical reputation enjoyed near universal acclaim. Increasingly, Louis XI is represented as a great and authoritative French king. Conversely, the actions of his adversaries appear to be unjustified attacks on the central authority of the crown. This interpretation is most clearly presented in Cardin Le Bret's work, *De la Souveraineté du roy*.[86]

Cardin Le Bret was born in 1558 into an important robe family. His grandfather was ennobled by Henri III, and Henri IV further facilitated the rise of the Le Bret clan. Cardin Le Bret followed his father's path into the magistracy, and he enjoyed considerable success, finally attaining a place on the *Conseil d'état*. From around 1590 to the early 1620s he was the *avocat-général* first for the *Cour des Aides* then for the Parlement of Paris. During the 1620s he undertook a series of diplomatic missions. After the publication of *De la Souveraineté du roy* in 1632, Le Bret devoted himself to conciliar duties on the *Conseil d'état* and, in that regard, his *parlementaire* outlook, gained during his years with the sovereign courts, gave way to a royalist viewpoint. Until his death in 1655, at the age of 97, Le Bret worked "à defendre les droits du Roi," both in theory and in practice, as a councillor to the king.[87]

Le Bret's work is the best known formulation of absolutist theory of its time, and it is indeed uncompromising in its discussion of an all-encompassing and unquestionable royal authority. Le Bret's view is summed up with his statement in the first chapter that the French kings can do no wrong: "they have always governed their kingdom with all mildness and moderation, and they have been so considerate to observe this wise advice, that Pliny gave to Trajan: *cave dum princeps sis, ne sit Domino locus* (beware while you are prince, lest there be a place for a master) that rarely have they given their people cause to complain of their government." Le Bret continues that, if they have seemed to act harshly upon occasion, they were forced by the iron rod of necessity to engage in extraordinary measures.[88] At first, Le Bret's work does not seem so much a serious treatise supporting absolutism as it does a not very subtle panegyric to past kings. The issue of authority is not addressed, since all kings behaved, with a few unavoidable exceptions, with the proper moderation.

In the second chapter, Le Bret becomes even more unequivocal. He maintains that the French kings, as sovereigns, are answerable to God alone.[89] It is interesting to note, however, that Le Bret upholds the restraining power of fundamental law. In this sense, Le Bret is much closer than is Loyseau to the sixteenth-century absolutists. Other than fundamental law, Le Bret supports the idea of the king above the law. In Le Bret's eyes, the king is both legislator and judge. From this point on in the work, Le Bret follows along lines of absolutist theory already established by Bodin. The power of creating officers belongs solely to the king, as do considerations of war and negotiation of peace. Le Bret devotes a chapter to the specific sovereign rights regarding the establishment of the postal service, in which Louis XI figures prominently as the founder of the French postal system. Le Bret departs from a purely "Bodinian" form of absolutism, however, when he asserts, along with Loyseau, the exclusive right of the king to levy impositions. He reasons: "This right and power was given to kings in order that they have sufficient means to defend the state and peoples that God committed to them, to punish rebels and reward those of merit."[90] Yet although Le Bret advocates unlimited authority in the area of finances, he strikes a note of kingly self-restraint. The king must always exercise prudence and discretion; he must recognize the limit beyond which the exactions become unduly onerous upon his subjects. Le Bret blunts the impact of his words, however, when he writes that France has been fortunate because it has few examples of royal avarice. Even Louis XI's oppressive taxation, which is normally criticized by the sixteenth-century absolutists, is justified by the wars he was forced to undertake against the duc de Bourgogne.[91]

Le Bret then addresses the king's power of the sword over his subjects. Coupled with his view on taxation, his emphasis on the permissibility of royal violence against the people separates Le Bret from absolutists like Bodin and Innocent Gentillet, who can only justify their view of absolutism on the grounds that the king will, of his own accord, act morally. In direct contrast to the common assertion that the king rules more effectively if he is loved rather than feared, Le Bret declares that it is necessary for kings to possess unlimited use of the sword,

> in order to excite reverence and fear in their subjects, to promptly dissipate tumults and seditions that can arise at any moment among the people, to prevent attempts on their sacred persons, which we have often seen occur as a result of the negligence of their guards; and finally to restrain the populace when they appear in public, which the ancients called *submotionem*.[92]

The final chapter of the work deals with the relationship between the estates general and the king. Le Bret believes the assembly is wholly dependent upon the monarch for its very existence. Again, in an echo of the "Bodinian" view, Le Bret contends that the institution serves to add lustre to the sovereign authority. He points out that the documents sent to the king from the assembly are always phrased in the form of supplications, never demands. Le Bret cites the now familiar example of the assembly at Tours convoked by Louis XI to act as arbitrator in the disagreement between him and his brother, Charles. Though they were judges, "nevertheless their resolution was not couched in these terms, 'we ordain,' but rather that the king would be humbly entreated to grant to Charles his brother, etc." Le Bret's version of the events contains none of the mildly accusatory tone of Bodin and even Loyseau, who base their arguments supporting Louis XI's authority on the fact that he manipulated the assembly into doing his will. With Le Bret, the estates general are presented as naturally accepting their exclusively supplicatory role in their relationship to the crown. Their appeal to Louis XI was worded in such a way because both the estates and the king recognized the central truth of absolutist government: kings are only obliged to follow the advice of the estates, "if natural reason, if civil justice and if the well-being and utility of the kingdom are suited to it, circumstances which brighten royal authority with a marvellous lustre."[93]

Le Bret understands and appreciates the crown's right to use all methods to achieve order and stability in the realm. Unlike Matthieu and other writers moving toward a more pragmatic view of politics, however, Le Bret does not believe that sovereign use of the sword must be justified as dictated by necessity. For Le Bret it is a positive good to instil in one's subjects the proper reverence and obedience which ensures the safety and felicity of the state.

Although the use of the general term "absolutism" in a discussion which ranges from the mid-sixteenth to the late seventeenth centuries has been deliberate and purposeful, it is worthwhile to reiterate the differences that distinguish varieties of absolutism. Absolutist theory in the seventeenth century, while echoing many of the ideas already articulated by Bodin, Gentillet and Belloy, emphasizes the untrammelled nature of royal authority. The reluctant recognition made by the *politiques* that royal power was, potentially speaking, virtually limitless, was seized upon and vigorously confirmed by later absolutist writers. Moreover, the fact that actions could be justified on other than moral grounds, first attempted by the *politiques*, albeit in the throes of painful exigency, set the stage for the emergence of a much more broadly-conceived political pragmatism on the part of seventeenth-century writers. The works of Loyseau, Baricave and Le Bret all illustrate some of the ways in which seventeenth-century absolutism differed from the ideas developed during the course of the Religious Wars. Loyseau emphasizes the connection between power and property and strengthens the idea of absolute monarchy through his arguments concerning sovereignty and the possession of the French "domain." Baricave frees the kings from the restraint of fundamental laws which had hitherto bound the monarchs according to the sixteenth-century absolutist view. Moreover, both Loyseau and Baricave steered the discussion about the nature of French government away from the topic of origins and endorsed the process of change. By doing so, the absolutists could extricate themselves from a debate that was framed by the constitutionalists and in which the absolutists were arguing from an essentially defensive position. By supporting legitimization through usage, seventeenth-century writers could re-define the parameters of the discussion on more favourable terms. Although Le Bret differs from Baricave in that Le Bret believes in the force of fundamental laws, it is not perhaps surprising that fundamental laws in his view work to support the authority of the sovereign rather than to limit it. Le Bret's belief that the king, as sovereign, is answerable to God alone, reiterates the view of earlier divine-right theorists, but he also amplifies it so that the sanctity of the monarch becomes unassailable.

By the end of the century, after more than fifty years of Louis XIV's rule (with whom Louis XI was so often compared), portraits of the Spider King by royalist writers became positively panegyrical. A case in point is the manuscript work of Joachim Legrand. Born in 1653, Legrand studied philosophy at Caen, then entered the Oratory. After six years, he went to Paris and began a career in diplomacy, for which he proved himself eminently suitable. In 1692, he accompanied the abbé d'Estrées on an ambassadorial mission to Portugal, after which the marquis de Torcy appointed him to a post in the ministry of foreign affairs. Alongside his bureaucratic duties, throughout the 1690s Legrand was engaged in research for a history of Louis XI which was, however, only completed in 1720. He died at the age of eighty in 1733.

It is not clear why Legrand's biography of Louis XI was never published. Contemporaries certainly knew of its existence; it is the last entry under the heading of Louis XI in Jacques Le Long's *Bibliothèque historique de la France*, published in 1719. According to Le Long, Legrand made a deliberate choice not to publish his biography, because "M. Le Grand believed he could not permit himself to expose yet another work [on Louis XI] to the eyes of the public if his research did not go much farther than that of others who had already written of Louis XI before him."[94] To that end, alongside all the chronicles used by previous authors, Legrand assiduously read private letters exchanged between principal participants, edicts and manifestos. Still, such authorial modesty seems misplaced in an individual who had already published numerous pamphlets and propaganda pieces in support of Louis XIV's domestic and foreign policies.[95]

Legrand's governmental sympathies correspond with his positive vision of Louis XI. The intensity of Legrand's admiration is, however, slightly unexpected. His huge *Vie et Histoire de Louis XI*, running to over nine hundred folio pages, is a monument to its subject. It is as if Legrand intended to refute all those aspersions cast on Louis XI's character by so many authors since Commynes. Legrand begins by discussing Louis XI's personality, incidentally demonstrating how he was influenced by the pragmatic view of politics developed in the first half of the century. Legrand does not deny that Louis XI was cruel at times, but he contends that the king's harshness was a necessary response to the troublesome era. Moreover, Legrand reiterates the ideas of early seventeenth-century absolutists concerning Louis XI's expenditure on the national welfare, justifying the onerous taxation by maintaining that, even if taxes were greater under Louis XI than they had ever been, nevertheless the revenue was expended in accordance with the best interests of France. Most importantly, Louis XI was indefatigable in his efforts on behalf of the kingdom, working relentlessly to secure peace and prosperity for France.[96]

The first three books of the work deal with Louis XI's years as dauphin. Book four sketches the propitious circumstances in France at the time of Louis's accession:

> Never had a prince succeeded to the throne in more favourable circumstances, nor with more appropriate qualities to be able to profit from them. He had passed the first follies of youth. He had experience and capacity, his reputation was well established both within and outside [the borders of France] . . . [97]

Legrand's discussion of the War of the Public Weal indicates a strongly anti-noble bias. It is abundantly clear that Legrand believes Louis XI was not the cause of the conflict, as others had argued, but rather it was the rapacity of the magnates that had brought about the struggle. Far from acting tyrannically in the early years of his reign, Louis XI showed himself to be both moderate and reasonable. During the first phase of the conflict, when troubles arose between Louis XI and the duc de Bretagne, Louis called an assembly of notables. At that assembly, Louis demonstrated his respect for the liberties of his advisors by assuring greater freedom of speech through his absence from the first sitting. Jean Dauvet, *premier président* of the Parlement of Toulouse, was so clear and convincing on the king's behalf "that the princes and lords avowed that they had come to Tours predisposed against the king, but that they were obliged to recognize that the king was right and the duc de Bretagne was wrong."[98]

Legrand evinces little sympathy for the noble cause; at one point he appears to demean the war by characterizing it as little more than a generational conflict. When Legrand cites Louis XI's response to the nobles' manifesto in which they claim to be working for the people, he appears to be not only recounting the words of Louis XI's spokesman in the assembly, but expressing his own opinions about the real intentions of the nobles as well: "With great promises to comfort the people, they desolated the countryside, they interrupted commerce, they pillaged and stole, they put everyone into dungeons . . . "[99] The envoy goes on to explain that, if Louis XI had given in to the nobles and allowed them to continue abusing their vassals, these same nobles would never have uttered a single protest on behalf of the public good.

Legrand makes much of the nobles' insincerity in claiming to fight for the public good. The War of the Public Weal should have been called the war of the public ill, as the comte de Dammartin had written to the comte de Charolais. Legrand comments that it was the enormous pensions which Louis XI was forced to pay to the nobles that resulted in greater taxation. The Treaty of Conflans, between Louis XI and the rebelling nobles, is roundly condemned by Legrand. In his view, it only provided for the particularist aims of the rebels; consequently it was not destined to endure long. It was ignominious, not only because of the burden of noble pensions assumed by the crown (and ultimately the people), but also because it left

France open to invasion, with the capital, Paris, on the borders of France proper, and thus exposed to the threat of sack by foreign armies.[100] Legrand asserts that Louis XI was forced to accept peace terms which he recognized as detrimental to the people, and later, the implied connection of the people's interests with those of the king is picked up and amplified by a number of nineteenth-century writers. The reference to exposed borders may well be a reflection of contemporary concerns: Legrand may be expressing the anxiety about foreign alliances against France, spearheaded by the Emperor on the one hand and William III of England on the other, which ostensibly lay behind France's foreign policy during the last years of Louis XIV's reign.

Legrand challenges the most common interpretations of Louis XI once again when he discusses the estates general of 1467. According to Legrand's account, after having condemned the alienation of Normandy to Louis's brother, Charles, the estates turned their attention to domestic affairs, which were in disarray. In direct contradiction to sixteenth-century versions, Legrand maintains that Louis XI *asked* the assembly to appoint a commission to help him set France's house in order. Moreover, Legrand believes that Louis XI's request was sincerely made.[101]

After having dealt exhaustively with the so-called War of the Public Weal and its aftermath, and settling the blame for the conflict firmly on the shoulders of the nobles, Legrand proceeds to recount the events of the rest of Louis XI's reign. In several instances, Legrand's account differs substantially from the versions put forward by writers negatively disposed to the king. With regard to the duc de Berry's untimely death in 1472, for example, Legrand seems content to assign the cause of death to quartian fever, despite the death of Charles's mistress just one month earlier which, Legrand freely admits, was the result of deliberate poisoning. The only reference Legrand makes to the possible poisoning of Charles is to condemn the comte de Charolais's willingness to spread groundless rumours by publishing a manifesto designed to inflame the public against a supposedly murderous king.[102]

Perhaps the most interesting aspects of Legrand's work occur at the very end, after Legrand recounts the death of Louis XI. Legrand launches into a eulogy of his fallen hero, asserting that "France has had few kings who have more of the qualities necessary for governing well." Despite the fulsome praise, Legrand denies writing an apologia for Louis XI. Legrand's somewhat disingenuous disclaimer is followed by a comparison of Louis XI and Louis XIII, in which the former is portrayed as more able:

If ever one wanted to make the parallel [between these two kings], one would find that the first [Louis XI] had advantages over the other; with less considerable forces, he overcame greater obstacles, he made more conquests and he secured them by good treaties whereas Louis XIII and his minister Cardinal Richelieu left the kingdom, upon their deaths, in cruel wars that were only terminated several years later.[103]

Clearly, the implied comparison is between Louis XI and Louis XIV, since both faced similarly tumultuous circumstances upon their accession to the throne, and through the force of their abilities were each able to overcome troubles to establish peace and prosperity, the twin pillars of greatness.

Given Louis XI's many contributions to the kingdom of France, Legrand argues that he deserves much better from posterity. Legrand blames Louis XI's black reputation on two individuals: Charles, duc de Bourgogne, and Louis XII. Legrand's attempt to discredit the "myths" about Louis XI promulgated under these two rulers demonstrates more than anything else his commitment to establishing Louis XI as a model monarch. The duc de Bourgogne, through his toady, Thomas Basin, fostered the idea of Louis XI as a tyrant, a Nero. Throughout his history, Basin was determined "to give the most sinister interpretations to each action or to each word." What is worse, this negative portrait of Louis XI was adopted and embellished by Claude Seyssel, under the approving eye of Louis XII:

> One would be surprised that, in order to make his own eulogy, this prince had allowed the memory of his predecessor to be defamed, if one did not know that he was suckled with the milk of hatred which he always retained against Louis XI and against his children.[104]

In fact, according to Legrand, Louis XI had treated Louis XII's mother, Marie de Cleves, exceedingly well, especially given her opposition to Louis XI during the War of the Public Weal. It is clear that Legrand views Louis XII as an ingrate. During his reign, not only Seyssel, but all writers dealing with the reign of Louis XI, were forced to adopt a biased position: "It is the testimony of these partial writers which has formed an idea of the reign of Louis XI that hardly conforms to the truth." In the end, Legrand argues that, if one were to compare these two kings, taking into account the state of the realm at the time Louis XII mounted the throne and its corresponding condition at his death, "the one is called a good man and Louis XI, despite all the faults with which one could reproach him, was a great king."[105]

Images of Louis XI evoked by absolutists of all stripes from the mid-sixteenth to the late seventeenth centuries demonstrate two related points. First, the consistent, one might say ubiquitous, use of Louis XI by absolutists of the sixteenth and seventeenth centuries provides solid evidence for the validity of a broad concept such as absolutism. The use of the term as an over-arching historical construct does not, however, deny the different ways in which absolutist ideas were formulated. It is clear that seventeenth-century absolutism was, in many ways, a less compromising conception of monarchical authority than that articulated by *politique* absolutists in the sixteenth century. Although the principle of monarchical self-limitation that is at the heart of absolutist theory remained intact, the scope of that self-limitation was constricted over the course of one hundred and fifty years. Fundamental law continued to bind the king's actions, but it was similarly diminished. The private property rights of individual citizens, hitherto protected by natural law, could be circumvented, even denied entirely, in the interests of the state. The notion of the state as an entity with its own needs and interests began to emerge in the course of the seventeenth century, but these early statist formulations still identified the state with the king.[106] This transitional entity – the king-state – divested itself of the personalized moral responsibility that was the *sine qua non* of sixteenth-century absolutism. In the course of this evolution from *politique* to statist absolutism, Louis XI was transformed from a morally-flawed but effective monarch into a political sage. The idea of "mettre les rois hors de page," which carried a negative connotation among the sixteenth-century resistance theorists, becomes in the seventeenth century a positive achievement, though no less evocative for its recharacterization. By way of contrast, the "guerre du bien public," a prime example of laudable and justified resistance to tyranny, becomes in the seventeenth century nothing more than an ill-conceived ruse employed to disguise the intent to usurp the power and authority of the king. This may be due to the manner in which the absolutist view came to dominate the intellectual environment under the first Bourbon kings.

Finally, one should take into account the new attention paid to the force of necessity in politics. Although, by and large, the new pragmatism developing in the seventeenth century seems to be most evident among absolutists, in some instances an appreciation of circumstances mitigates the harsh judgement of Louis XI offered by constitutionalists. Indeed, the appeal to necessity, along with the new emphasis on the "true" interests of the state, developed into a coherent theory known as *raison d'état*, whose promoters contribute more than any other group to the rehabilitation of Louis XI's historical reputation, so that for a brief period the Spider King enjoys almost universal acclaim.

5 "Qui nescit dissimulare, nescit regnare"

Louis XI and *raison d'état*

During the reign of Louis XIII, there emerged in France a set of ideas about the state, the manner in which it could be preserved, and how its needs could best be fulfilled.[1] Although the notion of the state's primary importance was already incipient in the thought of *politique* writers during the last quarter of the sixteenth century, *raison d'état*, which refers both to actions taken on behalf of the state and the justifications for such actions, became much more clearly formulated during the 1630s and 1640s, largely due to the efforts of writers commenting on Richelieu's policies. Despite the fact that a considerable amount of scholarship has been devoted to the study of *raison d'état*, or reason of state, the concept remains elusive. It can be seen from the organicist viewpoint as a form of thought superior to ordinary assumptions. Friedrich Meinecke, pursuing a strand of the Hegelian tradition, credits the state with a disembodied rationality, seldom perceptible to human reason. Modern interpretation of this kind makes much of seventeenth-century discussion of the mysteries of statecraft, or *arcana imperii*.[2] A more usual approach is to see *raison d'état* as characterized by a set of rules concerning the conduct of government which differ, sometimes greatly, from those rules which are traditionally believed to regulate private conduct. A spectrum from natural law to pragmatic views of morality allows wide differences within these parameters. Two of the best known scholars of French *raison d'état*, W. F. Church and Etienne Thuau, disagree quite markedly in their views of the relationship between religion and politics, which lies at the heart of any definition of *raison d'état*. While Church believes that *raison d'état* is essentially an attempt to justify exceptional actions on the part of the government within a Christian moral framework,[3] Thuau interprets the theory to mean a complete separation of politics from accepted Christian codes of ethics and morality.[4]

Another dimension is added to the analysis of *raison d'état* thought when the historical references commonly found in *raison d'état* treatises are examined. A comparison of references to Louis XI in different works, for example, highlights the shifts of emphasis found within the corpus of *raison d'état* literature. Among *raison d'état* writers, Louis XI's reputed pragmatism and political acumen made him a worthwhile object of interest and a useful example to support their arguments. This is especially true because of the maxim allegedly spoken by Louis XI, "qui nescit dissimulare, nescit regnare" ("he who does know how to dissemble, does not know how to reign"). The phrase was used already by sixteenth-century theorists to demonstrate Louis XI's reprehensible view of politics. It is even more commonly found in *raison d'état* literature but, by contrast, *raison d'état* writers present the statement as an established political maxim. Simply through the re-interpretation of this single phrase, Louis XI is transformed from a villain to a sage.

Although the phrase is probably classical in origin, few seventeenth-century authors concerned themselves with its proper attribution.[5] Moreover, it is never made clear in what context Louis XI supposedly uttered the saying, other than teaching it to his son, the future Charles VIII. "Qui nescit dissimulare, nescit regnare" was considered to be Louis XI's motto, despite the fact that the phrase did not originate with him, and, in fact, the king may never have actually uttered the words. It became a central axiom of *raison d'état* thought and Louis XI its most illustrious practitioner.

Defining the precise role of Louis XI for *raison d'état* writers is, however, complicated by the contradictory goals of these authors. The different ways in which the reputation of Louis XI is evoked reflects the complex nature of *raison d'état* thought, and specifically its relationship to Machiavellism and Tacitism.[6] Clearly, in modern scholarship, *raison d'état*, Machiavellism and Tacitism are not interchangeable terms. In contrast to *raison d'état*, Machiavellism and Tacitism refer to modes of personal as well as public conduct. It could be argued, however, that seventeenth-century writers identified Machiavellism and Tacitism as two terms roughly synonymous with *raison d'état*, connoting either a pejorative or positive interpretation of *raison d'état* principles. The references to Louis XI, so often linked with the Emperor Tiberius, amply demonstrate the intersection of Machiavellism, Tacitism and *raison d'état*. The connection between Louis XI and Machiavellism is far from clear cut. As a group, *raison d'état* writers seem unsure about how the lessons of Louis XI ought to be applied, i.e. whether his ideas and actions supported or refuted Machiavelli. Louis XI was used by some writers to distinguish *raison d'état* principles from the far more reprehensible doctrines of Machiavelli. On the other hand, there were *raison d'état* theorists who willingly characterized their principles as Machiavellian, believing that critics of Machiavelli had misinterpreted him. These supporters of Machiavelli employed Louis XI to demonstrate not only that Machiavellian ideas, properly understood, had operated to the benefit of France, but also to show that the Florentine had only articulated principles which were already advocated by others. Louis XI was invoked by *raison d'état* writers of all shades of opinion, from the most committed *étatistes* who argued that the good of the state required a separate political morality, to those writers earnestly trying to argue that *raison d'état* principles were congruent with accepted Christian ethics. How these writers refer to Louis XI indicates the rich diversity of opinion within the *raison d'état* camp.

Gabriel Naudé, the bibliophile secretary of Cardinal Mazarin, was perhaps the most clear-thinking and articulate of the *raison d'état* theorists. Born in 1600 into a modest but respectable family, Naudé's love of learning was quickly revealed during his studies while at the Collège du Cardinal Lemoine and then at the prestigious Collège de Navarre. In 1620 he published, at his own expense, *Le Marfore ou discours contre les libelles*, in which he both defended the duc de Luynes and argued for the king's right to choose his own favourites. As one biographer wrote, Naudé presented himself as the "ardent champion of a strong and resolute ruler beset on all sides by ignorant demagogues."[7] Already in *Le Marfore*, Naudé's positive views regarding Louis XI are revealed. In the context of his attack on the "calumniators," Naudé asserts that Louis XI embodied that monarchical attribute which best reflected the Divine Sovereign: the ability and willingness to better the lot of the poor through the distribution of royal largesse:

> King Louis XI (with whom Philippe de Comine shared the same opinion) said he passed the time making and unmaking, elevating and lowering, giving to and taking away from, those he saw fit: Princes seem to do this in imitation of the Sovereign monarch, called that because, apart from his goodness and mercy, in Psalm 122, he "raises the pauper out of filth into wealth."[8]

Although Naudé originally intended to pursue a career in medicine, attending the universities of both Paris and Padua, his medical studies were relegated to a secondary interest when he entered the service of Cardinal Bagni in 1631. It was during his period of tenure as a librarian and Latin secretary to Bagni that Naudé wrote and published his most famous work, *Considérations politiques sur les coups d'estat* (1639). It is very likely that Richelieu and Naudé were acquainted at the time the *Considérations* was published, and after the death of Antonio Barberini (for whom Naudé worked after Cardinal Bagni), Naudé entered Richelieu's service to take charge of his private library. After Richelieu's death, Naudé passed rather smoothly into the service of his successor, Cardinal Mazarin and, in his post as the first minister's librarian, Naudé engaged in a vigorous enterprise of book acquisition. During the Fronde, Naudé again demonstrated his loyalty both to his employer and to the idea of a strong state in his book, *Mascurat* or *Jugement de tout ce qui a esté imprimé contre le Cardinal Mazarin* (1649). While Mazarin was in self-imposed exile, Naudé laboured at the court of Queen Christina of Sweden, but when Mazarin returned to power, Naudé himself set out to return to France. He died on the journey in 1653.

In his *Considérations politiques sur les coups d'estat*, Gabriel Naudé provides us with the clearest exposition of *raison d'état* theory. Naudé praises prudence as a virtue. Rather like the neo-Stoics, to whom he openly acknowledged an intellectual debt, Naudé distinguishes between types of prudence, although he specifies only two sorts, as opposed to Lipsius's three.[9] "Easy and ordinary" prudence, which conforms to the accepted tenets of Christian morality, characterizes governmental behaviour in most situations. "Extraordinary" prudence, which encompasses those actions that seem contrary to morality, is employed only when conditions are so urgent as to require a *coup d'état*. While Naudé insists that this second form of prudence is to be followed only when the situation is dire, unlike the neo-Stoics, he not only countenances the more extreme variation of prudence, but endorses it as sometimes necessary for the preservation of the state:

> He has an easier and freer pace because of the great, weighty and danger-
> ous duty he carries; that is why it suits him to walk with a gait which
> might seem to others disordered and unbalanced, but which is to him
> necessary, fair and legitimate.[10]

Naudé asserts that, in certain circumstances, subterfuge and dissimulation are indeed permissible. He endorses, for example, the use of spies in order to ascertain the intentions of foreign princes. He then provides an historical example: "Louis XI, the wisest and most sensible of our kings, held as a principal maxim of his government, that he who does not know how to dissemble, does not know how to reign."[11] Clearly, the famous utterance is invested with a newly positive significance. It is telling, as well, that Naudé refers to Louis XI as "le plus sage . . . de nos roys." The *raison d'état* theorists have found their exemplar.

It becomes increasingly obvious just why subsequent writers perceived an affinity of purpose between Louis XI and Richelieu; the cardinal's own group of writers saw the fifteenth-century monarch as an object for emulation. Louis XI is not the sole recipient of such accolades, however. "Le Tyran," Charles IX, is similarly rehabilitated. The St Bartholomew's Day Massacre, denounced by Protestants and Catholics alike, is dismissed by Naudé as necessary, even just, given the dire situation.[12] Whereas in François Hotman's tirade, *De Furoribus Gallicis*, Louis XI and Charles IX are linked in infamy, for Naudé they are two examples of skilful monarchs.[13]

In discussing those "masterstrokes" which may be employed in times of peril, Naudé cites the actions of several French kings as re-establishing order out of confusion. Naudé points out that, despite Charles VII's adroit use of Joan of Arc, France remained at the time of his death "like those unhealthy and consumptive bodies that only breathe with laboured effort . . . " Since that time, however, France has recovered and been maintained in glory "by the means of stratagems practised by Louis XI, François I, Charles IX and yet by those who succeeded them."[14]

The phrase "qui nescit dissimulare, nescit regnare" alludes to another way in which Louis XI's reputation benefited from the emergence of *raison d'état* theory. Louis XI was criticized by sixteenth-century writers because he did not provide an adequate education for his son and successor, Charles VIII.

This issue is addressed by Naudé in his *Addition à l'histoire de Louis II* [*sic*] (1630). Naudé states that Louis XI has been maligned about his lack of regard for education by those proponents of learning as the necessary prerequisite for a just and effective monarch. He believes that the general assumption of Louis XI's ignorance is based upon the failure of both the historian, Pierre Matthieu, and the memorialist, Philippe de Commynes, to provide information about the king's childhood. To those determined to deal harshly with Louis XI, this lack of treatment indicates the desire of the two authors to hide some deficiency of education. Naudé launches a two-pronged attack against this negative characterization. First, Naudé asserts that Louis XI did indeed follow the proper course of education for a young prince, contrary to the accepted portrait of him as an ignorant malfeasant. Second, knowing much more than the famous five words of Latin, Louis XI actively chose, for understandable reasons, not to force a rigorous, and possibly irrelevant, course of study on his son.[15]

The *Addition* effectively complements the *Considérations politiques* as a work espousing *raison d'état* views. The monarch must always retain a flexible view of the world, his mind neither clouded with esoterica nor his actions confined within an irrelevant moral framework. Louis XI acts as a guide in both respects, his actions bespeaking intellectual agility unhampered by dogma, and an understanding of both the necessary and the just, and the best means of bringing the two as closely together as possible.

The *Addition* concentrates on dispelling the myth of Louis XI's ignorance, but along the way it also illuminates the new interpretation of his method of government. This is notable in Naudé's discussion of "qui nescit . . . nescit." Naudé's approbation is evident as well in Chapter Three of the *Addition*, which examines Louis XI's education in languages and the "ordinary sciences." Naudé says that, if the science of government "consists of making oneself obeyed, there is no doubt that Louis XI was the most knowledgeable Prince who ever reigned in France, because he was the best obeyed."[16] (Naudé seems to have conveniently forgotten that Louis XI's reign was singularly troubled by a noble rebellion and a notably recalcitrant parlement!) Naudé goes on to say that Louis XI "placed the kings his successors beyond restraint." In contrast to the condemnations voiced by Hotman, Beza and Buchanan, Louis XI receives the accolades of *raison d'état* writers for having put French kings *hors de page*!

The newer laudatory light in which Louis XI is portrayed is reflected as well in the comments by other authors on the *Addition*, included at the beginning of the work. Naudé and his subject are closely connected in Colletet's verse, which begins: "Considering the facts of eternal memory / of a Prince that Heaven made equal to itself / I admired his grandeur, and said to myself / that one could add nothing to his glory."[17] Despite his belief that Louis XI's glory was such that it could not be further amplified, Colletet, after reading Naudé's new history, is convinced that only Naudé is capable "of brightening the sun and of whitening ivory." According to Colletet, the historical figure and the contemporary writer benefit by association: "By him your name acquires great honours here, / by you, his vanquishes time and forgetfulness; / But between the virtues that you are elevating / when you make us see that he is full of knowledge, / you show us how much your mind is learned."

The pragmatism of Louis XI, as demonstrated in the oft-repeated phrase attributed to him in which he endorses the use of dissimulation, is even more amply illustrated by the association, forged in the minds of seventeenth-century theorists, of Louis XI with the Emperor Tiberius. The enduring quality of this association is quite remarkable and it reflects the growth of interest in the historian Philippe de Commynes and in Tacitus.

Even prior to the full flowering of *raison d'état* theory, the two models of dissimulation were found in tandem. In Pierre Matthieu's history of Louis XI, the Spider King is linked with Tiberius, though in a somewhat incidental manner. According to Matthieu, with the death of the king's brother, Charles of France, the treaty between Louis XI and the rebelling princes was broken. Charles le Téméraire, duc de Bourgogne, wishing to re-ignite the conflagration so recently dampened, attempted to raise the towns against Louis XI with written attacks on the king. Matthieu writes that the duke "spoke more unworthily of [Louis XI] than did King Artaban of Persia, of Tiberius, describing him as a tyrant over his people, a murderer of his brother, and perjured of his promises, and in this fury, he began to make war by fire, which he had never done."[18] Though the connection is tenuous here, perhaps even coincidental to this discussion, the association appears more deliberate if one notes Rodolphe Le Maistre's statement that Henri IV commanded him to write *Le Tibère françois* just as he had commanded Matthieu to compose a history of Louis XI. In his preface to *Le Tibère françois*, dedicated to Louis XIII, Le Maistre writes that Louis XIII's father, Henri IV, surpassed all the other kings "in prudence and good judgement, not less than in valour." Henri le Grand, as he was called, believed in the usefulness of history and commissioned Le Maistre and Matthieu to examine the two historical figures who would provide the most illustrative examples.[19] In Henri IV's mind, at least, these two monarchs served as dual pillars of effective government. It seems probable that Matthieu, like Le Maistre, was aware of the king's admiration for these two historical figures and therefore presented them in tandem to heighten the effect. Indeed, the connection of Tiberius and Louis XI has not gone unnoticed by modern scholars. Etienne Thuau clearly perceives the links made by seventeeth-century writers, both those supporting *raison d'état* theories and those espousing the more traditional morally-grounded view of *politiques*: "In effect, Tiberius, Nero, Louis XI, objects of repulsion for the humanists, are, for the defenders of the state, examples to consider and to follow."[20]

Gabriel Naudé makes the connection between Tiberius and Louis XI in his *Considérations politiques*. Not surprisingly, the association of the two figures is made with regard to the dissimulation practised by both kings.

Naudé cites both Louis XI's maxim on the topic and the statement made about Tiberius, "that he valued none of his virtues more than his ability to deceive."[21]

Some *raison d'état* writers were more overt in their attempts to rehabilitate Machiavelli through identification with Tacitus and Commynes. Louis XI and Tiberius were presented by these authors as the best personification of Machiavellian ideas. Despite the general opprobrium with which Machiavelli's ideas were received in France in the early seventeenth century, it is clear that Machiavelli was not universally execrated, and Louis XI plays a role in the attempt to make Machiavelli more acceptable to political thinkers and the literate public alike. In his manuscript work, *Apologie pour Machiavelle en faveur des princes et les ministres d'estat* (1643), Louis Machon intends to prove that Machiavellian doctrine is not as repugnant as it has been made out to be by its critics.[22] Machon maintains not only that Machiavelli has been misinterpreted by later commentators but also that many of the ideas he espoused were already accepted as tenets of government. Machiavelli's statements about the value of good ministers, for example, merely reiterated what most members of the court already knew:

> Philippe de Commines, nicknamed the French Tacitus, even though he never knew a word of Latin, said in his history of Louis XI that one usually found next to princes some clerics or men of the robe who are valuable when they are good and very dangerous when they are bad, who have a story every other minute, in the best of which one might find benefits from bad advice.[23]

It is indicative that Commynes is here referred to as "le Tacite français," especially since he had also been called "notre Machiavel." The connection of these three authors underscores the complicated and sometimes contradictory nature of Louis XI's place in seventeenth-century *raison d'état*.

The connection between Louis XI and Tiberius is also found in the discussion of Maxime Six, "Dissimuler, pour bien regner:"

> Louis XI said to his son Charles VIII that he knew enough Latin, and that [Charles] would know enough when he understood well this maxim: he does not know how to reign, who does not know how to dissimulate. The Emperor Tiberius loved none of his virtues more than dissimulation, as the most useful and the most necessary . . .[24]

It is important to note here that Machon cites Commynes via Pierre Matthieu's *Histoire de Louis XI*, and it is therefore not surprising that the reference to Louis XI is immediately followed by one to Tiberius.

In his efforts to refute the attacks made by Machiavelli's critics, Machon directs himself specifically to Innocent Gentillet's *Discours contre Machiavel* (1576). What is ironic and highly interesting from the point of view of Louis XI's historical reputation is that both Gentillet and Machon use a positive portrait of Louis XI to support their contradictory assertions.

Gentillet wants to prove Louis's success as a monarch who did not resort to Machiavellian methods, while Machon argues that Louis's ability to overcome numerous obstacles to establish peace and security for France not only confirms the validity of Machiavelli's ideas but, moreover, it proves that the concept of pragmatism in politics was not unique to the doctrines of Machiavelli. The juxtaposition of these two works shows the complexity of the relationship between the reputation of Louis XI and Machiavelli within the context of the development of *raison d'état* in France.

References to Louis XI can be found in the works of other, more moderate, *raison d'état* writers as well. Jean de Silhon (159?–1667) discusses Louis XI in the context of his justification for Richelieu's policies, which forms the core of the work, *Le Ministre d'estat* (1631). In a general sense, the careers of Silhon and Naudé are similar. Not much is known about Silhon's early life, but, like Naudé, he became a secretary, first to Richelieu and then to Mazarin. And like Naudé, during the Fronde, Silhon felt compelled to compose a defence of Mazarin, *Esclaircissement sur quelques difficultés touchant l'administration du Cardinal Mazarin* (1650).[25] Unlike Naudé, however, who had been exposed to, and influenced by, the worldly views of the Italian ecclesiastical luminaries, Silhon was profoundly religious. Silhon's work demonstrates the conflict between traditional faith and a necessary political pragmatism. Of all the *raison d'état* writers, Silhon was perhaps the most determined to fit the new theory of politics into the traditional Christian framework.[26]

Nevertheless, Silhon was committed to the idea of *raison d'état*; he recognized that there were times when exigency forced the government to act in a seemingly unjust manner. In his *Panegyrique au Cardinal de Richelieu sur ce qui s'est passé aux derniers troubles de France* (1629), Silhon offers a justification for the harsh treatment of some of the Huguenots. Moreover, his early ideas on *raison d'état* already contain references to Louis XI. In a letter to the bishop of Nantes, Philippe Cospean, in which Silhon expressed his thanks that Cospean liked his work, Silhon outlines his main ideas about the relationship between religion and politics and the necessary role of dissimulation in government:

> Finally, on this saying so much recommended and practised by Louis XI –
> that he who does not know how to dissemble does not know how to reign
> – I will research the cases in which dissimulation can be permitted, and
> amply discuss the nature and usage of equivocation: the abuse of it is so
> great, and commerce and society are so offended by it, that no one had
> ever aired so dangerous a matter.[27]

Silhon's most important work, and the work in which his ideas are most clearly expounded, is *Le Ministre d'estat*. The last discourse of the work justifies Richelieu's actions in attempting to crush the Huguenot opposition. Silhon argues that Richelieu used prudence in choosing the greatest good for the state, even if that may have caused hardship for some. The rest of the work is directed to a more general examination of the qualities possessed by a worthy minister of state. Silhon seems poised between the *étatiste* and traditionally moral viewpoints. He begins by asserting that a good minister derives great benefit from learning, especially with regard to the knowledge of the moral. Silhon goes on to modify these moral considerations, noting in the title of the eleventh discourse of Book One, "That a minister must regulate his conduct by the interest of the state and of the Prince," with the proviso that "he not offend justice."[28] Despite a certain reluctance on Silhon's part to allow *raison d'état* free rein, it seems apparent that Silhon recognizes prudence and pragmatism as cornerstones of effective government. With regard to prudence, Silhon makes reference again to "qui nescit . . . regnare," a phrase which had begun to epitomize *raison d'état* theory. In the fourteenth discourse of Book Two, Silhon discusses how to deal with agents of the pope, "and if it is lawful to use dissimulation, and how." Silhon asserts that, indeed, dissimulation is permitted in cases where one must defend oneself. He does some fancy footwork to justify dissimulation, and it is clear that Silhon does not feel as comfortable as Naudé in justifying amoral behaviour solely on the basis of the good of the state. Dissimulation, according to Silhon, may be used "not to deceive, but to protect oneself from deceit, and not to make a poison out of what must be only a preservative. In this sense, it is still true that dissimulation is permitted and that he who does not know how to dissemble, does not know how to reign."[29]

Louis XI is very highly praised by Silhon for his ability to conduct the affairs of France with stratagems that avoided exposing it to the ruinous condition of war:

> The life of one of our kings who deserved the appellation of wise is not less considerable than the lives of those who have worn the title of conqueror, and a neighbouring Prince gave him this praise, that never did a king have so few armies as he did, and never did a man give him so much trouble. The difficulties which troubled him, the artifices he was forced to combat, the conspiracies from which he had to protect himself and the enterprises of strangers, rendered useless by his prudence, have made him worthy of a title given to lesser persons: that of the Great. Few princes have had greater affairs in hand than Louis XI, nor more enemies arrayed against them: his principal officers betrayed him, the princes of his blood abandoned him. He saw England, Burgundy, Flanders and Brittany conspiring for his ruin. And nevertheless his skill overcame these difficulties, without the deployment of armies or the conducting of battles. He vanquished his enemies, without making much noise nor rigorous efforts . . . [30]

It is important to note as well that Silhon's laudatory appraisal of Louis XI follows closely on the heels of a brief mention of Tiberius and his dissimulating tactics.[31]

Silhon feels compelled, however, to modify his positive portrait of Louis XI and, in the thirteenth discourse of Book One, which discusses the need for ministers to be educated, Silhon asserts that Louis XI's particular skills, though valuable, were by no means those qualities which should be most highly admired. His virtues were corrupted by a lack of moderation; his courage, for example, "lacked rule and order."[32] Moreover, Silhon roundly criticizes Louis XI for not taking advice from his counsellors and relying too heavily on his own judgement. Silhon cites the famous anecdote that Louis XI boasted he owned the strongest horse in the world because it could carry himself and all his council.[33] As a result of his unwillingness to heed the advice of others, "he sometimes made such enormous errors . . . that all the world took notice."[34]

In a more general sense, Silhon is also demonstrating his uncertainty about the precise role dissimulation should play in government when he says, "there are nobler maxims for reigning, and more exalted principles than dissimulation."[35] Silhon is much less willing than is Naudé to admit that a different set of precepts governs public behaviour. He appears to want to continue operating within a moral framework consistent with that which defines private behaviour. Nevertheless, realizing that the interests of the state often require a certain ruthlessness and even deceit, Silhon seems ready to blur the edges of the outline in order to bring aspects of amorality into government. Silhon's view of Louis XI, although generally positive, indicates the ambivalence which is apparent on the more theoretical level: while recognizing that the security of the state may require extraordinary measures on the part of the monarch, and consequently praising Louis XI for his effective management of state affairs in what can only be termed desperate circumstances, Silhon remains reluctant to abandon completely those moral strictures which provide some safeguard against the wanton abuse of power.

Unlike Naudé and Machon, who make references to Louis XI and Tiberius within their defence of Machiavelli, Silhon employs Louis XI (and to a lesser extent Tiberius) as positive figures in an effort to refute the charges of Machiavellism so often levelled at *raison d'état* writers by the anti-*raison d'état* camp. Moderate *étatistes*, like Silhon, wanted to present the ideas of Tacitus and Commynes as an "antidote" to the viciously motivated doctrines of the Florentine. Consequently, Tiberius and Louis XI were praised in an effort to stem the tide of Machiavellism by adopting and diluting some of its least morally offensive maxims.

The use of Louis XI, and his biographer Commynes, to prove the erroneousness of Machiavelli's assertions, is even more amply demonstrated in Didier Herauld's *Fragment de l'examen du Prince du Machiavel* (1633). As its title implies, the work is designed to point out the falsities contained within *The Prince*, although Herauld is not zealously anti-Machiavellian. In the opening chapter, in fact, Herauld tries to strike a balance between those who praise Machiavelli and those who execrate him. Nevertheless, although Herauld admits that Machiavelli possessed a formidable knowledge about politics, he maintains that the latter's arguments were hampered by a lack of knowledge about science and letters.

Herauld begins by taking issue with Machiavelli's definition of a prince. He argues that Machiavelli's prince is not a well-established monarch but rather a petty potentate who can only hold on to power through oppression and violence. Many of Machiavelli's assertions, according to Herauld, are built on this narrow and fundamentally mistaken characterization. With regard to his council, for example, a tyrant will place little faith in it and ultimately destroy it, while a true prince will maintain his councillors in their dignities even if, because of dire circumstances, he is forced to limit his council to only a few men.[36]

Herauld then begins a lengthy section in which he discusses the virtues necessary to a minister. The four essential qualities of a good minister are prudence, integrity, loyalty to king and country, and popularity with the people. With regard to the first of these qualities, Herauld asserts that prudence will consist of "a general knowledge of worldly affairs, a particular familiarity with the affairs of the prince, and of his state, and especially, good sense and solid, assured judgement."[37] As an example of insufficient prudence, Herauld cites Louis XI's decision to meet the duc de Bourgogne at Péronne:

> At the same spot where Philippe de Commynes quite rightly elevates common sense over all the worldly sciences, as we said previously, he notes that king Louis XI had perfectly good common sense (which was the very term he used) and besides this still he was otherwise lettered; and nevertheless, the same historian remarks that this prince, for not knowing enough, made very great errors, among which can be counted when he went to find the duc de Bourgogne at Péronne, where he received the greatest affront that a prince of his quality could have received.[38]

Citing Commynes further, Herauld points out how basic common sense can be undermined through a lack of familiarity with history. Nevertheless, Herauld admits that, in the case of the famous meeting at Péronne, such a risk was taken because the situation was so dire "that there was no other possibility to save [Louis XI's] life or his state."[39]

Herauld's stance as a moderate advocate of *raison d'état* is indicated by his discussion of the second quality of a good minister. In true *raison d'état* style, Herauld presents virtue and integrity as relative terms whose precise definition is circumscribed by the situation:

> A particular minister or confidant of a Prince must be a good man, but in the courtly manner, that he must have the virtues and qualities that are particularly required in a minister, but it is not necessary that he have all the qualities of a man so exactly scrupulous and conscientious: which qualities, on the contrary, one considers incompatible with the others . . .[40]

Herauld utilizes Commynes's *Mémoires* as a source of anecdotes with which to point out the errors in Machiavelli, but he does not seek to denounce the pragmatism characterizing *raison d'état*. Rather, it appears that Herauld wants to divorce the oppressive form of rule which he believes to be advocated in *The Prince* from the useful political observations contained in the work. Thus expurgated, Machiavelli's ideas, coupled with those of Commynes, can inform both ministers and monarchs as how best to promote the interests of the state.

The analysis of Louis XI's importance to early seventeenth-century theorists is complicated still further by his positive portrayal by writers less positively disposed to *raison d'état*. In general, Louis XI remained an exemplary figure whose actions should be emulated. Honorat de Meynier (1570–1638) advocated a limited role for prudence in government, but on the whole his *Les Demandes curieuses et les reponses libres* (1635) extolled the virtues of sincere royal piety and adherence to traditional Christian virtues. The potential tension between "prudence" and "justice" lies at the heart of the discussion which follows the query: "In what fashion must one understand Seneca's sentence, 'qui nescit dissimulare, nescit regnare,' that Louis XI . . . gave as a single lesson in Latin to his son, Charles VIII, king of France after him?"[41] Meynier responds by asserting that, although there are some instances in which dissimulation may be permitted, the key to the meaning of the phrase lies in the recognition that dissimulation may only be used sparingly and in situations of great necessity:

> It is thus useful in order to reign, that the Prince know how to dissimulate if one must, with whom, on what occasion and when it is good to do it in order to conserve his honour, his state and his life. But one must guard against deceiving for the sole desire to do harm to others. Because in the last instance, dissimulation can only be very damaging to him, and especially if it is common for him to dissimulate in all instances, with all sorts of persons, for all subjects, in all places and at all times . . .[42]

Louis XI is used to indicate some "good" uses of dissimulation. Meynier demonstrates his ignorance of the events of Louis XI's reign when he cites Louis's efforts to deceive the great princes when he was besieged in Paris during the War of the Public Weal (he was never so besieged). Meynier is also in error when he refers to Louis XI's success in fooling the duc de Bourgogne and thus escaping from his captor at Péronne (the duke allowed Louis XI to return to Paris only after he forced the king to accompany him on his expedition against the Liègeois). Notwithstanding Meynier's gross distortion of the facts, Louis XI functions as a figure for emulation in the appropriate use of dissimulation:

> All these examples clearly show to all Princes who find themselves powerfully surprised, that they must dissimulate in order to gain time, rather than rashly plunge themselves into vengeance when they do not have the means.[43]

Meynier uses Louis XI to demonstrate that such instances in which dissimulation is permissible are severely circumscribed. In both cases, Louis

XI feared for his life, and this justified his use of deceit. Clearly, despite his willingness to acknowledge the necessity for dissimulation, Meynier does not belong to the *raison d'état* camp.

Moreover, Louis XI is sometimes used to support arguments made by even the most ardent defenders of the traditional moral framework against the contemptible doctrines of the *étatistes*. He is portrayed as a successful monarch who, though unscrupulous at times, managed for the most part to stay within that traditional moral framework. It is hard to fathom how these "traditionalists" could characterize Louis XI as an example of moral rectitude, yet this indeed seems to be the case. An anonymous pamphlet entitled *La Voix gemissante du peuple chrestien et catholique* (1640) incorporates a positive view of Louis XI into a vehement attack on the policies of Cardinal Richelieu. In the chapter in which kings are exhorted "to leave the marks of their grandeur in order to go as a private person to learn the sufferings of their people," the author praises Louis XI's unwillingness to go to war with his enemies since the ruin of one's enemies is not a necessary prerequisite for the conservation of the state. Rather ironically, the author seems to have plagiarized the section of Silhon's *Le Ministre d'estat* in which Silhon extolled the virtues of Louis XI. The author further embellishes Silhon's accolades, however, when he remarks that Louis XI "spared the blood of his people and that of his neighbours. Wisdom conserved his estates and his crown, which arms had perhaps weakened."[44]

In general, the work is absolutist in tone, focusing its attack on ministerial malfeasance rather than monarchical tyranny. It is not surprising, therefore, that a more positive picture of Louis XI might emerge. Yet, at the same time, the opposition to *raison d'état* so vehemently expressed in the work would lead one to expect a hostile interpretation of Louis XI. It appears that the anti-Richelieu writers were employing some of the same stratagems as their adversaries. By presenting Louis XI as a moral monarch, they effectively deprived the *raison d'état* theorists of their prime role model.

Louis XI occupies a peculiar place in the history of *raison d'état* theory. He is clearly embraced by the theory's supporters, and equally reviled by some outspoken opponents of *étatiste* doctrines. There is a middle ground between these two extremes, however, where interpretations of Louis XI cannot so easily find their footing. This considerable muddling of positive and negative portraits seems to have much to do with the paradoxical relationship between the Spider King and Machiavelli. Among moderate *raison d'état* writers, for whom Machiavelli personified the more objectionable extremes of pragmatic politics, Louis XI, along with Tiberius, sometimes acted as a model of balance. He demonstrated "prudence" but was not necessarily deceitful. Moreover, among a few writers who completely revile Richelieu and *raison d'état*, Louis XI functions as an example of an effective monarch who yet demonstrated his adherence to universal moral precepts. What can account for the general approbation Louis XI appears to have received from all quarters during the first half of the seventeenth century? In an intellectual environment heavily favouring strong centralized authority, it is logical that Louis XI should be positively portrayed. It could be argued that those supporting the circumscription of politics by morality sought to deprive their opponents of a powerfully emblematic figure. By proving the intrinsic morality of Louis XI, the advocates of moral politics could capitalize on the popularity of the king while simultaneously undermining the historical examples supporting *raison d'état* ideology.

In any case, it is clear that, in contrast to the sixteenth century, during which there was considerable disagreement as to Louis XI's merits both as a king and as a man, the first half of the seventeenth century witnessed the almost universal rehabilitation of his reputation. Although this brief period of general acclaim was not to last long, Louis XI's historical reputation benefited from the new legitimacy accorded pragmatism, an attribute which all agreed Louis XI possessed in large measure.

Part III

"Le roi à cheval"

Much like a subtle spider which doth sit
In middle of her web, which spreadeth wide;
If aught do touch the utmost thread of it,
She feels it instantly on every side.
                              (Sir John Davies, *The Immortality of the Soul*)

6 The repentant ghost

There has been a resurgence of scholarly interest in the Fronde recently, due in large measure to the new attention paid to the pamphlets produced during the period, collectively known as the Mazarinades.[1] These renewed attempts to understand a complex and convoluted period of French history have focused less on how the manipulations or miscalculations of individual historical agents brought about a crisis in the French polity, than on how unified action at different points during the Fronde masked the distinctiveness of goals motivating diverse social groups.

In examining the images of Louis XI presented in the Mazarinades, no clear-cut interpretation of the monarch emerges. Rather, the conflicting views of Louis XI espoused by the almost always anonymous authors of these pamphlets testify to the complex interplay of ideas that paralleled the bewildering shifts and shuffles in the political arena. Some important points emerge from the examination of the monarch's reputation among Fronde pamphleteers, however. The surprising frequency with which Louis XI appears in these pamphlets is in itself significant, for it indicates that his name still retained considerable evocative power. More importantly, despite the fact that there is little consensus regarding the views of Louis XI among Fronde pamphleteers, references to the monarch tend overall to be contained within a group of pamphlets dealing with the specific issue of the authority of the Parlement of Paris. As such, the contrasting views of the monarch provide an insight into the essential ambivalence of the *parlementaire* position during the Fronde, an issue which has been touched upon by a number of scholars but which has never been fully investigated.[2] The importance of Louis XI for authors concerned with the role of the Parlement of Paris will be discussed in the first half of this chapter. Louis XI also figures prominently in several pamphlets known as "dialogues des morts." The second half of the chapter will examine these so-called dialogues of the dead in an attempt to understand what function this small group of pamphlets was intended to serve and why the historical figure of Louis XI worked so effectively in this style of pamphlet.

Any attempt to provide a synoptic account of the Fronde is greatly hampered by the bewildering array of characters and the rapidity with which they switched sides. It is not without reason that this tumultuous period was labelled the "Fronde," referring to the slings with which children played. The appellation signifies a certain contemporary flippancy about the struggles among the royal faction, led by Anne of Austria and the minister Mazarin, the courts, the Condéan faction, and the group led by the troublemaking co-adjutor of Paris, Cardinal de Retz. The wars possessed a theatrical quality; the complicated and ever-changing alliances often seemed analogous to the manner in which the combination of characters in a play changes from scene to scene.

The Fronde was, nevertheless, a serious conflict indeed, the roots of which reached back into the reign of Louis XIV's grandfather, Henri IV. The venality of offices became an entrenched characteristic of French administration with the introduction of the *paulette* in 1604 which, upon annual payment of one sixtieth of an office's value, endowed the officeholder with the right to sell and bequeath his office.[3] The *paulette* had to be periodically renewed, however, and in its renewal the king possessed a weapon with which to threaten a recalcitrant magistracy.

Throughout the later years of Louis XIII's reign and during the minority of Louis XIV, repeated crop failures and the mounting cost of the continued war against the Habsburgs conspired to place the administration in desperate financial straits. The fiscal expedients employed by the government were met with resistance by the people, whose ability to pay the increased taxes was curtailed by the decline in their real incomes. The sovereign courts were also opposed, because they viewed the manner in which the new taxes were established and collected as being part of a much larger effort by the royal council to more narrowly circumscribe the authority of the courts within government.[4] The stability of the French state during the reign of Louis XIII and the minority of Louis XIV was undermined as well by recurrent princely revolts, beginning with the large-scale revolt of the princes of the blood in 1615–16 and erupting periodically every few years, up to and culminating in the Fronde.[5]

All these problems became more intense during the regency of Anne of Austria from 1643 onward. The difficult balancing act of the Parlement of Paris as agent and critic of the royal government became immediately and persistently apparent when, in 1643, it overturned Louis XIII's will stipulating that all state policies had to be approved by a majority of the members of the *conseil d'état* which included Anne, Gaston d'Orléans, and Condé, among others. The parlement confirmed Anne's absolute authority in exchange for a recognized voice in matters concerning the good of the state. From the very beginning of the new reign, the Parlement of Paris placed itself in an untenable position because the court's desire to involve itself in affairs of state ran up against its own acknowledgement of Anne's authority. This was to form the crux of the struggle between the royal administration and the sovereign courts during the remaining years of Louis XIV's minority. This latent struggle became overt whenever a *lit de justice*, wherein the king appeared in parlement to force the magistrates to register an edict, was held in order to force the registration of the financial measures which Michel d'Emery, *surintendant des finances*, urged upon the regent. These *lits de justice*, became more frequent in the later years of the 1640s and were the focus of much debate, since it was not clear that such a procedure was valid during the minority of a king.[6]

When yet another *lit de justice* was held on 15 January 1648, all the tensions within the state were placed in sharp relief. Once again questions arose regarding the legitimacy of a *lit de justice* held during a minority. Moreover, there was debate concerning whether its function had been perverted through overuse. Despite the registration of edicts concerning the implementation of certain fiscal measures, the parlement continued to examine these edicts and, in some instances, either modified them or sent remonstrances to the regent. Although eventually the parlement gave in on the subject of the modification of edicts after they had been registered in a *lit de justice*, relations between the sovereign courts and the regent remained difficult. In an effort to teach the obstreperous courts a lesson (and to acquire some more revenue), it was decided that the renewal of the *paulette* for officers of courts other than the parlement, among them the *chambres des comptes* and the *cours des aides*, would be conditional upon the forfeiture of four years' wages. By the time the government recognized this gross miscalculation, and agreed to renew the *paulette* for all magistrates uncondi-tionally, the damage was done. In a rare demonstration of magisterial unity, the parlement called for a plenary session of the sovereign courts of Paris to be held in the Chambre Saint Louis. Having achieved their goal of the renewal of the *paulette*, and not wishing to appear to be motivated solely by private interest, the magistrates turned their attention to the larger and much more explosive issue of fiscal reform.[7] The beginning of the Fronde is generally pegged to the assembly of the Chambre Saint Louis, which began meeting on 30 June 1648.

The summer of 1648 was the first of several instances during the Fronde when the goals of different groups within society coalesced to form a much more threatening type of opposition to the crown. Simultaneously encouraged by the parlement's negotiations with the regent and frustrated by the slow progress of these talks, the people of Paris raised the barricades in late August. The royal family fled to Saint-Germain-en-Laye. Although the family returned to Paris briefly in the autumn, and parlement issued a declaration in October incorporating many of the reforms proposed by the Chambre Saint Louis, tensions in the city heightened considerably towards the end of the year as reports of events in England reached the French capital. Once more in January of 1649, the royal family, along with Mazarin, fled Paris and, after their departure, the Prince de Condé laid siege to Paris on their behalf. In April of 1649, the Treaty of Rueil was signed between the regent and the parlement and the first phase of the Fronde came to a close.

Passions and expectations had both been raised, however, and the struggles over the ultimate control of the state continued unabated. From 1649 to 1652, the Fronde continued, primarily a revolt of *les grands* in which the two major noble factions led by Condé and de Retz wrangled with each other and with the supporters of the regent and Mazarin. The parlement's role was less overt during the latter stages of the conflict, but the presence of "Condéans," "Frondeurs" and Mazarinists among the membership of the sovereign court greatly hampered its efforts to maintain an already precarious balance between support of the government and criticism of governmental policies. The whole period following the Treaty of Rueil, and especially after the imprisonment of Condé and his brother, Conti, in January of 1650, was made even more anarchic by the periodic eruptions of violence in the provinces, in which the provincial parlements often played a pivotal role.[8] Towards the end of 1650, the Parlement of Paris, the Condéans and the Frondeurs briefly united, bound by their common hatred of Mazarin; early in 1651 the princes were freed and Mazarin was forced into exile. The conflict took on a more serious hue after Louis XIV reached his majority in September of 1651, since it could no longer be argued that the opposition was directed against ministers controlling government during a royal minority. Consequently, the parlement felt compelled to condemn the Prince de Condé when he led a second uprising against the crown. With Condé's condemnation in December of 1651, Mazarin returned to France, resulting in a renewed opposition to the government. Condé returned to Paris in 1652 and re-established control over the city, while Anne and Mazarin fled to Saint-Germain-en-Laye once more. Finally, in October, Mazarin went into exile a second time and the royal family was able to return to Paris. The Fronde officially ended with a *lit de justice* on 22 October 1651.

The contrasting references to Louis XI found in the Mazarinades underscore the confusion of ideas during the Fronde and especially the ambivalent position assumed by the Parlement of Paris throughout much of the conflict. While the historical reputation of Louis XI was almost uniformly positive in the first forty years of the century, interpretations of the monarch during the Fronde were considerably more mixed. One central factor emerges in all these contrasting views of Louis XI, however. Opinions about the role of the Parlement of Paris in government appear to correspond with assessments of Louis XI's character and accounts of his reign. Moreover, in contrast to sixteenth-century writers who tended to focus on Louis XI's relationship with the estates general, Fronde pamphleteers concentrated on his attitude toward the Parlement of Paris. Although the estates general had come to be regarded by some as a moribund institution (not having been assembled since 1614–15) and consequently figured less prominently in the political literature of the Fronde than it had in that of the sixteenth century, it continued to be a resonant symbol for a number of Fronde authors. The institution's continued importance in any discussion of the nature and structure of French government, and especially the competition between the estates general and the Parlement of Paris, strongly influenced how these writers interpreted the reign of Louis XI.

In a number of pamphlets published during the early months of 1649, Louis XI is presented in a harshly critical light. In *Lettre d'Avis à Messieurs du Parlement de Paris*, which the nineteenth-century bibliographer Célestin Moreau cites as causing a great furore,[9] the author echoes the opinion of Louis XI previously held by sixteenth-century constitutionalist writers. The work is virulently anti-monarchical, but is also hostile to the Parlement of Paris for not having more effectively checked the abuses of the regent's government.[10] The author criticized the parlement for not recognizing its intrinsic power. Had the parlement of Paris recognized the full extent of its own authority, it would never have permitted the indignities heaped upon it during the regency of Anne of Austria.[11] The author compares the parlement to the Roman Senate, maintaining that kings can do nothing of consequence without their consent.[12]

The second factor which explains the parlement's inability to counter the wilfulness of the regent is the existence of venality. Robbed of their independence because of the *paulette*, the magistrates feel compelled to register edicts which are contrary to justice. In the context of this discussion, the author refers to Louis XI as a tyrant who used the threat of the multiplication of offices (thereby decreasing the value of individual offices) to keep recalcitrant courts in line. Louis XI is once again criticized for having placed the French kings "hors de page," beyond the restraining reach of institutions like the courts and the estates general. Like the sixteenth-century constitutionalist writers François Hotman and Theodore Beza, the author of *Lettre d'Avis* characterizes Louis XI as the architect of French tyranny because, prior to his reign, no French king had ever levied any taxes on his subjects without the consent of the estates general or, if such consent was lacking, the authorization of the parlement.[13]

It is interesting to note here that the author appears to place the authority of the estates general above that of the parlement of Paris. The latter institution, however, still possesses enough authority to inhibit the actions of the king and the author condemns the parlement for not exercising that authority. It seems, then, that the author's view of Louis XI is coloured in part by the importance he attaches to the estates general and, although he seems to imbue the Parlement of Paris with the same authority as that august institution (perhaps for lack of a better alternative), he does not place a great deal of trust in a corporate body which seemed all too willing to negotiate with the corrupt regency government.

In another pamphlet from 1649, *Manuel du bon citoyen*, the issue of the relationship between the estates general and the sovereign courts is once again discussed. The author of this pamphlet, however, refutes the idea that the convocation of an estates general would be beneficial to the state. He maintains that, too often, these assemblies have been controlled by royal favourites "who hold the purse-strings, [and,] out of ambition and vanity, produce only splendour."[14] While the convocation of a "free" assembly would indeed be worthwhile, according to the author, such an assembly would take years to organize. Furthermore, the author asks rhetorically, are not the provincial parlements composed of the very same people who would attend an estates general? The author argues that the estates general need not be convoked because its role in protecting the common good is adequately carried out by the provincial parlements (acting in concert with other elements of society such as "les notables Bourgeois," the clergy and the nobility). The author emphasizes the need for cooperation among the various elements of the organic entity which is the state, rather than focusing on the authority of the Parlement of Paris *per se*.[15]

The discussion of Louis XI's character corresponds to the author's opinions about the need for the harmonious efforts of all members of society. The lack of balance in Louis XI's personality resulted in a lamentable lack of balance within the state. Noting that the character and reign of Louis XI have been much discussed, the pamphleteer points to Louis XI's increasing moroseness, especially towards the end of the king's life, and his jealousy and suspicion of his son and successor, Charles VIII.[16] These character flaws made Louis XI less responsive to the needs of his people.[17] The author's emphasis on the cooperation of all members of French society is underscored by the example of Louis XI, whose deficiencies of character worked to the detriment of the people of France.

The *Epilogue, ou dernier appareil du bon citoyen* is a follow-up to the *Manuel*, appearing in the last days of March 1649. Hubert Carrier asserts that the anonymous writer was directly influenced by Huguenot monarchomach writers such as François Hotman and Duplessis-Mornay.[18] Given the inspiration for the *Epilogue*, it is not surprising that, once again, Louis XI is cast not only as a tyrant but also as a usurper who undermined the contract established between his ancestor, Hugues Capet, and the French people.[19] The author asserts that royal policies which are contrary to God's law may be legitimately resisted, but he specifies that such resistance must be manifested by a group and not by an individual. Laws which are unjust in themselves but not necessarily contrary to divine law should be endured. The all-important exception is when the king uses violence to force the adherence of the populace to an unjust law. Should such an event take place, "there is no longer a Prince or subjects, and things are reduced to their first state."[20]

According to the author, Hugues Capet had been elected by the estates of France to reign with equity, following the laws of the country, and having sworn a solemn oath to that effect. If Louis XI had undertaken anything contrary to that contract, he sinned against his honour and duty. Consequently, the estates of Tours, held at the beginning of Charles VIII's reign, behaved appropriately and with full authority in re-establishing the contract as it had existed prior to its perversion by Louis XI.[21]

The idea that the reign of Louis XI was pivotal in the emergence of French tyranny is perhaps most baldly stated in a pamphlet entitled *La Guide ou Chemin de la Liberté* (1652) which Carrier describes as "authentiquement révolutionnaire." The central assertions of the pamphlet are that the French people were originally free, and that their liberty was preserved throughout much of French history up until the time of Louis XI.[22] The author unequivocally condemns the king, asserting: "Louis XI is that one among the kings who, placing the kings beyond restraint, put the people under tyranny."[23]

Louis XI was not, however, totally execrated during the period of the Fronde. There are a number of pamphlets in which the king was praised. A pro-Mazarin pamphlet from 1649 entitled *Lettre d'un Parisien, envoyee de Rome à Paris à un sien Parent*, takes its cue from the laudatory appraisals of Louis XI by *raison d'état* writers. The anonymous author of *Lettre d'un Parisien* writes that, although he previously followed the generally negative opinion of Mazarin, after travelling to Rome he came to appreciate the contributions of Italians in general and Mazarin in particular. The author then proceeds to outline the reasons for retaining Mazarin as first minister. The reason the author finds most persuasive is the need to keep a continuity in officials from king to king. In the context of this discussion the author refers to Louis XI as "one of our greatest and wisest kings" because he established the perpetuity of offices. It is highly ironic that the perpetuity of offices, something for which Louis XI has been reluctantly praised by those wanting to restrain monarchical power, is here being utilized to argue for Mazarin's retention as advisor!

While it is to be expected that Louis XI is praised in works espousing a royalist viewpoint, the fact that he is also portrayed positively in pamphlets calling for reforms in administration and at least implicitly attacking the crown is much more significant. The *Request de la Noblesse pour l'assemblée des Estats* (1651), for example, attempts to bolster its arguments in support of the convocation of the estates general by culling examples from French history that demonstrate how the convocation of the estates was beneficial to the state. The reference to Louis XI and the convocation of the estates in 1467 occupies a substantial place in this pamphlet. According to the author, the estates were assembled in order to reform abuses in the realm and to adjudicate the differences between Louis XI and the great nobles who had risen up against him during the War of the Public Weal. The author writes that, given the success of these estates in addressing the problems at hand, especially in light of the tumultuous circumstances, there is no reason why Louis XIV could not enjoy similar or even greater success if he convoked an assembly of the estates. Furthermore, if Louis XI, who was so little loved by his people, received so much satisfaction from his estates and whose authority was thus amplified, how much more true would it be of Louis XIV, so cherished by his people?[24] To a lesser degree this particular pamphlet possesses the same internal tension that characterized the works of

Hotman and Beza. By trying to elevate the estates general, the author asserts that even Louis XI felt compelled to convoke the assembly, thus undermining the argument that Louis XI was unresponsive to the needs of the people.

A publication that more clearly demonstrates the manner in which the reputation of Louis XI was used to enhance arguments concerning the authority of the Parlement of Paris is *Declarations des roys Louis XI et Henri III* (1648). Although the work was produced by the "Imprimeurs et Librairies ordinaires du roy," its intention is clearly to press the claims, both of privilege and of power, increasingly voiced by the Parlement of Paris. The tract reproduces a declaration made by Henri III in 1585 in which he states that members of the sovereign courts are exempt from billeting or victualling the king's soldiers.[25] Also included are some of the articles from the ordinances given at Blois in 1579. These articles stated that contentious issues which had come under scrutiny in the council of state were to be handed back to the judges of the sovereign courts. Furthermore, *arrêts* from parlement could not be retracted.[26] Finally, Louis XIV's declaration of 24 October 1648 contained references to Louis XI's ordinance of 1467 establishing the perpetuity of offices.[27]

A far more important pamphlet for a number of reasons is *Les Veritables maximes du gouvernement de la France* (1652), which Carrier attributes to Louis Machon.[28] The work resurfaced in a slightly altered form during the eighteenth century under the title *Judicium Francorum*, at which time it greatly influenced the development of *parlementaire* theory.[29] Louis Machon presents the Parlement of Paris as possessing the right, indeed the duty, to restrain the exercise of the royal will when necessary. Machon believes that the institution of parlement is coterminous with the founding of the French state and that, consequently, its authority is grounded in the fundamental laws of France.[30] It is significant that Machon identifies the modern institution of parlement rather than the estates general with the earliest Frankish assemblies held under the Merovingians. This discussion of origins which lay at the heart of the competition between the two institutions was much more fully developed during the eighteenth century, but in Machon's work we can already perceive the outlines of the debate. It is in the rising heat of this competition that an alternative interpretation of Louis XI is forged.

Despite the fact that Machon is elevating parlement's authority in relation to that of the crown, he is nevertheless favourably disposed to Louis XI despite the latter's reputed hostility toward the sovereign courts. While a number of sixteenth-century writers had asserted that Louis XI tried to coerce and threaten his parlement into doing what he wanted, Machon maintains that Louis XI recognized the authority of the sovereign court and willingly accepted its remonstrances and adjusted his edicts to suit their requirements. Referring to the famous incident in which Louis XI encountered opposition from the courts regarding the registration of a royal edict, Machon writes:

Louis XI, though more jealous of [his] authority than any of his predecessors, thanked the parlement for having refused the edicts that he had sent to it for verification, because they had gone against the well-being and repose of his people and vowed that he would never force it to do anything against its conscience.[31]

Machon presents a king who, while still anxious to maintain his authority, nevertheless acknowledges the authority of the parlement successfully to countermand his wishes in the best interests of the state. This is quite a different picture from that presented by sixteenth-century constitutionalists, who characterized Louis XI as a tyrant who had corrupted the constitution of France by manipulating institutions like parlement and the estates general, whose role it was to act as defenders of the public good against the wanton abuse of royal power.

Turning from pamphlets to more general works of political theory, we find a truly startling portrait of Louis XI by one of the most well-known mid-century opponents to absolutism, Claude Joly. In his most famous work, *Recueil des maximes veritables et importantes pour l'institution du roy*, Joly outlines a theory considerably at odds with the general trend of absolutism in the seventeenth century. Joly places a great deal of emphasis on the limited nature of the king's authority and the necessary involvement of institutions such as the estates general and parlement in the governmental process. One would expect, therefore, that Joly would view Louis XI with contempt. Surprisingly, this is not the case. In fact, Louis XI is, in many instances, held up as an exemplar of royal sagacity and majestic government. While Joly does criticize Louis XI in some places, the overall tone of the work is approbatory. Joly's work is an anomaly and it is worthy of close examination, especially given the attention Joly pays to the fifteenth-century monarch.

Joly is explicit in his view of the nature of monarchical authority. In chapter two, Joly cites the statement of Philippe de Commynes: "that the power of kings is finite and limited, and that they cannot do with their subjects solely according to their will and pleasure."[32] In chapter five, Joly asserts that the king was established to render justice; it follows that he himself must be subject to the law. He even comes close to the more extreme constitutionalist position regarding the role of the people in creating the monarchy when he says that kings were made only for the people and, while the latter existed without the former, the reverse was not true.[33] Echoes of the contract theory outlined in the *Vindiciae contra tyrannos* can also be found in Joly's work. Joly maintains that, although the king's power comes from the people, this does not preclude the power being simultaneously granted to the king by God. As soon as the contract between the king and the people is signed, by which the king agrees to do justice and protect the people, "God ratifies and approves him, and gives him all the necessary force to execute [the contract], and consequently the prince takes all his authority from this divine virtue and approbation which is like the seal of this synallagmatic act." [34] Finally, Joly takes a determined stand against those who would argue that the rules which govern private morality are inoperable in the political arena. (This is not a surprising position for Joly, given that one of his primary targets in the work is Cardinal Mazarin who, along with Richelieu, was perceived as the foremost practitioner of *raison d'état* politics.) Joly asserts: "It is a very great error, of which kings must be warned, to believe that politics and Christian piety are incompatible, and that it is impossible to accommodate the laws of the state with those of the Gospel."[35]

Joly is clearly against the absolutist form of government and the digression from Christian precepts which it sometimes entails. What, then, is Joly's impression of Louis XI, the archetypal absolute monarch, so often characterized as wilful and arbitrary, an amoral tyrant? The picture which emerges from the *Recueil des maximes veritables et importantes* is anything but negative. Louis XI is presented therein as wilful but not oppressive, hard but not cruel. Joly finds in Louis XI much that deserves the attention and approbation of posterity.

Louis XI's relationships with both the estates general and the parlement, previously characterized as tense at the very least, and acrimonious at worst, are re-cast in a much more favourable light. This is particularly significant because of the importance Joly places on these institutions as checks against the arbitrary exercise of royal power. Regarding the estates, two related events in Louis XI's reign are deemed significant by Joly. First, when the nobles rebelled against Louis XI, they recognized that they would be considered seditious if they did not prove their dedication to the public good by demanding the convocation of an estates general.[36] Second, Louis XI himself acknowledged the importance of the assembly when he used it to carry out his war against the comte de Charolais. Although Louis XI was disposed to convoke an assembly because he knew the deputies were willing to fall in with his wishes regarding war with Burgundy, Joly argues that this also implies that he recognized the importance of the estates.[37]

Joly's attempts to re-characterize Louis XI's reign are even more evident in his discussion of Louis XI's relationship with the parlements. Whereas other writers have portrayed Louis XI scurrying back to Paris with his tail between his legs after the debacle at Péronne, using the need to register the treaty in parlement as a pretext for his hasty withdrawal, Joly sees in this incident a genuine desire to follow through on the appropriate procedure regarding the registration of treaties.[38] Although Louis XI did at one time manifest some hostility to the parlement, he came to recognize its importance to the state. Joly believes that, in his heart, Louis XI had a true esteem for the court, as evidenced by his injunction to the dauphin not to change any officers in the realm (including those in the judiciary). The remonstrance was duly registered in the parlement, further demonstrating Louis XI's respect for the institution.[39]

Apart from his relationship with the estates and the parlement, Louis XI is praised by Joly for other aspects of his character and reign. Louis XI receives Joly's approval in the area of war and peace because he was always circumspect in his decisions regarding the prosecution of war. The preservation of one life was worth the greatest inconvenience to Louis XI, according to Joly, and this deserves praise because it is foolish to put one's subjects at risk for unimportant or trivial gains.[40] Even when discussing those royal virtues which, according to most historians, appear to have been either perverted or totally lacking in Louis XI, Joly finds room for a more positive reassessment. Faith, the foremost of these virtues, was demonstrated by Louis XI (though Joly acknowledges he was normally "fin et cauteleux") when he did not break the safe conduct he offered to the comte de Charolais in order that they might resolve their differences.[41] Another royal virtue, liberality, though possessed by Louis XI, was less effective because, in his case, it was not tempered by prudence. Finally, the royal virtue of clemency, though not demonstrated in Louis XI's actions, was described as necessary by the king in his instructions to the dauphin which are found in the *Rosier des Guerres*.

Therein lies the answer to the puzzle of Joly's positive interpretation of Louis XI. In the face of such established battle lines for and against, Joly draws his information regarding Louis XI almost exclusively from Commynes's *Mémoires* and the *Rosier des Guerres*, allegedly Louis XI's own instructions to the dauphin.[42] It is highly unlikely that Louis XI actually authored the piece. While it is true that early manuscript editions of the *Rosier* did name Louis XI as the author, by the time of the 1616 edition the *Rosier* was attributed to Pierre Choinet. Nevertheless, Joly based his analysis of Louis XI, at least in part, upon the assumption that Louis XI was indeed the author of the *Rosier des Guerres*.[43]

The lack of any reference to this important work prior to Joly appears somewhat surprising, at least initially. To my knowledge, none of the sixteenth-century authors I have read mention the *Rosier des Guerres* at all. Indeed, for constitutionalists like François Hotman and Theodore Beza, this may very well have been a deliberate omission. The *Rosier des Guerres* sits squarely within the late medieval tradition of handbooks for princes; of its nine chapters, the first seven describe the moral attributes of an ideal prince. If Louis XI was indeed the tyrant the constitutionalists painted him to be, he could not possibly have been the author of the moral sentiments espoused in the *Rosier des Guerres*. The lack of attention paid to the work by absolutists, on the other hand, is harder to comprehend. But if we consider that the absolutists' appreciation of Louis XI was predicated upon his ability to exercise control over the kingdom at a particularly turbulent time and not upon his adherence to an ideal of the virtuous prince, one can see that the *Rosier des Guerres* would not have been a particularly relevant source for absolutists either.

For Joly, the views expressed by Louis XI in the *Rosier des Guerres* more than outweigh the king's actions during his reign, which were at the very least, morally suspect. The way in which the sentiments espoused in the

Rosier des Guerres supersede earlier actions is clearly indicated in the discussion of Louis XI's celebrated wilfulness:

> Louis XI was one of our kings most concerned to be considered independent and less subject to the laws of his kingdom, as in effect one could say he gave much evidence of that; and that is why also one says of him that he placed kings *hors de page*. Nevertheless, we see that at the end of his days, whether experience had made him realize that he had not acted prudently, or he repented of it, he left to his son in the *Rozier des Guerres* a particular lesson to make good laws but even more to observe them well.[44]

With regard to the importance of good counsel, again Joly places more emphasis on the sentiments expressed in the *Rosier des Guerres* than on the circumstances of Louis XI's reign.[45] Rather ironically, Louis XI advises his son on the need to distinguish worthy from unworthy royal counsellors. In the *Rosier des Guerres*, Louis XI remarks that a king who holds disloyal men in as high regard as his faithful adherents will not reign long.[46] Finally, in what might well be the most ironic twist of all, Joly is effusive in his praise for the chapter on "justice" in the *Rosier des Guerres*, precisely that aspect of Louis XI's reign which is most execrated: "All this old language seemed to me so energetic, so grave and so royal that I did not want to take anything away from it."[47]

Joly's dependence on the *Rosier des Guerres* results in an interpretation of Louis XI considerably at odds with the portrait of the king which one would expect from an opponent of absolutism. It is important to remember, however, that Joly's praise for Louis XI stems from his injudicious reliance on a work he attributed to the direct authorship of the king. If Joly had placed more emphasis on the reign of Louis XI, rather than on a possibly apocryphal work, it is likely that his conclusions about the Spider King would have been much more in line with the standard negative appraisal of Louis XI shared by other constitutionalists.

Evidence from Claude Joly's *Recueil des maximes importantes*, Louis Machon's *Les Veritables maximes* and other *parlementaire* pamphlets indicates that appraisals of Louis XI made during the Fronde are much less clear cut than those of sixteenth-century polemicists. Although the ideas of François Hotman, Theodore Beza and later Leaguer theorists do find an echo in several Mazarinade pamphlets, the new focus on the role of the Parlement of Paris results in a more complex assessment of Louis XI.

The impact of the *parlementaire* claims on the historical reputation of Louis XI can be further illustrated through an examination of three Mazarinades written in the form of a dialogue between Louis XI and Louis XII which appeared in 1649 and 1653. These three works belong to a group of pamphlets known as *dialogues des morts*.[48] The participants in these "dialogues of the dead" are famous historical figures, some recently deceased, others

having lived and died centuries before. Engaged in often heated debate one
with another, the characters comment on contemporary political circumstances. During the period of the Fronde, this type of pamphlet appears to
have been quite a popular format for polemic; the historical figures employed
by polemicists ranging from Julius Caesar to Louis XIII, from Solon to
Richelieu. The dialogues between Louis XI and Louis XII fit squarely into
this sub-genre of political literature and constitute an excellent starting point
for further investigation into this type of pamphlet. Moreover, with regard to
the historical reputation of Louis XI, these three pamphlets demonstrate once
more how *parlementaire* ideas imbued the portrait of the king with more
variegated hues than those found in sixteenth-century versions.

The *Remonstrance du Roy Louis XII au Roy Louis XI sur leur differente façon de
regner* appeared in 1649. It is a slight work, devoid of any substantial theory,
but it is interesting because of its attempt to present the differences between
Louis XI and Louis XII in the clearest and simplest terms. In his catalogue
of the *Mazarinades*, Moreau notes that this pamphlet plagiarizes the other
pamphlet dealing with these two kings which also appeared in 1649, the
Dialogue entre le Roy Louys XI et Louys XII sur leur differente façon de regner.[49]
Although the titles of the two pamphlets are indeed similar, they are really
quite different in substance because they approach the comparison of the two
kings from different perspectives.

The *Remonstrance* begins with Louis XII stating, "Happy the princes to
whom God gives a mind of judgement and of discernment, and makes them
know that they are men and therefore capable of weakness."[50] Throughout
the work, Louis XII is often surprised at Louis XI's attachment to his
miserable earthly existence, as evidenced by the latter's attempts to extend it
through the assistance of mystics and doctors. Clearly, Louis XII advocates
keeping one's sights firmly fixed on the eternal, and acting with a view to
best ensuring a felicitous afterlife. Louis XII is articulating the much-
vaunted political tenet that it is better to be loved by one's subjects than to
be feared. Not only will royal justice to one's people during life be rewarded
with heaven after death, but that joy will be heightened by the knowledge
that the people of France will continue to remember one with love and
gratitude. Louis XII criticizes Louis XI for his method of governing through
fear and points out to his predecessor the irony of the pitiful state of virtual
imprisonment to which Louis XI was reduced in the last years of his reign.[51]
Louis XI responds to this attack by arguing that, above all, a king must
guard his authority even if the price paid to posterity is one of infamous
reputation. Moreover, he maintains, great kings have always had their
naysayers and critics. Louis XI's arguments have little effect on his adversary
who continues to assert that fear is less efficacious than love in assuring the
security of king and realm. The last word is given to Louis XII, who
summarizes the thrust of the pamphlet:

> Our successors will be able to judge in the different methods of our
> government whether it is more expedient to reign with force and absolute

power, or with a mild and tranquil authority. I avow that the first [method] renders a prince redoubtable during his lifetime, but the other grants him a glory which perpetuates itself for posterity.[52]

Clearly, the author wants to impress upon the boy-king Louis XIV that, if he follows Louis XII's advice and reigns with restraint and love, he will share his predecessor's glorious memory.

In the other dialogue from 1649, the criteria for judging Louis XI have expanded to include the king's relationship with the courts. Although *Dialogue entre Louys XI et Louys XII* bears a superficial resemblance to the *Remonstrance*, it is more sophisticated in its discussion and more pointed in its intent. The *Dialogue* is clearly a *parlementaire* work, focusing on the two monarchs' views of the role the courts play in government. Louis XI begins the dialogue with an uncompromising condemnation of parlement's too-lofty ambitions. He laments the mistakes of his predecessors in even instituting these courts and according them such involvement in government that the magistrates have dared to fashion themselves "guardians of kings, which means, in a word, to share with us the glory of our sceptre, that suffers no such division." Louis XI therefore felt compelled to take action "in order to keep them down and destroy their presumption."[53]

Louis XII responds by stating that he would like to make parlement's powers broader, since the kingdom was never better served than when parlement was able to exercise its votes freely, without the threat of royal coercion or overruling by way of "jussions." This is clearly a reference to the struggle between the regent and the Parlement of Paris over the latter's unwillingness to register financial edicts. In the years immediately preceding the Fronde, the government forced the parlement to register edicts that the sovereign court considered unjust, by using "jussions" or "lits de justice" with increasing frequency.

Louis XI remains adamant in the face of his opponent's arguments. He continues to maintain that "it is to be only half a king when one allows one's authority to be shared."[54] Interestingly, Louis XII's arguments are premised more on utility than on a principled defence of constitutionalism. He agrees that kings possess the right and authority to raise taxes, create new officers and declare edicts, "but in order to do these things with more reason and appearance of Justice, we voluntarily submit ourselves to having them verified and examined by the sovereign courts."[55] At the same time, Louis XII places added emphasis on the parlement by asserting that it represents the assembly of the three estates which cannot meet for all affairs of importance. Louis XI counters with the standard divine-right argument that God made kings wiser than other men precisely so that they could manage the state without the need of counsel. Louis XII then responds by recounting the La Vacquerie episode, in order to undermine Louis XI's position by reminding him of the time he was made to see things the parlement's way.[56]

Unaffected by Louis XII's harangue, Louis XI sums up his own position, which disregards any institutional check upon the king. "I know by experience that arms maintain the authority of kings and that finances are the nerves of war." By way of conclusion, Louis XII laments that he has not altered Louis XI's viewpoint but *le père du peuple* still maintains that "It is nevertheless sometimes very necessary that Princes be controlled in their actions and in their will."[57]

The *Dialogue entre Louys XI et Louys XII* differs from the *Remonstrance* in that it possesses a generally absolutist tone, albeit muted. One might argue that this strongly corresponds with the parlement's position in the opening days of the Fronde. Though unwilling to alienate the regent (and her ministers) entirely by denying unlimited royal authority, the magistrates nevertheless felt compelled to press their claim as counsellors to the king. The contrast between Louis XI and Louis XII is thus not drawn as starkly as it might have been. Louis XI is not presented as tyrannical but rather as misguidedly wilful. His arguments are presented reasonably and, although Louis XII's responses are designed more than adequately to counter the former's points, the piece lacks the derogatory tone directed at Louis XI in the *Remonstrance*.

The last of these three dialogues is the *Dialogue d'estat ou entretiens des roys Louys XI et Louys XII es Champs Elisées* published in 1652. It is an expanded version of the 1649 *Dialogue*, touching on a number of issues not discussed in the earlier pamphlet. The role of parlement in government remains a central issue, however. The exchange between the two kings is preceded by an introduction in which the author acknowledges that the method of ruling is largely dependent upon the disposition of the people. Unfortunately, people are normally insolent and can therefore only be restrained through intimidation and fear. He even goes so far as to say that "The clemency of kings often gives rise to revolts by subjects, and although it is ordinarily a virtue, nevertheless it can sometimes be the cause of crimes."[58] Still, the author maintains that government characterized by gentleness is better.

The dialogue itself begins with a rapid-fire exchange on the respective merits of fear and love as motivating forces behind the operation of government. Within that exchange, Louis XI is made to utter once more the statement which summarizes the achievement of his reign: "You know also how I was obeyed and made my successors avow that I had placed the kings of France *hors de page*."[59] He goes on to note how fortunate Louis XII had been to live in halcyon days, while he himself had lived during "perpetuelle inquietude" which forced him to exert rigorous, unchecked control. Louis XII agrees that sometimes force must be used to prevent attempts against the king, but the king is still subject to God's law. Louis XI's position as the advocate of absolutely unbridled royal authority is made clear in his response:

Kings are above the laws, they give them but they do not receive them and often it works out badly if they await the formalities of justice in order to punish a rebellion, when it is necessary to prevent the attempt by an accelerated punishment.[60]

An added element in this last pamphlet which is not present in the other dialogues is the attack both on *raison d'état* theory and on Cardinal Mazarin. Regarding *raison d'état*, Louis XI notes the many good ideas he had which, although not necessarily corresponding to the accepted tenets of morality, nevertheless resulted in benefits for France. He cites, by way of example, the time he sent a valet disguised as a herald to negotiate with Edward IV. Louis XII's response is significant. He argues from the normative Christian standpoint that the merits of an enterprise ought not to be judged according to its end result because, so often, success has more to do with luck than anything else.[61] Louis XII denies the validity of Louis XI's misguided credo, "qui nescit dissimulare, nescit regnare." In that regard, Louis XII clearly follows the traditional Christian viewpoint when he says "This was the same maxim practised by Emperor Tiberius, who was a tyrant and left behind him the very bad odour of his actions." Taking the *raison d'état* view of Tiberius, Louis XI responds that, nevertheless, Tiberius was considered to be a clever man.[62]

The attack on Mazarin is less direct, but noticeable nonetheless. In a section which does not appear in either of the other two pamphlets, the two kings discuss the virtues and vices of venality, the legitimacy of the royal confiscation of property, and the role of prelates in government. On this last issue, Louis XI argues that princes of the church need to maintain a certain level of splendour to encourage veneration of the church and to give them personal dignity. Louis XII argues that, generally speaking, men of the church make bad ministers.[63] Although Mazarin himself is not mentioned, in the context of an attack on *raison d'état* it is very likely that both Mazarin and his predecessor, Richelieu, were targets of criticism.

The *Dialogue d'estat* is evidently an amalgam of the two 1649 pamphlets. This is clearly demonstrated in the conflation of the endings. The *Dialogue d'estat* ends with Louis XII asserting that God and Louis XI's own conscience will be the latter's judges (repeating the last note of the *Remonstrance*) but that, nevertheless, it is sometimes beneficial to restrain a king (thus reiterating the main point of the second pamphlet). These three pamphlets taken as a group indicate some important points. First, it is clear that, for the author(s) of these pamphlets, Louis XI functioned as an illustrative figure to argue one side of a set of issues but, by and large, he does not represent the bogeyman of French tyranny. Louis XII's arguments invariably demonstrate the fallacy of Louis XI's views, but his comments are almost never designed to incite the reader against the form of government Louis XI had come to represent. Indeed, there is the recognition that, under unusually tumultuous conditions, the harsh rule advocated by Louis XI may in fact be necessary, even beneficial, for the state. Second, the pamphlets underscore how new criteria had emerged to evaluate Louis XI's reign. These new elements gave rise to a picture of Louis XI which is somewhat at odds with the portrait of the monarch handed down by sixteenth-century writers.

Collectively, the references to Louis XI within the *Mazarinades* do not provide a coherent set of clues about his significance for these pamphleteers. On the one hand, Louis XI is cited for his cruelty and abuse of power by those wishing to justify the Fronde. At the other extreme, he is presented in a positive light by the supporters of Mazarin. The picture is muddled, however, by the inconsistent use of Louis XI by *parlementaire* writers. He is both lauded and execrated by advocates of the sovereign courts; he is interpreted as both oppressing and protecting parlement's privileges.

Mid-seventeenth century *parlementaire* theory already contains deep ambiguities and inconsistencies, as evidenced by the contradictory portraits of Louis XI presented by advocates of the sovereign courts. Is the primary role of the Parlement of Paris to act as a pillar of royal authority? Or is it an abridgement of the three estates, charged to protect the people? Is it the guardian of existing law, or an agent in the creation of new law? For *parlementaire* writers the problem was not how to choose from among these characterizations but how to be all of these things simultaneously. By the eighteenth century, these inconsistencies become so magnified that they effectively stymie any *parlementaire* action either on behalf of the people or the crown. The murkiness of parlement's corporate identity, amply demonstrated during the Fronde, fosters the entangling of constitutionalist and absolutist thought that characterizes French political thinking from then until the Revolution.

7   Louis XI and the idea of counsel

In his highly-praised book, *Inventing the French Revolution*, Keith M. Baker describes political ideology in the eighteenth century as consisting of three competing discourses. For Baker these three are: the discourse of will, articulated by Jean Jacques Rousseau and the abbé Sieyès; the discourse of reason, expounded by various royal ministers; and the discourse of justice, pronounced primarily by the Parlement of Paris.[1] Baker's work definitively rejects worn-out models premised upon the interpretation of constitutionalism and absolutism as discrete and opposing theories. Baker presents a more complicated and satisfying picture of several rival discourses created from the "disaggregation of the attributes traditionally bound together in the concept of monarchical authority." As significant as Baker's work is, however, the schema he outlines invites some adjustment and reorientation. This chapter, then, serves to complement Baker's analysis, first by offering an alternative interpretation of *parlementaire* theory as centring on the idea of counsel. This emphasis on what one might call the "discourse of counsel" need not displace Baker's discourse of justice, although I would argue that the idea of counsel is at least as important to *parlementaire* theorists as is a concern about the rule of law. From the larger perspective, it seems worthwhile to consider these different discourses as strands within a larger discursive web. Throughout the course of the eighteenth century, I would argue, rather than moving away from each other, these strands become increasingly entangled. Eventually, the web became a discursive "knot," a knot so snarled that, by the eve of the Revolution, it could not be untied – and so had to be severed.

In this discussion of "counsel," I take as my starting point the work of John Guy on the notion of counsel in English political thought.[2] Guy asserts that the metaphor of counsel functioned as an "inspirational myth" wherein the tension between sovereignty and the need for consultation could apparently be resolved.[3] Guy further elaborates two rhetorical modes for discussing counsel: the humanist–classical mode, with its emphasis on the need for virtuous, public-spirited men to advise the king; and the feudal–baronial mode, which delineated some men, by birth, as "natural" counsellors to the king. I would argue that these characteristics of conciliar rhetoric

– its apparent ability to resolve the authority/limitation dilemma and its incorporation of humanist and feudal interpretations of counsellors – made it even more ideally suited to the French context and very appealing to the ideologically-conflicted magistrates of the Parlement of Paris. French *parlementaire* writers manifested deep affinity for the rhetoric of counsel but, ironically, throughout the course of the eighteenth century, the frequent use of conciliar rhetoric was ultimately to demonstrate how false the apparent resolution of the tension between *imperium* and *consilium* really was.[4]

The discourse of counsel employed by *parlementaire* writers overlaps in some important ways with the noble/royal debate over the origins of the French monarchy.[5] Most of these writers took up a decidedly *nobiliaire* position, arguing that the Frankish conquest, with all its constitutional ramifications, and the existence of some sort of national assembly at the Champs de Mars under the first race of French kings, are of crucial importance. They sought to anchor their claims about parlement's role in providing kingly counsel to the existence of the French monarchy itself. But by relying on pedigree for legitimization, the Parlement of Paris opened itself up to supplantation by another assembly that laid claim to the same lineage: the estates general. Moreover, those who called for the convocation of the estates general used the rhetoric of counsel very reluctantly. Instead, the role of the estates general was increasingly premised upon the idea of *souveraineté nationale*. The tentativeness of conciliar rhetoric, with its balance of *imperium* and *consilium*, could not compete with the bold vision of representative government; the discourse of counsel gave way before the discourse of will.

Parlementaire theorists in search of historical examples to support their assertions, both about the importance of counsel and about the sovereign court's ability and duty to function in this capacity, need look no further than the reign of Louis XI. By the eighteenth century, one of the stock stories surrounding Louis XI was about his horse: "Did you know that Louis XI owned the strongest horse in all the kingdom?" "No. Why was Louis XI's horse considered the strongest in the kingdom?" "Because it could carry Louis XI and all his counsel!" While this may seem a feeble witticism to us, it nevertheless indicates a commonly held perception about Louis XI's contempt for counsel. Yet this anecdote about a king deriding the need for consultation must be balanced against repeated references to Louis XI's willingness to allow the Parlement of Paris to advise, and even chastise him, in the interests of the kingdom. It seems surprising that magistrates would look to Louis XI for support of their conciliar pretensions, given the ambiguous evidence about Louis XI's relationship with the sovereign court; yet they did cite Louis XI, and with remarkable regularity. Significantly, *parlementaire* writers examined events in Louis XI's reign quite different from those so often cited by sixteenth- and seventeenth-century constitutionalists. Rather than focusing on the "guerre du bien publique," the *parlementaire* theorists emphasize two other episodes. The confrontation between Louis XI and the Parlement of Paris, under the leadership of *premier président* La Vacquerie, and the ordinance of 1467, which acknowledged the perpetuity of offices, are objects of intense interest and scrutiny during the eighteenth century. With the new attention paid to these events, Louis XI's reputation enters a new phase. One aspect remains constant, however: the Spider King continues to sit squarely within the web of French political discourse.

There is little doubt that *parlementaire* pretensions were on the rise during the first half of the eighteenth century. The estates general had been defunct since the abortive assembly of 1614–15; by the end of Louis XIV's reign, the parlements had enjoyed one hundred years of monopoly as the only institution which could claim to be the protector of the commonwealth. Indeed, only fifty years after the last estates general, the Parlement of Paris was already beginning to cloak itself in the mantle of guardianship.[6] By the early years of the eighteenth century, *parlementaire* ideas were given a further positive impetus when the Parlement of Paris's right to remonstrate, which had been revoked by Louis XIV in 1673, was revived in 1715 by Philippe d'Orléans in the attempt to gain *parlementaire* support for his regency.

Throughout the late seventeenth and especially during the eighteenth centuries, Jansenism played a crucial role in the struggles between the crown and the sovereign court. Some of the most prolific *parlementaire* writers, such as Louis Adrien Lepaige, were certainly Jansenist, but the movement found broader support as well because of the long-held Gallicanism of many magistrates. The sovereign court was unwilling to countenance the sort of papal incursions into French ecclesiastical affairs manifested by the bull *Unigenitus*. The monarchy's support for *Unigenitus* brought it into direct conflict with the Parlement of Paris on repeated occasions and it is no coincidence that the major judicial crises of the first half of the eighteenth century centred on Jansenism and the triangular relationship between king, church and judiciary.[7] Moreover, the theological doctrines of Jansenism lent the religious movement a powerful political dimension. "Figurism," which stated that contemporary events had been prefigured in the Old and New Testaments, propelled Jansenists into the political arena.[8] Finally, for our purposes, perhaps the most important aspect of Jansenism was its conciliarism; the Jansenist appeal to a general council of the Church had a considerable impact on the magistrates' perception of the sovereign court's relationship to the monarchy.[9] Indeed, most arguments for greater *parlementaire* involvement in government were premised upon the pressing need for kingly counsel. The Parlement of Paris was in the best position to provide such counsel because of its ancient origin and because fundamental law protected parlement's right to exist and to issue remonstrances to the king.

The ancient origin of parlement received a great deal of attention from *parlementaire* theorists. The anonymous *Essay historique concernant les droits et prérogatives de la cour des pairs qui est le Parlement séant à Paris*, written in 1721, contains a clear statement of the ancient origin of the sovereign courts. The author asserts, in no uncertain terms: "The origin of parlement or of the court of peers is so ancient that it would be more appropriate to say that it is born with the monarchy and that it has the same foundations."[10] The identification of the modern Parlement of Paris with a court of peers is significant because of the clear responsibility these "peers" had as natural counsellors of the king. Here the author of the *Essay historique* is employing what John Guy has called the feudal/baronial rhetorical mode to assert the parlement's role in providing counsel.

Moreover, the author uses the claims of ancient institutional lineage to attack the legitimacy of the estates general and to deny it the role of protecting the interests of the people.[11] Even if the estates general had come into existence under the first race of kings, as most of its proponents argued, parlement still possessed a better claim to represent the nation, being contemporaneous with the birth of the French monarchy itself. For one thing, the author argues, the national estates are held very rarely and only when it pleases the king. For another, the outcome of these assemblies can easily be determined through manipulation by influential royal ministers. This was certainly not the case for the truly ancient institution of parlement. "Thus, one can say that the parlement is better placed to render service to the nation than these controlled assemblies."[12] The discourse of counsel is once again very evident in the distinction drawn between unsuitable counsellors, namely flatterers and those who can be manipulated on the one hand, and virtuous men whose counsel is public-spirited on the other.

The ancient quality of parlement is also unequivocally stated in another anonymous manuscript, *Pour l'autorité du Parlement dans les affaires publiques*. At the very beginning of the work, the author outlines the *parlementaire* view of the ancient constitution: "The parlements were formerly meetings of the princes, officers of the crown, prelates, the greatest lords and notable persons of the church and the nobility, assembled in order to deliberate the affairs of states and to render sovereign justice to the subjects of the king."[13] Here again we find the equation of the parlement with a court of peers, called together not only to render justice but also to provide counsel.

Probably one of the best-known of the *parlementaire* tracts is the *Mémoire touchant l'origine et l'autorité du Parlement de France, appellé Judicium Francorum*, published in 1732.[14] The author of the *Judicium Francorum* has a great deal to say about the origins of parlement. As in the *Essay historique*, the *Judicium Francorum* contains the assertion that parlement is coterminous with the foundation of the French state. Because parlement represents the assembly of the Franks,

> it is as old as the crown, it was born with the state; one finds no letters of its institution because it represented the entire monarchy when it was assembled every year in the *champs de mars*, under the first race [of French kings] . . . [15]

The author of the *Judicium Francorum* believes that the parlement was not only born at the same time as the French state, but was, in its original form, that assembly from which the estates general also claimed descent. The author maintains that, under the first race of French kings, the Franks assembled to discuss and vote upon all matters of importance to the nation, including all laws, issues of war and peace, alliances, "and all of the great affairs of the kingdom." Under the second race, with the addition of conquered lands, both the geographic expanse and the increased population of the kingdom prohibited the continuation of direct suffrage enjoyed by the French people under the Merovingians. This altered form of the assembly continued as well under the Capetians. The author concludes his brief history: "There was no other tribunal for the affairs of state and for the general administration of the kingdom. That is why our historians call these assemblies courts of the Franks." Finally, at the time of Philippe-Auguste, the name of the institution was changed to "parlement." Nevertheless, its authority remained unchanged. Similarly, though the procedure for bringing matters of importance to parlement's attention changed to one of appeal under Philippe le Bel, parlement continued its involvement in the great affairs of state. In fact, as if to punctuate his assertions about the continued role of parlement, the author openly draws the conclusion to which all his arguments had been directed: "And in fact we see that the parlement has always been an abridgement of the three estates."[16]

Louis-Adrien Lepaige's work, *Lettres historiques sur les fonctions essentielles du parlement* (1753–4) is arguably the most important *parlementaire* work of the eighteenth century.[17] It appeared at a climactic point in the on-going triangular struggle between the Parlement of Paris, the ecclesiastical hierarchy and the crown, which had intensified with the promulgation of the papal bull *Unigenitus* in 1713. Constitutional principles were inextricably bound up in the controversy over *Unigenitus*, which once again condemned Jansenism as a heresy. Although far from uniformly Jansenist in its religious composition, parlement felt compelled to oppose the rigorous implementation of *Unigenitus* because the members perceived it to be both an attack on the liberties of the Gallican church and consequently on the authority of the crown, and also a challenge to the authority of the court and an assault on the privileges of its members.

Lepaige's work appeared amid the tumult over the church's active policy of refusing last rites to those who did not acknowledge *Unigenitus* or could not produce a "billet de confession" proving that they had been absolved by a properly orthodox cleric.[18] It is not surprising, then, that Lepaige's ideas, tempered in the heat of the debate, should be the most clearly thought out and articulated of any *parlementaire* writer. Lepaige intends to prove, first, that the ancient constitution envisioned the existence of parlement,[19] and, second, that the modern parlement is the same as that ancient constitution, possesses the same responsibilities, and fulfils the same function.[20]

In a way, Lepaige conflates the *thèse royale* and the *thèse nobiliaire*, deriving some elements from both of the opposing theories. While Lepaige believes that the Franks did indeed conquer Gaul and became a class distinct from the Gallic inhabitants, he argues that the latter were "happy serfs." But their serfdom consisted only in their exclusion from parlement and participation in public affairs.[21] According to Lepaige, parlement was originally the assembly of all the nobles in the kingdom. The so-called *Cour du roi*, consisting of those nobles who remained with the king at all times, was a truncated version of the *parlement général*, and eventually this council took over the role and function of the full parlement, becoming in fact that institution from which the modern parlement clearly descends.[22] The manner by which the powers of the *parlement général* were transmitted to the *Cour du roi* is explained by the emergence of feudalism. Since, after the death of Charlemagne, the kingdom was divided and the hierarchical feudal structure was created, fewer nobles owed direct fealty to the king. Consequently there were fewer members of both *parlement général* and the *Cour du roi*. The two bodies merged to become one.[23] Lepaige further argues that, despite changes in the institution – for example, Philippe le Bel's establishment of parlement as sedentary in Paris – the functions and authority of parlement were in no way impaired under either the Carolingians or the Capetians.

Lepaige not only outlines the historical development of parlement, he does so with an eye to refuting similar historical claims made by advocates of the estates general. He is emphatic that the Parlement of Paris, not the estates general, is the heir of the ancient assemblies held at the Champs de Mars under the early Merovingians. In a footnote to his discussion of the *Cour du roi*, Lepaige states the case for parlement unequivocally:

> The estates general, that began under Philippe le Bel, are decidedly not the ancient parlements; they are only an imperfect copy. The authority and the functions of these ancient assemblies stayed with the parlement, so much so that far from ceasing to exercise them during the convocation of the estates, on the contrary, the parlement exercised this authority over the estates themselves; it repressed with its *arrêts* all that was passed that was contrary to the laws of the kingdom of which it is both depository and guardian, as alone representing the ancient parlements.[24]

Despite his strong endorsement for parlement's active involvement in government, Lepaige's work, perhaps more than any of the others discussed, demonstrates the ambivalence at the base of the *parlementaire* position. Lepaige appears to argue simultaneously for unlimited monarchical authority and monarchical authority limited by law. This is most evident in his recapitulation of the ideas expressed in the first four chapters. The first point Lepaige makes in his summary is the need for a monarch in whom "all the legislative and coactive power" resides. All the powers in the realm exercised by other bodies derive from the power of the king alone. Lepaige qualifies his apparent endorsement of absolute monarchy, however: "no matter how extended his authority, far from being unjust or arbitrary, it is essentially regulated by the supreme laws of equity, as by those of the state."[25] As the repository of the laws, parlement counsels the king on whether his actions are or are not legal. Yet its authority comes from the king himself.

This uncertainty is manifested as well in Lepaige's interpretation of Louis XI. As Claude Joly did a century earlier, Lepaige sees Louis XI as a strong but not arbitrary monarch, intensely aware of the need for royal self-restraint. Moreover, like Joly, Lepaige refers frequently to Louis XI's instructions to his son, encapsulated in the *Rosier des Guerres*. Louis XI's admonition to his son to always protect the liberty of the people, found in chapter three of the *Rosier des Guerres*, is cited by Lepaige in the context of his discussion of the need for the king willingly to restrain his own power for the good of the state.[26]

Lepaige's positive view of Louis XI is echoed in almost all of the *parlementaire* literature, as is his essentially ambivalent view of parlement's relationship to the crown. While arguing that parlement is as old as the monarchy itself, and therefore in some sense partaking of the power established at its inception, Lepaige also recognizes the other important aspect of such an argument: that, in a very real sense, the fate of parlement rests with that of the monarchy itself. As we shall see, the ultimate inability to distinguish itself from the governmental machinery with which it co-existed resulted in *parlementaire* criticisms of the government that always stopped just short of all-out frontal attack.

Nevertheless, parlement did feel an urgent need to press its claims regarding its role as caretaker of the commonwealth. The other important pillar of *parlementaire* argument was the protection afforded by fundamental law.[27] *Parlementaire* writers like the author of the *Judicium Francorum* argued that the corpus of fundamental law indicated the rationale of parlement and specifically defined its responsibilities and authority. This is a significant departure from the traditional assumptions about the character of fundamental law. The standard view was that fundamental laws were those which laid out basic tenets of the French constitution, such as the succession or the inalienability of the domain. Given that these were the only laws that absolutists agreed limited the king's sphere of action, they were narrowed or broadened in scope, according to the manner in which the theorist conceptualized the French monarchy: constitutionally-limited or absolute.[28] Yet even such famous advocates of constitutionalism as Hotman and Beza tended not to define fundamental law as a corpus of specific regulations detailing the administration of the French government,[29] which is precisely what the *parlementaire* writers appear to be arguing. From the *parlementaire* viewpoint, the right to issue remonstrances is unquestionable, since it is incorporated in the fundamental law of the realm. The *Judicium Francorum* spells out the reliance on fundamental law:

It is a fundamental law that nothing can be imposed upon the subjects of
the king and that one can make no new laws without the consent of the
parlement, which represents the general consent of the people. Such is the
essential form of French government.[30]

This particular quotation is also of interest in demonstrating the author's
unflinching stance that the institution of parlement represents the people.
The author's view on fundamental law is significant in that he argues that it
not only expresses the general assertion of popular sovereignty but it also
specifies parlement as the vehicle through which that sovereignty is most
properly exercised.

While *parlementaire* writers cited examples from early French history to
buttress claims that parlement occupied an integral place and fulfilled a
necessary function in government, they also referred to more recent episodes
in history, frequently pointing to events which took place during the reign
of Louis XI. In stark contrast to the sixteenth-century resistance theorists
who employed the Spider King as a warning against the excesses which
follow almost inevitably from absolute monarchy, the *parlementaire* writers
often evoked the memory of Louis XI as a means to bolster their conciliar
claims.

The primary concerns of *parlementaire* writers can be seen in the attention
paid to the famous La Vacquerie episode. The contretemps between Louis XI
and his sovereign court is referred to in many tracts. For the most part, prior
to the eighteenth century, the event was interpreted as yet another in a series
of attempts by the tyrannical king to impose his will on the kingdom and to
crush all opposition in the process. The particularly vitriolic attack on Louis
XI, found in the sixteenth-century pamphlet *Le Reveille-Matin des François et
de leurs voisins*, portrays the officers of parlement as potential martyrs for the
cause of constitutional government, choosing death before submitting to the
tyranny of Louis XI.[31] The confrontation is thus used to demonstrate the
extreme behaviour of Louis XI and, by extension, that of all arbitrary rulers
who care little for the laws of the realm.

By contrast, the *parlementaire* writers place a wholly new interpretation on
the occurrence. Far from using the episode to demonstrate the tyranny of
Louis XI, these theorists focus on the actions of the parlement, arguing that
Louis XI's acquiescence serves to highlight the importance of the institution
in French government. While acknowledging Louis XI's reputation as wilful
and jealous of his authority, the *parlementaires* turn this characterization to
their own advantage by pointing out that parlement's authority to
remonstrate must have been unequivocally established if even a monarch of
Louis XI's wilful disposition would accede to their advice.

Almost all the *parlementaire* pamphlets already mentioned, as well as a
number of others, discuss the La Vacquerie incident in some detail. In the
Judicium Francorum, the author employs the figure of Louis XI to demonstrate the continued importance of the parlement even under the Capetians,
who were generally portrayed as arbitrary and absolute. For this particular

parlementaire writer, Louis XI represents a positive role model. It is interesting that Louis XI has become a hero to those who wish to re-establish or at least re-affirm the limitations on kingship. In the *Judicium Francorum*, Louis XI's attitude during the confrontation and the years following it are recounted. Not only did he thank parlement for not registering the offending edict, he added that he would never force the court to do anything against its conscience. Moreover, Louis XI appears to have always remembered and been affected by the incident: "When he was dying, Louis XI exhorted his son never to undertake anything without the consent of his peers and of his parlement. He even wanted Charles VIII to have his admonition registered."[32]

There is a notable absence of any reference to Louis XI's alleged attempts at coercion. By contrast, earlier works, like *Le Reveille-Matin*, place a great deal more emphasis on Louis XI's strong-arm tactics and less on the resolution of the conflict. According to the account in the *Judicium Francorum*, the incident was not actually characterized by conflict at all, but rather by cooperation between the two components of government, without which the legislative process could not be carried out. A similar interpretation of the event can be found in the manuscript, *Pour l'autorité du Parlement dans les affaires publiques*. While recognizing that Louis XI possessed an authoritarian bent, perhaps even emphasizing it to heighten the impact of his actions, the author depicts Louis XI as extremely acquiescent in his relationship with the sovereign court. After President La Vacquerie and the other officers made their remonstrance to the king, "Louis XI responded that he held them to be his loyal servants and thanked them, adding that he would be their good king and never constrain them to do anything against their consciences."[33] Louis XI is presented here as almost mild-mannered and eager not to antagonize parlement. What a difference from the portrait of the blackhearted tyrant painted by the author of *Le Reveille-Matin*!

The importance of the La Vacquerie episode as a weapon in the arsenal of *parlementaire* members themselves is attested to by the description of the event in a remonstrance dated 1718. While the document included both the expected protestations of unswerving loyalty and the equally expected recognition of the king as "the sole legitimate power in France," the document does promote a more assertive role for parlement. Like many of the other works discussed, the 1718 remonstrance alludes to the modern parlement's connection to an older version of the institution which was more actively involved in the making of laws.[34] The avowed purpose of the remonstrance is to convince the Regent that even those kings who most jealously guarded their authority adhered to the counsel of parlement. In this regard, the author of the remonstrance wrote:

> Louis XI, despite being more jealous of his authority than had been any of his predecessors, thanked his parlement for having refused the edicts that he had sent for verification because they went against the well-being and repose of his peoples.[35]

Interestingly, this remonstrance was bound together with, among other *parlementaire* works, the *Judicium Francorum*. Perhaps even more significant for the purposes of this study, another work included in the collection is the *Accomodement entre le Roy Louis XI et son Parlement*.

The *Accomodement* is actually an extract from François de Bouchel's *La Bibliothèque ou Trésor du Droit François*, which was first published in 1615 and then again in 1671. Though we cannot be certain, since the pamphlet bears no publication date, it is not unlikely that the excerpt appeared sometime early in the eighteenth century. Its inclusion with the remonstrance from 1718 in the collection of works dating from the first twenty-five years of the century supports this assertion. The *Accomodement* confirms the importance of Louis XI to proponents of increased *parlementaire* authority.

As one might suspect, the "accommodation" to which the pamphlet's title refers is the resolution of differences between Louis XI and his parlement, led by *premier président* La Vacquerie. In this account, all evidence of conflict between Louis XI and parlement is effaced. In fact, the two parties were falling over each other to appear courteous and accommodating. When La Vacquerie relayed parlement's refusal to register the edict to Louis XI, "he asked the king to take in good part the refusal of the court to verify his edict and not to interpret [the court] as lacking respect, fidelity or obedience." Louis XI, for his part, went to great lengths to assure his officers that he held them to be his good and affectionate servants and that he had no intention of removing them from their offices or otherwise retaliating against them. In the face of their determination, Louis pledged "by his life, he would not constrain them to do anything against their consciences; and from this time forward, he held his promise to them inviolable."[36] The editor, Bouchel, adds his own comments on Louis XI's actions:

> I will say frankly that this Prince demonstrated in this act a trait of great prudence, and practised well a proverb that he usually had on his lips, and that merits not being forgotten: that when pride and presumption go first, shame and injury follow soon after.[37]

Viewed in this manner, Louis XI is a champion of *parlementaire* thought. He recognizes the necessity of parlement's active involvement in government; he readily agrees to, even encourages, the participation of the court in the legislative process, and obviously values the counsel he receives from the court.

Louis XI is praised by *parlementaire* writers for another important reason. Counsel can only be useful when it is not coerced or manipulated, but freely given. The parlement was concerned to demonstrate its freedom from undue royal influence. Because of this, the perpetuity of offices was held to be an inviolable right of the sovereign court. Arguments concerning the perpetuity of offices through prescription are different from arguments for legitimacy based on origins, as with the ancient assemblies. This apparent contradiction does not appear to disturb *parlementaire* theorists. Both sorts of argument bolster the claims of the court to participate actively in public affairs on behalf of the people: origin arguments assert the legitimacy of the institution, while the perpetuity of offices establishes its integrity and efficacy when considering questions concerning the nation as a whole, since they are not swayed from their duty by private interests.

The 1467 ordinance is of such significance because it established parlement as a body of impartial officers who can remain independent of the crown's influence (unlike the estates general which, as pointed out in the *Essay historique*, could be manipulated). The *Judicium Francorum* thus concludes that the parlement is the only institution capable of discussing contentious issues:

> We have an authentic proof of this truth in the 1467 ordinance of Louis XI. This prince, speaking about his officers, said that they are an essential part of the government and members of that body of which he is the chief.[38]

Another extremely interesting work which emphasizes the importance of the ordinance of 1467 comes much later in the century. The *Lettres sur l'état de la magistrature en l'année 1772* by the First President of the Parlement of Normandy, Hue de Miromesnil, is dedicated to restoring Louis XVI's faith in parlement. Miromesnil's letters were written in response to Chancellor Maupeou's "reform" of the judiciary. Clashes between the crown and the courts had intensified after 1750, reaching a climax in December of 1770 when, in a *lit de justice*, Louis XV pushed through the registration of an edict which diminished the efficacy of issuing remonstrances and condemned the *parlementaire* use of "strikes" as a weapon to force the king to withdraw objectionable legislation. When parlement did not submit to the restrictions placed on the court by the edict, Maupeou convinced the king to exile all the magistrates from Paris. During the course of the Maupeou "reform," which lasted from 1771 to 1774, some of the provincial parlements were suppressed altogether and the judicial purview of the Parlement of Paris was drastically narrowed. Moreover, Louis XV abolished venality of office in the *parlements*. The exiled magistrates were only reinstated in their offices after the accession of Louis XVI in 1774.[39]

Miromesnil's purpose is to convince the king that the existence of parlement poses no threat to his authority. Rather, the support of the court strengthens the foundation of royal absolutism. In some ways, the work echoes the uncertain tone of Lepaige and others in so far as it illustrates the ambivalence of *parlementaire* writers in their desire to remain loyal to the monarchy while simultaneously trying to preserve and, if possible, expand the role of parlement in government.[40]

Unlike some of the other *parlementaire* writers, Miromesnil vehemently condemns France's feudal past. He decries the feudal period in French history, and praises the Capetians for beginning the process of reuniting the great *seigneuries* to the crown. Louis XI stands in good stead for his efforts in this regard, as well as for establishing additional *bailliages* and *sénéchaussées*, according fiscal and political privileges to the towns and setting up fixed parlements in several provinces.[41] From this absolutist standpoint, Miromesnil argues that the magistrature, as the fourth order of the realm, has contributed to increased royal authority. While the Merovingian and Carolingian kings were troubled by feudal violence, with the help of the parlements the Capetians were able to deal with internal conflict much more easily. Miromesnil attributes Charles VII's success in chasing the English out of France to the internal stability maintained by the existence of the "fourth estate," the magistracy. In fact, it is with the help of parlement that Charles VII

> gave Louis XI the means to put kings beyond restraint (as Mézeray said); means of which Louis XI did not take as full advantage as he could have (though he did great things) if he had used less finesse and more nobility and steadfastness in his conduct.[42]

The criticism of Louis XI is mild indeed, but what is astonishing is the implication that it was through the efforts of parlement that Louis XI and his successors were placed "hors de page"! This is a complete reversal from sixteenth-century constitutionalist treatises, which not only placed an entirely negative connotation on the phrase but also stated that it came about through the actions of the tyrant, Louis XI.

Appended to the *Lettres sur la magistrature* (and discussed in the sixteenth and final epistle) is a document entitled *Recherches des principales ordonnances concernant l'établissement et les fonctions des Officiers des Parlemens*. Not surprisingly, the ordinance of 1467 is given considerable attention. While Louis XI is criticized for rather impetuous behaviour early in his reign when he replaced the ancient, "natural" counsellors with upstarts and flatterers, thereby causing himself and the kingdom a great deal of trouble, he is praised for his ability to correct his error and repair the damage. Louis XI set out to win back the hearts of the great nobles, the *bourgeoisie* and the magistrates, this last group through the promulgation of the ordinance confirming the perpetuity of offices. Miromesnil acknowledges that, at first, Louis XI's efforts may have seemed to be merely a ploy to gain popularity, devoid of any real commitment to the magistrates, but the king proved his sincerity by "the precaution that he took on his death bed of making his son and successor swear to maintain the execution [of the edict]."[43]

Miromesnil's work is an important contribution to *parlementaire* theory for a number of reasons. First, it may provide an inkling as to why, despite assertions which, at least by logical extension, question monarchical sovereignty, most *parlementaire* writers continued to write from a vantage point within the established "system." Unlike proponents of the estates general, *parlementaire* writers did not see support for the institution as necessarily threatening the *status quo*. Perhaps, then, it is not so surprising that, at times, their interpretations of Louis XI parallel those promoted by absolutists in the first half of the seventeenth century.

For the magistrates themselves, the ordinance of 1467 occupies a central place in their arsenal.[44] The document is considered germane to much more than just the perpetuity of offices. It is used as an emblem of a whole range of privileges and responsibilities which parlement tried to protect against perceived encroachment by both the crown and the Church. Regarding the controversy over *Unigenitus*, for example, parlement published several remonstrances condemning the clerical practice of refusing to administer the last rites to those who would not endorse the papal bull. The confrontation intensified when, in March of 1751, Monsieur Clément stood up toward the end of a court session and roundly denounced a certain Father Bouettin, *curé* of Saint-Etienne-du-Mont, who had refused to perform the last rites for a member of parlement on the grounds that he could not present a "billet de confession."[45] With the incident as a starting point, the parlement issued a remonstrance which went far beyond merely commenting on the incident itself. Perceiving the actions of the priest as an insult to the court, the framers of the remonstrance trumpeted the prestige of the institution, employing the ordinance of 1467 as proof of its importance:

> Nevertheless, Sire, what is this tribunal? You are its chief; the judgments that it pronounces are entitled with your august name.
>
> In what manner did Louis XI, who perhaps of all the kings your predecessors best understood the means of assuring his authority, explain this in one of his ordinances of 21 October 1467?
>
> "In our officers, consists our authority, the direction of deeds by which the public good of our kingdom is undertaken and administered and who are the essential ministers like members of the body of which we are the head."[46]

A few years later Louis XI's ordinance again figured prominently in a remonstrance issued by the Parlement of Paris. This time the parlement responded to a perceived attack on one of its provincial counterparts, the parlement at Besançon. In the remonstrance, the Parlement of Paris claims that the ordinance of 1467 guarantees that

> Magistrates cannot be troubled or disturbed in the exercise of their functions, by *lettres des cachets*, or otherwise, nor would they lose the exercise of their charges except by death, voluntary resignation or forfeiture, before being judged and declared judicially and according to the terms of justice by competent judges.[47]

What is particularly interesting about this quotation is that it is part of a written exchange between the crown and parlement regarding the true meaning of the ordinance. Through his chancellor the king responds that, while he recognizes the protection afforded magistrates by the ordinance, "one should not thereby question the suppression of offices when the good of the subjects and the reform of some parts of the public order demands it."[48] Not satisfied with the king's response, the parlement decided to adopt a set of articles, including the declaration that any law trying to dispossess the magistrates of their offices "would reverse all magistracy and destroy that free and entire function of their jurisdiction in which our kings wanted their officers to be maintained." Such a law would be contrary to the most ancient laws of the realm which had been reiterated by the ordinance of 1467.[49] In short, if the perpetuity of offices was not maintained, the magistrates could not truly or effectively give kingly counsel.

Finally, in 1788, when Louis XVI staged a *lit de justice* for the creation of a plenary court, which would take on the duties of parlement, the ordinance of 1467 again became the focus of scrutiny by both sides. Not surprisingly, parlement held up the ordinance as protection against the judicial reforms proposed by the king, which would result in considerable reduction of parlement's authority and responsibilities. In the words of an incredulous President Séguier:

> A new court of peers . . . could it replace the ancient parlements where the assembled nation deliberated on the formation of ordinances and accorded to its king the subsidies that the necessity of the times forced him to levy on his people?[50]

The king tried to assuage the anxieties of the officers, assuring them that he would do "nothing to the contrary of the wise and celebrated ordinance of Louis XI of 21 October 1467." Louis XVI interpreted the ordinance to mean quite a different thing from that understood by the magistrates, however. The ordinance guaranteed the irremovability of officers, not the perpetuity of the offices themselves. Therefore, reasoned Louis XVI, in reducing the number of offices, rather than depriving individuals of their offices and awarding them to others, he was doing nothing contrary to the ordinance of 1467. Parlement could find no protection under that particular law. Parlement then countered by criticizing the king's interpretation as hair-splitting: "to suppress an office is to deprive the officer when one takes away his functions . . . " Parlement quoted the pertinent clause of the ordinance in full, and then remarked: "fifteen years after having published this ordinance, the same king, before dying, made his son Charles VIII swear to its execution. He sent the authentic act of this oath to his parlement in order for it to be published and registered."[51]

President Séguier's remarks about the "assembled nation" echo and amplify a secondary voice within much of *parlementaire* theory. Only a whisper at the beginning of Louis XV's reign, the call for an estates general grew throughout the course of the eighteenth century so that, by the eve of the Revolution, the whisper had become a vigorous chorus to which many magistrates lent their voices. In the same way that the Parlement of Paris was uncertain about the nature of its relationship to the crown (an uncertainty for which conciliar rhetoric seemed particularly well suited), the sovereign court was also unsure about an institution that could be perceived as a direct rival: the estates general. And although there was a struggle between the Parlement of Paris and the estates general throughout much of the early modern period, the repeated and intense clashes between the crown and the sovereign court (especially after 1750) tended to overshadow older, more nebulous corporate rivalries. Indeed, by the late 1780s, magistrates did not denigrate the estates general but rather supported its convocation as they began to believe that *parlementaire* self-interest was best served through the convocation of a national assembly. Correspondingly, as the conciliar rhetoric of *parlementaire* theorists was shown to lack weight and efficacy, it was abandoned in favour of the stronger constitutional language of, among others, the abbé Sieyès. If we look briefly at portraits of Louis XI drawn by a few proponents of the estates general, we can clearly see how powerful are the discursive strands of "will" with which the more fragile threads of counsel became entangled.

In contrast to the portrayal of the king in the *parlementaire* works discussed, Louis XI casts a long, dark shadow in the works by advocates of the estates general. He is a sinister persona whose presence serves as a reminder to the reader of the tyranny which has existed in France during the past and which continues to menace the people as long as there are no institutions which represent the nation's interest and place limitations on the exercise of the royal will.

An example of the clear correlation between negative portraits of Louis XI and advocacy of the estates general can be found in the works of Gautier de Sibert. Born in 1720 into a family of tax-farmers, Gautier de Sibert abandoned the family business to pursue a literary career.[52] For the most part, his contributions to literature were not distinguished. Nevertheless, two of his treatises do provide us with a clear picture, both of the potential role of the estates general in government and of how a writer with a high regard for the assembly might portray Louis XI's contribution to the development of the French monarchy.

In the *Considerations sur l'ancienneté de l'existence du Tiers-etat* (1789), Gautier de Sibert clearly and forcefully proposes that the monarchy is essentially dependent on the third estate. The work begins with the assertion that all men are equal, the third estate being the representatives of the city dwellers and free country farmers. These people possess certain rights "that have been suspended by a reversal of natural law, as ancient as the feudal regime is modern."[53] Gautier de Sibert is vehement in his denunciation of *nobiliaire* writers like Boulainvilliers;[54] the custom of dividing the realm in the years after Charlemagne eventually led to the ruinous development of feudal government, under which the rights of free citizens (including that of representation in the national assembly) were often suppressed by the new petty princes.[55]

Rather surprisingly, Gautier de Sibert praises the Capetian kings, who have so often been criticized as the architects of French absolutism. He accords the third race of French kings a great deal of credit for pulling France out of the feudal chaos into which it had fallen: "in a word, they overcame the feudal hydra, that monster formed from the pride of *les grands* and the weakness of previous kings . . . "[56] In order to accomplish this goal, the Capetians created localities with considerable autonomy called communes, to which they gave many privileges by charter. These kings, then, fostered the growth of prosperous urban groups from which emerged many individuals who rendered tremendous services to the state through their industry and talent. From the contributions made by these individuals and the third estate as a whole, Gautier de Sibert concludes that "it was just that they have suffrage, because they provided for the needs of the state with a proportion of their property."[57]

After Gautier's views on the mutually-beneficial relationship of the king and the third estate, one would expect him to praise Louis XI. His depiction of the interdependent relationship of the king and the third estate presages ideas which would be more fully developed during the first half of the nineteenth century in works which deal much more favourably with Louis XI. But in fact, Gautier de Sibert's opinion of Louis XI is anything but favourable. If we examine Gautier de Sibert's major work, *Variations de la Monarchie Françoise dans son gouvernement politique, civil et militaire* (1765), we find an intensely negative portrait of Louis XI. He is, for Gautier de Sibert, the archetype of tyranny.

The four-volume work, divided into nine epochs, charts the course of French history from Clovis to Louis XIV. The reign of Louis XI falls into the seventh epoch (1315–1515), of which the defining event, according to Gautier, is the emancipation of the serfs. The author characterizes the last years of Charles VII's reign as internally tranquil, and he faults Louis XI for not capitalizing on the fortunate state of affairs when he succeeded to the throne:

> Louis XI, sovereign of a kingdom where he could work with success to the well-being and glory of the nation, did none of these things. Concerned to reign as an absolute king, he sacrificed everything to this idea, rendering himself unjust and cruel.[58]

Gautier de Sibert blames Louis XI for the outbreak of the War of the Public Weal. Gautier acknowledges that Louis is considered by many to be among the greatest "politiques," and that he is regarded by some as a great king. Nevertheless, Gautier comments, "he seems to me not to merit either of these titles." The author goes on to paint a portrait of Louis XI in the harshest possible tones:

> A monarch who played with the lives of men, who liked no one, who vexed his subjects, who violated his treaties, who preferred utility to honesty, who degraded his dignity with baseness, who was liberal only to deceive, who promised in order to seduce, who was pious in a peculiar fashion, who believed that in making pilgrimages he would achieve

divinity, who held captive a respectable queen, who left the successor to the throne in ignorance in a chateau isolated from the court: a monarch of this ilk must have no apologist. Such was Louis XI . . . [59]

In Gautier's view, Louis XI was the embodiment of all those abuses which follow in the wake of absolute rule. It is significant that someone who endorses the estates general so strongly should also portray Louis XI in such an unflattering light. Nor, as we shall see, is Gautier de Sibert unique in possessing a negative view of Louis XI while pledging an allegiance to the third estate and its political vehicle, the estates general.

In his work, *Catéchisme du citoyen ou élémens du droit public françois* (1775), Guillaume-Joseph Saige espouses many of the views expressed by Gautier de Sibert regarding the importance of the third estate and its corporate representatives in the estates general. Not much is known about Guillaume-Joseph Saige, one of three members of the Saige family who were politically active in the period before and during the French Revolution. Guillaume-Joseph Saige was born in Bordeaux in 1746, where he lived most of his life. He became an *avocat* in the Parlement of Bordeaux in 1768. Little is known of his life between 1789 and his death in 1804.[60]

In a series of questions and answers, Saige proceeds to outline his vision of the French constitution. From the general discussion of various political configurations, Saige moves on to a more detailed examination of the French constitution. Saige asserts that the legislative power resides in the assembly of the estates general, composed of the king and representatives from the three orders. Although the king participates in the estates general, he is the least important component of the assembly, being, in effect, only an administrator.[61]

Saige's interpretation of French history is also very similar to that of Gautier de Sibert. Charlemagne receives the highest accolades for his successful attempts to restore the powers and liberties of the French people, who had been oppressed by his grandfather, Charles Martel: "This was also the most brilliant epoch in the history of the nation: the Franks, filled with the ardor and courage that is the natural effect of liberty, extended their conquests over all of Europe."[62] Unfortunately, the civil wars which followed Charlemagne's reign resulted in a descent into feudalism. Like Gautier de Sibert, Saige demonstrates an anti-noble stance when he denies the existence of the nobles under the first race of French kings. From all of the respondent's answers, the questioner concludes, "You have made me understand that the nobility owes its origin to an abuse of government, to the usurpations of the principal magistrates and to the perversion of the constitution." These usurped rights and privileges only became legitimate under the reign of Charlemagne, and were made so by the consent of the nation.[63] Saige acknowledges that the powers of the king waxed and waned considerably during the very early period of the French monarchy. Proper limitations were placed on monarchical authority by Charlemagne, however, and these limitations continue to operate as the boundary circumscribing the king's power. Saige summarizes the king's present-day powers: "The king is the first person in the state, the chief of the nation and, in this capacity, its first judge; he presides, or is supposed to preside, over the supreme tribunal of the kingdom, which is the court of peers . . ."[64]

The questioner then ponders the reign of Louis XI: if the limits of royal authority are really those described by the respondent, how does one explain the accumulation of authority accomplished by Louis XI and several of his successors? The answer is not surprising:

> These accretions, whether they are passing or, through the negligence of the nation, they become permanent, are true usurpations and must be considered as assaults which can, in no fashion, take away from the law.[65]

Other references to Louis XI are contained within the "Fragments Politiques," which follow the notes at the end of the work. In the first of these fragments, entitled "Reflections on the right of the estates general, relative to the concession of subsidies," Saige states that "one cannot levy taxes on the nation without the consent of the assembled nation." The assertion is entirely predictable given Saige's position on the primitive contract protecting the property of the citizens. According to Saige, Charles VII was just and moderate, convoking frequent assemblies during his reign, wherein "no imposition was established without their consent."

On the other hand, this virtuous king was succeeded by:

> Louis XI, crowned villain, man at once cowardly and violent, the most deceitful, the most cruel and the most despicable of tyrants. Nothing was sacred to him. Unashamedly, he crushed the rights of his peoples and the privileges of particular men beneath his feet; and, justifying his oppressions by crimes, he inundated the kingdom with the blood of his subjects. This monster, who marked each day of his life with depredations or assassinations, appears to have been put upon the earth only to alert and to frighten people about the dangers of too great power in the hands of one man, and to make them sense how much it is necessary to confine the authority of monarchy within an unshakeable barrier.[66]

This last sentence provides the key to Saige's view of Louis XI. As for Gautier de Sibert, Louis XI functions as nothing more than a symbol, the archetype of tyranny. Saige's indictment of Louis XI is placed within a context which appears to be nothing more than a pretext for the attack; Saige does not even refer to Louis XI's behaviour regarding taxation, ostensibly the focus of the "reflexion." Louis XI is employed as a didactic tool in Saige's attempt to educate the public about its rights and responsibilities under the French constitution. If the body politic does not properly exercise its sovereignty through the assembly of the estates general, a monarch with evil intentions could easily transform the French monarchy into a despotism, and the people might then find it difficult to re-establish their true liberties. In the work of Gautier de Sibert and Guillaume Saige we perceive the results of an unravelling of the discourse of counsel – no longer are these authors writing, at least indirectly, to the king in an attempt to convince him of the need continually to seek the advice of virtuous counsellors; instead, Frenchmen are being warned about the dangers of royal tyranny.

The use of Louis XI as the symbol of tyranny reaches its apogee in Jean-Baptiste Britard's work, *Discours historique sur le caractère et la politique de Louis XI*, published in 1794 (although it was clearly written before the republic was declared). Composed during the tumultuous revolutionary period, and marked by an understandable intensity missing from the works of both Gautier de Sibert and Saige, the *Discours historique* amplifies many of the same ideas of the earlier works. Britard states his purpose clearly in his dedicatory epistle to his fellow citizens: "Frenchmen, I offer you the tableau of despotism; read and see if you must cherish liberty."[67]

Britard maintains that he has read everything ever written about Louis XI, even manuscript works like that of Joachim Legrand.[68] Britard expresses regret that the work about Louis XI penned by Montesquieu has been lost:

> If the flames had not devoured the portrait that the French Tacitus had painted of the Tiberius of France, there would remain nothing for us to say; we would have a masterpiece; and never would the Academy have considered reproducing a subject exhausted by Montesquieu.[69]

What is particularly interesting here is the recurrence of the connection between Louis XI and Tiberius, which is so common in works produced during the first half of the seventeenth century. Louis XI is also compared by Britard to Nero.[70] Britard places part of the blame for the emergence of a tyrant such as Louis XI on the French people themselves. The people deliberately chose to place more power in the hands of Charles VII, and, although this desire was understandable in light of the circumstances, they were foolish not to have realized the dangers of despotism to which they would be exposed by increasing the powers of the king.[71] For his part, Charles VII wanted to convoke the estates general to re-establish limits on the king before his son came to the throne: "It is a great fault that he did not put these means in the constitution. What evils he would have prevented; how much we have the right to reproach him!"[72]

Upon his accession to the throne, Louis XI sought to undo all that his father had accomplished; his most heinous crime was the destitution of all officers who had been loyal to Charles VII. The War of the Public Weal, which was undertaken in response to Louis XI's actions, was "the forerunner of the great revolutions: well directed, this revolution, born of excesses of evil and oppression, could have finally produced liberty and well-being in France."[73] Britard thus portrays the War of the Public Weal as a harbinger of great things to come, and he establishes a spiritual kinship between those resisting tyranny in the fifteenth century and those who Britard asserts have successfully abolished it in the eighteenth century.

Britard holds no special regard for the nobility. He is disgusted with the great lords of the League of the Public Weal because they abandoned the people as soon as their particular interests were satisfied. The willingness of the people to tolerate Louis XI's excesses was a result of their belief that only a strong monarch could protect them from oppressive feudal rule:

> [Louis XI] bound himself to respect the public power, to cure the injuries of France, to chain up the hundred arms of the feudal hydra who still desolated the most beautiful lands.
>
> The people, who had need of a defender against the subaltern tyrants, considered it worse to restrain royal prerogative that to extend it. In elevating the throne, they sought under its shadow a refuge against the oppression of the nobles by whom they had been victims for so long.[74]

If the people found some protection from noble oppression in the increase of Louis XI's power, they did not long enjoy it; vanquishing the nobles resulted in the absence of any effective means to counter Louis XI's despotic behaviour. This became even more the case when Charles le Téméraire, duc de Bourgogne, died. Increasingly, Louis XI put his own capricious will in the place of law:

> Thus, he no longer recognized bridles or restraint. he crushed beneath his feet all laws, the most sacred rights; without decency, he scoffed at the life of citizens and, abandoning himself to all the perversity of his character, dirtied himself with all sorts of crimes without remorse.[75]

After ten years of ruse and pretence, Louis XI was free from constraint. Far from freeing the people from the burden of noble oppression, Louis XI succeeded only in creating an equality of the oppressed in the face of tyranny: "To his eyes, everyone was equal, but in the sense that a lesser despot of our own day said, when asked to soften the conditions for a famous unfortunate: 'in the Bastille all prisoners are equal.' "[76]

The result of Louis XI's despotism was a change in the nature of the French state. The nation was deprived of its right to assemble and to discuss matters pertinent to its interest. By degrees, Louis XI transformed the character of a nation, he destroyed public spirit and debased the French soul.[77] Britard summarizes the consequences of Louis XI's victory over the nobles and his establishment of complete tyranny over France:

> All rights were destroyed: security, property, liberty; nothing existed any longer. The sword struck the most elevated heads and menaced all. Fortune, rank, virtue, nothing was sacred. Innocence was not a safeguard and wealth was a crime. Nothing escaped the suspicions and worry of the despot; everyone bent beneath a yoke of iron.[78]

Britard concludes his diatribe against Louis XI by stating that divine justice was exercised against the tyrant because in the last three years of his life he was unhappy, tortured by overwhelming paranoia. His self-imposed imprisonment was worse than any he had inflicted on his enemies. France was finally relieved of its suffering with the death of Louis XI in 1483: "In effect, with his death, France breathed again: the Bastille was forced to open its maw and surrender its victims. The assembled nation took repossession of its rights."[79]

And yet, Britard was not a radical republican; he was determined to show that there are good kings, such as Louis XVI, who cooperate with the estates general for the benefit of all Frenchmen. The succession of an evil king to the throne, however, could result in national calamity, and Britard's lengthy exposé of Louis XI's tyranny is intended to accomplish two related goals. First, Britard wants to paint a portrait of despotism in order to make the French people cherish the presence of a virtuous monarch such as Louis XVI. Second, Britard feels compelled to alert the citizens of France both to their rights and their responsibilities. If they do not preserve their sovereign authority intact, if they give undue power and control to the monarch because of circumstances, they will find it difficult to reclaim the full extent of their liberty. They will reap the miserable harvest of tyranny which they themselves have sown. Saige, Gautier de Sibert and especially Britard all call upon the diabolical spectre of Louis XI in order to frighten the people of France into carrying out their full responsibilities as part of the governmental machinery. In their view, Louis XI's reign was the unfortunate result of the people's surrender of their rightful authority as the price for restored order. All three authors are convinced, however, that the price was too high; in order to prevent the recurrence of the atrocities committed against the nation under Louis XI, the people must re-assume their positions as counsellors to the king and protectors of the commonwealth.

As we have seen, however, Louis XI did not lack his share of supporters during the eighteenth century. He is portrayed positively by *parlementaire* theorists intent upon "re-establishing" the authority of parlement in government. Several factors contributed to Louis XI's positive portrayal by *parlementaire* writers. First, by focusing on Louis's relationship with his officers, and not on the War of the Public Weal, the *parlementaire* view incorporated new episodes from his reign which tended to shed a much more favourable light on the monarch. Perhaps their desire to distinguish the goals of the *noblesse de robe* from those of aristocratic opposition, led by writers like Boulainvilliers, motivated them to ignore the unfortunate confrontation between Louis XI and the great magnates. Most importantly, although the *parlementaire* writers wanted to see the authority of parlement enhanced, their intention was not to change the existing system but rather to "fine-tune" the balance between the component parts of an essentially sound governmental structure. And, while one could argue that the advocates of the estates general were trying to accomplish these same goals, there is one important difference between the positions of the two sets of theorists. The estates general had not been called since 1614 and were essentially defunct. To call for their re-activation as part of the legislative process was much more potentially threatening to the *status quo* than were appeals on behalf of the parlement, which was firmly entrenched in governmental process. Despite their avowed loyalty to the monarchy, writers like Saige and Gautier de Sibert were promoting ideas which could very easily upset the applecart – as indeed they did.

Throughout the early modern period, the historical reputation of Louis XI was inextricably bound up in the debates characterizing political theory. The consistent evocation of Louis XI for the purposes of political argument testifies to the importance of historical examples in the polemical exchange which continued unabated up to, and to a lesser extent beyond, the French Revolution.

In charting the historiography of Louis XI, it has been crucial to keep in mind the important shifts and changes in political theory between the beginning of the sixteenth and the end of the eighteenth centuries. Obviously, the Renaissance monarchy was something quite different from the *ancien régime* in 1789, and political theory, emerging from, and responding to, the socio-political context, was consequently much altered throughout the course of the early modern period. In light of its established link with political theory, it is to be expected that the historical reputation of Louis XI should be employed to different ends at different times.

During the sixteenth century, when the religious wars radicalized the intellectual elite, resulting in a bifurcation of political theory into seemingly irreconcilable principles of constitutionalism and absolutism, Louis XI was drawn into the fray as the straw tyrant by one camp, and consequently portrayed as a maligned hero by the other. The resistance theorists pointed to Louis XI as an example of the worst sort of tyrant, whom one might legitimately disobey and even resist. They also employed the reputedly wilful and paranoid Louis XI to show that France's government possessed a constitutional configuration which continued to operate under the most unfavourable conditions and the most determined of tyrants. By contrast, the absolutists, who acknowledged that the king was not unlimited but denied that limitations came in an institutional form, evoked the memory of Louis XI to argue that France was most effectively governed by a king who willingly submitted himself to the law and listened to the advice of his counsellors. Such being the case, those who advocated disobedience and sometimes even armed resistance were motivated by nothing more than an evil desire to destroy the monarchy, or at the very least to establish an illegitimate control over the king.

The first quarter of the seventeenth century witnessed a large-scale rehabilitation of Louis XI's historical reputation, due to a number of factors. First, with the triumph of the Bourbons, the positive view of Louis XI expounded earlier by *"politique* absolutists" like Bodin and Gentillet became the most-accepted view of royal authority. Second, the emergence of *raison d'état* ideology seemed to provide the theoretical justification for many of

Louis XI's actions and his conduct in general. Indeed, the early seventeenth century was a period of almost universal admiration for Louis XI, during which time even those opposed to *raison d'état* and absolutism tried to blunt the force of their opponents' arguments by maintaining that Louis XI was a committed constitutionalist and a highly moral individual. Throughout the latter half of the seventeenth century, however, opposition to absolutism re-emerged. In the scores of pamphlets flooding into France from outside its borders, Louis XI and Louis XIV were condemned in tandem: twin pillars holding up the edifice of French tyranny. There was also an emphasis on reform from within and, as the end of Louis XIV's reign drew nearer, the hopes of writers such as Fénelon were placed in the future succession of a reform-minded monarch. These hopes were dashed with the death of the Duke of Burgundy, but the desires for administrative reform remained and, during the eighteenth century, these were recast with the long-held aspirations of the nobility in mind. Louis XI was condemned by these *nobiliaire* writers, not surprisingly, given his conflicts with the nobility in his own time. Louis XI brooked no administrative involvement by the nobility, denying the great lords their rightful place at the council table. Writers like Boulainvilliers saw in Louis XI the culmination of an unfortunate series of events by which the nobility were deprived of their privileges and authority, to the detriment of all Frenchmen.

The extent to which the constitutionalist and absolutist threads had become entangled is evidenced by Louis XI's often laudatory treatment at the hands of *parlementaire* writers, beginning in the mid-seventeenth century. Louis XI's supporters among proponents of the Parlement of Paris did much to undermine the hard and fast association of Louis XI with tyranny. These writers evoked the memory of Louis XI to bolster their arguments concerning the authority and autonomy of the courts. Their treatment of the Spider King illustrates the gulf separating *parlementaire* writers from their counterparts advocating the ideology of the *noblesse d'épee*. It also points to important differences between advocates of the sovereign courts and their rivals for the support of the people, the proponents of the estates general. This last group reverted to many of the arguments articulated by the sixteenth-century resistance theorists concerning the sovereignty of the people and the importance of the estates general as the vehicle by which the will of the people could be manifested in government. Along with their belief in the sovereignty of the people, the eighteenth-century advocates of the estates general inherited the vigorously negative view of Louis XI held by writers like Hotman and Beza. In the case of Britard, his interpretation of Louis XI was laced with a vitriol lacking even in the sixteenth-century portraits of the monarch.

The tortuous path of Louis XI's historical reputation between 1560 and 1789 mirrors the twists and turns in French political thought during the same period. Although it continues to be useful when appraising the evolution of French political thought to think in terms of constitutionalism and absolutism, one can no longer consider these as discrete and opposing theories. Clearly, there remains the essential difference between constitutionalism and absolutism, namely where sovereignty resides within the French state – with the king or with the people. This fundamental disagreement forms a chasm that bifurcates the entire landscape of *ancien régime* political thought. What is unexpected and, to my mind, quite remarkable, is the number of "bridges" built by both constitutionalists and absolutists across this chasm between the sixteenth and eighteenth centuries. These bridges are not, however, constructed for mutual benefit, but rather as the means by which constitutionalist and absolutist thinkers could make lightning raids into enemy territory to steal or sabotage polemical weaponry. In the seventeenth century, for example, absolutists made use of the concept of fundamental law to turn the tables on their opponents: fundamental law was evoked to shore up the authority of the king rather than to place fences around that authority. In the eighteenth century, constitutionalist writers retrieved *le peuple* from royalist writers who, having laid claim to some of the higher moral ground of *salus populi* occupied by the resistance theorists, now based the need for absolute monarchy on the protection of *le peuple*. Finally, writers like Sieyès built the strongest bridge, made from an alloy of *le peuple* and *la nation*, by which constitutionalist forces could finally overrun and take possession of absolutist territory.

Let us return to this book's defining (and less combative) metaphor of a web. Historians such as Baker have illuminated the value of considering political discourse both as the ebb and flow of ideas and the manner in which ideas are created, appropriated and transformed. In this study of Louis XI's historical reputation I have attempted to illuminate a discursive web constructed of constitutionalist and absolutist strands that become increasingly entangled. The rhetoric of counsel is an example of how these seemingly contradictory strands are spun together into a pattern so intricate that one cannot easily pick out individual threads. I am hopeful that the reader will perceive not only the obvious supporting weave spun from the reputation of Louis XI, but also the lighter, gossamer threads of *ancien régime* political thought.

Epilogue

"Le roi bourgeois"

This investigation into the historical reputation of Louis XI, with its central focus on the relationship between interpretations of Louis XI and the on-going intellectual battle concerning the nature of the state, concludes rather appropriately with the French Revolution. As for so many other things, the Revolutionary and Napoleonic period forms a turning point in the historiography of Louis XI. One could persuasively argue that the conflict between constitutionalism and absolutism which, in its various configurations, had determined the basis of almost all discussion about Louis XI, had all but ended by 1815 with the apparent victory of the constitutionalist forces. The Bourbon restoration, founded on the Charter of 1814, effectively put an end to absolute monarchy, both as an idea and as a governmental form.[1]

With the establishment of the constitutional monarchy, the issue of indivisible sovereignty was, if not resolved, at least indefinitely shelved by most political thinkers, although the heirs of the Jacobins continued to argue for popular sovereignty. As the "doctrinaires" put it, the location of sovereignty was irrelevant; they based their ideas on the belief in divisible sovereignty and the necessity for cooperation between component elements of the government.[2] With the issue of sovereignty pushed aside, many of the events of Louis XI's reign that had been interpreted in the light of this debate were divested of their theoretical significance. The League of the Public Weal, for example, could no longer be effectively employed as a constitutional struggle against the usurping efforts of the tyrant, Louis XI. Similarly, Louis's confrontation with President La Vacquerie and the Parlement of Paris was less relevant to the requirements of Restoration France than it had been in the struggle to establish institutional limitations on the monarch prior to the Revolution.

The period after the Restoration nevertheless witnessed an explosion of interest in the fifteenth-century monarch. Writers seemed fascinated by Louis XI; their intense interest in the king is reflected in the remarkable number of works about him, both literary and historical, which appeared in the 1820s and after. Moreover, despite the fact that the theoretical debate that had largely determined the basis of discussion about Louis XI prior to the Revolution had ceased to be truly relevant to contemporary politics, his reputation was still, to a great degree, a function of political arguments.[3] During the nineteenth century, as the interest in class struggle altered the approach to history, Louis XI's reign, and in particular his relationship with the *bourgeoisie*, became the object of scrutiny. The intensity of interest in issues of class in French history, and the emergence of the *bourgeoisie* in particular, provided an added element to the discussion of Louis XI which was not evident in prior interpretations of the monarch, and which consequently separates the views of nineteenth-century writers from their pre-Revolutionary predecessors.

Louis XI's relationship with the *bourgeoisie* became the central focus of a considerable debate. Even prior to the Revolution, there were intimations of the importance of this issue. Much of absolutist thought in the eighteenth century had claimed that the *raison d'être* of absolute monarchy was the protection of *le peuple*. Of course, the specific identification of the king with the *bourgeoisie* was not yet apparent in works from the eighteenth century. Although some writers praised Louis XI for his "common touch," others criticized the Spider King for having oppressed the third estate just as he had the nobles. After the Restoration, in contrast, Louis XI was most often portrayed as having fostered the emergence of the *bourgeoisie*, thereby actually contributing to the first stirrings of freedom that eventually led to the Revolution.[4]

Although Louis XI's relationship with the *bourgeoisie* was often cited with approbation by writers during the Restoration and the July Monarchy, ironically, the first work dealing directly with this issue had appeared under Napoleon and condemned the monarch for his revolutionary legacy. In *Le Règne de Louis XI et de l'influence qu'il a eue jusque sur les derniers temps de la troisième dynastie* (1811), Alexis Dumesnil bewailed the "revolution" of Louis XI because it planted the seed of liberty in the people which eventually grew into the anarchy of the Revolution. Dumesnil was born in 1783 into a family of magistrates who were very loyal to the monarchy. He entered the royal army at the age of sixteen and fought until the pacification. He began to write under the Empire, and his criticism of Napoleon, contained in the work on Louis XI, brought him under the scrutiny of the authorities.[5] After the Restoration, he was appointed as a *commissaire extraordinaire* in Normandy, and, in later life, wrote a substantial number of pamphlets.

Dumesnil begins *Le Règne de Louis XI* with a vehement denunciation of the monarch: without real talents or virtues, Louis XI was still fortunate enough to become king, but he was only able to maintain himself on the throne through dissimulation and excess. He owed his celebrity to the astonishing variety of his crimes and a cruelty hitherto unknown.[6] Even though Dumesnil despises Louis XI's character, he applauds the king's efforts to bring down the nobility, despite the fact that the king's efforts had lamentable results for the people. Dumesnil cites Louis XI's successful attempt, while still dauphin, to discipline the nobles under his direct administration in Dauphiné.[7] Once he became king, Louis XI launched an all-out attack on the independent nobles and he was willing to submit himself to the people to accomplish this goal;

> Thus Louis no longer counted royal majesty at all; he submitted himself to everyone, he wanted to appear to obey, he would have voluntarily disposed of his crown in order to retake the hands of the nation . . . As the true force of this prince was entirely in the people, [Louis XI] neglected nothing to attach himself to them. Often he would go alone in the streets and enter a simple citizen's house, an artisan's house and sit at his table if it was the dinner hour. He frequently called them to his own home.[8]

The emphasis here is clearly on the involvement of the people, and it is with their fate in mind that Dumesnil recounts the consequences of the "revolution" effected by Louis XI. Book six begins by acknowledging the accuracy of some historians who have attributed the immense power enjoyed by his successors to the accomplishments of Louis XI himself. In depriving the nobles of their power, Louis did indeed contribute to the expansion of the royal authority, which Dumesnil believes to be necessary for "true" liberty, not to be confused with equality, which Dumesnil abominated.[9] But Louis also created a vacuum, and when, under Henri II and his successors, the crown began to weaken, "the people, having become more forward, took to themselves a portion of that power that the great nobles had in other times possessed."[10] Dumesnil characterizes the activities of the Catholic League as "the first act of the power of the people" and declares that the period ending with the Revolution was one of decline, unrelieved even by the reign of Louis XIV. The anarchic potency of the people, given its opportunity by the actions of Louis XI, eroded the foundations of the monarchy. Liberty diminished as the people's demands for equality, which is absolutely contrary to liberty, intensified. (In this sense, though in much cruder form, Dumesnil's ideas approximate those of Tocqueville, later in the century.) Dumesnil blames Louis XI for creating a set of circumstances in which the people could gradually increase their power and create a society marked by equality but also by a lack of liberty. Although his interpretation of the relationship between Louis XI and the people is quite different from the views of most writers after the Restoration, his focus on that relationship set the groundwork for the many references to Louis XI in the works of subsequent nineteenth-century historians.

The clearest exposition of the relationship between Louis XI and the bourgeoisie is found, not unexpectedly, in Augustin Thierry's *Essai sur l'histoire de la formation et des progrès du Tiers Etat*. Not only does Thierry recognize the association forged between king and people during the reign of Louis XI, he also notes the ambivalence most modern scholars feel about the monarch. Interestingly, Thierry characterizes the third estate as a divided group with contradictory goals. He maintains that, within the third estate, there were two fundamentally opposed "spirits" which infused the people. The commercial classes were motivated by a liberal, municipally-focused view, while the magistrature was much more intimately connected with the forces of government. In other words, the former were drawn to the cause of liberty, the latter to that of order. The struggle of these two spirits, according to Thierry, resulted in slow but steady progress to France's present happy state, wherein the people enjoy "civic equality, national unity and unity of government."[11]

Thierry praises the reign of Charles VII as a period of great popular progress but, like all such movements in history, it could not be sustained, because the unified effort of many individuals dissipates quickly. In order to preserve the advances made under Charles VII, the power to continue the effort had to be placed in the hands of one energetic person: "This one man, this jealous, active, obstinate personality was Louis XI. If, in history, there are personages who seem marked with a seal for a providential mission, the son of Charles VII was one of these . . . "[12] Thierry successfully balances the contributions made by Louis XI, which were necessary for the preservation of the advances made under his predecessor, with the recognition that his actions in that regard were often immoral:

> His reign was a struggle every day for the unity of power and the cause of social levelling, a struggle sustained in a savage manner, by shrewdness and cruelty, without courtesy or mercy. From that comes the blend of interest and repugnance that this strange original character excites in us.[13]

In his *Histoire de France*, Henri Martin follows Thierry's interpretation of Louis XI quite closely, even quoting directly from Thierry's *Essai sur l'histoire de la formation et des progrès du Tiers Etat* about the king.[14] The importance of Louis XI to Martin is indicated as well on the title page of his *Histoire de France populaire*. The engraving shows the Spirit of France placing her left hand on the shoulder of Louis XI and pointing with her sword to his name on a list of great persons which also includes those of Vercingetorix, Charlemagne, St Louis and Joan of Arc.[15] Perhaps nothing could more amply testify to the immense contributions allegedly made by Louis XI to France than to place him among such company.

Martin, like Thierry, is reluctant to attribute much of the progress of *le peuple* to the efforts of the king, despite the undeniable bond of common interest which united them. In the case of Louis XI, for example, Martin is careful to demonstrate that the convocation of the estates general in 1467, though necessary to the state and beneficial to the *bourgeoisie*, was not welcomed by Louis XI. The king called the assembly because he recognized the strength of the people, the support of whom he desperately needed if he was successfully to withstand the noble pressure regarding the grant of Normandy to his brother Charles.[16] The assembly at Tours was nonetheless significant in spite of Louis XI's lack of enthusiasm for the event. Martin compares it to the assembly of Philippe le Bel in his struggle against the pope: "in 1302, it had been a question of the independence of the kingdom; it was a question of national unity in 1468."[17]

Martin goes on to describe the specific contributions that Louis XI made to France, including the numerous territorial gains and the defeat of the feudal nobles. Moreover, Louis XI encouraged the industrial and commercial forces in the realm. Martin is quick to point out, however, that "if the accretion of national power was immense, if social progress was, in certain respects, incontestable, nevertheless despotism also progressed . . . "[18] Martin laments that the undeniable benefits for France possessed such unwelcome side-effects. His view on the progress of the arts is indicative. While he asserts that the arts were indeed beginning to flourish, they did so in a desiccated moral landscape. Consequently, the advances of the fifteenth century were not as brilliant as those which occurred in the Renaissance.[19] In a somewhat romantic vein, Martin sums up the character and significance of Louis XI: "He was the incarnate reaction against the middle ages, against its morality and its idealism as much as against its aberrations; against its liberties as much as against its anarchy."[20] Louis XI was in many ways a contradiction, not the least of which was the tension produced by contemptible conduct in pursuit of laudable goals. Martin sums up succinctly: "This bad man was not at all a bad Frenchman."[21]

François Guizot was perhaps the greatest of Louis XI's nineteenth-century admirers. He possessed an evolutionary view of French history, and of European civilization in general. According to Guizot, the fifteenth century was especially important in the history of Europe because the process of gradual change accelerated and intensified; the late medieval period held a special appeal for Guizot as the "door" to the modern world.[22] Guizot's belief in evolutionary change in history reflects his faith in government through cooperation and compromise. In his view, all elements of society must work together; the French Revolution was the violent but necessary corrective to a disruptive period of social conflict during which the monarchy lost its ability to act as the focus of the desire for unity and social cohesiveness.[23]

Guizot's view of history reflected his experiences as a political player in Restoration France. Born in 1787 in Nîmes, he moved to Paris in 1805. After becoming a professor of history at the University of Paris in 1812, he made the acquaintance of Royer-Collard, who helped him to obtain his first governmental post as secretary-general for the Ministry of the Interior. When he was dismissed from his position on the *Conseil d'état* in 1820 in the conservative reaction, he lectured on representative government and published his *Essais sur l'histoire de France* (1823). His lectures on European and French civilization attracted a large political audience in the years preceding the July Revolution. Thereafter he was wholly engrossed in politics under Louis-Philippe. His political career reached its peak in the 1840s but, as the decade wore on, Guizot was increasingly viewed as a conservative and was ousted from power during the Revolution of 1848. After that time, Guizot returned to history and to journalism and did not re-enter the political scene. He died in 1874.

Guizot perceived history to be as much the product of economic progress as it was of evolution to representative political institutions. In this respect, Guizot approaches the economic determinism of Marx, but this element of the class struggle is, for the most part, muted in his work. Guizot's emphasis on economic issues could account, in part, for his extremely positive view of Louis XI. In the eleventh lesson of his *Histoire de la civilisation en Europe*, where he discusses the fifteenth century, Guizot acknowledges the importance of Louis XI in the emergence of the middle classes.

> One often spoke of the struggle of Louis XI against the great nobles of the kingdom and of his favour towards the *bourgeoisie* and the common men. There is truth in this, although it has been exaggerated and the conduct of Louis XI towards diverse classes of society often troubled more than served the state.[24]

The way in which Guizot refers to Louis XI's contribution to the rise of the middle classes illustrates the fact that, by the time Guizot was writing, the association of Louis XI with the *bourgeoisie* had become almost a commonplace assertion. Guizot recognizes the importance of Louis XI's efforts, but he maintains that Louis accomplished something even more significant in terms of France's political development. Louis XI succeeded in substituting the "politics of intelligence" for the "politics of force." Granted, he also employed trickery and deceit in pursuit of political goals, but the abandonment of force was a tremendously important advance, nonetheless. Guizot maintains that, although the greater "revolution" in politics came later, when justice and intelligence supplanted self-aggrandizement and "égoïsme" as the goal of politics,

> It is nonetheless true that it was already a great step to renounce the continual use of force, to invoke especially superior intelligence, to govern by the handling of minds and not by the shattering of lives. It is this [process], in the midst of all his crimes and faults, and despite his perverse nature, by the merit of his lively intelligence that Louis XI began.[25]

Guizot's evolutionary view of history, with its emphasis on economic progress, translated into a laudatory appraisal of Louis XI. Moreover, this appreciation of the forces of historical development led him to re-interpret Louis XI's manipulative tactics as a positive step taken in the direction away from the barbarous politics associated with feudalism. Guizot's desire to place events within a much larger analytic framework led him to re-evaluate Louis XI as a shining example of incipient modernity.

Louis XI's popularity in the nineteenth century was also due, in large measure, to the emergence of the romantic movement in France in the 1820s, somewhat later than its counterparts in Germany and England. It is recognizably difficult to provide a precise definition of romanticism, and no two scholars are likely to agree, but, generally speaking, the romantics were moved by a spirit of restless individualism and a distaste for the oppressive ideological structures of order and rationality. In revolt against the so-called universal norms touted by the *philosophes*, the romantics emphasized a sensual experiencing of the world and endorsed each individual's expression of his or her own subjective, personal reality. Although French romantics spanned the political spectrum from Bourbon conservatism to social utopianism, they shared an organicist vision of the French polity, wherein each individual had an established place and function to fulfil. Coupled with their elevation of untamed nature over mechanized industry, this organicist perspective led French romantics to manifest an appreciation of, and in some cases a longing to return to, the pre-industrial paradise of the Middle Ages. For French romantics, Louis XI, whose complex personality reflected his position balanced on the cusp between the Middle Ages and modernity, was a fascinating, vaguely repellent figure.

Louis XI's popularity can be more specifically linked with the tremendous success and influence of Sir Walter Scott's novel *Quentin Durward*.[26] *Quentin Durward* first appeared in France in 1823 when romanticism was already in full flower. With its vividly drawn portraits, its tales of intrigue and its medieval setting, *Quentin Durward* possessed tremendous appeal, and Scott's characterization of Louis XI as the wily and unscrupulous manipulator influenced many subsequent nineteenth-century portraits of the king, and indeed continues to exert an influence on modern opinions about Louis XI.

Much has been written about Scott's use of historical events,[27] but the historical veracity of *Quentin Durward* is seldom discussed in these works, perhaps because of the patently dubious scholarship behind the romance. Scott drew his portrait of Louis XI almost entirely from Nathaniel Wraxall's *Memoirs of the Kings of France of the Race of Valois* (1777).[28] Nevertheless, *Quentin Durward* was both commercially and critically successful, and it spawned numerous works of both fiction and non-fiction in which Louis XI occupied a central place.

The fascination with Louis XI appears to have peaked in 1827 when no less than four works about the king were published. Scott's view of Louis XI as the shrewd and villainous king was echoed in two plays: Casimir Delavigne's *Louis XI, Une Tragédie* and Mély-Janin's *Louis XI à Peronne*. In both works the villainy of Louis XI is a device used to heighten the dramatic effect.[29] In the same year, a history of Louis XI by Pigault-Lebrun also appeared which again seems to have been highly influenced by Scott's interpretation. Not surprisingly, given Pigault-Lebrun's prolific production of rather salacious novels, the "biography" was not a product of serious scholarship and was completely lacking in source citations. Finally, Isidore Moustardun published his *Discours sur le règne de Louis XI*, also in 1827. Moustardun's work broke from the view propounded by Scott; he praised Louis XI for destroying the feudal nobility, thus facilitating the emergence of a more temperate monarchy. Moustardun's opinion points to the most important aspect of nineteenth-century interpretations of Louis XI: his involvement in fostering the emergence of the modern French state, primarily through his encouragement of the aspirations of the *bourgeoisie*. Interest in Louis XI abated only slightly after the peak in 1827.[30]

The influence of *Quentin Durward* can also be found in the work of French novelists. Victor Hugo's portrait of Louis XI in *Notre Dame de Paris* was said to have been modelled on that drawn by Scott.[31] Moreover, it has recently been argued that Scott influenced the novels of Honoré de Balzac as well.[32] Though Scott's impact on Alexandre Dumas and Stendhal is perhaps less pronounced, Louis XI also makes brief appearances in their novels, respectively *The Three Musketeers* and *Le Rouge et le Noir*. In both cases the impression of Louis XI, master manipulator, popularized by Scott, is evoked by the authors in order to underscore and clarify a point made about or by one of the characters.[33] It is clear that, in all aspects of literary romanticism, Scott played a pivotal role and Louis XI was generally characterized along Scott's lines.[34]

Finally, Scott's work was influential for a number of romantic historians.[35] To historians like Prosper de Barante, who believed that the spirit of an age was of central importance and could be evoked through vivid individual characterizations, Scott's novels provided worthy examples.[36] Prosper de Barante's *Histoire des Ducs de Bourgogne* was particularly indebted to Scott's *Quentin Durward*. Both C. A. Sainte-Beuve and F. R. Toreinx, contemporary critics, acknowledged the importance of Scott's historical novels to the development of the historical discipline in general, and on Barante's work in particular. Sainte-Beuve praised Scott's work as a much-needed step in the direction away from the excessive "present-mindedness" of eighteenth-century histories. Comparing Barante to Scott, Sainte-Beuve maintained that, although the former was at a disadvantage because he could not venture into fiction as could Scott, nevertheless "His Louis XI, for reality and life, agreed with *Quentin Durward*."[37] In his *Histoire du Romantisme en France* (1829), Toreinx went even farther in praising Barante. While admitting that Scott's works generally demonstrated all the best qualities of a novel, Toreinx was less pleased with *Quentin Durward*, saying "the figure of Louis XI is incomplete: there is only weakness and pettiness; the genius, the firm resolution are not there."[38] Barante himself noted the appeal historical novels had hitherto possessed over serious history, since the former could take liberties with the truth in the effort to make the past seem more alive. Barante's intent was to imbue history with that vivacity which characterized historical novels:

> I have attempted to restore to history the attraction that the historical novel had taken from it. It must be, above all, exact and serious, but it seems to me that it could be lively and real at the same time.[39]

Barante's view of Louis XI's unmitigated villainy parallels that of Scott. One particularly interesting aspect of Barante's discussion of Louis XI is his examination of both contemporary sources and subsequent histories of the monarch. He maintains that servants of the king were too close to him to be able to see beyond the dazzling array of tricks Louis XI employed to achieve a goal. Authors like Commynes did not believe themselves capable of penetrating into the inner workings of Louis XI's "genius," and therefore they did not question either his methods or the ends to which they were directed.[40] Barante himself was under no illusions about the nature of his reign: "The kingdom was ruined; the people were at the lowest level of misery; the prisons were full; no one was certain of his life or his posses-sions . . . "[41] Barante's harshest criticism is reserved for Charles Pinot Duclos and others who:

> viewing the past as a spectacle of disorder, ignorance and barbarism, in
> some fashion excused Louis XI at the expense of the epoch in which he
> lived, finding in him a clearer mind, a more sensible viewpoint, a more
> mocking language than in those who surrounded him.[42]

The most famous, and complex, of the romantic historians was, of course, Jules Michelet. Michelet's exuberant and dramatic style comes through as clearly in his treatment of Louis XI as almost anywhere else in his great *Histoire de France*. It should not be surprising after all, since, in Louis XI, Michelet finds a character of considerable complexity and drama; Louis XI was the shadow following closely behind the bright figure of Joan of Arc.[43]

Michelet's view of Louis XI changed through the years as he gained access to different source materials. In the early 1830s, Michelet was more positively disposed to Louis XI; his lectures at the Collège de France were filled with admiration for the monarch. His *Précis de l'histoire de France* (1833) portrayed Louis XI in the most flattering light:

> [Louis XI] became the depository of the hopes of the poor people, the
> artisan of a policy of progress who was supported by the *bourgeoisie* in
> order to hasten the ruin of the feudality, the liberator of France, for whom
> a ruse was worth more than the untimely bravery of the *chevaliers* of Crècy,
> the intelligent enemy of Charles the Rash, who [Louis XI] let wear
> himself out in the pursuit of chimeras.[44]

After he had travelled to Brussels and examined various Burgundian sources, Michelet modified his view of the king. As a romantic historian, moreover, Michelet expressed a preference for the vibrant style of the Burgundian chronicler Chastellain (whose work had only recently been published for the first time) over what he considered to be the dry, lifeless prose of Com-mynes.[45] Yet even after he changed his view of Louis XI somewhat, Michelet still advanced an interpretation of Louis which was considerably at odds with the general opinion of the monarch passed down to nineteenth-century writers. In a letter written to Michelet upon the publication of the sixth volume of the *Histoire de France* (which included the section on Louis XI), a friend commented on Michelet's success in shedding new light on the monarch.

> I think that your remarkable work on Louis XI is very suitable for making one appreciate the reign and influence of this prince who, without being morally inferior to other kings who were his contemporaries, was superior to them in his capacity to govern. Your book perfectly shows that he was one of the most energetic agents for the destruction of the old feudal organization, which was destined to perish. As such, he merits a high rank among modern sovereigns, if it is true that one must esteem political action according to whether it favours, at any given moment, the spontaneous evolution of societies.[46]

Michelet devotes considerable attention to the discussion of how Louis XI made his presence felt throughout all of France with the extension of royal power. The nobles were, of course, especially alarmed by the succession of Louis XI; their glory days as independent magnates were over. "The great nobles mourned the dead king; they mourned themselves. The funeral of Charles VII was their funeral: with him ended their control of royal authority."[47]

In true romantic fashion, Michelet chose to make his point about Louis XI's suppression of the nobles by emphasizing seemingly mundane matters rather than large-scale events. With regard to Louis XI's attack on the nobles, Michelet focuses on the monarch's efforts to curtail noble privileges associated with the hunt: "Under the pretext of regulating the chase, he was going to touch *seigneurie* at its most delicate point, to hamper the noble in his most cherished liberty, that of vexing the peasant."[48] Louis XI's circumscription of noble hunting privileges was the quotidian reflection of a sweeping "revolution monarchique." Michelet discounts the story bruited by two chroniclers that Louis XI had the ear of a gentleman cut off as punishment for illegal hunting; he gives more credence to the assertion that Louis's men often replaced the nobles as vexatious burdens on the people. Michelet is as quick to point out, however, that Louis XI willingly provided restitution to "les pauvres gens" who had suffered some injury at the hands of his men. Michelet remarks that, on the basis of the numerous such small tokens and gifts which one finds in Louis XI's accounts, "one would be tempted to believe that this sensible politician will have often had the vague desire, in his war against the great nobles, of making himself the king of the 'little people'." In this one sentence, Michelet has summed up the interpretation advanced by a number of his contemporaries whose emphasis on the relationship between Louis XI and "les petits" largely determines the nineteenth-century view of the monarch.

Louis XI's dark and complex personality and the manner in which he exercised power attracted the romantics. At the same time, new political assumptions, as suggested in Michelet's history, added a fresh dimension to discussions of the monarch. In place of the old debate between constitutionalism and absolutism which, as we have said, effectively ended with the Revolution, a controversy developed concerning the exact nature of popular representation in government. Moreover, while the principle of a constitution was accepted, there appeared to be some need to prove the historical legitimacy of the middle classes, who benefited in proportion to their wealth from the establishment of a franchise based on property. Thus, although the sovereignty issue had been set aside, history could still be used for political purposes, as indeed it was.

Louis XI continues to exert a strong hold on both the scholarly and popular imagination – the twentieth century has produced still more books about this enigmatic monarch. But despite the abundance of published material about Louis XI, including exhaustive biographies, thoroughly researched articles delving into all aspects of his life and reign, and primary source collections of letters and ambassadorial dispatches, people still sum him up dismissively as "le roi araignée," or possibly as "le roi bourgeois." In the long run, the image of Louis XI as tyrant has won out, perhaps because, as some historians believe, we are still living with the Revolution, a revolution that definitively rejected the portrait of Louis XI as political sage.

Appendix

Chronological list of works referring to Louis XI, 1560–1795

1566   Jean Bodin, *Method for the Easy Comprehension of History*
1567   *De la Nécessité d'assembler les Estats*
1567   *Mémoires des occasions de la guerre, appellée le Bien-Public, rapportez à l'estat de la guerre presente*
1573   François Hotman, *De Furoribus Gallicus*
1573   François Hotman, *Francogallia*
1573   Theodore Beza, *Du Droit des Magistrats*
1576   Innocent Gentillet, *Discours contre Machiavel*
1576   Innocent Gentillet, *Remonstrance au Tres Chrestien Henry III de ce nom Roy de France et de Pologne*
1576   Jean Bodin, *Les Six Livres de la République*
1576   Jean Bodin, *Recueil de tout ce qui s'est negocié en la compagnie du tiers-état de France . . . en la ville de Blois au 15 Novembre 1576 . . .*
1579   *Vindiciae contra tyrannos*
1582   George Buchanan, *Rerum Scoticarum Historia*
1585   Pierre Belloy, *Apologie Catholique contre les libelles declarations, advis, et consultations faictes, écrites et publiées par les Liguez perturbateurs du repos du Royaume de France . . .*
1587   Pierre Belloy, *De l'Authorité du Roy*
1589   *Dialogue du Royaume*
1589   *L'Atheisme de Henri de Valoys: où est monstré le vray but de ses dissimulations et cruautez*
1591   Jean Boucher, *De justa Abdicatione Henrici Tertii*
1593   *Satyre Ménippée de la vertue de Catholicon d'Espagne et de la tenue des estatz de Paris*
1608   Charles Loyseau, *Traité des Seigneuries*
1609   Charles Loyseau, *Cinq livres du droit des offices*
1610   Charles Loyseau, *Des Ordres et simples dignités*
1610   Pierre Matthieu, *Histoire de Louis Onze*
1614   M. I. Baricave, *La Defence de la monarchie françoise et d'autres monarchies, contre les detestables et execrables maximes d'estat des Ministres Calvinistes*

1616   Rodolphe Le Maître, *Le Tibère françois ou le six premiers livres des Annales de Cornelius Tacitus*

1620   Gabriel Naudé, *Le Marfore ou discours contre les libelles*

1630   Gabriel Naudé, *Addition à l'histoire de Louis XI*

1631   Jean de Silhon, *Le Ministre d'estat avec le veritable usage de la politique moderne*

1632   Cardin Le Bret, *De la souveraineté du Roy*

1633   Didier Herauld, *Fragment de l'examen du prince de Machiavel*

1635   Honorat de Meynier, *Les Demandes curieuses et les responses libres*

1640   *La Voix gemissante du peuple chrestien et catholique*

1643   Louis Machon, *Apologie pour Machiavelle en faveur des princes et les minstres d'estat*

1648   *Declarations des roys Louis XI et Henry III*

1649   *Dialogue entre le Roy Louys XI et Louys XII sur leur differente façon de regner*

1649   *Epilogue, ou dernier appareil du bon citoyen*

1649   *Lettre d'avis à Messieurs du Parlement de Paris, escrit par un Provincial*

1649   *Manual du bon citoyen ou bouclier de defense legitime contre les assauts de l'ennemi*

1649   *Remonstrance du Roy Louis XII au Roy Louis XI sur leur differente façon de regner*

1651   *Request de la Noblesse pour l'Assemblée des Estats generaux*

1652   *La Guide au Chemin de la Liberté*

1652   *Le Dialogue d'estat*

1652   *Les Veritables maximes du gouvernement de la France*

1652   Claude Joly, *Recueil des maximes veritables et importantes pour l'institution du roy*

1689   *Les soupirs de la France esclave, qui aspire après la Liberté*

1690   *Entretien de Louis Onze et de Charle Hardi Duc de Bourgogne*

1694   *Avis d'un amy à l'autheur du Miroir historique de la ligue de l'an 1464*

1694   *Miroir historique de la ligue de l'an 1464 ou peut se reconnoitre la ligue de l'an 1694*

1694   *Pensées sur l'avis d'un amy à l'auteur du Miroir historique de l'an 1464*

1697   Pierre Bayle, *Dictionnaire historique et critique*

1699   Fénelon, *Télémaque*

c. 1700 Fénelon, *Dialogues des morts*

c. 1700 Joachim Le Grand, *Histoire de Louis XI*

c. 1720 *Accomodement entre le Roy Louis XI et son Parlement*

c. 1720 *Pour l'autorité du Parlement dans les affaires publiques*

1721   *Essay historique concernant les droits et prérogatives de la cours des pairs qui est le Parlement séant à Paris*

1721   *Tres humbles et tres respecteuses iteratives remonstrances que presentens au Roy*

1727   Henri de Boulainvilliers, *Histoire de l'ancien gouvernement de la France*

1732   Henri de Boulainvilliers, *Essais sur la noblesse de France*

1732   *Mémoire touchant l'origine et l'autorité du Parlement de France, appellé Judicium Francorum*

1745   Charles Pinot Duclos, *Histoire de Louis XI*

1748   Montesquieu, *L'Esprit des lois*

1753/4 Louis-Adrien Lepaige, *Lettres historiques sur les fonctions essentielles du parlement*

1764   Marquis d'Argenson, *Considérations sur le gouvernement ancien et present de la France*

1765   Gautier de Sibert, *Variations de la Monarchie Françoise dans son gouvernement politique*

1768   Damiens de Gomicourt, *Mélanges historiques et critiques*

1772   Hue de Miromesnil, *Lettres sur l'état de la magistrature en l'année 1772*

1777   Pierre Louis Gin, *Les Vrais principes du gouvernement françois*

1788   Abbé Sieyès, *Qu'est-ce que c'est le tiers-état?*

1788   Guillaume-Joseph Saige, *Catéchisme du citoyen ou élémens du droit public françois*

1789   Gautier de Sibert, *Considérations sur l'ancienneté de l'existence du Tiers-état*

c. 1794 Jean-Baptiste Britard, *Discours historique sur la caractère et la politique de Louis XI*

1797   Pierre Louis Gin, *Origine des malheurs de la France*

Notes

INTRODUCTION: "LE ROI ARAIGNÉE"

1 Catherine Legros, *Je ne suis pas celui que vous croyez* (Dijon: Edition de l'Aleï, 1985).

2 The most recent and even-handed biography of Louis XI is Paul Murray Kendall, *Louis XI: The Universal Spider* (New York: W. W. Norton & Co., 1971).

3 This is not to say that, prior to the 1970s, historians were not concerned with an individual king's contemporary and historical image; see, for example, Raymond Ritter, *Henry IV lui-même, l'homme* (Paris: Michel, 1944). It does seem, however, that only in recent years has there been sustained attention paid to the power of a particular king's image, in both contemporary and historical contexts. Two particularly interesting additions to the growing number of studies devoted to the creation (and manipulation) of the monarch's image are: James Smither, "Myth and Reality of Kingship during the French Wars of Religion" (PhD dissertation, Brown University, 1989) and Nancy Davenport, "Maenad, Martyr, Mother: Marie Antoinette Transformed," *Proceedings of the Consortium on Revolutionary Europe 1750–1850* 15 (1985): 66–84.

4 Michel Tyvaert, "L'Image du roi: légitimité et moralité royales dans les histoires de France au XVIIe siècle," *Revue d'histoire moderne et contemporaine* 21 (1974): 521–47.

5 See Nannerl O. Keohane, *Philosophy and the State in France* (Princeton, NJ: Princeton University Press, 1980), pp. 3–22.

6 The limitations of absolute monarchy are admirably addressed in J. H. Burns, "The Idea of Absolutism," in *Absolutism in Seventeenth-Century Europe*, ed. John Miller (New York: St. Martin's Press, 1990), pp. 21–42.

7 Julian Franklin defines constitutionalism as possessing three necessary elements: "the notion of the supremacy of law . . . the idea of a sovereign community from which all authority derives, and the institutionalization of that sovereignty through control of governmental power by the people and their representatives." *Constitutionalism and Resistance in the Sixteenth Century* (New York: Pegasus Books, 1969), p. 12.

8 W. F. Church, *Constitutional Thought in Sixteenth-Century France* (Cambridge, Mass: Harvard University Press, 1941), especially chapter three.

9 For a discussion of this institutional rivalry and how it was manifested in political ideology, see my "Meddling Chaperons: The Involvement of the Parlement of Paris in the Estates General of 1593," in *Politics, Ideology and the Law in Early Modern Europe: Essays in Honor of J. H. M. Salmon*, ed. Adrianna E. Bakos (Rochester, NY: University of Rochester Press, 1994), pp. 91–105.

10 James Tully, ed., *Meaning and Context: Quentin Skinner and his Critics* (New York: Polity Press, 1988); David Boucher, *Texts in Context: Revisionist Methods for Studying the History of Ideas* (The Hague: Martinus Nijhoff, 1985); Anthony Pagden, ed., *The Languages of Political Theory in Early Modern Europe* (Cambridge, England: Cambridge University Press, 1987).

11 Quentin Skinner, "Meaning and Understanding in the History of Ideas," in Tully, pp. 29–78.

12 J. G. A. Pocock, "The Concept of a Language and the *métier d'historien*: Some Considerations on Practice." in Pagden, pp. 19–38.

13 This synoptic treatment is based largely upon the relatively short but well-written account of Louis's reign in Ernest Lavisse, gen. ed., *Histoire de France*, 9 vols (Paris: Librairie Hachette, 1902), vol. 4, part 2: *Charles VII, Louis XI et les premières années de Charles VIII 1422–1492*, by C. Petit-Dutaillis; also on the brief biography by Charles Tyrrel, *Louis XI* (Boston: Twayne Publishers, 1980). A more extensive treatment can be found in Paul Murray Kendall, *Louis XI: The Universal Spider*.

14 There is a rather unsophisticated psychological study of Louis XI by Chalfant Robinson, contained in the 1916 annual report of the American Historical Association.

15 Ironically, though perhaps not surprisingly, some of those who had encouraged Louis to rebel against his father were among those who later revolted against Louis himself. Jean II, duc d'Alençon, and Antoine de Chabannes, comte de Dunois, are important examples of *seigneurs* seemingly intent on rebelling against Louis XI, despite the fact that they had intrigued with him twenty years before.

16 For an extensive discussion of Louis XI's efforts to undermine the feudal structure in France see Henry Montaigu, *La Fin des féodaux: Le pré carré de roi Louis* (n.p.: Olivier Orban, 1980).

17 This tendency has been noted with regard to Louis's relationship with the duc de Bretagne in Barthelèmy-Amedée Pocquet du Haut-Jusse, "A Political Concept of Louis XI: Subjection instead of Vassalage," in *The Recovery of France in the Fifteenth Century*, ed. P. S. Lewis and trans. G. F. Martin (London: Macmillan, 1971), pp. 196–215.

18 At the time of Louis XI's succession, there had been some murmurings to have Louis by-passed in favour of his younger brother, Charles, but the embryonic conspiracy came to nothing. These ideas, however, would seem to indicate that Charles did have designs on the crown quite apart from any concerns he might have had regarding the welfare of the realm. Petit-Dutaillis, p. 322. See also Henri Stein, *Charles de France, frère de Louis XI* (Paris, 1921).

19 The duc de Bourgogne wanted Louis XI to give Champagne to Charles, and he attempted to insert a clause into the Treaty of Péronne to this effect. Louis XI resisted the insertion of the clause into the treaty but agreed to draw up a separate agreement. After the Treaty of Péronne was concluded, however, he asked how the duke would respond if, because Charles was not satisfied with the appanage, Louis was forced to bestow a province other than Champagne upon his brother. The duke washed his hands of the tiresome affair by saying that, if Charles could be satisfied in some other way, he would not intervene. In the end, Charles was "persuaded" to take Guyenne instead of Champagne, a much more advantageous resolution of the issue for Louis since it was considerably farther from Burgundy than was Champagne. See Kendall, pp. 213–26 for a discussion of the negotiations for Charles's appanage.

20 After being granted Normandy, Charles came into conflict with his new neighbour, the duc de Bretagne, over some disputed border territories. Seizing the opportunity, Louis reportedly said to the duc d'Alençon: "Je croy qu'il me

faulra reprendre ma duché de Normandie. Il me fault aler secourir mon frère."
Petit-Dutaillis, p. 352.

21   Louis XI's relationship to the Holy See is discussed by Paul Ourliac, "The
Concordat of 1472: An Essay on the Relations between Louis XI and Sixtus
IV," in P. S. Lewis, ed. *The Recovery of France in the Fifteenth Century*.

22   See René Gandlihon, *La Politique economique de Louis XI* (Rennes, 1940); Henri
Sée, *Louis XI et les villes* (Paris, 1891); Gaston Zeller, "Louis XI, la noblesse et la
marchandise," *Annales E. S. C.* 1 (1946): 331–41.

23   In his invaluable *Bibliothèque Historique de la France* (Paris: G. Martin, 1719),
pp. 377–80, Jacques Le Long lists forty-one separate items, both manuscript
and published accounts of the reign of Louis XI. He includes a number of
contemporary chronicles, like that of Monstrelet, memoirs of individuals such
as Jacques de Clercq, Seigneur de Beauvoir en Ternois, and histories written by
sixteenth- and seventeenth-century authors, such as Bernard de Girard, Sieur
du Haillan and Pierre Matthieu. Interestingly, although Le Long mentions Jean
Godefroy's edition of Commynes's *Mémoires* (Brussels, 1713), in which
Godefroy included a number of other contemporary accounts alongside that of
Commynes, Le Long cites no sixteenth-century editions of Commynes's
Mémoires.

24   I have relied here on documents published in the relevant volumes of *Documents
historiques inédits sur l'histoire de France*, edited by J. J. Champollion-Figéac and
published in 1843.

25   J. J. Champollion-Figéac, *Documents historiques inédits sur l'histoire de France*, 4
vols (Paris, 1843–48), 2: 196.

26   " . . . ayde et conseil des princes et seigneurs de son sang et aultres notables
hommes de *son royaulme*." (emphasis mine) Ibid., 2: 315. The editor also noted
the peculiar usage but attempted to explain it through the fact that Berry was
heir presumptive since Louis XI had no male offspring at that time. However,
it becomes possible to see it as a more deliberate indication of intent when one
takes into account the confession of the Seigneur de Crèvecoeur, in which he
states that Charolais and other nobles "estoient deliberez, eulx assemblez, faire
un regent, ensemble un connestable, oudit royaulme, et donner ordre, provision
et police au gouvernement et regime dudit royaulme." p. 352. According to
Crèvecoeur's testimony, Berry was to be regent, while the position of the
constable had not yet been decided upon.

27   Ibid., 2: 215.

28   See Kendall, pp. 119–20, for a discussion of the machinations involved in Louis
XI's acquisition of Roussillon.

29   Champollion-Figéac, 2: 441.

30   Modern historians such as J. Russell Major consider the 1484 assembly to be
significant because it was the first time meetings were held in the *bailliages* and
sénéchaussées to elect deputies to send to the estates general. Two other proposed
innovations, the creation of provincial estates in regions which were previously
governed by *élus* and the establishment of a two-year limit on the granting of
the *taille*, were never realized. J. Russell Major, *From Renaissance Monarchy to
Absolute Monarchy: French Kings, Nobles and Estates* (Baltimore: Johns Hopkins
University Press, 1994), p. 16. See also J. Russell Major, *Representative
Institutions in Renaissance France, 1421–1559* (Madison, Wisconsin: University
of Wisconsin Press, 1960), pp. 58–116.

31   Jean Masselin, *Journal des Etats-Généraux tenus à Tours en 1484*, ed. A. Bernier
(Paris: Imprimerie Royale, 1835), p. 3.

32   Ibid., pp. 139–41.

33   Ibid., p. 147.

34 After discussing the Parisian nominees, the assembly agreed that the most desirable form of council would be composed of thirty-six members, of whom twelve would be from the Parisian list. However, on 6 February, they were presented with a list of councillors which Louis had apparently compiled as part of his last testament. The estates then maintained that they would retain twelve members from this "ancienne liste" and add twenty-four more deputies of their own choosing. Their freedom to choose was further diminished when they were presented with a *rôle* which contained sixteen names (four nobles, four clergy, four "gens des finances" and four merchants). Those speaking for the king were now laying down the law with little regard for the rights of the estates. As well, at this time, the assembly was given an even clearer sign of the end of royal favour: one morning in mid-February the deputies walked into the main assembly room only to find that it had been thoroughly despoiled of ornaments, including such small items as the designs which decorated the backs of chairs. Although discussion seems to have turned more to the issue of taxation from this point on, it seems apparent that the assembly's spirit of independence was slowly but surely undermined and, in the end, the council reflected less the choice of the assembly than the successful machinations of the court nobles. Ibid., pp.101–310.

35 Ibid., p. 419.

36 Ibid., p. 355.

37 According to Jacques-Charles Brunet, *Manuel du Libraire et de l'amateur de livres*, 6 vols (Paris: Firmin Didot, 1860), Chastellain's *Chronique des ducs de Bourgogne* was published for the first time in Buchon's *Collection des Chroniques françaises* (Paris, 1827).

38 Georges Chastellain, *Oeuvres historiques inédits*, J. A. C. Buchon, ed. in *Choix de chroniques et mémoires sur l'histoire de France* (Paris: Librairie Charles Delagrave, 1883), p. 130.

39 Ibid., p. 356.

40 Another possibility for the identity of the woman is that she is the personification of France. The hypothesis that the image represents Mary is supported by the statement made by the apparition that, because Louis is a "non-homme" who despoils all the dignity that is in man, "c'est raison que tu vois droit cy, devant toi, lumiere de l'umain voyage et figure de *l'image divine* que tu ignores, que tu comtempnes et mescongnois . . . " (my emphasis). Ibid., p. 356. As well, Louis was known to be devoted to Notre Dame de Clèry – this vision could be a veiled reference to the hypocrisy of that piety.

41 Ibid., p. 359.

42 The hypothesis of a collaboration between Chastellain and Meschinot was first propounded by A. La Borderie, who based his assertions upon the fact that Chastellain's verses, *Les Princes*, form the core of each of Meschinot's *Ballades*. La Borderie rejects the possibility of plagiarism on the part of Meschinot since in one of the ballads Meschinot speaks directly to his unnamed source to express his gratitude for the latter's imput: "Touteffois j'ay faict diligence / Et par vostre commandement / De cy monstrer mon inscience, / Mais donnez y amendment." Cited by Christine Martineau-Genieys in her introduction to Jean Meschinot, *Les Lunettes des Princes* (Geneva: Droz, 1972), pp. xlii–xliii.

43 Considerez le temps qui present court.
Les loups sont mis gouverneurs des oueilles;
 . . . Les bestes sont, les corbins et corneilles,
Mort de faim, dont peines non pareilles
Ont pouvres gens: qui ne l'entend est sourd!
 . . . Seigneur puissant, sainson n'est que sommeilles,
Car tez subjectz prient que tu t'esveilles,

> Ou aultrement leur temps de vivre est court.
>
> (Cited by A. Borderlie, "Jean Meschinot: sa vie et ses oeuvres,"
> *Bibliothèque de l'Ecole des Chartres* lvi (1895): 294–5)

44 La Borderie, pp. 301–2. Martineau-Genieys maintains that the apparition in Chastellain's chronicle and Meschinot's *Dialogue* is the personification of France. See also above, note 42.

45 Jacques-Charles Brunet lists the following editions in *Manuel du Librairie et de l'amateur de livres*: Nantes, 1493; four subsequent undated editions probably appearing before 1495; Paris, 1495 – the first edition to include the *Vingt-cinq ballades*; two editions published in Paris, 1499; Paris, 1501; an undated edition published in Rouen after 1500; an undated Paris edition; Paris, 1504; Paris, 1505; Paris, c. 1520; Paris, 1522; Paris, 1527; Paris, 1528; Rouen, 1530; Lyons, without date; Paris, 1534; Paris, 1539.

46 A. La Borderie notes that sixteenth-century authors who sang the praises of Meschinot's poetry include Etienne Pasquier, Noël du Fail and Jean Bouchet, who wrote in his *Temple de bonne Renommée*: "Si vous lisez des Princes les *Lunettes*, / Vous n'y verrez que matières très nettes / Pour acquérir les vertus cardinales, / Semblablement les trois théologales." Cited in "Jean Meschinot: sa vie et ses oeuvres," p. 132.

47 For a short comparison of Commynes and Basin with the Burgundian chroniclers, see Paul Archambault, *Seven French Chroniclers: Witnesses to History* (Syracuse, NY: Syracuse University Press, 1974). In his chapter on Basin, which directly follows his treatment of Chastellain and La Marche, Archambault notes Basin's strong moral didacticism: "The historian is both judge and participant; he can raise his voice, interpret, exhort, condemn." p. 89.

48 Cited by Archambault, p. 89.

49 Ibid., p. 85.

50 The last seven chapters of book seven were added to a revision made by Basin in 1484 (the original work being written between 1473 and 1484). A revised manuscript of 1487 does not contain these chapters. It has been argued that they were omitted from the second revision because of their excessively condemnatory language, but this seems an unlikely reason because Basin had written quite enough to earn himself an execution without these added chapters. It could be, however, that Basin hoped to avoid angering Anne de Beaujeu by removing the most vitriolic attacks on Louis XI from his work. See Charles Samaran, Introduction to *Histoire de Louis XI* by Thomas Basin, 3 vols (Paris: Les Belles Lettres, 1963–72), I: xii–xiii.

51 Basin, III: 301.

52 Basin discusses Louis XI's elaborate spy system through which he was able to be informed about all incidents of slander or malignant references to him. The perpetrators were then brought before the courts and could only escape retribution if they had the financial resources to bribe the judges. Basin also asserts that some individuals were summarily thrown into the river without ever having appeared before a judge. Ibid., III: 323–7.

53 Ibid., III: 339.

54 To his credit, Basin does note that not all nobles were so altruistically motivated. Some were indeed concerned with personal gain, but Basin quickly states that this fact cannot discredit the entire rebellion. Ibid., I: 227.

55 Ibid., I: 177.

56 Ibid., I: 181.

57 Basin himself obviously viewed his ideas on legitimate resistance as more than a justification for a specific historical event. In his *Histoire de Charles VII* he elucidated his general views on resistance. "As free men, let us freely obey any prince who governs justly and legitimately for the good of all, and let us give

him our allegiance. But if one governs neither justly or legitimately nor for the general welfare, but in order to sacrifice the republic to his private, iniquitous and unjust passions, and to reduce his subjects to abject slavery, it is far better not to obey him. If the power to resist him were given us, we should be doing a far worthier thing, than if, with a dumb patience, we were to put up with his wild and unjust lusts and passions, as if we were approving them." Cited by Archambault, p. 96.

58 The secondary literature on Commynes's life and his *Mémoires* is vast. In recent years, Jean Dufournet has established himself as the premier scholar on Commynes. As well as producing a critical edition of the *Mémoires*, Dufournet has written three full-length studies of the author and his works: *La Destruction des myths dans les Mémoires de Philippe de Commynes* (Geneva: Publications romanes et françaises, 1966); *Études sur Philippe de Commynes* (Paris: Bibliothèque du Quinzième Siècle, 1975); and most recently *Philippe de Commynes. Un historien à l'aube des temps modernes* (Brussels: DeBoeck Université, 1994), which includes an excellent selected bibliography, pp. 299–312.

59 Commynes, *Mémoires*, ed. Jean Dufournet (Paris: Gallimard, 1979), Book I: Prologue, pp. 91–2.

60 The first edition of 1524 included only the first six books of the *Mémoires*, recounting events up to the death of Louis XI. In 1528, the last two books of the *Mémoires* appeared separately. In 1540 the first complete edition of Commynes's *Mémoires* appeared.

61 According to Kenneth Dreyer, there were no fewer than 120 French editions and ten translations of the work published between 1544 and 1643. Kenneth Dreyer, "Commynes and Machiavelli: A Study in Parallelism," *Symposium* (1951): 38.

62 Commynes, I: 358.

63 Ibid., I: 359.

64 Ibid., I: 360–1.

65 For a discussion of what constituted "normal" politics at this time see J. H. Hexter, *The Vision of Politics on the Eve of the Reformation* (New York: Basic Books, Inc., 1973).

66 Jean Dufournet, *Sur Philippe de Commynes* (Paris: Société d'Edition d'Enseignement Supérieur, 1982), pp. 111–46.

67 A number of scholars have investigated the striking similarities between Commynes and Machiavelli. Both André Stegmann and Kenneth Dreyer see similarities between the two writers in terms of method and perspective. With regard to method, Stegmann writes that, like Machiavelli, Commynes "n'entend traiter que de l'histoire dont il connaît avec certitude les protagonistes, les événements, les dessous du jeu, mais aussi, comme pour Machiavel, parce que son experience l'a conduit à un pessimisme nécessaire pour aborder lucidement la politique." "Commynes et Machiavel," *Studies on Machiavelli*, ed. Myron P. Gilmore (Florence: G. C. Sansoni, 1972), p. 271. Kenneth Dreyer notes that the most striking similarity between the two writers is their appreciation of normally unattractive character traits. "Commynes and Machiavelli: A Study in Parallelism," p. 49.

68 André Stegmann, "Le Tacitisme: programme pour un nouvel essai de définition," *Machiavellismo e Antimachiavellici nel Cinquecento* (Florence: Leo S. Olschki, 1969): 117–30. See also Kenneth C. Schellhase, *Tacitus in Renaissance Political Thought* (Chicago: Chicago University Press, 1976). See my discussion of the relationship between Louis XI and Machiavellism in Chapter 5 of this book.

69 The biographical information provided here is primarily derived from Donald Kelley's introduction to Claude de Seyssel, *The Monarchy of France*, trans. J. H.

Hexter (New Haven and London: Yale University Press, 1981), pp. 3–8. The most recent full-length biography of Seyssel is Alberto Caviglia, *Claudio di Seyssel (1450–1520)* (Turin, 1928).

70 *Ad . . . Angliae regem Henricum Septium Oratior* (Paris, 1506), cited by Jacques Poujol in the Introduction to *La Monarchie de France* by Claude de Seyssel (Paris: Librairie D'Argences, 1961), p. 14.

71 While Seyssel acknowledges that Charlemagne accomplished great things for France, his glory is somewhat tarnished by the fact that some of his endeavours were not undertaken for the glory of God. Moreover, Charlemagne waged more battles than did Louis XII and therefore lost more men and *matériél*. Furthermore, Seyssel applauds Louis XII's sage refusal of the imperial title which Charlemagne had first worn. All in all, Seyssel says: "ie veux dire pour verité, que la conduicte et le regne du Roy Loys ont esté plus profitables au royaume de France que ceux dudict roy Charles, et qu'iceluy royaume a esté et est plus grand repos et prosperité soubs le gouvernement du roy Loys qu'il fut soubs celuy du roy Charles." Claude de Seyssel, *Histoire du Roy Loys Douziesme, Pere du Peuple* (Paris: Jacques du Puys, 1587), pp. 24(r-v).

72 Ibid., pp. 36(r-v). It seems likely that Seyssel is referring here to Commynes's *Mémoires*. I have yet to find, other than in Commynes, these positive portraits of Louis XI.

73 Ibid., p. 37(r).

74 Ibid., p. 51(v).

75 J. G. A. Pocock, "Texts as Events: Reflections on the History of Political Thought," in Kevin Sharpe and Steven Zwicker, eds, *Politics of Discourse: The Literature and History of Seventeenth-Century England* (Berkeley, CA: University of California Press, 1987), pp. 21–34.

CHAPTER 1: THE ARCHITECT OF TYRANNY

1 See Donald R. Kelley, *The Foundations of Modern Historical Scholarship* (New York: Columbia University Press, 1970).

2 For the English side, see J. G. A. Pocock, *The Ancient Constitution and the Feudal Law* (Cambridge, England: Cambridge University Press, 1957); Glenn Burgess, *The Politics of the Ancient Constitution* (University Park, PA: Pennsylvania State University Press, 1993). J. P. Sommerville critiques Pocock's assertions about the "common-law mind" in *Politics and Ideology in England 1603–1640* (London: Longman, 1986).

3 Richard Tuck, *Natural Rights Theories: Their Origin and Development* (Cambridge, England: Cambridge University Press, 1979).

4 Richard Tuck takes a somewhat different view of the French Calvinist writers whom he characterizes as influenced by legal humanism of the law schools where many of them were educated. "Like the humanists, specific constitutional remedies were at the focus of their concern. If we are to understand the developments in rights theories during the sixteenth and early seventeenth centuries, then we must group the Calvinist theorists with such men as Alciato, and see them all as engaged in a retreat from the position where the natural law and natural rights enjoyed primacy to one where the major concern was human law designed by men for common utility either under their own initiative or under the command of God." Ibid., pp. 42–4. While I agree that Hotman and other Calvinist resistance theorists were more concerned with the specifics of the French context, I do not think we should discount their interest in natural rights theories as thoroughly as does Tuck.

5 For a brief discussion of the consequences of the massacre see J. H. M. Salmon, *Society in Crisis: France in the Sixteenth Century* (London: Methuen, 1975), pp. 183–95.

6 Donald Kelley discusses the importance of the St Bartholomew's Day Massacre both as a major contribution to the "mythology" of an international conspiracy intent on the complete extermination of the Huguenots and as an event which successfully re-energized the Protestant martyrological tradition. Kelley believes the effect of the massacre on political theory was even more dramatic. Donald Kelley, "Martyrs, Myths and the Massacre: The Background of St. Bartholomew," *American Historical Review* 77 (1972): 1323–41. Similarly, in his *Myths of the St. Bartholomew's Day Massacre 1572–1576* (Cambridge, Mass: Harvard University Press, 1988), Robert Kingdon examines the way in which writers discussing the massacre tried to accomplish three main goals: to describe the massacre itself and memorialize its victims (in keeping with the Protestant tradition of martyrology), to "spread and to internationalize further the conflict in which these massacres were an episode," and to use the event as a springboard to a much broader examination of the nature of government. The book lays heavy emphasis on the *Memoires de l'estat de France sous Charles IX*, compiled by Simon Goulart, but Kingdon also examines other major works like the *Francogallia* and the *Du Droit des magistrats*, making the important point that often these works were not narrowly Protestant in tone but rather were directed to a broader constituency of the disaffected.

7 For a discussion of the *regalians* see chapter 2 of W. F. Church, *Constitutional Thought in Sixteenth-Century France* (Cambridge, Mass: Harvard University Press, 1941).

8 A substantial section of the pamphlet is devoted to recounting the "evidence" to support the assertion that Charles was in fact involved in the massacre at all stages of its planning and execution. *Le Reveille-Matin des François et de leurs voisins* ("Edinburgh," 1574), pp. 50–72. Advocates and opponents of the premeditation theory have managed to keep the controversy about the origins of the St Bartholomew's Day Massacre alive for over four hundred years. For a recapitulation of the most recent scholarship on the subject, see Barbara Whitehead, "Revising the Revisionists: Louis-Pierre Anquetil and the Saint Bartholomew's Day Massacre," in *Politics, Ideology and the Law in Early Modern Europe*, p. 160, n. 3. The most recent (and most exhaustive) account of the St Bartholomew's Day Massacre is by Denis Crouzet, *La nuit de la Saint-Barthelèmy: un rêve perdu de la Renaissance* (Paris: Fayard, 1994).

9 J. H. M. Salmon, *Society in Crisis*, p. 186.

10 Ibid., p. 187.

11 *Le Reveille-Matin*, p. 75.

12 Ralph E. Giesey dissents from most other historians of the period and asserts that the St Bartholomew's Day Massacre did not contribute overwhelmingly to the "politicizing" of Huguenot theory. He maintains that the political content in their writings (as opposed to a purely religious emphasis) was already assuming more importance in the decade before the massacre. Ralph E. Giesey, "The Monarchomach Triumvirs: Hotman, Beza and Mornay," *Bibliothèque d'Humanisme et Renaissance* 32 (1970): 41.

13 Julian H. Franklin, "Constitutionalism in the Sixteenth Century: The Protestant Monarchomachs," in *Political Theory and Social Change*, ed. David Spitz (New York: Atherton Press, 1967), p. 121.

14 It is possible that this extract from Commynes, published in 1567, before the resistance theory of the Huguenots was fully formulated, influenced the general understanding of Commynes's ideas in the latter half of the sixteenth century. Of course, writers like Hotman were likely to have read all of Commynes's

work; new editions of the work were available throughout the sixteenth century. The passages reprinted in *De la necessité*, however, are precisely those most frequently cited by later writers, and the influence of this pamphlet should not, therefore, be underestimated.

15 *De la Necessité d'assembler les Estats* (n.p., 1567), Aii(r).
16 Ibid., Aiii(r).
17 See Chapter 4, p. 101, of this book.
18 Ibid., Bi(v) – Bii(r).
19 Ibid., Ciii + 1(r).
20 *Memoires des occasions de la guerre, appellée le Bien-Public, rapportez à l'estat de la guerre presente* (n.p., 1567), p. 6.
21 Ibid., pp. 6–7.
22 Ibid., p. 11.
23 Ibid., p. 18.
24 It should be noted that not all scholars see the Huguenots as placing such a great emphasis on the estates general as an *actual* means of checking the power of the king. See, for example, Ralph E. Giesey, who argues that "In sum, then, the modern Estates is impotent in Hotman's scheme, as likely as not ineffectual in Beza's, and superseded in Mornay's" in "The Monarchomach Triumvirs," p. 44.
25 For biographical data on François Hotman see Ralph E. Giesey and J. H. M. Salmon, Introduction to *Francogallia*, by François Hotman (Cambridge: Cambridge University Press, 1972). For a full biographical study see Donald R. Kelley, *François Hotman: A Revolutionary's Ordeal* (Princeton, NJ: Princeton University Press, 1973).
26 On John Ponet in particular see Winthrop S. Hudson, *John Ponet (1516?– 1556) Advocate of Limited Monarchy* (Chicago: Chicago University Press, 1942) and more recently Barbara Peardon, "The Politics of Polemic: John Ponet's *Short Treatise of Politic Power* and Contemporary Circumstance," *Journal of British Studies* 22 (1982): 35–49.
27 See Jean Louis Thireau, *Charles Du Moulin 1500–1566* (Geneva: Droz, 1980).
28 The resolution of this controversy is further hampered by considerations of the conditions under which the *Francogallia* was written. For the most part, Ralph E. Giesey deals with these issues in his article "When and Why Hotman Wrote the *Francogallia*," *Bibliothèque d'Humanisme et Renaissance* 29 (1967): 581–611. Giesey maintains that the chronology of its composition indicates that the *Francogallia* "is not a systematic work, but a bundle of separate essays on important aspects of French public law . . . ", p. 609. Nevertheless, Giesey does maintain that Hotman did intend the work to possess a certain amount of political content and it is in this respect that the work is considered here.
29 *Francogallia*, p. 233.
30 Ibid., p. 291.
31 Ibid., p. 333.
32 Ibid., p. 459.
33 Ibid., p. 325.
34 The legendary Aragonese coronation oath was a sort of contract between the king and the people which the successor was required to take before he would be acknowledged king. It stated that the king would adhere to the conditions imposed on his rule by the people that were designed to protect their ancient liberties. If the king did not abide by these rules, the people were no longer obliged to obey. The oath was a standard weapon in the Huguenot arsenal, referred to by Beza and the author of the *Vindiciae* as well as by Hotman. For a discussion of the oath see Ralph E. Giesey, *If Not, Not: The Oath of the Aragonese*

and the Legendary Laws of Sobrarbe (Princeton, NJ: Princeton University Press, 1968).

35 Ibid., pp. 441–3.

36 "Et fut cette guerre depuis appellée le Bien Public pource qu'elle s'entreprenoit *soubs couleur de dire que c'estoit pour le bien public du royaume* (my emphasis)." Commynes, *Mémoires*, 1: 98.

37 The concept of the thirty-six deputies (or ephors) is common in most constitutional theory. It was mentioned in the *Mémoires des occasions*, written before the *Francogallia*, as well as a number of other works from the 1570s. Nor was it merely an abstract concept. In his journal, Masselin notes the desire of the deputies at the estates of 1484 to appoint thirty-six counsellors who would advise the king on what reforms needed to be made. The concept of the thirty-six reformers or tutors was propounded as well at the close of the estates of 1576–77.

38 *Francogallia*, p. 447.

39 For a discussion of Beza's role as activist preacher in Calvinist Geneva, see Robert M. Kingdon, *Geneva and the Consolidation of the French Protestant Movement, 1564–1572* (Geneva: Droz, 1967). See also Kingdon's introduction to the modern edition of Beza's *Du Droit des Magistrats* (Geneva: Droz, 1970). The only full-length biographical study of which I am aware is Henry M. Baird's *Theodore Beza, The Counsellor of the French Reformation* (New York: Burt Franklin, n.d.)

40 Theodore de Bèze, *Du Droit des Magistrats*, ed. Robert M. Kingdon (Geneva: Droz, 1970), p. 33.

41 Ibid., p. 41.

42 Ibid., p. 42.

43 Emile Littré, *Dictionnaire de la langue française*, 6 vols (Chicago: R. R. Donnelly and Sons Co., 1987), 3: 3031. The *Trésor de la langue française* makes the connection between *hors de page* and sovereignty more explicit: "Etre hors de page (vieilli). Etre entièrement son maître." The *Trésor* provides an example of this usage from Chateaubriand's *Mémoires*: "Ces deux princesses crurent que la royauté, hors de page, était enfin affranchie des entraves que le gouvernement représentatif attache au pied du souverain."

44 Authorship of the *Vindiciae contra tyrannos* has never been conclusively established. Almost since the publication of the work itself, speculation has centred on two individuals: Hubert Languet and Philippe du Plessis Mornay. Those scholars supporting Languet's authorship include E. Barker, "The authorship of the *Vindiciae Contra Tyrannos*," *Cambridge Historical Journal* 3 (1929–31): 164–81 and M. N. Ratière, "Hubert Languet's authorship of the *Vindiciae contra Tyrannos*," *Il pensiero politico* 14 (1986): 395–420. On the other side, Graham Jagger supports the contention that Mornay is the author: "On the Authorship of the *Vindiciae contra tyrannos*," *Durham University Journal* 60 (1968): 73–80. A useful overview of the evidence is provided by George Garnett in his introduction to the recent modern edition of the *Vindiciae, contra tyrannos* (Cambridge, England: Cambridge University Press, 1994), pp. lv–lxxvi. After a careful examination of contemporary anecdotal evidence and modern scholarly interpretations, Garnett comes to the conclusion that the most satisfactory answer to the question of authorship is a possible collaboration between Languet and Du Plessis Mornay.

45 [Stephanus Junius Brutus], *Vindiciae contra Tyrannos*, ed. A. Jouanna *et al.* (Geneva: Droz, 1979), p. 119.

46 Ibid., p. 62.

47 Ibid., p. 109.

48 Ibid., p. 228.

49 Louis XI's posthumous fame (or infamy) was definitely not a uniquely French phenomenon. English interest in the Spider King is especially notable, perhaps due in part to the large number of French political treatises referring to Louis XI that were translated into English in the last decades of the sixteenth century. Regrettably, despite its intrinsic interest, a discussion of Louis XI's foreign reputation cannot figure in this book about political thought in France.

50 George Buchanan, *Rerum Scoticarum Historia* (n.p., 1668), p. 420.

51 For a brief treatment of the events of the 1580s see Mark Greengrass, *France in the Age of Henri IV: The Struggle for Stability* (New York: Longman, 1984), pp. 1–58. For more extensive coverage of this decade as well as a discussion of the development of the League, see Salmon, *Society in Crisis*, pp. 196–276. The major secondary work dealing with the political theory of the Leaguers is Frederic J. Baumgartner, *Radical Reactionaries: The Political Thought of the French Catholic League* (Geneva: Droz, 1975). For a discussion of the League in Paris, see Elie Barnavi, *Le Parti de Dieu: étude sociale et politique des chefs de la Ligue* (Brussels, 1980).

52 Jean Boucher, *De justa Abdicatione Henrici Tertii* (n.p., 1591), p. 45.

53 Ibid., p. 46.

54 *Dialogue du Royaume* (Paris, n.p., 1589), p. 36.

55 Ibid., pp. 70–1.

56 *L'Athéisme de Henri de Valoys: où est monstré le vray but de ses dissimulations et cruautez* (Paris: n.p., 1589), p. 3. The subject of Henri III's image in contemporary pamphlet literature is examined in some depth by James Smither, "Myth and Reality of Kingship during the French Wars of Religion" (PhD dissertation, Brown University, 1989). See also Keith Cameron, *Henri III: A Maligned or Malignant King?* (Exeter: University of Exeter Press, 1978).

57 *L'Athéisme de Henri de Valoys*, p. 5.

58 Ibid, pp. 27–9.

59 Ibid., p. 30.

CHAPTER 2: A SPIDER AT VERSAILLES

1 See Part II, Chapters 4 and 5 of this book, on Louis XI's reputation among late sixteenth- and seventeenth-century absolutists and on the rehabilitation of Louis XI by *raison d'état* writers, respectively.

2 For a brief biography of Fénelon, see Thomas Merton, introduction to *Fénelon Letters*, ed. John McEwen (London: Harvill Press, 1964).

3 This theme is most evident in book eighteen, when Telemachus visits the underworld in his continuing search for Ulysses and, while there, meets a number of tortured souls in Tartarus.

4 François de Salignac de la Mothe-Fénelon, *Oeuvres*, ed. Jacques Le Brun (Paris: Gallimard, 1983), 1: 1386, n.2.

5 Ibid., 1: 1338.

6 Ibid., 1: 445.

7 See Gabriel Naudé's point-by-point refutation of Louis XI's alleged lack of education in Chapter 5, pp. 125–6 of this book.

8 Fénelon, *Oeuvres*, 1: 446.

9 Ibid., 1: 447.

10 Ibid., 1: 448.

11 Ibid., 1: 453.

12 See the recent biography of Louis XII by Frederic J. Baumgartner, *Louis XII* (New York: St. Martin's Press, 1994), especially pp. 245–53, in which Baumgartner discusses Louis XII's "legacy" and briefly surveys his historical

reputation in the almost three centuries between his death and the French Revolution.

13 Fénelon was probably aware of the dialogues between Louis XI and Louis XII which had been composed earlier, especially since *Le Dialogue d'Estat ou entretiens entre des roys Louys XI et Louys XII es Champs Elisées* (1652) was republished in 1691. See Moreau, I: 319. For a further discussion of the Fronde dialogues, see Chapter six of this book.

14 Fénelon, *Oeuvres*, p. 455.

15 Ibid. p. 497.

16 Ibid., p. 498.

17 *Entretien de Louis Onze et de Charle Hardi Duc de Bourgogne* [sic] (Amsterdam, 1690). Louis XI refers specifically to a dialogue between old enemies François I and Emperor Charles V. To my knowledge, no such dialogue between these two figures from this period is extant. The *Dialogues entre Charles Quint et François Premier dans les Champs Elisees sur le projet de la Paix* appeared sometime in the second decade of the eighteenth century prior to the death of Louis XIV. Louis XI's reference to a conversation between the two kings is so specific, however, that the existence of such a pamphlet (even if only in manuscript form) would seem to be strongly indicated.

18 Ibid., p. 17.

19 Ibid., p. 31.

20 Ibid., p. 32.

21 Here Charles makes an interesting aside when he states that "Just Lipse me dit un jour ici que Comine étoit digne des Alexandres, quoiqu'il ne sut pas bien le latin." Ibid., p. 40. The admiration of Lipsius and the neo-Stoics for Commynes is well known and goes a long way in explaining the more positive portrait of Louis XI presented by early seventeenth-century authors.

22 Ibid., p. 55.

23 Bayle discusses the authorship of these pamphlets in the entry on Louis XI. He maintains that the pamphlets were probably written by the author who also penned the well-known pamphlet, *Le Salut d'Europe*, i.e. the Huguenot exile, Pierre Jurieu.

24 *Miroir historique de la ligue de l'an 1484 ou peut se reconnoitre la ligue de l'an 1694* (Cologne, 1694), pp. 3–4.

25 Ibid., p. 22.

26 Ibid., pp. 50–1.

27 *Avis d'un amy à l'autheur du Miroir historique de la ligue de l'an 1464* (Cologne, 1694), p. 4.

28 Ibid., p. 18.

29 *Pensées surs l'avis d'un amy à l'auteur du Miroir historique de l'an 1464* (Basel, 1694), pp. 22–3.

30 Although there have been several studies of Huguenot exile literature in general, notably Guy Howard Dodge, *The Political Theory of the Huguenots of the Dispersion* (New York: Columbia University Press, 1947) and Elisabeth Israels Perry, *From Theology to History* (The Hague: Martinus Nijhoff, 1973), I have not found much work specifically directed to a study of the pamphlets written by Bayle, Jurieu and their respective adherents. A relatively recent exception is the article by Elisabeth Labrousse, "The Political Ideas of the Huguenot Diaspora (Bayle and Jurieu)," in *Church, State and Society under the Bourbon Kings*, ed. Richard M. Golden (Lawrence, Kansas: Coronado Press, 1982). Even Labrousse, however, does not analyse the individual pamphlets exchanged between these two writers in any great detail. Dodge does provide bibliographic information about many of these pamphlets, pp. 119–38, especially nn. 69–72. Given the

intensity of the debate between Bayle and Jurieu (both personal and political), such a study would be a welcome addition to the scholarship.

31 A concise account of Bayle's life and work can be found in Elizabeth Labrousse, *Bayle*, trans. Denys Potts (Oxford: Oxford University Press, 1983).

32 Pierre Bayle, *Oeuvres diverses*, 4 vols (La Haye, 1727), 2: 168.

33 Ibid., 3: 98.

34 Ibid., 3: 99.

35 Pierre Bayle, *Dictionaire {sic} Historique et Critique*, 3rd edn, 4 vols (Rotterdam: Michel Bohm, 1720), 2: 1767.

36 Ibid, 2: 1768.

37 Ibid., 2: 1769, n. (L).

38 Ibid., 2: 1772.

39 Ibid., 4: 2797.

40 In footnote (Q) Bayle cites from a number of authors, including Commynes, Seyssel, Matthieu and Mezeray, on the subject of Louis XI's cruelty.

41 The authorship of this famous pamphlet is disputed. Gotthold Reimann, *Der Verfasser de "Soupirs de la France Esclave qui aspire après la liberté"* (1689–90) (Berlin, 1938), attributes authorship to Michel Levassor, but, as Dodge points out, Levassor was never suggested as the author by contemporaries. Bayle certainly accused Jurieu of having penned the piece. Jurieu maintained that there was no proof for attributing the piece to him, but he never at any time explicitly denied writing it. For an extended discussion of external and internal evidence establishing Jurieu as the author of *Les Soupirs*, see Dodge, pp. 140–6. For an opposing view see Labrousse, "The Political Ideas of the Huguenot Diaspora," pp. 253, 277, nn. 70–2.

42 See J. H. M. Salmon, *The French Religious Wars in English Political Thought* (Oxford: Oxford University Press, 1959), p. 150.

43 *Les Soupirs de la France esclave, qui aspire après la Liberté* (n.p., 1690), pp. 41–2. A fascimile reprint edition of *Les Soupirs* has been produced by Editions d'Histoire Sociale (Amsterdam, 1976).

44 Ibid., p. 99.

45 Ibid., p. 125.

46 Ibid., p. 162.

47 Ibid., p. 198.

48 For a discussion of the cultural construction of absolutism, see Peter Burke, *The Fabrication of Louis XIV* (New Haven, CT: Yale University Press, 1992).

CHAPTER 3: LOUIS XI AND THE FRENCH NATION

1 Saint-Simon, Louis de Rouvroy, duc de, *Memoirs*, trans. Katharine Prescott Wormeley, 4 vols (Boston, 1902), III: 238.

2 In his article, "Was there an Aristocratic Reaction in Pre-Revolutionary France?", *Past and Present* 57 (1972): 97–132, Doyle challenges the long-held belief in noble decline under Louis XIV, upon which the whole notion of an eighteenth-century aristocratic reaction is based. The older vision of a reactionary nobility is most ably represented in Franklin Ford's *Robe and Sword: The Regrouping of the French Aristocracy after Louis XIV* (Cambridge, Mass.: Harvard University Press, 1953).

3 G. Chaussinand-Nogaret, *La Noblesse au XVIIIème siècle* (Bruxelles: Edition Complexe, 1984), chapter one.

4 Montesquieu's status as a *nobiliaire* writer is, of course, problematic. He is as critical of Henri de Boulainvilliers' historical schema as he is of Boulainvilliers' main royalist opponent, the abbé Dubos. Nevertheless, I would argue that he is ideologically much closer to the *nobiliaire* camp in that he believes that the

nobility shared sovereign authority with the king and he sought to prove this through delving into the French past.

5 See Louis Lemarié, *Les Assemblées franques et les historiens réformateurs du XVIIIe siècle* (Paris: Imprimerie Bonvalot-Jouve, 1906); Nannerl O. Keohane, *Philosophy and the State in France* (Princeton, NJ: Princeton University Press, 1980), p. 347.

6 Pierre Nora, "Nation," in *A Critical Dictionary of the French Revolution*, ed. Mona Ozouf and François Furet, trans. Arthur Goldhammer (Cambridge, Mass.: Belknap Press of Harvard University Press, 1989), p. 744.

7 See, for example, Jacques Godechot, "Nation, Patrie, Nationalisme et Patriotisme en France au XVIIIe siècle," *Annales historiques de la Revolution Française* no. 206 (1971): 481–501 and earlier works by Robert R. Palmer, "The National Idea in France before the Revolution," *Journal of the History of Ideas* 1 (1940): 95–111; Boyd C. Shafer, "Bourgeois Nationalism in the Pamphlets on the Eve of the French Revolution," *Journal of Modern History* 10 (1938): 31–50.

8 In his review essay, "Recent Works on Early Modern French National Identity," *Journal of Modern History* 68 (1996): 84–113, David Bell reviews six new works dealing with early modern expressions of French "nationalism": Colette Beaune, *The Birth of an Ideology: Myths and Symbols of Nations in Late-Medieval France*, trans. Fredric L. Cheyette (Berkeley and Los Angeles: University of California Press, 1991); Suzanne Citron, *Le mythe nationale: L'histoire de France en question* (Paris: Editions Ouvrières, 1987); Liah Greenfeld, *Nationalism: Five Roads to Modernity* (Cambridge, Mass: Harvard University Press, 1992); Jean-Yves Guiomar, *La nation entre l'histoire et la raison* (Paris, 1990); Pierre Nora, ed. *Les lieux de mémoire*, pt. 3: *Les France*, 3 vols (Paris: Gallimard, 1993); and Peter Sahlins, *Boundaries: The Making of France and Spain in the Pyrenees* (Berkeley and Los Angeles: University of California Press, 1989). Perhaps even more important than his trenchant comments on the individual books under review, Bell provides a very useful introduction to the question of early modern national identity by "laying out a number of conceptual axes along which to locate differing definitions." At the end of the essay he proposes some interesting paths for further investigation into early modern national identity, including a more "fractured" approach to French society. Clearly, not all Frenchmen began to perceive themselves as partaking in the same national identity or at precisely the same moment. Bell's excellent essay should be the starting point for anyone interested in the thorny issue of early modern French identity.

9 Bell, "Recent Works on Early Modern French National Identity," pp. 94–6.

10 Along with works by Ford and Chaussinand-Nogaret already cited above in notes 2 and 3, see also J. Q. C. Mackrell, *The Attack on "Feudalism" in Eighteenth-Century France* (London: Routledge and Kegan Paul, 1973) and Jacques Barzun, *The French Race* (New York: Columbia University Press, 1932).

11 André Devyver, *Le Sang Epuré: Les préjugés de race chez les gentilhommes français de l'Ancien Régime (1560–1720)* (Brussels: Editions de l'Université de Bruxelles, 1973).

12 Vincent Buranelli, "The Historical and Political Thought of Boulainvilliers," *Journal of the History of Ideas* 18 (1957): 475–94.

13 Harold Ellis, *Boulainvilliers and the French Monarchy: Aristocratic Politics in Early Eighteenth-Century France* (Ithaca, New York: Cornell University Press, 1988), pp. 6–11.

14 Ellis, p. 64. While Ellis's work seeks to place Boulainvilliers firmly within the political context in which he lived and developed his ideas, a more strictly biographical work is the excellent study by Renée Simon, *Henry de*

Boulainvilliers: Historien, Politique, Philosophe, Astrologue: 1658–1722 (Paris: Boivin, 1941).

15 Ellis, p. 209. The *affaire du bonnet*, while a seemingly trivial disagreement over whether members of the sovereign courts ought to remove their hats in the presence of dukes and peers, was symbolic of the deep divisions between sword and robe nobility that went far beyond skirmishes over social pre-eminence. See Ellis, *Boulainvilliers and the French Monarchy*, for a discussion of the constitutional implications of the *affaire du bonnet*. The *affaire des princes* concerned the controversy over Louis XIV's decision to legitimize and place in the royal succession his natural children, the duc du Maine and the comte de Toulouse. Ellis also discusses the larger constitutional context in which the *affaire des princes* was played out in chapter six of his book.

16 Henri de Boulainvilliers, *Essais sur la noblesse de France* (Amsterdam, 1732), pp. 3–5.

17 Ibid., p. 1.

18 Ellis refutes André Devyver's ideas about Boulainvilliers as an exponent of racism, based on his status as part of the "proletarianized nobility." Ellis maintains that Boulainvilliers was not a "race conscious *hobereau*" in that his family was reasonably well off. Furthermore, Boulainvilliers "developed no explicitly biological theory of noble excellence or 'virtue' ", pp. 17–30.

19 For a discussion of the nobility's evolving self-perception in an earlier period, see Ellery Schalk, *From Valor to Pedigree: Ideas of Nobility in France in the Sixteenth and Seventeenth Centuries* (Princeton, NJ: Princeton University Press, 1986). The contrast between self-centred noble "honour" and civic-minded bourgeois "virtue" was often highlighted for polemical gain later in the century as in the Véron-Morangiès legal case examined by Sara Maza in "The Véron-Morangiès Affair, 1771–1773: The Social Imagery of Political Crisis," *Historical Reflections / Reflexions historiques* 18 (1992): 101–35.

20 Boulainvilliers, *Essais*, 13.

21 Ibid., pp. 16–17.

22 In this regard Louis Lemarié wrote: "Boulainvilliers et ses continuateurs trouvèrent dans Hotman un modèle et une méthode . . . Boulainvilliers, Mably et Lepaige ont contribué à faire éclore ces germes de liberté que la monarchie croyait définitivement étouffés depuis la tentative infructeuse d'Hotman et des autres pamphletaires du XVIe siècle." *Les Assemblées franques et les historiens réformateurs du XVIIIe siecle*, p. 73.

23 Boulainvilliers, *Essais*, p. 19.

24 Boulainvilliers, *Histoire de l'ancien gouvernement de la France*, 3 vols (La Haye/Amsterdam, 1727), I: 25.

25 "Il est absolument contraire à la verité et au caractère des anciens François d'imaginer que le droit Royal fut parmi eux souverain et monarchique ou despotique, en sorte que les Particuliers lui fussent sujets pour la vie, les biens, la liberté, l'honneur et la fortune; au contraire encore un coup tous les François étoient libres, et par consequent non sujets à prendre ce terme à la rigueur." Ibid., I: 29.

26 Ibid., I: 29.

27 Ibid., I: 109.

28 The *Lettres historiques* also appeared as a separate work entitled *Histoire des anciens parlements de France, ou Etats Généraux du Royaume* (London: John Brindley, 1737).

29 Boulainvilliers, *Histoire de l'ancien gouvernement*, I: 215–17.

30 Ibid., III: 161–2.

31 Ibid., III: 198–9.

32 Boulainvilliers, *Histoire des anciens parlements de France*, p. 179.

33 "Louis XI a été le premier qui, pour gouverner plus arbitrairement, aprocha de sa personne et employa dans les négocations des gens de petite fortune . . . C'étoit l'entreprise la plus forte que l'on put faire contre les droits de l'ancienne Noblesse." Boulainvilliers, *Essais*, pp. 202–10.

34 Ibid., pp. 233–6. The Order of St. Michel, instituted in 1470, was modelled on the earlier Burgundian order of the Golden Fleece and on the English Knights of the Garter. Its members swore oaths of loyalty to the king, and were ostensibly dedicated to the defence of the Church and the preservation of chivalric ideals. In reality, it was another means by which Louis XI sought both to appease the nobles and bind them more closely to himself.

35 "Depuis ce tems-là la solde pécuniaire des troupes est devenue le nerf principal de la puissance monarchique, et les Rois se sont accoustumez à juger les services de tous leurs Sujets leur sont également profitables, considerant que l'ancien Noble ne peut rien faire à meilleur marché que le Roturier, et même au contraire, que les nouveaux annoblis sont plus riches et plus en état de se passer de secours, que l'ancien Noble attend de la liberalité du Souverain. Cela le rend odieux ou importun. On cesse dès-lors de regarder le Gentilhomme d'ancienne race comme un membre considerable de l'Etat. Ni l'intérêt general du Gouvernement, ni l'intérêt particulier des plaisirs du Prince, ne l'aprochent de sa personne par aucune consideration d'utilité." Ibid., pp. 269–70.

36 Montesquieu's views were strongly influenced by his *parlementaire* background as Elie Carcassonne makes clear in *Montesquieu et le problème de la constitution française* (Paris: Presses Universitaires de France, 1927).

37 For a concise biography of Montesquieu see Iris Cox, "Montesquieu and the History of French Laws," in *Studies on Voltaire and the Eighteenth Century* (Oxford: The Voltaire Foundation, 1983), pp. 51–70. For a more exhaustive treatment there is the excellent political biography by Robert Shackleton, *Montesquieu, A Critical Biography* (Oxford: Oxford University Press, 1961).

38 Albert Mathiez, "La Place de Montesquieu dans l'Histoire des Doctrines Politiques du XVIIIe siècle," *Annales historiques de la Révolution Française* VII (1930): 97–112.

39 For further discussion of the ways in which Montesquieu combined ideas from both Boulainvilliers and Dubos, see Iris Cox, *Montesquieu and the History of French Laws*, pp. 30–41.

40 Montesquieu, *The Spirit of the Laws*, trans. and ed. Anne Cohler, Basia Miller and Harold Stone (Cambridge, England: Cambridge University Press, 1989), book xxx, p. 662.

41 Shackleton, *Montesquieu*, p. 331.

42 Mark Hulliung, *Montesquieu and the Old Regime* (Berkeley and Los Angeles, University of California Press, 1976).

43 Montesquieu, *The Spirit of the Laws*, book xxxi, pp. 669–77.

44 Ibid., book xxxi, p. 695.

45 Ibid., book xxxi, p. 708.

46 Montesquieu wrote of this work about Louis XI in a letter to the abbé Octavien de Guasco in which he suggests that the abbé write about the state of arts and letters during the reign of Louis XI in his bid to enter the *Académie Française*. Montesquieu says he would have entered the essay competition himself "si les mémoires sur lesquels je travaillai l'*Histoire de Louis XI* n'avoient point été brulés" in *Oeuvres complètes de Montesquieu*, 3 vols (Paris: Les Editions Nagel, 1950–55), III: 1097.

47 *Pensées et fragments inédits*, 2 vols (Bordeaux: G. Gounouilhou, 1899–1901), p. 335.

48 Ibid., p. 337.

49 Ibid., p. 338.

50 Ibid., p. 340.

51 For a discussion of the connections between Montesquieu and Tacitus see Catherine Volpilhac-Auger, *Tacite et Montesquieu* in *Studies on Voltaire and the Eighteenth Century* (Oxford: The Voltaire Foundation, 1985). On the relationship between Montesequieu and Machiavelli see Robert Shackleton, "Montesquieu and Machiavelli: a reappraisal," in *Essays on Montesquieu and the Enlightenment* (Oxford: The Voltaire Foundation, 1988).

52 Montesquieu, *Oeuvres complètes*, p. 539.

53 The most complete monograph on the abbé Dubos remains the work by A. Lombard, *L'Abbé Du Bos: Un initiateur de la pensée moderne* (Paris: Hachette, 1913).

54 Ford, *Robe and Sword*, p. 232.

55 No full-length study of Damiens de Gomicourt exists. Basic information about his life can be obtained from: *Biographie Universelle* (Paris: C. Desplaces, 1857), 17: 135; *Dictionnaire de Biographie Française* (Paris: Librairie Letouzey et Ané, 1982–85), 16: 537.

56 August-Pierre Damiens de Gomicourt, *Mélanges historiques et critiques*, 2 vols (Paris, 1768), I: 3–4.

57 Ibid., I: 7.

58 Ibid., I: 11.

59 "J'ai essayé de faire voir dans l'ouvrage que je donne aujourd'hui au Public, que ce partage d'autorité n'avoit jamais existé en France; qu'au contraire nos Rois ont eu légitimement et sans interruption le droit d'établir des règles générales qu'on nomme loix." Ibid., I: 12.

60 Ibid., I: 17.

61 "Nous ne pensons pas, après ce que nous venons de dire, que ce systême de M. de Boulainvilliers puisse se soutenir. Nous croyons avoir suffisamment prouvé que la souveraine puissance residoit seule dans les Rois Mérovingians, d'ou on peut conclure, que n'ayant pas été usurpée, les Rois de France ont toujours dû avoir légitimement une autorité absolue." Ibid., I: 106.

62 Ibid., I: 20.

63 Ibid., I: 59.

64 Ibid., I: 69.

65 Ibid., I: 78.

66 *Biographie universelle*, 17: 135.

67 *Mélanges historiques*, I: 209–10.

68 "Ce ministre aussi grand politique que Louis XI, plus entreprenant et plus conséquent que lui, executa sous un Roi foible, le project que le Roi le plus décidé de tous les Rois de la Monarchie, n'avoit pu qu'ébaucher. Il est certain que pour le faire réussir, il falloit en suivant les mêmes principes que Louis XI, ôter aux Grands les moyens de faire valoir à la Cour les prétentions d'independance qu'ils avoient, et pour cela il falloit les priver des ressources infinies que la possession des grandes dignités leur offroit sans cesse pour se faire des partisans." Ibid., I: 211–12.

69 See Chapter 5 of this book.

70 *Mélanges historiques*, I: 59.

71 Ibid, I: 10.

72 Keohane, *Philosophy and the State in France*, p. 377.

73 Arthur Ogle, *The Marquis d'Argenson* (London: T. Fisher Unwin, 1893), passim.

74 Marquis d'Argenson, *Considerations sur le gouvernement ancien et present de la France* (Amsterdam: Marc Michel Rey, 1764), pp. 215–20. Keohane discusses d'Argenson's ideas concerning the balance of interests in *Philosophy and the State in France*, pp. 376–82.

75 D'Argenson, *Considerations*, p. 137.

76 Ibid., p. 152.
77 Ibid., p. 204.
78 Ibid., p. 319.
79 *Dictionnaire de Biographie Française* (Paris, 1967), 11: 1268–70.
80 Charles Pinot Duclos, *Histoire de Louis XI*, 3 vols (La Haye, 1745), I: 201 [mispaginated as 301], 239.
81 Ibid., I: 244.
82 Ibid., I: 287.
83 Ibid., I: 293. Duclos cites some pension totals to demonstrate the effects of the war in terms of increased taxation: in 1465, the total amount of distributed pensions was 108,564 *livres*; in 1466, that number jumped to 266,900 *livres*.
84 Ibid., I: 263.
85 Ibid., II: 508.
86 Ibid., II: 509.
87 See Chapter 7 of this book for Jean-Baptiste Britard's scathing indictment of Duclos's enthusiastic endorsement of tyranny. On the other hand, by the nineteenth century Duclos was somewhat rehabilitated. In his lectures on eighteenth-century French literature Abel Villemain complained that, although Duclos was objective, he lacked the requisite passion to be a truly exceptional historian along the lines of Voltaire. *Cours de Litterature Française* (Brussels: A. Jamar, 1840), 148.
88 Voltaire, *Essai sur les moeurs*, ed. Rene Pomeau, 2 vols (Paris: Garnier Frères, 1963), II: 2–8.
89 Ibid., II: 7.
90 Ibid., II: 6.
91 Ibid., II: 8–9.
92 Ibid., II: 10.
93 Joël Félix, *Les Magistrats du Parlement de Paris (1771–1790): dictionnaire biographique et geneologique* (Paris: Sedopols, 1990), p. 103.
94 Pierre Louis Claude Gin, *Les Vrais principes du gouvernement françois* (Geneva, 1777), p. v.
95 Ibid., p. 31.
96 Ibid., pp. 54–5.
97 "J'ai fait l'édit, je veux qu'il s'observe, ma volonté devoit servir de raison, on ne la demande jamais à un prince en un état obéissant. Je suis roi maintenant, je vous parle en roi, je veux être obéi." Ibid., p. 295.
98 Gin, *Les Vrais principes*, pp. 169–70.
99 Ibid., p. 96.
100 Gin, *Origine des malheurs de la France*, p. 39.
101 David Bell, *Lawyers and Citizens: The Making of a Political Elite in Old Regime France* (Oxford and New York: Oxford University Press, 1994), passim.
102 "Celui de nos rois qui avoit le plus abusé de ce pouvoir, Louis XI, y mit lui-même des bornes en renouvellant par l'ordonnance de 1467 la disposition du capitulaire de Charles le Chauve, dans lequel ce prince s'étoit engagé à ne conferer aucun office, s'il n'étoit vacant par mort, démission volontaire, ou forfaiture 'jugée et declarée judiciairement et selon les termes de justice par juge competent;' loi si sage aux yeux de Louis XI lui-même, qu'il se transporta peu de temps avant sa mort au château d'Amboise, accompagné des princes de son sang et des principaux seigneurs de sa cour, pour en faire jurer l'observation à Charles VIII son fils, dont il fut dressé un acte revêtu de lettres-patentes addressées à toutes les cours souveraines du royaume." Gin, *Les Vrais principes*, p. 220.
103 This ambivalence of the Parlement of Paris is examined in greater depth in Chapter 7 of this book.

104 Ibid., p. 29.
105 "Cette puissance du monarque ne donne atteinte ni à la liberté, ni à la propriété de ses sujets. L'époque du rétablissement de l'autorité royale est celle de l'anéantissement de la servitude dans toutes les parties du royaume." *Les Vrais principes du governement françois*, p. 288. See also *Origine des malheurs de la France*, pp. 38–9.
106 Jean-Denis Bredin, *Sieyes. La Clé de la Révolution française* (Paris: Éditions de Fallois, 1988).
107 Sewell provides a useful and succinct account of Sieyès's life in *A Rhetoric of Bourgeois Revolution: The Abbé Sieyes and What is the Third Estate?* (Duke University Press, 1994), pp. 18–20.
108 In the flood of scholarship that accompanied the bicentennial of the French Revolution, a not insignificant amount of attention has been directed at Sieyès. Book-length studies include (along with that of Bredin) Murray Forsyth, *Reason and Revolution: The Political Thought of the Abbé Sieyès* (Leicester: Leicester University Press, 1987) and Paul Bastid, *Sieyès et sa pensée* (Paris: Hachette, 1970). The essays of Lynn Hunt, Keith Baker and Bronislaw Baczko in vol. 2 of *The Political Culture of the Old Regime* (Oxford: Pergamon Press, 1987) all discuss aspects of Sieyès's thought. See also Keith Baker, *Inventing the French Revolution* (Cambridge, England: Cambridge University Press, 1990), pp. 224–51.
109 In *A Rhetoric of Bourgeois Revolution*, William Sewell engages in a deep textual analysis of *What is the Third Estate?*. He begins with a discussion of Sieyès's argument, pointing out its overall coherence and apparent "seamlessness," but then proceeds to an examination of the "fissures" and disjunctures with the text. These fissures are, in Sewell's view, reflective both of Sieyès's own conflicted life as a relatively minor member of the clergy and of the ambivalent stance of the politically-attuned segments of the Third Estate in 1788/89.
110 "If we have no constitution, it must be made, and only the nation has the right to make it. If we do have a constitution, as some people obstinately maintain, and if, as they allege, it divides the National Assembly into three deputations of three orders of citizens, nobody can fail to notice, at all events, that one of these orders is protesting so vigorously that nothing can be done until its claim is decided." *What is the Third Estate?*, pp. 119–20. I am relying here on the English translation by M. Blondel (London: Pall Mall Press, 1963).
111 Although Sieyès believes that the Third Estate can form the national assembly on its own, he is concerned that such an action may be too "abrupt." An interim step proposed by Sieyès is that the Third Estate, having apprised the public of the need for and the means of creating a national assembly, would confine itself to preparing for such an assembly and would act solely in a curatorial capacity, without actual authority to make final decisions. Ibid, pp. 150–4.
112 See especially Murray Forsyth, *Reason and Revolution*, pp. 69–70.
113 Ibid., pp. 59–60.
114 Ibid., p. 66.
115 See especially Pasquale Pasquino, "Le concept de nation et les fondements du droit public de la Révolution: Sieyès." in François Furet, *L'Héritage de la Révolution française* (Paris: Hachette, 1989).
116 Sieyès proposed an "Assembly of the Recognized and Verified Representatives of the French Nation," while Mirabeau suggested calling the assembly the "Representatives of the French People." See Lynn Hunt, "The National Assembly," in Keith M. Baker, *The French Revolution and the Creation of Modern Political Culture*, vol. I, pp. 410–13.

117 Ibid., p. 61.
118 *Le Moniteur Universel*, 6 July 1791.

CHAPTER 4: UNFETTERED KING, UNLIMITED GREATNESS

1 See Sarah Hanley, *The* Lit de Justice *and the Kings of France: Constitutional Ideology in Legend, Ritual and Discourse* (Princeton, NJ: Princeton University Press, 1983), pp. 226–7.

2 William Beik, *Absolutism and Society in Seventeenth-Century France* (Cambridge and New York: Cambridge University Press, 1985); Hilton L. Root, *Peasants and King in Burgundy: Agrarian Foundations of French Absolutism* (Berkeley: University of California Press, 1987); Daniel Hickey, *The Coming of French Absolutism: The Struggle for Tax Reform in the Province of Dauphiné, 1540–1640* (Toronto: University of Toronto Press, 1986); François Xavier Emmanuelli, *Un myth de l'absolutisme bourbonnien: l'intendance du milieu du XVIIème siècle à la fin du XVIIIème siècle* (Aix-en-Provence: Publications Université de Provence; Paris: H. Champion, 1981).

3 Among this group, Roger Mettam's *Power and Faction in Louis XIV's France* (Oxford: Basil Blackwell, 1988) provides a cogently argued revisionist thesis. In his attempt to discredit the "absolutist" school, however, Mettam seems unwilling to recognize and incorporate evidence which does point to the centralization and consolidation of power in certain areas of government. Moreover, he tends to dismiss as mere sycophancy the willingness of some of Louis XIV's contemporaries to endorse absolute authority.

4 Andrew Lossky, "The Absolutism of Louis XIV: Reality or Myth?" *Canadian Journal of History* 19 (1984): 1–15; Phyllis K. Leffler, "French Historians and the Challenge to Louis XIV's Absolutism," *French Historical Studies* 14 (1985): 1–22.

5 See Jean-Louis Thireau, *Les Idées politiques de Louis XIV* (Paris, 1973).

6 See Roland Mousnier, *Les Institutions de la France sous la monarchie absolue*, 2 vols (Paris: Presses Universitaires de France, 1974, 1980).

7 The *politiques* were so named because of their moderate stance on religious questions and their belief that support for the monarchy should take precedence over confessional loyalties. They were equally opposed to radical Protestantism and the ultra-Catholic policies of the League. For a further discussion of the *politiques*, see Mack P. Holt, *The Duke of Anjou and the Politique Struggle during the Wars of Religion* (Cambridge and New York: Cambridge University Press, 1986).

8 "Un Calviniste zêlé, mais d'un mediocre savant et d'un très petit Politique," *Les Satires personelles qui portent le titre l'Anti* (Paris, 1689), cited in A. D'Andrea, "The Political and Ideological Context of Innocent Gentillet's *Anti-Machiavel*," *Renaissance Quarterly* 23 (1970): 398.

9 In the *Anti-Machiavel*, Gentillet elucidates the main tenet of *politique* thought: that, at the base, Catholicism and Protestantism are similar faiths. In a famous passage, Gentillet recounts the story of a Protestant and a Catholic who exchange views about their respective faiths. In the end, they discover, as expressed by the Protestant, "That the Catholike and we differ not in Religion, but do agree in all points necessary for our salvation." Although this anecdote is followed by another story meant to poke fun at the more ridiculous aspects of monasticism, it does not indicate Gentillet's essential hostility to the Catholic faith, thereby undermining the sincerity of his previous assertions espousing toleration, as asserted by C. Edward Rathé. Rather, it seems little more than good-natured, albeit well-directed, mockery.

10 D'Andrea, "The Political and Ideological Context of Innocent Gentillet's *Anti-Machiavel*," pp. 402–3.

11 C. Edward Rathé, "Innocent Gentillet and the First 'Anti-Machiavel' ", *Bibliothèque d'Humanisme et Renaissance* xxvii (1965): 186–225.

12 " . . . cercha tous les moyens qu'il luy fut possible pour appaiser ceste guerre, suyvant en ce l'advis et conseil de Francisque Sforza duc de Milan son bon amy, quy luy conseilla pour avoir paix de ne refuser rien de tout ce qu'on luy demandoit." Innocent Gentillet, *Remonstrance au Tres Chrestien Henry III de ce nom, Roy de France et de Pologne* (Aygenstain: Gabriel Iason, 1576), pp. 61–2.

13 Gentillet's devotion to the cause of peace is demonstrated as well in his *An Apology or Defence for the Christians of France*, trans. Sir Iherom Bowes (London, 1579) in which he tries to prove that Protestant rather than Catholic theology adheres more closely to the Scriptures and even to the ancient canons of the Roman Church. As in the *Remonstrance au Roy Tres Chrestien Henri III*, however, much of the work extols the virtues of peace: "If we considered the monstrous wasting and spoyling of things which civill warres are wont to breede (whereof we have seene but too many by experience) the heare [sic] of our heads would stand up at it." Epistle to Henri II, King of Navarre, n.p.

14 It should be noted, however, that this absolutist interpretation of Gentillet's work is not universally agreed upon. For example, C. Edward Rathé states that "Gentillet had arrived unconsciously at a view of sovereignty based on the popular will." p. 219. See also A. D'Andrea and P. Stewart, introduction to Innocent Gentillet, *Discours contre Machiavel* (Florence: Casalini Libri, 1974).

15 Gentillet, *Discours contre Machiavel*, p. 49.

16 "Il est certain qu'un Prince peut bien faire guerre et imposer tailles sans le consentement de ses sujets, par une puissance absolue, mais il seroit meilleur qu'il usast de puissance civile, et en seroit tousjours mieux obey." Ibid., p. 60.

17 For a discussion of Gentillet's contribution to the development of anti-Machiavellism in France, see Edmond M. Beame, "The Use and Abuse of Machiavelli: The Sixteenth-Century Adaptation," *Journal of the History of Ideas* 43 (1982): 41–5.

18 Saint Beuve cited by Kenneth Dreyer, "Commynes and Machiavelli: A Study in Parallelism," *Symposium* (1951): 38.

19 Gentillet, *Discours contre Machiavel*, p. 18.

20 Ibid., p. 172.

21 Ibid., p. 236.

22 " . . . il levoit de grands deniers sur ses sujets, voire au triple qu'avoyent fait ses predecesseurs. Mais il ne les despendoit en bombances, ny autres dissolutions, ny à exercer liberalité à gens indignes, ains à bons usages et pour les afaires du Royaume: comme pour acheter paix avec ses voisins, et pour corrompre les personnes estrangeres qui luy pouvoyent servir en cela, ou en ses autres afaires." Ibid., p. 432.

23 Ibid., p. 250.

24 "Or il est certain que s'il est question qu'il faille estre foulé, qu'on ayme mieux l'estre d'un seul que des plusieurs, et que les sujets le portent plus patiemment de leur Prince que des particuliers: veu mesme que ceste foule qu'on souffre du Prince est destinee a estre employée pour le bien public, et qu'elle est aucunement adoucie par l'entretenement d'une bonne paix et justice." Ibid., p. 478.

25 According to Commynes, in 1475 Nicola di Montforte, the comte de Campobasso, was shown favour by the duke and given a commission to go to Italy and raise troops. Campobasso notified the king twice that he would kill or imprison the duke as the king desired. Louis told the duke of the plan but the duke did not believe him and in fact showed Campobasso even more favour than before. Subsequently, Campobasso deserted the duke on the field of battle

at Nancy, when the Burgundians were fighting the Swiss, and the duke was killed on the spot. Commynes, *Mémoires*, books four and five.

26 Gentillet, *Discours contre Machiavel*, p. 383.

27 Ibid., pp. 39–40.

28 Ibid., pp. 44–5.

29 See, for example, Julian Franklin, "Jean Bodin and the End of Medieval Constitutionalism," and J. H. M. Salmon, "Bodin and the Monarchomachs," both in *Verhandlungen der internationalen Bodin Tagung in Munchen*, ed. Horst Denzer (Munich: C. H. Beck, 1973).

30 K. D. McRae, "Introduction," to Jean Bodin, *Six Bookes of a Commonweale* (1606 edn; facs. reprint edn, Cambridge, Mass: Harvard University Press, 1962).

31 For example, Summerfield Baldwin has argued that Bodin was in fact an orthodox Catholic for most of his life and that his support of the League thus posed no conflict to his religious views. Summerfield Baldwin, "Jean Bodin and the League," *Catholic Historical Review* xxiii (1937/8): 160–84. For a different interpretation of Bodin's religious views, see Paul Lawrence Rose, *Bodin and the Great God of Nature* (Geneva: Droz, 1980).

32 Jean Bodin, *The Method for the Easy Comprehension of History*, trans. Beatrice Reynolds (New York, 1945), pp. 172–3.

33 Ibid., p. 202.

34 Ibid., p. 254.

35 Ibid., p. 103.

36 Ibid., p. 384. See also Gentillet, *Discours contre Machiavel*, pp. 176–82.

37 Bodin, *The Method*, pp. 191–2.

38 Jean Bodin, "Recueil de tout ce qui s'est negocié en la compagnie du tiers-état de France, en l'assemblée générale des trois états, assignee par le roi en la ville de Blois au 15 Novembre 1576 . . ." *Des Estats Généraux et Autres Assemblées Nationales*, ed. Charles-Joseph Mayer, 18 vols (Paris: Buisson, 1788–9) 13: 215–328.

39 For example, on the second to last day of February 1577 a group of thirty-two deputies from the third estate met secretly "pour s'opposer tant qu'ils pourroient à ce que le tiers-état ne demandant la paix . . . ." Bodin maintained that they had no power because they were meeting in secret without the command to assemble given by the king. Bodin stated "c'étoit crime capital de s'assembler sans mandement du roi, et de traiter de la paix ou de la guerre, cas reservés à la souveraineté, et moins pouvoient-ils encore s'autoriser en leurs protestations, n'ayant ni corps, ni college, ni magistrat, ni greffier, ni tabellion." Ibid., p. 307.

40 Ibid., p. 279.

41 See my discussion of the constitutional wrangling between the estates general and the Parlement of Paris in, "Meddling Chaperons: The Involvement of the Parlement of Paris in the Estates General of 1593," in *Politics, Ideology and the Law in Early Modern Europe*, ed. Adrianna E. Bakos (Rochester, NY: University of Rochester Press, 1994), pp. 91–105.

42 Anonymous, *Satyre Ménippée de la vertue de Catholicon d'Espagne et de la tenue des estatz de Paris*, ed. Ch. Marcilly (Paris: Garnier Frères, n.d.), p. 243.

43 Pierre de Belloy, *Apologie Catholique contre les libelles declarations, advis, et consultation faictes, écrites et publiées par les Liguez perturbateurs du repos du Royaume de France . . .* (n.p.: E.D.L.I.C., 1585), p. 44(r).

44 Ibid., p. 83(v).

45 Ibid., p. 65(v). Well before the reign of Louis XI, France endured a troublesome relationship with the papacy. Already at the very beginning of the fourteenth century, a power struggle between Philippe IV and Boniface resulted in the papal bull *Unam Sanctam* (1302) in which it was stated that

216 *Notes*

obedience to the Holy See was necessary for salvation. Boniface excommunicated Philippe IV when the latter appealed to a general council of the Church. A century later, in 1407, Charles VI issued an ordinance which established the liberties of the French Church, and in 1438 the Pragmatic Sanction was promulgated which asserted that a general council was superior to the pope. The Pragmatic Sanction also endorsed the ecclesiastical election to higher clerical offices and restricted the payment of annates to Rome. What Pierre Belloy does not say in his *Apologie Catholique* is that Louis XI had revoked the Pragmatic Sanction in 1462 in order to gain papal support for policies in Italy. In 1467 he was only reaffirming a set of laws he himself had abrogated five years earlier.

46 *De l'Autorité du Roy* (n.p., 1587), p. 22(r).
47 Ibid., p. 70(r).
48 Ibid., pp. 63(r-v).
49 Ibid., p. 67(r).
50 Ibid., pp. 68(r-v).
51 Biographical information about Loyseau is provided by both Roland Mousnier, *The Institutions of France under the Absolute Monarchy 1598–1789*, trans. Brian Pearce (Chicago: University of Chicago Press, 1979), pp. 4–5, and by Howell A. Lloyd, "The Political Thought of Charles Loyseau (1564–1627)," *European Studies Review* 11 (1981): 53–4.
52 Howell Lloyd has recently edited and translated a new edition of Loyseau's *Des ordres et simples dignités: A Treatise of Orders and Plain Dignities* (Cambridge and New York: Cambridge University Press, 1994).
53 In his article on Loyseau, Lloyd provides a helpful overview of different interpretations of Loyseau's political thought. He notes that, by emphasizing different aspects of his works, modern scholars have arrived at diverse conclusions about the writer. Myron P. Gilmore, for example, was most interested in Loyseau's ideas on the "theory of office" and how it related to the continued importance of Roman law in French political thought. W. F. Church examined Loyseau's use of legal theory to support arguments about royal prerogative. On the sociological front, Roland Mousnier and Boris Porschnev disagreed about Loyseau's views of French society: the latter presents Loyseau as an advocate of the *bourgeoisie*, while the former maintains that, far from elucidating a "class" view of society, Loyseau described a "society of orders." Lloyd, "The Political Thought of Charles Loyseau," p. 55.
54 Lloyd remarks (p. 57) that Loyseau's intention was "not to underwrite a 'constitutional balance', but to justify a monarchy absolute in its own sphere." Later, in describing Loyseau's views on sovereignty, Lloyd writes (p. 68): "The sovereign's power was 'absolute' in that it absolved him from recognizing any superior under God and any law or contract made by any previous sovereign. Time did not limit it, and no member of the state was excluded from its scope." Church comments that Loyseau and the other legists lent the doctrine of absolutism a precision it had previously lacked: "With the appearance of these complete legal systems embodying the major tenets of royal absolutism, the seventeenth-century conception of kingship may be regarded as having achieved predominance in political thinking." W. F. Church, *Constitutional Thought in the Sixteenth Century*, p. 316.
55 See W. F. Church's discussion of Charles Loyseau in chapter six of *Constitutional Thought in the Sixteenth Century*. He makes a brief comparison of Bodin and Loyseau, though he does not, I believe, make enough of the differences between the two theorists.
56 Charles Loyseau, "Traité des Seigneuries," in *Oeuvres* (Lyon: Compagnie des Librairies, 1701), p. 3. Loyseau defines *seigneurie* as follows: " . . . *in abstracto*

tout droit de proprieté, ou puissance proprietaire, qu'on a en quelque chose, qu'à l'occasion d'icelle on peut dire sienne: L'autre, de signifier *in concreto* une terre seigneuriale."

57 "Cette Souveraineté est la propre Seigneurie de l'Estat. Car bien que toute Seigneurie publique deust demeurer à l'Estat, neanmoins les Seigneurs particuliers ont usurpé la Suzerainete: mais la Souverainete est du tout inseparable de l'Estat, duquel si elle estoit ostee ce ne seroit plus un estat, et celui qui l'auroit, auroit l'Estat, en tant qu'il auroit la Seigneurie souveraine . . . " Ibid., p. 8.

58 Ibid., p. 3.

59 Ibid., p. 6.

60 Ibid., p. 8. W. F. Church is hesitant to place too much emphasis on Loyseau's discussion of the proprietary quality of kingship, pointing out that a ruler may still not will away his realm, divide it or alienate it without the consent of the estates or parlement. See Church, *Constitutional Thought in the Sixteenth Century*, p. 319.

61 Loyseau, "Traité des Seigneuries," p. 14.

62 Loyseau asserts that it is only by the king's permission that customary laws may be allowed to function throughout France. Furthermore, Loyseau clearly dismisses the declaratory power of parlement when he says "Quant aux Arrests des Parlemens et autres Cours Souveraines, ce ne sont pas loix, mais plutost c'est observation et l'execution des loix." Ibid., p. 14.

63 Ibid., p. 16.

64 Ibid.

65 Ibid., pp. 16–17.

66 Ibid., pp. 21–2.

67 M. I. Baricave, *La Defence de la monarchie françoise et d'autres monarchies, contre les detestables et execrables maximes d'estat des Ministres Calvinistes* (Toulouse: Dominique Bose, 1614). The work is essentially a sustained attack on the *Vindiciae contra tyrannos*. Baricave cites passages from the work, following them with lengthy refutations of its central thesis.

68 Speaking specifically of divine-right theorists, Church writes, "the extreme absolutists reduced drastically the traditional significance of fundamental law, of the distinction between king and the crown, and even of the coronation ceremony, and based their fundamental theory of kingship simply upon the personal divine right of the reigning monarch." *Constitutional Thought in the Sixteenth Century*, p. 309.

69 Baricave, pp. 585–6.

70 Robert Gaguin, *Les chroniques de France* (Paris, 1515).

71 Ibid., p. 821.

72 Ibid., p. 823.

73 There is even a little known pamphlet entitled *Les Rois hors de Page* (1617) which, although bearing no mention of Louis XI, indicates that the phrase had become part of the common political parlance. Nor is it inconceivable, given Louis XI's long association with the phrase, that overt reference to the Spider King was no longer required, his abuse of the estates being of sufficient renown.

74 Pierre Matthieu, *The History of Lewis the Eleventh*, trans. Edward Grimeston (London: George Eld., 1614), n.p.

75 Ibid.

76 See Chapter 5, p. 127, of this book.

77 Matthieu, *The History of Lewis the Eleventh*, n.p.

78 "This was all that the king did for hee held it not fit to hazard anything, hee knew this great and gaping breach would exhale contagious vapors, that it

would not be closed up with the death of one man alone, but would swallow a million, that he rather save his subjects then vanquish his enemies. So great a conspiracie would that choller should straine the sinewes of his soule, and that he sould refuse peace to them who demanded nothing but warre, but he represented unto himselfe the deadly bitings of incensed necessitie; that the bloud which should be spilt in this warre flowed from his veines, that the blowes would fall uppon his members, and upon his bowels: That it is a goodly thing to suffer himselfe to bee vanquished, when the victorie is dangerous to the victor." Ibid., pp. 91–2.

79 Ibid., pp. 149–50.
80 Ibid., p. 133.
81 Ibid., p. 194.
82 Ibid., p. 178.
83 Ibid., p. 134.
84 Ibid., p. 206.
85 Ibid., p. 120.
86 Cardin Le Bret, *De la Souveraineté du Roy*, in *Les Oeuvres de Messire C. Le Bret* (Paris: Charles Osmont, 1689). An analysis of Le Bret's theory can be found in Gilbert Picot, *Cardin Le Bret (1558–1665) et la doctrine de la souveraineté* (Nancy, 1948).
87 Picot, pp. 31–56.
88 Le Bret, *De la Souveraineté du Roy*, p. 2.
89 Ibid., p. 3.
90 Ibid., p. 109.
91 Ibid., p. 110.
92 Ibid., p. 135.
93 Ibid., p. 165.
94 Jacques Le Long, *Bibliothèque historique de la France* (Paris: G. Martin, 1719), p. 380.
95 Joseph Klaits discusses at considerable length the pamphlets believed to have been written by Joachim Legrand in chapter eight of his work, *Printed Propaganda under Louis XIV: Absolute Monarchy and Public Opinion* (Princeton, NJ: Princeton University Press, 1976).
96 Joachim Legrand, *Vie et histoire de Louis XI* (B.N. MSS Fr. 6991), p. 2(r-v).
97 Ibid., p. 121(r).
98 Ibid., p. 297(r).
99 Ibid., p. 309(r).
100 Ibid., p. 349(r).
101 "Tous les deputés ne pouvoient pas douter que Louis ne parler sincerement luy tesmoignerent qu'ils etoient bien obligés à rendre Grace à Dieu d'[avoir] donné un Roy si sage, si prudent, si vertueux. Ils renouvelerent les protestations qu'ils avoient faites de lui estre toujours bons et fidels sujets et de donner tous ce qu'ils avoient et leur vie-même pour son service le pour obeir à ses commandemens." Ibid., p. 423(r).
102 Ibid., p. 544(r).
103 Ibid., p. 925(v).
104 Ibid., pp. 927(v)–8(r).
105 Ibid., p. 928(v).
106 But see Howell A. Lloyd's provocative thesis that the concept of the state actually evolved during the course of the sixteenth century in *The State, France and the Sixteenth Century* (London: George Allen and Unwin, 1983).

CHAPTER 5: "QUI NESCIT DISSIMULARE, NESCIT REGNARE"

1 I would like to thank the editors of the *Journal of the History of Ideas* for permission to include here, with only a few minor changes, my article, " 'Qui nescit dissimulare, nescit regnare': Louis XI and *Raison d'état* during the Reign of Louis XI," 52 (1991): 399–416.

2 Friedrich Meinecke discusses this organicist view in *Machiavellism*, trans. Douglas Scott (New Haven, Connecticut: Yale University Press, 1957), especially pp. 163–86. J. H. M. Salmon restates and summarizes Meinecke's view in "Rohan and interest of state," in *Renaissance and Revolt: Essays in the Intellectual and Social History of Early Modern France* (Cambridge, England: Cambridge University Press, 1987), pp. 98–116.

3 W. F. Church, *Richelieu and Reason of State* (Princeton, NJ: Princeton University Press, 1972), passim.

4 Etienne Thuau, *Raison d'état et pensée politique à l'epoque de Richelieu* (Paris: A. Colin, 1966), pp. 351–8.

5 Among seventeenth-century authors, Honorat de Meynier, *Les Demandes curieuses et les responses libres* (Paris, 1635), appears to be alone in attributing the phrase to Seneca. I have been unable to locate the phrase in any Senecan work, though the sentiment is expressed in Seneca's tragedy, *Thyestes*, as well as in *De Clementia*, which Seneca addressed to the Emperor Nero. In modern dictionaries of phrases, the attribution to Louis XI seems to be standard. For modern attributions, see *Larousse des Citations* (Paris: Larousse, 1976); P. Dupré, *Encyclopédie des Citations* (Paris, 1959); Maurice Maloux, *Dictionnaire des proverbes, sentences et maximes* (Paris: Larousse, 1995). In *Ways of Lying: Dissimulation, Persecution and Conformity in Early Modern Europe* (Cambridge, Mass: Harvard University Press, 1990), Perez Zagorin cites Hans Walther's characterization of the phrase as a medieval proverb in *Lateinische Sprichwörter und Sentenzen de Mittelalters in alphabetischer Anordnung*, 6 vols (Göttingen: Vandenhoeck and Ruprecht, 1963–1967), 4: no. 24329.

6 On Machiavellism in general and its relationship to growth of *raison d'état*, see the works by W. F. Church, Etienne Thuau and Friedrich Meinecke cited above. A more recent treatment can be found in Peter S. Donaldson, *Machiavelli and Mystery of State* (New York: Cambridge University Press, 1988), especially chapter 4. See also Maurizio Viroli, *From Politics to Reason of State* (Cambridge and New York: Cambridge University Press, 1992). A considerable amount of scholarship exists on the importance of Tacitus and Tacitean ideas in the sixteenth and seventeenth centuries. For example, Kenneth C. Schellhase, *Tacitus in Renaissance Political Thought* (Chicago: Chicago University Press, 1976), J. H. M. Salmon, "Cicero and Tacitus in Sixteenth Century France," *American Historical Review* 85 (1980), 307–31; Peter Burke, "Tacitism," in T. A. Dorey (ed.), *Tacitus* (London: Routledge and Kegan Paul, 1969). For a discussion focusing on the relationship between Tacitism and Machiavellism, see André Stegmann, "Le Tacitisme," in *Machiavellismo e Antimachiavellici nel Cinquecento* (Florence: Olschki, 1970) and Giuseppe Toffanin, *Machiavelli e il Tacitismo* (Padua: A. Draghi, 1921).

7 Jack A. Clarke, *Gabriel Naudé (1600–1653)* (Hamden, Connecticut; Archon Books, 1970), p. 4. Clarke provides a solid biographical background for Naudé. For an analysis of his writings, see James V. Rice, *Gabriel Naudé (1600–53)* (Baltimore: Johns Hopkins University Press, 1939).

8 Gabriel Naudé, *Le Marfore ou discours contre les libelles* (Paris, 1620), p. 11.

9 Lipsius subdivides *prudentia mixta* into three categories: light, middling and great. Light prudence consists of distrust and dissimulation; middling prudence is characterized by bribery and deceit; great prudence includes treachery and injustice. Lipsius advises the use of the first sort of prudence,

tolerates the second and utterly condemns the third. A description of the circumstances in which such prudence may be employed is set forth by Lipsius in book four, chapter fourteen, of *Politicorum sive civilis doctrinae libris sex*. For a discussion of neo-Stoicism, see Gerhard Oestreich, *Neostoicism and the Early Modern State*, eds Brigitta Oestreich and H. G. Koenigsberger, trans. David McLintock (Cambridge, England: Cambridge University Press, 1982); J. H. M. Salmon, "Stoicism and Roman Example: Seneca and Tacitus in Jacobean England," *Journal of the History of Ideas* 59 (1989): 199–225. More focused on neo-Stoicism in France is F. E. Sutcliffe, "La Notion de Raison d'Etat dans la pensée française et espagnole au XVIIe siècle," Roman Schnur (ed.), *Staatsräson: Studien zur Geschicte eines politischen Begriffs* (Berlin: Duncker and Humblot, 1975), pp. 213–24. On the connections between the idea of prudence articulated by Naudé and other *raison d'état* writers and those of Lipsius, Charron and other neo-Stoics, see F. E. Sutcliffe, *Politique et Culture 1560–1660* (Paris: Didier, 1973).

10 Gabriel Naudé, *Considérations politiques sur les coups d'estat* (n.p., 1667), p. 54. For an excellent extended discussion of the differences between "ordinary" and "extraordinary" prudence, see Julien Freund, "La situation exceptionelle comme justification de la raison d'état chez Gabriel Naudé," *Staatsräson*, pp. 141–64.

11 Naudé, *Considérations politiques*, p. 55.

12 Ibid., pp. 170–1.

13 In *De Fuoribus Gallicus* (1573), Hotman writes of Charles XI appearing before the Parlement of Paris two days after the St Bartholomew's Day Massacre, in order to receive the congratulations of the sovereign court. In the English translation of the same year Hotman, under the pseudonym Ernest Varamund, recounts how the president of the Parlement praised Charles for having "nowe with guile and subtilitie overcome these his enimies, whom he could never vanquishe by armes and battell, saying that therein the king had most fully verified the olde saying of Lewes the eleventh his progenitor King of France, which was wont to say that he knew never a Latine sentence but this one, Qui nescit dissimulare, nescit regnare, He that cannot skill to dissemble, cannot skill to be a King." pp. lxv–lxvi.

14 Ibid., pp. 154–5.

15 Gabriel Naudé, *Addition à l'histoire de Louis II* [sic] (Paris, 1630), p. 28.

16 Ibid., p. 52.

17 "Considerant les faicts d'eternelle memoire / D'un Prince que le Ciel fit seul esgal à soy. / J'admirois sa grandeur, et disois à part moy / qu'on ne pouvoit plus rien adiouster à sa gloire." "D'esclaircir le Soleil et de blanchir l'yvoire." "Par luy ton nom s'acquiert de grands honneurs icy, / Par toy le sien vaincra le temps et l'oubliance; / Mais entre les vertus que tu vas eslevant, / Lors que tu nous fais voir qu'il fut plein de science. / Tu nous monstres combien ton esprit est scavant." Ibid., n.p.

18 Pierre Matthieu, *Histoire de Louys XI* (Paris, 1610), p. 207.

19 "Tant adonné toutesfois à l'Histoire, qu'il [Henri IV] eut la curiosité de faire dresser pour son usage, et le vostre, le Loüys XI par le Sieur Mathieu son Historiographe, honneur des belles plumes de ce temps: Et me commander aussi quelque temps apres, d'essayer de mon costé, si le Tacite tant estimé entre les Ecrivains, se pourroit voir si bienhabillé à la Françoise, que la conservation nous en peust estre plus familiere." Rodolphe Le Maistre, *Le Tibère françois ou les six premiers livres des Annales de Cornelius Tacitus*, 2nd edn (Paris, 1616), n.p. See Chapter 4 of this book for a discussion of Pierre Matthieu.

20 Thuau, p. 40.

21 "... Nullam ex virtutibus suis magis quam dissimulationem diligebat." Naudé, *Considérations politiques*, p. 55.

22 For a brief biography of Machon, see Donaldson, *Machiavelli and Mystery of State*, pp. 186–7.

23 Louis Machon, *Apologie pour Machiavelle en faveur des princes et les ministres d'estat* (1643) B.N. Mss Fr. 19046, 19047, n.p.

24 Ibid., pp. 655–6.

25 Works about Jean de Silhon are few in number, but see the slim volume by René Kerviler, *Jean de Silhon* (Paris, 1876), and Gilbert Picot, *Jean de Silhon (1594?–1667) ou la recherche des certitudes en religion et en politique* (Nancy, 1980).

26 Silhon's first major work was devoted to the examination of the soul, *Les Deux verites, l'un de Dieu et de sa Providence; l'autre de l'immortalité de l'Ame* (1626). Kerviler perhaps overstates Silhon's religious convictions when he asserts that "il fit, toute sa vie, sa première préoccupation de défendre les principes religieux contre les athées et les rationalistes d'alors." Kerviler, p. 8.

27 Faret, *Recueil de lettres* (1640), cited by Kerviler, p. 12.

28 Jean de Silhon, *Le Ministre d'estat avec le veritable usage de la politique moderne* (Amsterdam, 1664), p. 74.

29 Ibid., p. 257.

30 Ibid., pp. 89–90.

31 Ibid., p. 89.

32 Ibid., p. 102.

33 See the discussion of kingly counsel in Chapter 7 of this book.

34 Ibid., p. 110.

35 Ibid., p. 101.

36 Didier Herauld, *Fragment de l'examen du prince de Machiavel* (Paris, 1633), pp. 17–18.

37 Ibid., p. 36.

38 Ibid., pp. 59–60.

39 Ibid., p. 73.

40 Ibid., pp. 76–7.

41 Honorat de Meynier, *Les Demandes curieuses et les reponses libres* (Paris, 1635), p. 350.

42 Ibid., p. 352.

43 Ibid., p. 381.

44 *La Voix gemissante du peuple chrestien et catholique* (Paris, 1640), p. 101.

CHAPTER 6: THE REPENTANT GHOST

1 Hubert Carrier is leading the effort to mine the rich source material of Fronde pamphlets, having edited a small but significant sample of Mazarinades, *La Fronde. Contestation democratique et misère paysanne: 52 Mazarinades* (Paris: EDHIS, n.d.), and having published an in-depth examination of the pamphlets and their authors, *Les Mazarinades*, 2 vols (Paris: Champion, 1987, 1992). His bibliography of the entire collection is anxiously awaited. Christian Jouhaud's important work, *Mazarinades: la Fronde des mots* (Paris: Aubier, 1985) calls for a new integration of history of literature into socio-political history.

2 Both Ernst Kossman and Lloyd Moote recognize and discuss the contradictory self-perception of the Parlement of Paris. In his book, *La Fronde* (Leiden: Universitaire Pers Leiden, 1954), Kossman makes the assertion that the Fronde never became a "positive" force for reform because the Parlement of Paris did not have the gumption to outline more definitively its role within government. Moote interprets the ambivalence of the *parlementaire* position in a more positive light, arguing that the Parlement sought to control the pace and extent of reform by characterizing itself both as "part of the crown" and, simultaneously, as the institution designed to check the abuses of royal

authority. See the introduction to *The Revolt of the Judges. The Parlement of Paris and the Fronde 1643–1652* (Princeton, 1971). Nevertheless, the role of the Parlement of Paris in the government of France, as perceived by its own members and proponents of the court, especially as regards its relationship with the estates general, awaits a full-scale treatment.

3   Roland Mousnier's comprehensive work, *La Venalité des offices sous Henri IV et Louis XIII* (Paris: Presses Universitaires de France, 1971), is an excellent source both for the development of the system of venality and how it functioned in French government.

4   See chapters two and three in Moote, *The Revolt of the Judges*, for a detailed account of fiscal policies employed by Michel d'Emery, *intendant des finances* during the last years of Louis XIII's reign and *surintendant des finances* after 1647.

5   For a brief but helpful introduction to the conditions in France prior to the outbreak of the Fronde, see Roland Mousnier, "The Fronde," in *Preconditions of Revolution in Early Modern Europe*, eds Robert Forster and Jack P. Greene (Baltimore: Johns Hopkins University Press, 1970). An excellent discussion of the princely revolt of 1614–15, combining an examination of the events with an exploration of the pamphlets produced during the course of the conflict, is Jeffrey Sawyer's *Printed Poison: Pamphlet Propaganda, Faction Politics and the Public Sphere in Early Seventeenth-Century France* (Berkeley: University of California Press, 1990).

6   The changing conception and function of the 'lit de justice' is expertly examined by Sarah Hanley, *The "Lit de Justice" of the Kings of France: Constitutional Ideology in Legend, Ritual and Discourse* (Princeton, NJ: Princeton University Press, 1983).

7   For a discussion of the series of events leading up to the assembly at the Chambre Saint Louis, see Kossman, *La Fronde*, pp. 45–52, and Moote, pp. 91–131. See also Orest Ranum's recent book, *The Fronde: A French Revolution, 1648–1652* (New York: W. W. Norton, 1993).

8   There are a number of studies devoted to the manner in which the Fronde was played out in the provinces. See, for example, Sharon Kettering, *Judicial Politics and Urban Revolt in Seventeenth-Century France. The Parlement of Aix, 1629–1659* (Princeton, NJ: Princeton University Press, 1978).

9   Although not exhaustive, C. Moreau's *Bibliographie des Mazarinades*, 3 vols (New York: Burt Franklin, 1965) is still an invaluable resource for students of the Fronde. Moreau has the following to say about the *Lettre d'Avis*: "Il n'y a peut être pas de Mazarinade qui ait fait plus de bruit dans les temps et reçu plus d'éloges." I: 358.

10   According to Hubert Carrier, the pamphlet was written by Jean Beaudeau, Marquis de Clanleu, the governor of Château-Chinon. The work was directed specifically against the magistrates' efforts to negotiate with the royal court.

11   The author writes, "La premiére cause que nous trouvions, est que vous ne faites pas assez de réflexion, sur ce que vous estes. Nous ne sommes généreux qu'autant que nous le croyons estre, comme nous ne sommes poltrons que pour avoir trop de défiance de nos forces; c'est pourquoi, dit-on, Dieu ne voulut pas donner aux animaux la connoissance de ce qu'ils pouvoient; autrement l'homme n'auroit iamais pu en venire à bout ny les dompter comme il fait." *Lettre d'avis à Messieurs du Parlement de Paris, escrit par un Provincial* (1649) in *Choix de Mazarinades*, ed. C. Moreau, 2 vols (Paris, 1853), I: 361.

12   Ibid.

13   "Prenez garde, Messieurs, comme il en est tousiours allé de pis en pis depuis que vos charges ont commencé à se vendre. Avant Louis XI, les Roys ne levoient rien sur leurs suiets que par le consentement des Etats, ou qui ne fust

du moins authorisé par la cour du Parlement; mais ce Prince qui les mit hors de page, commença de se servir en ses patentes des termes de certaine science, plain pouvoir et authorité; et pour imprimer de la crainte dans les esprits des Officiers de Iustice qui s'en formalisoient, il proposa à l'instigation de ses courtisans de mettre leurs charges en vente." Ibid., I: 365–6.

14 *Manuel du bon citoyen ou bouclier de defense legitime contre les assauts de l'ennemi* (22 mars 1649) in *Choix de Mazarinades*, I: 441–2.

15 " . . . C'est à sçavoir, le droict et la faculté qu'a ce peuple là de se gouverner et de se maintenir, se répand et se communique par tout le corps politique; la teste duquel s'appelle un Roy, un Empereur ou un Duc; les autres parties nobles et principales sont Conseillers, Magistrats, Governeurs, Capitaines, Consuls, Eschevins; celles d'au dessous sont Marchands, Laboureurs, Matelots, Artisans; et enfin les plus basses sont Manoeuvres, Portefaix, Mendians et autres personnes qui composent la multitude. De la composition de tous ces membres réussit un corps politique et moral, lequel ne sçauroit se bien porter, ny subsister, que par la parfaite correspondance, liason et continuité de tous ses membres." Ibid., I: 451.

16 Ibid., I: 443–4.

17 Because of these failings, Louis XI was rendered "moins accessible et moins pitoyable aux nécessitez de son peuple, dont il a merité le reproche et la malédiction iusques à nos iours; au lieu que nous adorons la bonté et la mansuétude de Louis XII, et que nous admirons la clémence de Henri IV . . . " Ibid., I: 443–4.

18 Carrier writes that the pamphlet is "un résumé très clair et très éloquent des thèses les plus avancées de la Fronde parlementaire sur la souveraineté populaire et l'idée de contrat." *La Fronde. Contestation democratique et misère paysanne: 52 Mazarinades*, introduction, I: 3.

19 See Chapter 1 of this book for a discussion of Hotman's appraisal of Louis XI.

20 *Epilogue, ou dernier appareil du bon citoyen* (n.p., 1649), p. 5.

21 Ibid., p. 8. The author asserts that the kings who followed "se sont maintenus dans une louable moderation." He mentions Louis XII and Henri IV with approval, praising the latter for consistently adhering to legality, despite chaotic conditions and abusive attacks on his person. It is, however, rather ironic that the turbulent reigns of Charles IX and Henri III are so casually overlooked!

22 The author maintains that the estates general of the kingdom were responsible for the transmission of royal authority from the Merovingians to the Carolingians and then to the Capetians. *La Guide au Chemin de la Liberté* (Paris, 1652), p. 6.

23 Ibid., p. 11.

24 *Request de la Noblesse pour l'Assemblée des Estats generaux* (1651) in Moreau, II: 235–7.

25 *Declarations des roys Louis XI et Henry III* (Paris: Par les Imprimeurs et Librairies ordinaire du Roy, 1648), pp. 3–6.

26 Ibid., pp. 6–9.

27 Ibid., pp. 10–11.

28 Carrier's attribution is supportable given Machon's established authorship of the manuscript, *Apologie pour Machiavel*. In the manuscript, which defends Machiavellism and *raison d'état* in general, Machon espouses a positive view of Louis XI very similar to that found in *Les Veritables maximes*.

29 See a further discussion of *Judicium Francorum* in Chapter 7 of this book.

30 *Les Veritables maximes du gouvernement de la France* (Paris, 1652), p. 8.

31 Ibid., p. 10.

32 Claude Joly, *Recueil de maximes veritables et importantes pour l'institution du roy* (Paris, 1663), p. 18.

33 Ibid., pp. 130–1.

34 Ibid., pp. 134–5.

35 Ibid., p. 63.

36 Ibid., p. 331. Joly cites Commynes's interpretation of the Leaguers as disguising their particularist aims with altruistic phrasing. He appears to agree with Commynes's assessment of the rebels' intentions without in any way diminishing his point about the importance of the estates.

37 Ibid., pp. 332–3.

38 Ibid., chapter 9.

39 Ibid., chapter 10.

40 Ibid., pp. 452–3.

41 Ibid., p. 505. It should be pointed out that, although Joly cites the famous maxime, "Que celuy qui ne sçait feindre et dissimuler, ne sçait pas regner," he minimizes its importance by noting in the margin that "Cecy n'est qu'un mot trivial, qui est attribué à Louys XI."

42 Several fifteenth-century manuscript editions of the *Rosier des Guerres* are extant in the Bibliothèque Nationale (FF. 442, 1238, 1239, 1240, 1965, 4986, 17273, 24261). The first published edition appeared in Paris in 1521. Two other editions appeared in 1522 and 1529, included in François Regnault's *Rozier historial de France*. For bibliographic information on the *Rosier des Guerres*, see Jean Kaulek, "Louis XI: Est-il l'auteur du *Rosier des Guerres?*" *Revue historique* 21 (1883): 312–22. After this initial flurry of editions, the *Rosier* fell into relative obscurity, although another edition did appear in 1616, which Claude Joly utilized in his discussion of Louis XI. There is also a modern edition, *Le Rosier des guerres: enseignements de Louis XI Roy de France pour le Dauphin son fils* (Paris: Bernouard, 1925) with an introduction by Maurice Diamantberger.

43 The question of authorship is addressed by Jean Kaulek, "Louis XI, est-il l'auteur du *Rosier des Guerres?*" Based on internal evidence and comparison with another work, *Livre des trois ages*, known to have been authored by Pierre Choinet, Kaulek establishes Choinet, a physician at the court of Louis XI, as the most probable author.

44 Ibid., p. 160.

45 Ibid., p. 172.

46 Ibid., p. 209.

47 Ibid., p. 163.

48 Very little attention has been devoted to the so-called *dialogues des morts*, and the few works that do exist tend to be literary rather than historical studies. See, for example, Johann S. Egilsrud, *Le "Dialogue des morts" dans les litteratures française, allemande et anglaise 1644–1789* (Paris, 1934). George Armstrong Kelly discusses eighteenth-century and revolutionary dialogues in chapter 4 of his *Mortal Politics in Eighteenth-Century France* (Waterloo, Canada: University of Waterloo Press, 1986).

49 Moreau, *Bibliographie des Mazarinades*, I: 319.

50 *Remonstrance du Roy Louis XII au Roy Louis XI sur leur differente façon de regner* (Paris, 1649), p. 3.

51 Ibid., pp. 4–5.

52 Ibid., pp. 13–14.

53 *Dialogue entre le Roy Louys XI et Louys XII sur leur differente façon de regner à sçavoir lequel est meilleur ou de les Gouverner par amour ou par force et puissance absoluë* (n.p., 1649). pp. 3–4.

54 Ibid., p. 5.

55 Ibid., p. 6.
56 Ibid., p. 9.
57 Ibid., p. 11.
58 *Le Dialogue d'estat* (Paris, n.d.), p. 4.
59 Ibid., p. 10.
60 Ibid., p. 12.
61 Ibid., p. 20.
62 Ibid., p. 13.
63 "Il me semble pourtant qu'il y a ie ne sçay quelque mesceance et incompatibilité, et que d'ordinaire le ministere des gens d'Eglise est arrogant, avare et sans humanité, sous pretexte de n'estre iusticiable que de Dieu ainsi qu'ils s'imaginent." Ibid., p. 30.

CHAPTER 7: LOUIS XI AND THE IDEA OF COUNSEL

1 Keith M. Baker, *Inventing the French Revolution* (Cambridge, England: Cambridge University Press, 1990), esp. pp. 25–7.
2 John Guy, "The Rhetoric of Counsel in Early Modern England," in *Tudor Political Culture*, ed. Dale Hoak (Cambridge, England: Cambridge University Press, 1995), pp. 292–310. To my knowledge, very little attention has been paid to the idea of counsel in French political thought.
3 Guy writes: "A belief that *imperium* and *consilium* were symbiotic sustained the role of 'counsel' as an 'inspirational myth'. An assumption that the vice and passion of rulers could be mitigated by the advice of good counsellors energized the process whereby the metaphor was refashioned and reinterpreted for rhetorical and political ends." Ibid., pp. 292–3.
4 I have deliberately chosen to employ the two different acceptable spellings of "counsel." "Counsel" is used to refer to the concept of giving or receiving advice; "council" refers to a more or less formal organization in proximity to the king, consisting of individuals whose purpose is to provide counsel. "Counsellor" and "councillor" are similarly applied to differentiate between individuals supporting and advising the king informally, on the one hand, and actual members of the king's council, on the other.
5 See the discussion of *nobiliaire* theory in Chapter 3 of this book.
6 See the work by Albert N. Hamscher, *The Parlement of Paris After the Fronde, 1653–1673* (Pittsburgh, PA: University of Pittsburgh Press, 1976). Even during the Fronde, *parlementaire* aspirations were repeatedly and vehemently voiced in a multitude of pamphlets; among these, *Les Veritables maximes du gouvernement du France, justifiées par l'ordre des temps . . . servant de response au pretendu arrest de cassation du Conseil du 18 janvier 1652* is perhaps the most significant and influential. See also the works of Claude Joly, including *Recueil de maximes veritables et importantes pour l'institution du roy*.
7 The continuing importance of Jansenism in the struggle of the magistrates right up to the Revolution is discussed in a series of excellent articles by Dale Van Kley, including: "The Religious Origins of the Patriot and Ministerial Parties in Pre-Revolutionary France," *Historical Reflections/Réflexions historiques* 18 (1992): 17–63; and "The Jansenist Constitutional Legacy in the French Prerevolution, 1750–1789," *Historical Reflections/Réflexions historiques* 13 (1986): 393–453.
8 On the importance of "figurism" in the political dimension of Jansenism see Catherine Maire, "L'Église et la nation: Du dépot de la vérité au dépot des lois: la trajectoire janséniste au XVIIIe siècle," *Annales. Économies, Sociétés, Civilisations* 46 (1991): 1177–205.

9 See Dale Van Kley, "The Estates General as Ecumenical Council: The Constitutionalism of Corporate Consensus and the *Parlement's* Ruling of September 25, 1788," *Journal of Modern History* 61 (1989): 1–52.

10 *Essay historique concernant les droits et prérogatives de la cours des pairs qui est le Parlement séant à Paris*, 1721. (B.N. Mss. Fr. n.a. 1503), p. 9.

11 The author makes no effort to hide his contempt for the assembly: "L'experience nous apprend qu'il n'y a presque rien plus infructueux à la nation que ces assemblées." Ibid., p. 275.

12 Ibid., pp. 275–6.

13 *Pour l'autorité du Parlement dans les affaires publiques*, n.d. (Bibliothèque de l'Arsenal Mss. 5860), p. 1.

14 "Mémoire touchant l'origine et l'autorité du Parlement de France, appellé Judicium Francorum" in Mezeray, *Mémoires historiques et critiques* (Amsterdam, 1732). It is significant that the *Judicium Francorum* is, to a great extent, actually a reprint of a Fronde treatise entitled *Les Veritables Maximes du gouvernement de la France*. There are important differences between the two works, however. *Les Veritables Maximes* is obviously a *pièce de circonstance*: it demonstrates a clear-cut animus against Cardinal Mazarin and appears to be directed towards countering the power of the *Conseil d'Etat* (especially with regard to the council's attempt to block parlement's *arrêt* against Mazarin). Most of these elements are missing from the *Judicium Francorum*, while new passages concerning parlement's authority during the regencies of Louis XIII and Louis XIV have been added. More importantly, the *Judicium Francorum* differs from the earlier version in paying less attention to the details of a particular political context than to the exposition of general principles of *parlementaire* authority.

15 Ibid., p. 122.

16 Ibid., pp. 114–16.

17 Biographical information on Lepaige and thoughtful analysis of his works are provided throughout David Bell's *Lawyers and Citizens: The Making of a Political Elite in Old Regime France*. See also Dale Van Kley, *The Damiens Affair*, Princeton, NJ: Princeton University Press, 1980), pp. 117–79, 184–94.

18 For a brief introduction to the controversy over the refusal of sacraments, see Daniel C. Joynes, "Parlementaires, Peers and the *Parti Janséniste*: The Refusal of Sacraments and the Revival of the Ancient Constitution in Eighteenth Century France," *Proceedings of the Annual Meeting of the Western Society for French History* 8 (1980): 229–38. More extensive discussion can be found in Dale Van Kley, *The Damiens Affair and the Unraveling of the "Ancien Régime"* and in Jean Egret, *Louis XV et l'opposition parlementaire 1715–1774* (Paris: Armand Colin, 1970), both of which are invaluable in terms of their discussion of the refusal of sacraments issue as well as the larger question of *parlementaire* politics in the eighteenth century. Recently, in *Louis XV and the Parlement of Paris, 1737–1755* (Cambridge, England: Cambridge University Press, 1995), John Rogister has written on the Parlement of Paris's struggles with the crown in the critical period between 1737 and 1755, and has adeptly placed the issue of Jansenism alongside the endemic conflicts over fiscal reform.

19 "Concluons-en qu'on ne peut assez admirer, la sagesse qui a presidé à la Constitution primitive de notre Gouvernement, et qui a établi tout à la fois cette Puissance Monarchique dont la justice et l'équité sont la regle; et ce Parlement aussi ancien que la Monarchie même, dont la fonction éminente est d'être le dépositaire et le conservateur des Loix constitutives de l'Etat." Louis-Adrien Lepaige, *Lettres historiques sur les fonctions essentielles du parlement*, 2 vols (Amsterdam, 1753–4), I: 32.

20 From the earliest times, parlements have changed their form but have always "subsisté dans ce qu'elles ont de fondamental, et dans ce qui caractérise la

nature fonciere des anciens Parlemens Germains, c'est-à-dire, dans leurs fonctions importantes par rapport au Gouvernement." Ibid., I: 35.

21 Ibid., I: 38.

22 Ibid., I: 142.

23 Ibid., I: 183–4. Lepaige makes no judgement about the development of feudalism in France. Its emergence did not affect the institution of parlement, except to contribute to the fusion of the *parlement général* and the *Cour du roi*. Although Lepaige is clearly not hostile to the old aristocracy, he does recognize that a division exists between robe and sword, and he tries to address the complaints of sword nobles regarding the *parvenu* status of most of parlement's members. Lepaige maintains that the *noblesse d'épée* should not worry about potential competition from the new robe aristocracy. In fact, compared with the composition of the parlement at the time it became sedentary, the sword nobles are better represented on the modern court because there are fewer ecclesiastics. Moreover, despite the fact that elder sons of the sword usually pursued a military career, the ancient nobility was more than adequately represented in parlement by brothers and younger sons. Ibid., II: 21–4. Lepaige's attempt to allay the anxieties of the sword nobles is significant because it provides evidence that, at least in the eyes of contemporaries, a rift did indeed exist between robe and sword which continued into the second half of the eighteenth century. The best representation of the "fusion thesis" is put forward by Franklin L. Ford, *Robe and Sword: The Regrouping of the French Aristocracy after Louis XIV* (Cambridge, Mass.: Harvard University Press, 1953).

24 Lepaige, *Lettres historiques*, I: 142. For further discussion of this conflict between the estates general and the parlement, see my "Meddling Chaperons: The Involvement of the Parlement of Paris at the Estates of 1593," in *Politics, Ideology and the Law in Early Modern Europe* (Rochester, NY: University of Rochester Press, 1994). Dale Van Kley has found, however, that Lepaige was not always so antagonistic to the estates general, especially after the Maupeou coup revealed "the fragility of these venal royal officers' constitutional position and ability to represent the nation." "The Estates General as Ecumenical Council," p. 25.

25 Lepaige, *Lettres historiques*, I: 150.

26 "Et c'est où se réduit aussi cette belle Instruction, que Louis XI lui-même laissa en mourant, à Charles VIII son fils, sous le nom de *Rosier des Guerres* (c. 3 de Justice) *Quant les Rois ou les Princes ne ont {sic} regard à la Loi, en ce faisant ils font leur peuple serf, et perdent le nom de Roi; car nul ne doit être appellé Roi, fors celui qui régne et seigneurie sur les Francs; car les Francs de nature, aiment leur Seigneur; mais les serfs naturellement les héent, comme les Esclaves leurs Maîtres. Un Roi régnant en droit et en justice, est Roi de son peuple: et s'il regne en iniquité et en violence, combien que ses sujets le tiennent à Roi, toutefois leur volonté et leur courage s'encline à un autre.*" Ibid., I: 27–8.

27 For a good introduction to the evolution of the concept of fundamental law, see Martin P. Thompson, "The History of Fundamental Law in Political Thought from the French Wars of Religion to the American Revolution," *American Historical Review* 91 (1986): 1103–28. André Lemaire, *Les lois fondamentales de la monarchie française d'après les théoriciens de l'Ancien Régime* (Paris: A. Fontemoing, 1907) provides the best overview of the French context.

28 For a discussion of the alternate contraction and expansion of the corpus of fundamental law and how this relates to changes in the nature of absolutism, see Chapter 5 of this book.

29 François Hotman does, however, outline eight fundamental laws in Chapter 25 of the 1586 edition of *Francogallia*, some of which do approach the specificity

characterizing the eighteenth-century parlementaire definition of fundamental law.

30 *Judicium Francorum*, p. 117.

31 [Eusebe Philadelphe Cosmopolite], *Le Reveille-Matin des François et de leurs voisins* (Edinburgh?: Jacques James, 1574).

32 *Judicium Francorum*, p. 120.

33 *Pour l'autorité du Parlement dans les affaires publiques*, p. 2(v).

34 *Tres humbles et tres respecteuses iteratives remonstrances que presentens au Roy, notre tres-honore et souverain seigneur, les gens tenans sa cour de Parlemens*, 26 juillet 1718, p. 61(r).

35 Ibid., p. 62(r).

36 *Accomodement entre le Roy Louis XI et son Parlement*, pp. 2–3.

37 Ibid., p. 2.

38 *Judicium Francorum*, p. 135.

39 The best secondary sources on the exile of the magistrates are Jules Flammermont, *Le Chancelier Maupeou et les parlements* (Paris: Alphonse Picard, 1883), and Durand Echeverria, *The Maupeou Revolution: A Study in the History of Libertarianism* (Baton Rouge: Louisiana State University Press, 1985), pp. 1–34. In his article, "The Parlements of France and the Breakdown of the Old Regime," *French Historical Studies* VI (1970): 415–58, William Doyle argues that, in carrying out his "reform," Maupeou was motivated by personal ambition rather than by any real desire to establish greater monarchical control over the courts. By contrast, in his article, "In Defense of Reform: French Government Propaganda during the Maupeou Crisis," *French Historical Studies* 8 (1973): 51–76, David Hudson argues that the ideological conflict between parlement and the crown underlay both Maupeou's actions and parlement's response, and he believes that Doyle has underestimated its importance. More recent articles have focused on the impact of the Maupeou coup on the mobilization of public opinion on a scale hitherto unknown. The new importance accorded public opinion was to have lasting effects and contribute in no small measure to the outbreak of the Revolution. See the special issue of *Historical Reflections/Reflexions historiques* 18 (1992) entitled *The Maupeou Revolution: The Transformation of French Politics at the End of the Old Regime*, comprising articles by Dale Van Kley, Shanti Singham and Sarah Maza, and an introduction by Keith M. Baker.

40 "L'autorité doit être absolue parce que c'est elle seule qui doit et qui peut contenir tous les ordres de l'Etat dans le devoir: mais cette autorité absolue doit avoir pour l'objet de tout réunir de tout conserver et de ne jamais rien détruire." [Hue de] Miromesnil, *Lettres sur l'etat de la magistrature en l'année 1772* (B.N. Mss. Fr. 10986), p. 5.

41 Ibid., pp. 5–8.

42 Ibid., p. 13.

43 Ibid., p. 172.

44 There is a general consistency of interpretation between the *parlementaire* pamphleteers and remonstrances of the magistrates which indicates a unity of purpose and uniformity of ideas between the two groups (though this is not too unexpected, since theorists like Lepaige were often themselves members of the courts). The prominence and frequency of references to Louis XI in the remonstrances of the Parlement of Paris attest to the power of that king's image in the rhetorical battle waged by the sovereign court throughout the eighteenth century.

45 Along with a number of other "orthodox" clerics under the leadership of the Archbishop of Paris, Christophe de Beaumont, Father Bouettin zealously applied the tactic of refusing sacraments in order to hunt down priests

suspected of Jansenist sympathies. Bouettin himself repeatedly clashed with parlement over this issue during the early 1750s and was even, on one occasion, incarcerated for an hour or so on the order of the sovereign court. Dale Van Kley provides an admirable summary of the activities of Bouettin and the other "constitutionary" clerics, and how the struggle between the Church and parlement coloured the trial of François Damiens, who had attempted, in 1757, to assassinate Louis XV by stabbing him with a penknife. Dale Van Kley, *The Damiens Affair and the Unraveling of the "Ancien Regime" 1750–1770*, passim.

46 Flammermont, *Remonstrances du parlement*, 1: 423.
47 Ibid., 2: 180–1.
48 Ibid., 2: 185–6.
49 Ibid., 2: 191.
50 Ibid., 3: 765.
51 Ibid., 3: 767–9.
52 *Dictionnaire de Biographie Française* (Paris: Librairie Letouzey et Ané, 1982), 15: 855.
53 Gautier de Sibert, *Considerations sur l'ancienneté de l'existence du Tiers-etat, et sur les causes de la suspension de ses droits pendant un temps* (Paris, 1789), n.p.
54 "In vain does the comte de Boulainvilliers, who built his system of servitude on the falsity advanced by Loyseau; in vain do the partisans of his work want, like him, to support Clovis, who became sovereign of the greater portion of provinces of Gaul [and reduced to servitude the ancient inhabitants of these rich lands]." Ibid., p. 4.
55 Ibid., p. 70.
56 Ibid., p. 74.
57 Ibid., p. 113.
58 Gautier de Sibert, *Variations de la Monarchie Françoise dans son gouvernement politique, civil et militaire*, 4 vols (Paris: Saillant, 1765), 3: 172.
59 Ibid., 3: 204.
60 What little biographical information there is about Guillaume Saige is discussed by Keith Baker, "A classical republican in eighteenth-century Bordeaux: Guillaume-Joseph Saige," in *Inventing the French Revolution. Essays on French Political Culture in the Eighteenth Century* (Cambridge, England: Cambridge University Press, 1990), pp. 128–52, and Clarke W. Garrett, "The *Moniteur* of 1788," *French Historical Studies* 5 (1968): 267–8. Garrett notes that the main biographical reference works are useless because they confuse the lives of the three Saige family members.
61 Guillaume-Joseph Saige, *Catéchisme du citoyen ou élémens du droit public françois* (n.p., 1788), pp. 24–5. In his article, "The *Moniteur* of 1788," Clarke Garrett expresses the view that Saige promotes the parlement rather than the estates general as the representative body which would protect the interests of the French people, but Keith M. Baker recognizes the importance of the estates general in the "political vision" of Saige in his article, "French Political Thought at the Accession of Louis XVI," *Journal of Modern History* 50 (1978): 279–303.
62 Saige, *Catechisme du citoyen*, p. 31.
63 Ibid., p. 70.
64 Ibid., pp. 43–5.
65 Ibid., p. 45.
66 Ibid., pp. 169–70.
67 [Jean-Baptiste Britard], *Discours historique sur le caractere et la politique de Louis XI; par un Citoyen de la section du Théatre Français* (Paris: l'an second de la Liberté), n.p.

68 Britard charges Charles Pinot Duclos with copying great chunks of Joachim Legrand's manuscript. Moreover, Duclos did not express the right political sentiments to suit Britard: "N'ayant eu, pour ainsi dire, que la peine d'écrire, du moins devoit-il revêtir son style des couleurs de la liberté, et s'armer contre la tyrannie, de cette courageuse Philosophie dont il se targuoit dans le monde, et c'est ce qu'il n'a pas fait." p. 6.

69 Ibid., p. 12.

70 In speaking of Louis XI's relationship with his brother, Charles, Britard writes: "Louis affecte la franchise et la joie. Il presse son frere contre son sein: il embrassa Charles . . . comme Nero embrassa Britannicus." Ibid., p. 69. Like Louis XI, Nero is ubiquitously employed as the personification of tyranny. See W. B. Gwyn, "Cruel Nero: The Concept of the Tyrant and the Image of Nero in Western Political Thought," *History of Political Thought* 12 (1991): 421–55.

71 Britard, p. 15.

72 Ibid., p. 22.

73 " . . . avant-coureur des grandes Révolutions: et bien dirigée, cette Révolution, née de l'excès des maux et de l'oppression, pouvoit enfin produire la Liberté et le bonheur de la France." Ibid., p. 34.

74 Ibid., p. 85.

75 Ibid., p. 98.

76 Ibid., p. 152.

77 Ibid., p. 116.

78 Ibid., p. 124.

79 Ibid., p. 169.

EPILOGUE: "LE ROI BOURGEOIS"

1 There are a great many works which deal with the Bourbon restoration and its aftermath. For a brief introduction to the Charter of 1814 and its effect on the nature of French restoration politics and society, see Irene Collins, *Government and Society in France 1814–1848* (London: Edward Arnold, 1970). For a general discussion of political theory in the restoration period, see Dominique Bagge, *Les Idées politiques en France sous la Restauration* (Paris: Presses Universitaires de France, 1952); Jean-Jacques Chevallier offers a rather synoptic treatment of the main trends in nineteenth-century political theory and their main proponents in his *Histoire de la pensée politique* (3 vols), vol. 3: "La grande transition: 1789–1848" (Paris: Payot, 1984).

2 The political ideas of the "doctrinaires," of whom Guizot and Royer-Collard were the prime examples, are described by Guizot's biographer, Douglas W. Johnson, in chapter two of *Guizot: Aspects of French History 1781–1874* (London: Routledge and Kegan Paul, 1963).

3 See Stanley Mellon, *The Political Uses of History* (Stanford, CA: Stanford University Press, 1958).

4 In his work, *Louis XI et les villes* (Geneva: Slatkine-Megariotis Reprints, 1974), Henri Sée endorses the view that Louis XI worked tirelessly on behalf of the *bourgeoisie*. He concludes his book with the summation of Louis XI's contributions: "Louis XI améliore la navigation fluviale; il crée de nouvelles foires; il essaie d'établir des compagnies de commerce; il ne conclut ni un traité ni une trève qui ne contienne des clauses commerciales . . . Plus qu'aucun de ses prédécesseurs, Louis XI prend souci de l'opinion publique, qui déjà devient rédoutable; à tout instant, il proteste de son désir 'd'aleger et soullaiger le peuple des grans et grafves charges qu'il a portées et soustenues' . . . Ainsi, au-dessous de l'Etat, Louis XI conçoit déjà l'existence d'une nation, qui se personnifie en la bourgeoisie." pp. 371–2.

5 In the "avant-propos" to the second edition of the work, published in 1819, Dumesnil recounts the difficulty he had in getting the work published originally. Labelled a "Bourbonnien," Dumesnil was forced to add the last paragraph which praised Napoleon before the work would be accepted. Dumesnil writes: "Le ministre [in charge of censorship] ne vouloit point que l'on montrât la révolution de peuple plutôt que de principes; ni qu'on parlât d'une intention malheureuse de liberté, toujours mal exprimée; ni qu'on fit à Louis XI le reproche d'avoir jeté dans la multitude le germe d'une funeste égalité." pp. xxiii-xxiv.

6 Alexis Dumesnil, *Le Règne de Louis XI et de l'influence qu'il a eue jusque sur les derniers temps de la troisième dynastie* (Paris: Maradan, 1811), p. 9.

7 Ibid., p. 14.

8 Ibid., pp. 73–5.

9 Ibid., pp. 145–6.

10 Ibid., p. 150.

11 Augustin Thierry, *The Formation and Progress of the Third Estate*, trans. Francis B. Wells, 2 vols in 1 (London: Thomas Bosworth, 1855), pp. 84–5.

12 Ibid., p. 109.

13 Ibid., pp. 108–9.

14 Henri Martin, *Histoire de France*, 4th edn (Paris: Furne, 1865), p. 531. Martin quotes from Thierry, "Le despote Louis XI n'est pas de la race des tyrans égoistes, mais de celle des novateurs impitoyables." p. 65 from *Essai sur l'histoire du Tiers Etat.*

15 The engraving is found on the title page of Henri Martin, *Histoire de France populaire* (Paris, 1868).

16 Ibid., VII: 29.

17 Ibid.

18 Ibid., VII: 154.

19 Ibid., VII: 155.

20 Ibid., VI: 530.

21 Ibid., VI: 531.

22 François Guizot, *Histoire de la civilisation en Europe*, 11th edn (Paris: Didier et Cie., 1871), p. 299. "Nous touchons à la porte de l'histoire moderne proprement dite, à la porte de cette société qui est la nôtre, dont les institutions, les opinions, les moeurs, étaient, il y a quarante ans, celles de France, sont encore celles de l'Europe, et exercent encore sur nous, malgré la metamorphose que notre révolution nous a fait subir, une si puissante influence."

23 J. H. M. Salmon, "The French Romantics on Comparative Revolution," *History of European Ideas* 11 (1989): 381–91.

24 Guizot, *Histoire de la civilisation en Europe*, p. 306.

25 Ibid., pp. 307–8.

26 The most important work dealing with the influence of Scott on his contemporaries and on authors writing in the years after him is Louis Maigron, *Le Roman historique à l'époque romantique: Essai sur l'influence de Walter Scott* (Paris: Hachette, 1898).

27 See, for example, the relatively recent work by James Anderson, *Sir Walter Scott and History* (Edinburgh: The Edina Press, 1981).

28 Orville W. Mosher, *Louis XI, King of France as he appears in history and literature* (Toulouse: Edouard Privat, 1925), p. 231. Although Mosher's book lacks both a clear theme and coherent structure, it is nevertheless useful in pointing to relatively unknown works about Louis XI.

29 In his book, *The French Romantic Knowledge of English Literature* (Paris: Librairie Ancienne Edouard Champion, 1924), Eric Partridge wrote that "All in

all . . . the great novelist provided the plot and the characters of many plays, of which very few had much literary merit, though some ran for a long time: the French playwrights were swept away by his tremendous vogue and the deceptive aptness of his stories." p. 229. Partridge cites a number of contemporary articles written about the vogue of *Quentin Durward* and the noticeable and largely positive effect it had on the plays of Delavigne in particular. According to Partridge, Eugene Briffaut wrote somewhat later in *Le Temps* (4 December 1838) that Delavigne's *Louis XI* was influenced greatly by Scott and that the playwright was moved to write the work in part by the great popularity of Scott's novel.

30 In 1830, another history of Louis XI appeared, this one by Charles Liskeme. Two more works about the monarch were published in 1841 and 1842, *Louis XI et Plessis les Tours* by W. H. Louyrette, and *Histoire de Louis XI* by M. J. J. E. Roye, respectively. The latter work reiterated Scott's black interpretation of Louis XI. Finally, much later in the century, Urbain Legeay published a two-volume history of the king (1874). Mosher, Part III: "Louis XI and the Historians," pp. 195–208.

31 Partridge quotes from a critic who wrote in *L'Artiste* I, 105 (early 1831) that Hugo's Louis XI was "le Louis XI de *Quentin Durward*." Partridge, p. 267.

32 Donald Haggis, "The Popularity of Scott's Novels in France and Balzac's *Illusions perdues*," *Journal of European Studies* xv (1985): 21–9.

33 In *The Three Musketeers*, Dumas referred to Louis XI in his discussion of Richelieu's decision to starve La Rochelle into submission: "Meanwhile [Richelieu] considered the plight of that unfortunate town, which contained so much misery and heroism, and recalled the maxim of Louis XI, his political predecessor, just as he was Robespierre's: 'Divide and rule.' " (Bantam Classic Edition, 1984, p. 426). In *Le Rouge et le Noir*, Stendhal has M. de la Mole musing about the character of Julien Sorel: "Non, il n'a pas le génie adroit et cauteleux d'un procureur qui ne perd ni une minute ni une opportunité . . . Ce n'est point un caractère à la Louis XI." *Oeuvres complètes*, 50 vols (Paris and Geneva: Slatkine Reprints, 1986), II: 373.

34 The romantic figure of Louis XI was presented in the visual arts as well. In his *Mémoires d'un Touriste*, Stendhal wrote that, while at Tours, he remembered the sculpture of Louis XI executed by Jean-Louis Nicholas Jaley, now in the Louvre.

35 On the influence of romanticism on historiography, see the recent works by John B. Roney, *The Inside of History: Jean Henri Merle d'Aubigné and Romantic Historiography* (Westport, Connecticut: Greenwood Press, 1996), and Stephen Bann, *Romanticism and the Rise of History* (New York: Twayne Publishers, 1995).

36 See Partridge's discussion of Scott's influence on French novels, pp. 258–89.

37 "Son Louis XI, pour la réalité et la vie, a soutenu la concurrence avec *Quentin Durward*." C. A. Sainte-Beuve, *Portraits contemporains*, 5 vols (Paris: Michel Levy Frères, 1870), IV: 52–3.

38 F. R. de Toreinx, *Histoire du Romantisme en France* (Paris, 1829 edn; facs. reprint Geneva: Slatkine Reprints, 1973), pp. 293–4.

39 Prosper de Barante, *Histoire des ducs de Bourgogne* (Paris, 1837), preface, p. 39.

40 Prosper de Barante, *Histoire des ducs de Bourgogne*, 3rd edn, 13 vols (Paris: L'Advocat, 1824–6), XII: 358–9.

41 Ibid., XII: 360.

42 Ibid., XII: 369.

43 In his introduction to Michelet's *Oeuvres complètes*, Paul Viallaneix quotes Michelet: "Après la lutte contre les Anglais vient la lutte contre la Maison de Bourgogne; après la Pucelle, Louis XI; après l'héroisme, la ruse; après le drame,

le fabliau." Paul Viallaneix, *Oeuvres complètes de Michelet*, 21 vols (Paris: Flammarion, 1971–), VI: 23.

44 Ibid.

45 At one of his lectures at the Collège de France in 1839, Michelet said, "Commines est l'historien de la politique froide et sèche, tandis que Chastellain est l'ecrivain du coeur, de la nation, de la sensibilité loyale, le serviteur d'une maison de beaucoup de chimères, mais généreuse, qui a dormi trente ans en paix, ce qui est rare dans l'histoire des sociétés humaines." Ibid., VI: 24.

46 Ibid., VI: 33.

47 Ibid., VI: 233–4.

48 Ibid., VI: 269.

Bibliography

MANUSCRIPTS

(a) *Bibliothèque de l'Arsenal*

"Pour l'autorité de Parlement dans les affaires publiques." Ms. 5860.

(b) *Bibliothèque Nationale*

Girard, Bernard de, Sieur Du Haillan. "Histoire de Louis XI." Mss. Fr. 17518.
"Essay historique concernant les droits et prerogatives de la cours des pairs qui est le Parlement seant à Paris." (1721) Mss. Fr. nouvelles acquisitions 1503.
Legrand, Joachim. "Vie et Histoire de Louis XI." Mss. Fr. 6991.
Machon, Louis. "Apologie pour Machiavelle en faveur des princes et les ministres d'estat." (1643) Mss. Fr. 19046, 19047.
Miromesnil, Hue de. "Lettres sur l'état de la magistrature en l'année 1772." Mss. Fr. 10986.
"Tres humbles et tres respecteuses iteratives remonstrances que presentens au Roy, nôtre tres-honoré et souverain seigneur, les gens tenans sa cours de Parlemens." (26 juillet 1718)

PUBLISHED PRIMARY SOURCES

Accomodement entre le roi Louis XI et son Parlement sur le refus de verifier un édit de ce prince inique et pernicieux. n.d.
Argenson, Marquis d'. *Considérations sur le gouvernement ancien et présent de la France.* Amsterdam: Marc Michel Rey, 1764.
Balzac, Guez de. *Le Prince.* n.p., 1631.
Barante, Prosper de. *Histoire des Ducs de Bourgogne.* 3rd edn., 13 vols. Paris: L'Advocat, 1824–6.
Baricave, M. I. *La Defense de la monarchie françoise et d'autres monarchies, contres les detestables et execrables maximes d'Estat des Ministres Calvinistes.* Toulouse: Dominique Bosc, 1614.
Basin, Thomas. *Histoire de Louis XI.* 3 vols. Ed. and trans. Charles Samaran. Paris: Les Belles Lettres, 1963–72.
Bayle, Pierre. *Oeuvres diverses.* 4 vols. La Haye, 1727.
—— *The Dictionary Historical and Critical.* 5 vols. London, 1736.
Belleforest, François de, ed. *Les Chroniques et annales de France dez l'origine des Francoys, et leur venues es Gaules.* By Nicole Gilles. Paris: Nicolas du Chemin, 1573.

Belloy, Pierre de. *Apologie Catholique contre les libelles declarations, advis et consultations faictes, écrites et publiées par les Liguez perturbateurs du repos du Royaume de France . . .* E.D.L.I.C., 1586.

—— *De l'autorité du roy.* n.p., 1587.

Bèze, Theodore de. *Du Droit des Magistrats.* Ed. Robert M. Kingdon. Geneva: Librairie Droz, 1970.

Bodin, Jean. *Method for the Easy Comprehension of History.* Ed. and trans. Beatrice Reynolds. New York, 1945.

—— "Recueil de tout ce qui s'est negocié en la compagnie du tiers-état de France, en l'assemblee générale des trois états, assigné par le roi en la ville de Blois au 15 Novembre 1576 . . ." *Des Estats Généraux et Autres Assemblées Nationales.* Ed. Charles Joseph Mayer. 18 vols. Paris: Buisson, 1788–9. Vol. 13, pp. 215–328.

—— *The Six Bookes of a Commonweale.* Ed. Kenneth Douglas McRae, trans. R. Knolles, 1606; facsimile reprint edn, Harvard University Press, 1962.

Bossuet, Jacques-Benigné. *Histoire de France*, in *Oeuvres complètes*. vol. 17. Paris: Gauthier Frères et Cie, 1828.

—— *Panegyrique de Saint François de Paule*, in *Oeuvres complètes*. vol. 7. Paris: Gauthier Frères et Cie, 1828.

Botero, Giovanni. *The Reason of State and the Greatness of Cities.* Trans. P. J. Waley and D. P. Waley. London: Routledge and Kegan Paul, 1956.

Boucher, Jean. *De iusta abdicatione Henrici Tertii.* n.p., 1591.

Boulainvilliers, Henri de. *Histoire de l'ancien gouvernement de la France.* La Haye/Amsterdam, 1727.

—— *Essais sur la noblesse de France.* Amsterdam, 1732.

—— *Histoire des anciens parlemens de France, ou Etats Généraux du Royaume.* London: John Brindley, 1737.

Britard, J. B. *Discours historique sur le caractère et la politique de Louis XI; par un citoyen de la section du Théâtre Français.* Paris [1793–4].

Champollion-Figéac, J. J., ed. *Documents historiques inédits sur l'histoire de France.* 4 vols. Paris, 1843.

Chastellain, Georges. *Oeuvres historiques inédites*, in J. A. C. Buchon, ed., *Choix de chroniques et mémoires sur l'histoire de France.* Paris: Librairie Charles Delagrave, 1883.

Commynes, Philippe de. *Mémoires.* Ed. Jean Dufournet. Paris: Gallimard, 1979.

Declarations des roys Louis XI et Henry III. Paris, 1648.

De la Nécessité d'assembler les Estats. n.p., 1567.

Dialogue d'estat ou entretiens des roys Louys XI et Louys XII es champs elisees. Paris, n.d.

Dialogue entre le Roy Louys XI et Louys XII sur leur differente façon de regner à sçavoir lequel est meilleur ou de les gouverner par amour ou par force et puissance absolue. n.p., 1649.

Duclos, Charles Pinot. *Histoire de Louis XI.* 3 vols. La Haye: Jean Neaulme, 1745.

Dumesnil, Alexis. *Le règne de Louis XI et de l'influence qu'il a eue jusque sur les derniers temps de la troisième dynastie.* Paris: Maradan, 1811.

Du Tillet, Jean, Bishop of Meaux. *Brefves Narrations des actes et faictez memorables advenus depuis Pharamond . . . continuées iusques à lan mil cinq cens cinquante et six.* Rouen: Jehan du Gord, 1556.

—— *Une Chronique abbregée contenant tout ce qui est advenu, tant en fait de Guerre, qu'autrement, entre le Roys et Princes, Republiques et Potentats estrangers*, in Jean Du Tillet, Sieur de la Bussière, *Recueil des Roys de France, Leur Couronne et Maison.* Paris: Jacques du Puys, 1580.

Du Tillet, Jean, Sieur de la Bussière. *Les Memoires et Recerches de Jean Du Tillet, Greffier de la Cour de Parlement à Paris.* Rouen: Philippe de Tours, 1578. Republished as *Recveil des Roys de France, Leur Couronne et Maison.* Paris: Jacques du Puys, 1580.

Entretien de Louis Onze et de Charle Hardi Duc de Bourgogne. Amsterdam, 1690.

Epilogue, ou dernier appareil du bon citoyen. n.p., 1649.

Fénelon, François de Salignac. *Les Aventures de Télémaque.* New York: Ivison and Phinney, 1855.

—— *Ecrits et Lettres Politiques.* Ed. Charles Urbain. n.p., 1921.

—— *Oeuvres.* Ed. Jacques Le Brun. Paris: Gallimard, 1983.

Flammermont, Jules. *Remonstrances du parlement de Paris au XVIIIe siècle.* 3 vols. Paris, 1888.

[Garasse, François]. *Les Recherches des recherches et autres oeuvres de M. Estienne Pasquier, pour la defense de Nos Roys, contre les outrages, calomnies, et autres impertinences dudit Autheur.* Paris: Sebastien Chappelet, 1622.

Gautier de Sibert. *Considérations sur l'ancienneté de l'existence du Tiers-état, et sur les causes de la suspension de ses droits pendant un temps.* Paris, 1789.

—— *Variations de la Monarchie Françoise dans son gouvernement politique, civil et militaire.* 4 vols. Paris: Saillant, 1765.

Gentillet, Innocent. *Remonstrance au Roy Tres Chrestien Henry III de ce nom Roy de France et de Pologne.* Aygenstain: Gabriel Iason, 1576.

—— *Discours contre Machiavel.* Ed. A. D'Andrea and P. D. Stewart. Florence: Casalini Libri, 1974.

Gin, Pierre Louis Claude. *Les vrais principes du gouvernement françois.* Geneva, 1777.

—— *Origine des malheurs de la France.* Hamburg, 1797.

—— *Discours sur l'histoire universelle depuis Charlemagne jusqu'à nos jours, fesant suite à celui de Bossuet.* 2 vols. Paris: Bertrand Pottier, 1802.

Girard, Bernard de, Seigneur Du Haillan. *De l'Estat et succez des affaires de France.* Paris: Jonathon Provence, 1613.

Gomicourt, Damiens de. *Mélanges historiques.* 2 vols. Paris, 1768.

Hay, Paul du Chastelet. *Recueil de diverses pièces pour servir à l'histoire.* Paris, 1635.

L'hellebore pour nos malcontents, cueilli au jardin d'un Anti-Machiavel et mis en lumière. Paris, 1632.

Herauld, Didier. *Fragment de l'examen du Prince de Machiavel.* 2nd edn. Paris, 1633.

Hotman, Francois. *Francogallia.* Trans. J. H. M. Salmon and Ed. J. H. M. Salmon and Ralph E. Giesey. Cambridge: Cambridge University Press, 1972.

—— [Ernest Varamund]. *A True and plain report of the Furious Outrages of Fraunce.* "Striveling, Scotland": 1573.

Joly, Claude. *Recueil de maximes veritables et importantes pour l'institution du roy.* Paris, 1663.

Le Bret, Cardin. *De la Souveraineté du Roy*, in *Les Oeuvres de Messire C. Le Bret.* Paris: Charles Osmont, 1689.

L'hermité, J. B. T. de Soliers. *Le Cabinet du roy Louis XI.* Paris, Quinet, 1661, in *Archives curieuses de l'histoire de France.* Ed. L. Cimber. Series 1, vol. 1. Paris: Beauvais, 1834.

Le Maître, Rodolphe. *Tibère français ou les six premiers livres des Annales de Cornelius Tacitus.* 2nd edn. Paris: Robert Estienne, 1616.

Lepaige, Louis-Adrien. *Lettres historiques sur les fonctions essentielles du parlement.* 2 vols. Amsterdam, 1753–4.

Le Reveille-Matin des Francois, et leurs voisins. "Edinburgh" [Basel?]: "Jacques James," 1574.

Lettre d'avis à Messieurs du Parlement de Paris, escrit par un Provincial. Paris, 1649.

Loyseau, Charles. *Oeuvres.* Lyon: Compagnies des Librairies, 1701.

Manifeste contenant les causes et raisons qui ont obligé ceuz de la ville de La Rochelle de prendre les armes . . . plus le serment de Louys XI. Rochelle, 1627.

Manuel du bon citoyen ou bouclier de defense legitime contre les assauts de l'ennemi. Paris, 1649.

Martin, Henri. *Histoire de France.* 4th edn. 17 vols. Paris: Furne, 1865.

Masselin, Jehan. *Journal des Etats Généraux de France tenus à Tours en 1484.* Ed. A. Bernier. Paris: Imprimerie Royale, 1835.

Matthieu, Pierre. *The History of Lewis the Eleventh.* Trans. Edward Grimestone. London, 1614.

Mémoires des occasions de la guerre, appellée le Bien-Public, rapportez à l'estat de la guerre presente. n.p., 1567.

Mémoires touchant l'origine et l'autorité du Parlement de France, appellé Judicium Francorum, in Mezeray, *Mémoires historiques et critiques.* 2 vols in 1. Amsterdam, 1732.

Meynier, Honorat de. *Les Demandes curieuses et les responses libres.* Paris: Pierre Billaine, 1635.

Michelet, Jules. *Oeuvres complètes.* 21 vols. Ed. Paul Viallaneix. Paris: Flammarion, 1971–.

Mignet, F. A. *De la Féodalité des institutions de St. Louis, de l'influence de la législation de ce prince.* Paris: L'Huillier, 1822.

Miroir historique de la ligue de l'an 1464 où peut se reconnoitre la ligue de l'an 1694. Cologne, 1694. Also included, *Avis d'un amy à l'autheur du Miroir historique de la ligue de l'an 1464* and *Pensées sur l'avis d'un amy à l'autheur du Miroir historique de la ligue de l'an 1464.*

Montesquieu, Le Baron Charles de Secondat. *Pensées et fragments inédits.* Ed. Le Baron Gaston de Montesquieu. 2 vols. Bordeaux: G. Gounouilhou, 1899–1901.

—— *Oeuvres complètes.* Ed. Andre Masson. 3 vols. Paris: Nagel, 1950–5.

Moreau, Charles, ed. *Choix de Mazarinades, publié pour la Société de l'histoire de France.* 2 vols. Paris, 1853.

Mounier, J. J. *Nouvelles observations sur les Etats-Généraux de France.* n.p., 1789.

Naudé, Gabriel. *Le Marfore ou discours contre les libelles.* Paris: Louis Boulenger, 1620.

—— *Addition à l'histoire de Louys XI.* Paris, François Targa, 1630.

—— *Considérations politiques sur les coups d'estat.* n.p., 1667.

—— *Mémoire confidentiel addressé à Mazarin apres la mort de Richelieu.* Ed. Alfred Franklin. Paris, 1870.

Pasquier, Etienne. *Les Lettres d'Estienne Pasquier . . . par lesquelles se voit plusieurs belles matieres et grand discours sur les affaires de la France, concernantes les guerres civiles.* Arras: Gilles Bauduyn, 1598.

—— *Les Recherches de la France.* Paris, 1665.

—— *Ecrits Politiques.* Ed. Dorothy Thickett. Geneva: Droz, 1966.

—— *Lettres Historiques.* Ed. Dorothy Thickett. Geneva: Droz, 1966.

Remonstrance du Roy Louis XII au Roy Louis XI sur leur differente façon de regner. Paris, 1649.

Request de la Noblesse pour l'Assemblée des Estats généraux. Paris, 1651.

Roederer, P. L. *Oeuvres.* 8 vols. Paris: Firmin Didot, 1853.

Saige, Guillaume-Joseph. *Catéchisme du citoyen ou elemens du droit public françois.* n.p., 1788.

Sainte-Beuve, C. A. *Portraits contemporains.* 5 vols. Paris: Michel Levy Frères, 1870.

Saint-Simon, Louis de Rouvroy duc de. *Memoirs.* Trans. Katharine Prescott Wormeley. 4 vols. Boston, 1902.

Satyre Ménippée de la vertue de Catholicon d'Espagne et de la tenue des estatz de Paris. Ed. Ch. Marcilly. Paris: Garnier Frères, n.d.

Scott, Sir Walter. *Quentin Durward.* London: Hurst, Robinson and Company, 1823.

Seyssel, Claude de. *Histoire du Roys Loys Douziesme, Père du Peuple.* Paris: Jacques du Puys, 1587.

—— *La Monarchie de France.* Ed. Jacques Poujol. Paris: Librairie D'Argences, 1961.

Silhon, Jean de. *The Minister of State.* Trans. by H. H. London: Thomas Dring, 1658.

Simonde de Sismondi, J. C. L. *Précis de l'histoire des français.* 3 vols. Paris, 1839.

Les Soupirs de la France esclave, qui aspire après la Liberté. n.p. 1690; facsimile reprint edn, Amsterdam: Editions d'Histoire Sociale, 1976.

Stendhal. *Oeuvres complètes.* 50 vols. Paris; Geneva: Slatkine Reprints, 1986.

Toreinx, F. R. de. *Histoire du Romantisme en France.* Paris, 1829; facsimile reprint edn, Geneva: Slatkine Reprints, 1973.

Varillas, Antoine. *Histoire de Louis Onze.* 2 vols. Paris: Claude Barbin, 1689.

—— *La Minorité de Saint Louis avec l'histoire de Louis XI et de Henri II.* La Haye: Adrian Moetjens, 1685.

Les Veritables maximes du gouvernement de la France. Paris, 1652.

Villemain, Abel François. *Cours de Littérature Française.* Bruxelles: A. Jamar, 1840.

Vindiciae contra Tyrannos. Ed. A. Jouanna. Geneva: Droz, 1979.

La voix gemissante du peuple chrestien et catholique. Paris, 1640.

Voltaire. *Essai sur les moeurs.* Ed. Rene Pomeau. 2 vols. Paris: Garnier Frères, 1963.

SECONDARY SOURCES

Allen, J. W. *A History of Political Thought in the Sixteenth Century.* London: Methuen and Co., 1928.

Archambault, Paul. *Seven French Chroniclers: Witnesses to History.* Syracuse, NY: Syracuse University Press, 1974.

Baker, Keith M. "French Political Thought at the Accession of Louis XVI." *Journal of Modern History* 50 (1978): 279–303.

—— *The French Revolution and the Creation of Modern Political Culture.* 3 vols. Oxford: Pergamon Press, 1987.

—— *Inventing the French Revolution.* Cambridge, England: Cambridge University Press, 1990.

Bakos, Adrianna E., ed. *Politics, Ideology and the Law in Early Modern Europe.* Rochester, NY: University of Rochester Press, 1994.

Baldwin, Summerfield. "Jean Bodin and the League." *Catholic Historical Review* 23 (1937/8): 160–84.

Barzun, Jacques. *The French Race.* New York: Columbia University Press, 1932.

Baumgartner, Frederic J. *Radical Reactionaries: The Political Thought of the French Catholic League.* Geneva: Droz, 1975.

Beame, Edmond M. "The Use and Abuse of Machiavelli: The Sixteenth-Century French Adaptation." *Journal of the History of Ideas* 43 (1982): 33–54.

Beik, William. *Absolutism and Society in Seventeenth-Century France.* Cambridge, England: Cambridge University Press, 1985.

Bell, David. *Lawyers and Citizens: The Making of a Political Elite in Old Regime France.* New York: Oxford University Press, 1994.

Bickart, Roger. *Le Parlements et la notion de souveraineté nationale au XVIIIe siècle.* Paris, 1952.

Bonney, Richard. *Society and Government in France under Richelieu and Mazarin.* New York: St. Martin's Press, 1988.

Bourrilly, V.-L. "Les idées politiques de Commynes." *Revue d'Histoire Moderne et Contemporaine* 1 (1899): 93–123.

Bouwsma, William J. "The Politics of Commynes." *Journal of Modern History* 23 (1951): 315–28.

Buranelli, Vincent. "The Historical and Political Thought of Boulainvilliers." *Journal of the History of Ideas* 18 (1957): 475–94.

Burgess, Glenn. *The Politics of the Ancient Constitution.* University Park, PA: Pennsylvania State University Press, 1993.

Burke, Peter. *The Fabrication of Louis XIV.* New Haven, Connecticut: Yale University Press, 1992.

Burns, J. H., ed. *The Cambridge History of Political Thought, 1450–1700*. Cambridge, England: Cambridge University Press, 1991.
—— "The Idea of Absolutism," in *Absolutism in Seventeenth-Century Europe*. Ed. John Miller. New York: St. Martin's Press, 1990.
Carcassonne, Elie. *Montesquieu et le problème de la constitution française au XVIIIe siècle*. Paris, 1927; Geneva: Slatkine Reprints, 1970.
Cardascia, Guillaume. "Machiavel et Jean Bodin." *Bibliothèque d'Humanisme et Renaissance* 3 (1943): 129–67.
Carlyle, A. J. and Carlyle, R. W. *A History of Medieval Political Theory in the West*. 6 vols. New York: Barnes and Noble, n.d.
Carrier, Hubert. *Les Mazarinades*. 2 vols. Paris: Champion, 1987, 1992.
——, ed. *La Fronde. Contestation democratique et misère paysanne: 52 Mazarinades*. Paris: EDHIS, n.d.
Chaussinand-Nogaret, G. *La Noblesse au XVIIIème siècle*. Bruxelles: Edition Complexe, 1984.
Cherel, Albert. "La pensée de Machiavel en France au temps de la Fronde." *Revue de littérature comparée* 13 (1933): 577–87.
Chevallier, Jean-Jacques. *Histoire de la pensée politique*. 3 vols. Paris: Payot, 1984.
Church, William Farr. *Constitutional Thought in Sixteenth Century France*. Cambridge, Mass.: Harvard University Press, 1941.
—— *Richelieu and Reason of State*. Princeton, NJ: Princeton University Press, 1972.
—— *Louis XIV in Historical Thought*. New York: W. W. Norton, 1976.
Clarke, Jack A. *Gabriel Naudé, 1600–1653*. Hamden, Connecticut: Archon Books, 1970.
Cox, Iris. *Montesquieu and the History of French Laws*. Oxford: The Voltaire Foundation, 1983.
D'Andrea, A. "The Political and Ideological Context of Innocent Gentillet's Anti-Machiavel." *Renaissance Quarterly* 23 (1970): 397–411.
Denzer, Horst, ed. *Verhandlungen der internationalen Bodin Tagung in München*. Munich: C. H. Beck, 1973.
Dodge, Guy Howard. *The Political Theory of the Huguenots of the Dispersion*. New York: Octagon Books, 1972.
Donaldson, Peter S. *Machiavelli and Mystery of State*. New York, 1988.
Doyle, William. "The Parlements of France and the Breakdown of the Old Regime." *French Historical Studies* 6 (1970): 415–58.
—— "Was there an Aristocratic Reaction in Pre-Revolutionary France?" *Past and Present* 57 (1972): 97–122.
Dreyer, Kenneth. "Commynes and Machiavelli: A Study in Parallelism." *Symposium* 5 (1951): 38–61.
Dufournet, Jean. *Etudes sur Philippe de Commynes*. Paris: Bibliothèque du Quinzième Siècle, 1975.
—— *Sur Philippe de Commynes*. Paris: Société d'Edition d'Enseignement Supérieur, 1982.
—— *Philippe de Commynes. Un historien à l'aube des temps modernes*. Brussels: DeBoeck Université, 1994.
Echeverria, Durand. *The Maupeou Revolution: A Study in the History of Libertarianism*. Baton Rouge, Louisiana: Louisiana State University Press, 1985.
Egilsrud, Johann. *Le "Dialogue des morts" dans les littératures française, allemande et anglaise 1644–1789*. Paris, 1934.
Egret, Jean. *Louis XV et l'opposition parlementaire 1715–1774*. Paris: Armand Colin, 1970.
Ellis, Harold A. *Boulainvilliers and the French Monarchy: Aristocratic Politics in Early Eighteenth-Century France*. Ithaca, NY: Cornell University Press, 1988.

Fernandez-Santamaria, J. A. *Reason of State and Statecraft in Spanish Political Thought, 1595–1640*. Lanham, Maryland: University Press of America, 1983.

Flammermont, Jules. *Le Chancelier Maupeou et les parlements*. Paris, 1883.

Ford, Franklin L. *Robe and Sword: The Regrouping of the French Aristocracy after Louis XIV*. Cambridge, Mass.: Harvard University Press, 1953.

—— *Political Murder: From Tyrannicide to Terrorism*. Cambridge, Mass.: Harvard University Press, 1985.

Forsyth, Murray. *Reason and Revolution: The Political Thought of the Abbé Sieyès*. Leicester: Leicester University Press, 1987.

Franklin, Julian. *Jean Bodin and the Sixteenth-Century Revolution in the Methodology of Law and History*. New York: Columbia University Press, 1963.

—— *Constitutionalism and Resistance in the Sixteenth Century*. New York: Pegasus, 1969.

—— *Jean Bodin and the Rise of Absolutist Theory*. Cambridge, England: Cambridge University Press, 1973.

Friedrich, Carl J. *Constitutional Reason of State*. Providence, RI: Brown University Press, 1957.

Garrett, Clarke W. "The *Moniteur* of 1788." *French Historical Studies* 5 (1968): 263–73.

Gidel, Gilbert. *La Politique de Fénelon*. Geneva: Slatkine Reprints, 1971.

Giesey, Ralph E. "When and Why Hotman Wrote the Francogallia." *Bibliothèque d'Humanisme et Renaissance* 29 (1967): 581–611.

—— *If Not, Not: The Oath of the Aragonese and the Legendary Laws of Sobrarbe*. Princeton, NJ: Princeton University Press, 1968.

—— "The Monarchomach Triumvirs: Hotman, Beza and Mornay." *Bibliothèque d'Humanisme et Renaissance* 31 (1970): 41–56.

Godechot, Jacques. "Nation, Patrie, Nationalisme et Patriotisme en France au XVIIIe siècle," *Annales historiques de la Revolution Française* 206 (1971): 481–501.

Gooch, G. P. *History and Historians in the Nineteenth Century*. 2nd edn. London: Longmans, Green and Company, 1952.

Greengrass, Mark. *France in the Age of Henri IV: The Struggle for Stability*. New York: Longmans, 1984.

Guy, John. "The Rhetoric of Counsel in Early Modern England," in *Tudor Political Culture*. Ed. Dale Hoak. Cambridge, England: Cambridge University Press, 1995.

Gwyn, W. B. "Cruel Nero: The Concept of the Tyrant and the Image of Nero in Western Political Thought." *History of Political Thought* 12 (1991): 421–55.

Haggis, Donald. "The Popularity of Scott's Novels in France and Balzac's *Illusions perdues*." *Journal of European Studies* 15 (1985): 21–9.

Hamscher, Albert N. *The Parlement of Paris After the Fronde 1653–1673*. Pittsburgh, Penn.: University of Pittsburgh Press, 1976.

Hanley, Sarah. "The *Discours Politiques* in Monarchomaque Ideology: Resistance Right in Sixteenth-Century France." *Assemblee de Stati e Istituzioni Rappresentative nella Storia de Pensiero Politico Moderno (secoli XV–XX)*. Rimini: Universita de Perugia, 1982.

—— *The "Lit de Justice" of the Kings of France: Constitutional Ideology in Legend, Ritual and Discourse*. Princeton, NJ: Princeton University Press, 1983.

Hexter, J. H. *The Vision of Politics on the Eve of the Reformation*. New York: Basic Books, Inc., 1973.

Holt, Mack P. *The Duke of Anjou and the Politique Struggle during the Wars of Religion*. Cambridge, England, and New York: Cambridge University Press, 1986.

Hudson, David. "In Defense of Reform: French Government Propaganda during the Maupeou Crisis." *French Historical Studies* 8:1 (1973): 51–76.

Hulliung, Mark. *Montesquieu and the Old Regime.* Berkeley, CA: University of California Press, 1976.

Johnson, Douglas W. *Guizot: Aspects of French History 1781–1874.* London: Routledge and Kegan Paul, 1963.

Joynes, Daniel C. "*Parlementaires,* Peers and the *Parti Janséniste*: The Refusal of Sacraments and the Revival of the Ancient Constitution in Eighteenth-Century France." *Proceedings of the Annual Meeting of the Western Society for French History* 8 (1980): 229–38.

Kaulek, Jean. "Louis XI, est-il l'auteur du *Rosier des Guerres?*" *Revue historique* 21 (1883): 312–22.

Kelley, Donald R. "Jean Du Tillet, Archivist and Antiquary." *Journal of Modern History* 38 (1966): 337–54.

—— *Foundations of Modern Historical Scholarship.* New York: Columbia University Press, 1970.

—— "Murd'rous Machiavel in France: A Post-Mortem." *The Political Science Quarterly* 85 (1970): 545–59.

—— "Martyrs, Myths and the Massacre: The Background of St. Bartholomew." *American Historical Review* 77 (1972): 1323–41.

—— *François Hotman: A Revolutionary's Ordeal.* Princeton, NJ: Princeton University Press, 1973.

Kelly, George Armstrong. *Mortal Politics in Eighteenth-Century France.* Waterloo, Canada: University of Waterloo Press, 1986.

Kendall, Paul Murray. *Louis XI.* New York: W. W. Norton, 1971.

Keohane, Nannerl O. *Philosophy and the State in France.* Princeton, NJ: Princeton University Press, 1980.

Kerviler, René. *Jean de Silhon.* Paris: Dumoulin, 1876.

Kingdon, Robert. *Geneva and the Consolidation of the French Protestant Movement.* Madison, Wisconsin: University of Wisconsin Press, 1967.

—— *Myths of the St. Bartholomew's Day Massacre.* Cambridge, Mass.: Harvard University Press, 1988.

Klaits, Joseph. *Printed Propaganda under Louis XIV.* Princeton, NJ: Princeton University Press, 1976.

La Borderie, A. "Jean Meschinot: Sa vie et ses oeuvres." *Bibliothèque de l'Ecole des Chartes.* 56 (1895): 99–140; 274–317; 601–38.

Labrousse, Elisabeth. "The Political Ideas of the Huguenot Diaspora (Bayle and Jurieu)," in *Church, State and Society under the Bourbon Kings.* Ed. Richard M. Golden. Lawrence, Kansas: Coronado Press, 1982.

—— *Bayle.* Trans. Denys Potts. Oxford: Oxford University Press, 1983.

Leffler, Phyllis K. "French Historians and the Challenge to Louis XIV's Absolutism." *French Historical Studies* 14 (1986): 1–22.

Lemaire, André. *Les lois fondamentales de la monarchie française d'après les théoriciens de l'Ancien Régime.* Paris: A. Fontemoing, 1907.

Lemarié, Louis. *Les Assemblées franques et les historiens réformateurs du XVIIIe siècle.* Paris: Imprimerie Bonvalot-Jouve, 1906.

Lewis, P. S., ed. *The Recovery of France in the Fifteenth Century.* Trans. G. F. Martin. London: Macmillan, 1971.

Lloyd, Howell A. "The Political Thought of Charles Loyseau." *European Studies Review* 11 (1981): 53–82.

—— *The State, France and the Sixteenth Century.* London: George Allen and Unwin, 1983.

Lombard, A. *L'Abbé Du Bos: Un initiateur de la pensée moderne.* Paris: Hachette, 1913.

Lossky, Andrew. "The Absolutism of Louis XIV: Reality or Myth?" *Canadian Journal of History* 19 (1984): 1–15.

Mackrell, J. Q. C. *The Attack on "Feudalism" in Eighteenth-Century France*. London: Routledge and Kegan Paul, 1973.

Maigron, Louis. *Le Roman historique à l'epoque romantique: Essai sur l'influence de Walter Scott*. Paris, 1896.

Maire, Catherine. "L'Église et la nation: Du dépot de la verité au dépot des lois: la trajectoire janséniste au XVIIIe siècle." *Annales. Économies, Sociétés, Civilisations* 46 (1991): 1177–205.

Major, J. Russell. *Representative Institutions in Renaissance France, 1421–1559*. Madison, Wisconsin: University of Wisconsin Press, 1960.

—— "The Renaissance Monarchy as seen by Erasmus, More, Seyssel, and Machiavelli," in *Action and Conviction in Early Modern Europe*. Ed. Theodore K. Rabb and Jerrold E. Seigel. Princeton, NJ: Princeton University Press, 1969.

—— *From Renaissance Monarchy to Absolute Monarchy: French Kings, Nobles and Estates*. Baltimore: Johns Hopkins University Press, 1994.

Martin, G. F. "A Political Concept of Louis XI: Subjection instead of Vassalage," in *The Recovery of France in the Sixteenth Century*. Ed. P. S. Lewis. London: Macmillan, 1971.

Martineau-Genieys, Christine, ed. "Introduction" to Jean Meschinot, *Les Lunettes des Princes*. Geneva: Droz, 1972.

Mason, Lester B. *The French Constitution and the Social Question in the Old Regime*. n.p., 1954.

Mathiez, Albert. "La Place de Montesquieu dans l'histoire des doctrines politiques du XVIIIe siècle." *Annales historiques de la Révolution Française* 7 (1930): 97–112.

McKenzie, Lionel A. "Natural Right and the Idea of Interest in Early Modern Political Thought: Francesco Guicciardini and Jean de Silhon." *History of European Ideas* 2 (1981): 277–98.

Meinecke, Friedrich. *Machiavellism*. Trans. Douglas Scott. New Haven, Connecticut: Yale University Press, 1957.

Mellon, Stanley. *The Political Uses of History*. Stanford, California: Stanford University Press, 1958.

Mettam, Roger, ed. *Government and Society in Louis XIV's France*. London: Macmillan, 1977.

Montaigu, Henry. *La Fin des féodaux: le pré carré du roi Louis*. Olivier Orban, 1980.

Moote, A. Lloyd. *The Revolt of the Judges. The Parlement of Paris and the Fronde 1643–1652*. Princeton, NJ: Princeton University Press, 1971.

Moreau, C., ed. *Bibliographie des Mazarinades*. 3 vols. New York: Burt Franklin, 1965.

Mosher, Orville W. *Louis XI King of France as He Appears in History and in Literature*. Toulouse: Edouard Privat, 1925.

Mousnier, R. *La Plume, la faucille et le marteau: Institutions et société en France du Moyen Age à la Revolution*. Paris: Presses Universitaires de France, 1970.

—— "The Fronde," in *Preconditions of Revolution in Early Modern Europe*. Ed. Robert Forster and Jack P. Greene. Baltimore: Johns Hopkins University Press, 1970.

—— *La Venalité des Offices sous Henri IV et Louis XIII*. Paris: Presses Universitaires de France, 1971.

—— *The Institutions of France under the Absolute Monarchy 1598–1789*. Vol. 1. Trans. Brian Pearce. Chicago: University of Chicago Press, 1979.

Oestreich, Gerhard. *Neostoicism and the Early Modern State*. Ed. Brigitta Oestreich. Trans. David McLintock. Cambridge, England: Cambridge University Press, 1982.

Ogle, Arthur. *The Marquis d'Argenson*. London: T. Fisher Unwin, 1893.

Ourliac, Paul. "The Concordat of 1472: An Essay on the Relations between Louis XI and Sixtus IV", in P. S. Lewis, Ed., *The Recovery of France in the Fifteenth Century*. Trans. G. F. Martin. London: Macmillan, 1971.

Ozouf, Mona. "Two Historical Legitimations of Eighteenth-Century French Society: Mably and Boulainvilliers," in *In the Workshop of History*, pp. 125–39. Ed. François Furet. Trans. Jonathan Mandelbaum. Chicago: Chicago University Press, 1984.

Ozouf, Mona and François Furet, eds. *A Critical Dictionary of the French Revolution*. Trans. Arthur Goldhammer. Cambridge, Mass.: Harvard University Press, 1989.

Pagden, Anthony, ed. *The Languages of Political Theory in Early Modern Europe*. Cambridge, England: Cambridge University Press, 1987.

Palmer, Robert R. "The National Idea in France before the Revolution." *Journal of the History of Ideas* 1 (1940): 95–111.

Partridge, Eric. *The Romantic Knowledge of English Literature*. Paris: Librairie Ancienne Edouard Champion, 1924.

Perry, Elisabeth Israels. *From Theology to History*. The Hague, 1973.

Petit-Dutaillis, C. *Charles VII, Louis XI et les premières années de Charles VIII, 1422–1492*. Vol. 4, pt. 2 of *Histoire de France*, ed. Ernest Lavisse. 9 vols. Paris: Librairie Hachette, 1902.

Picot, Gilbert. *Cardin Le Bret et la doctrine de la souveraineté*. Nancy: Société d'Impressions Typographiques, 1948.

Pocock, J. G. A. *The Ancient Constitution and the Feudal Law*. Cambridge, England: Cambridge University Press, 1957.

—— "Texts as Events: Reflections on the History of Political Thought," in *The Politics of Discourse: The Literature and History of Seventeenth-Century England*. Ed. Kevin Sharpe and Steven Zwicker. Los Angeles: University of California Press, 1987.

Ranum, Orest. *Artisans of Glory: Writers and Historical Thought in Seventeenth-Century France*. Chapel Hill, North Carolina: University of North Carolina Press, 1980.

—— *The Fronde: A French Revolution, 1648–1652*. New York: W. W. Norton, 1994.

Rathé, C. Edward. "Innocent Gentillet and the First 'Anti-Machiavel.' " *Bibliothèque d'Humanisme et Renaissance* 27 (1965): 186–225.

Reynolds, Beatrice. *Proponents of Limited Monarchy in Sixteenth Century France: François Hotman and Jean Bodin*. New York: Columbia University Press, 1931.

Rice, James V. *Gabriel Naudé, 1600–1653*. Baltimore: Johns Hopkins University Press, 1939.

Rose, Paul Lawrence. *Bodin and the Great God of Nature*. Geneva: Droz, 1980.

Rothkrug, Lionel. *Opposition to Louis XIV: The Political and Social Origins of the French Enlightenment*. Princeton, NJ: Princeton University Press, 1965.

Rowen, Herbert H. *The King's State: Proprietary Dynasticism in Early Modern France*. New Brunswick, NJ: Rutgers University Press, 1980.

Salmon, J. H. M. *The French Religious Wars in English Political Thought*. Oxford: Oxford University Press, 1959.

—— *Society in Crisis: France in the Sixteenth Century*. London: Methuen, 1975.

—— *Renaissance and Revolt: Essays in the Intellectual and Social History of Early Modern France*. Cambridge, England: Cambridge University Press, 1987.

—— "Stoicism and Roman Example: Seneca and Tacitus in Jacobean England." *Journal of the History of Ideas* 59 (1989): 199–225.

—— "The French Romantics on Comparative Revolution." *History of European Ideas* 11 (1989): 381–91.

Sawyer, Jeffrey. *Printed Poison: Pamphlet Propaganda, Faction Politics and the Public Sphere in Early Seventeenth-Century France*. Berkeley: University of California Press, 1990.

Schellhase, Kenneth C. *Tacitus in Renaissance Political Thought*. Chicago: Chicago University Press, 1976.

Schnur, Roman, ed. *Staatsräson: Studien zur Geschichte eines politischen Begriffs*. Berlin: Duncker und Humblot, 1975.

Sée, Henri. *Louis XI et les villes*. Geneva: Slatkine-Megariotis Reprints, 1974.

—— *Les Idées politiques en France au XVIIe siècle*. Paris, 1923; reprint edn, Geneva: Slatkine Reprints, 1978.

Sewell, William. *A Rhetoric of Bourgeois Revolution: The Abbé Sieyes and What is the Third Estate?* Durham, NC: Duke University Press, 1994.

Shackleton, Robert. *Montesquieu: A Critical Biography*. Oxford: Oxford University Press, 1961.

Shafer, Boyd C. "Bourgeois Nationalism in the Pamphlets on the Eve of the French Revolution." *Journal of Modern History* 10 (1938): 31–50.

Simon, Renée. *Henry de Boulainvilliers: Historien, Politique, Philosophe, Astrologue; 1658–1722*. Paris: Boivin, 1941.

Skinner, Quentin. *The Foundations of Modern Political Thought*. Vol 2. Cambridge, England: Cambridge University Press, 1978.

Sommerville, J. P. *Politics and Ideology in England 1603–1640*. London: Longman, 1986.

Stegmann, André. "Le Tacitisme: programme pour un nouvel essai de définition." *Machiavellismo e Antimachiavellici nel Cinquecento*. Florence: Leo S. Olschki, 1969, pp. 117–30.

—— "Commynes et Machiavel." *Studies on Machiavelli*. Ed. Myron P. Gilmore. Florence: G. C. Sansoni, 1972.

Stone, Bailey. *The Parlement of Paris, 1774–1789*. Chapel Hill, North Carolina: University of North Carolina Press, 1981.

Sutcliffe, F. E. *Politique et Culture 1560–1660*. Paris: Didier, 1973.

Thireau, Jean Louis. *Les Idées politiques de Louis XIV*. Paris: Presses Universitaires de France, 1973.

Thompson, Martin P. "The History of Fundamental Law in Political Thought from the French Wars of Religion to the American Revolution." *American Historical Review* 91 (1986): 1103–28.

Thuau, Etienne. *Raison d'Etat et Pensée Politique à l'Epoque de Richelieu*. Paris: Armand Colin, 1966.

Tuck, Richard. *Natural Rights Theories: Their Origin and Development*. Cambridge, England: Cambridge University Press, 1979.

Tully, James, ed. *Meaning and Context: Quentin Skinner and his Critics*. New York: Polity Press, 1988.

Tyrrel, Joseph M. *Louis XI*. Boston: Twayne Publishers, 1980.

Ulph, Owen. "Jean Bodin and the Estates General of 1576." *Journal of Modern History* 19 (1947): 289–96.

Van Kley, Dale. *The Damiens Affair and the Unraveling of the "Ancien Regime" 1750–1770*. Princeton, NJ: Princeton University Press, 1984.

—— "The Jansenist Constitutional Legacy in the French Prerevolution, 1750–1789." *Historical Reflections/Reflexions historiques* 13 (1986): 393–453.

—— "The Estates General as Ecumenical Council: The Constitutionalism of Corporate Consensus and the *Parlement's* Ruling of September 25, 1788." *Journal of Modern History* 61 (1989): 1–52.

—— "The Religious Origins of the Patriot and Ministerial Parties in Pre-Revolutionary France." *Historical Reflections/Reflexions historiques* 18 (1992): 17–63.

Volpilhac-Auger, Catherine. "Tacite et Montesquieu." *Studies on Voltaire and the Eighteenth Century*. Oxford: The Voltaire Foundation, 1985.

Walch, Jean. *Les Maitres de l'histoire 1815–1850*. Geneva and Paris: Slatkine Reprints, 1986.

Weill, Georges. *Les Théories sur le pouvoir royal en France pendant les Guerres de Religion*. New York: Burt Franklin, n.d.

Wolfe, Martin. "Jean Bodin on Taxes: The Sovereignty–Taxes Paradox." *Political Science Quarterly* 83 (1968): 268–84.

Index

and the romantic movement 185–9;
and the *Rosiers des Guerres* 149–50;
taxation policies 8, 10, 11, 12, 97,
113, 117, 118; compared with
Tiberius 71, 123, 127–8, 174;
Voltaire on 80–1
Louis XII 1, 20–1, 120; and the
dialogues des morts 48–9, 151–4
Louis XIII 66, 119, 140
Louis XIV 1, 20–1, 49–52, 57, 83, 87,
93, 106, 146, 158, 178; compared
with Louis XI 45–6, 51–2, 53–4,
58, 59
Louis XV 76, 166
Louis XVI 85, 166, 169, 176
Loyseau, Charles 106–10, 116, 216–17n

Machiavelli, N. 19, 95, 97, 123, 128–9,
131–3, 134, 199n
Machon, Louis 45, 128–9, 146–7, 150
magistrates 37–8, 39, 83–4, 168–9
Manuel du bon citoyen 143–4
Marie de Cleves 120
Marillac, Charles de 30
Martel, Charles 65, 172
Martin, Henri 183–4
Masselin, Jean 10–13
Matthieu, Pierre 111–13, 126, 127
Maupeou, Chancellor 74, 166
Maurepas, Jean 78
Maximilian I 49
Mayenne, duc de 103
Mazarin, Cardinal Jules 60, 124, 129,
140, 142, 145, 148, 154, 226n
Mazarinades pamphlets 23, 139, 142–7,
150–5
Meinecke, Friedrich 122
Mély-Janin 186
Mémoires des occasions de la guerre 31–2,
36–7
Merovingians 76, 82
Meschinot, Jean 14–15
Meynier, Honorat de 133–4
Michelet, Jules 9, 188–9
Miroir historique de la ligue de l'an 1464
51–3
Miromesnil, Hue de 166–7
Molinet 79
monarchy: authority of *see* absolutism;
authority of the crown;
constitutional 180
money, coining of 109
Montesquieu 60, 67–72, 81, 83,
206–7n, 209–10n

moral politics 122, 123, 131, 134–5
Moreau 151
Moulin, Charles Du 33
Moustardun, Isidore 186–7

Nantes, Edict of 82
nation, idea of 2, 61–2, 64–5, 72, 75,
84–6, 87–8
nationalism 61–2
natural law 94, 200n
natural rights 27–8, 37, 200n
Naudé, Gabriel 23, 45, 47, 57, 124–6,
127–8, 129
necessity: as force in politics 112–13,
121; as justification for Louis XI's
actions 112–13
Nero 174
nobiliaire ideology 3, 60–72, 157,
161, 178
nobility 9–10, 62, 66–7, 74–9 *passim*,
82–3, 84, 87–8, 118–19, 178,
181–2, 183–4, 189, 227n; pensions
of 118; rights of 10, 87–8; and
taxation 10, *see also* League of the
Public Weal
Nora, Pierre 61, 85
Normandy 7, 10

Orléans, Gaston d' 140
Orléans, Philippe d' 63, 158

papacy 8, 215–16n
Parlement of Brittany 74
Parlement of Paris 8, 23, 34, 35, 57, 59,
74, 95, 100, 139, 143, 146–7, 148,
152, 155, 221–2n; and the idea of
counsel 156–70 *passim*; defies Louis
XI under La Vacquerie 8, 57, 58,
100, 157–8, 164, 180; and estates
general 143, 159, 161, 170; during
reigns of Louis XIII and XIV 140–1,
142; right of registration 8, 73–4,
100, 165
parlementaire theory 83–4, 146, 156–70,
176, 178
Pasquier, Etienne 29, 57
paulette, introduction of the 140, 141
*Pensees sur l'avis d'un amy l'auteur du
miroir historique* 54
pensions, of nobility 118
Pepin 37, 65
Péronne, Treaty of (1468) 7, 195n
perpetuity of offices 83–4, 102, 109–10,
145, 158, 165–6, 167, 168–9